FOREWORD

It is with the greatest of pleasure that I write this foreword for Richard Suttle whom I have known for the past fifty years.

He has always been a keen and enthusiastic cricketer. His love and dedication for the game goes back some five decades when he played most of his cricket at the Wanderer's Cricket Club, "Bayland", St. Michael, Bridgetown, Barbados.

I shall always remember how well he organised youth cricket in which I participated, (between the age of 12-14) during my long summer holidays.

He has never played test cricket, but his wealth of experience in Club and League cricket has helped many youngsters to benefit from his coaching.

I wish him every success with his book entitled, *The Vicissitudes of a Cricketing Motivator* and I hope that all lovers of the game will give him the necessary support in this important field of endeavour.

Best wishes,

Sir Garry Sobers

FOREWORD BY DAVID STONE
(Lead Member for Leisure in Chesterfield)

As Lead Member for Leisure in Chesterfield it gives me great pleasure to write the foreword for Richard Suttle's new book.

I first met Dick nearly 40 years ago, when he started what was to become a long and distinguished service in organising and coaching cricket for youngsters in our area.

Over the years, numerous youngsters have owed a debt of gratitude to Dick for his dedication and devotion. Many of his protégés have gone on to represent Derbyshire C.C.C. and other County Cricket Clubs at various levels.

Finally, I wish Dick and his colleagues all the best for the future.

David Stone

INTRODUCTION

At the age of 66, I am attempting to write a story of my cricketing life, which spans five decades (1943-1993). I can vividly recall many events which took place over this period; but none more than my last trip to Barbados with the Chesterfield and District Touring Team in 1993, under the management of Mrs. Ann Wells, who took over this position, after the sudden death of our ex-Mayor of Chesterfield, Mr. Les McCulloch, who was a very keen and enthusiastic cricketer when he played for the A.G.D.C.C.

Dick Suttle
(N.C.A. Cricket Coach)

Our team was ably led by Mr. Tim Kirk, whom I coached from the tender age of 10. Tim had been on two previous tours to Barbados (1985 and 1988).

As you continue to read this book, you will discover what an ardent, astute and enthusiastic leader he is. He is a member of Chesterfield Cricket Club and was selected recently to represent the M.C.C.

Due to several years of being plagued with arthritis, I have had to retire recently, but I have been able to look back on half-a-century in my life with great pride, from which I can recall the wonderful friends I have made, the interesting people I have met as well as the places I have travelled in my homeland, Barbados, also Holland, Scotland and England; but best of all the young cricketers I have coached and encouraged during those unforgettable years.

If I could relive those treasured years, I would certainly do it all over again, as the advantages have definitely outweighed the inevitable disadvantages which lurk unfortunately in everyone's lifetime.

Finally, as the curtain slowly falls, I now look forward to enjoying my retirement and I sincerely hope that my attempt in writing this book, will enable someone to pursue whatever their field of endeavour is, with as much enthuriasm, fortitude, enjoyment and pleasure as I have enjoyed during those fifty wonderful years of cricket.

Best wishes and good luck in your future endeavours.

BMSuttle

MY CHILDHOOD YEARS

I was born on Monday, 10th December, 1928 and was christened Charles Richard William Suttle. I was told that I was the 6th child of my parents. My mother, Albertha Augusta Wright Linton gave birth to ten children, but I am the only one to survive.

My father, Cornelius Cleophas Smith Suttle, was a salesman for Johnson & Redman's Bakery. He was a very keen cricketer; but unfortunately in the 1930's in Barbados, a poor black man found it very difficult to reach the top in cricket, as opportunities were quite limited in those days.

From this humble background, I have tried to explain with some difficulty to people who simply marvel and seem surprised at my survival. They also wonder how my mother managed to cope and overcome such misfortune and adversity during those tragic years of her life.

As far back as I can remember, around the age of four-and-a-half, my mother used to take me to Mrs. Smith's Infant School, which was situated near the end of the junction of Beckles Road and Bay Street, approximately three-quarters-of-a-mile from the Bayland, where I was born.

However, on one occasion while taking me to school, she decided to ask a lady, who was passing in front of the school to take me there because when she started her journey with me she suddenly realised that her washing was nearly dried, when some thick dark clouds rapidly appeared in the sky.

As she returned home, the lady kindly offered but only took me part of the way. Some sixty-odd years on, I can still visualise the lady to whom I referred, leaving me to cross the road on my own. Unaware of the danger at so tender an age, I crossed the road but came face to face with the bonnet of a baby Austin, just inches away from me. This scared the life out of me, as I could have been run over and never have been able to tell the tale. Now with hindsight, I am convinced there must have been a guardian angel there, as I came to no harm.

When someone informed my mother of the incident, she vowed she would never again ask anyone to take me to school and surely that vow was never broken. Just imagine what a tragedy this would have been for her. Thank God, I have been spared to relate this story now sixty years on with almost pinpoint accuracy.

At this point, I can vividly recall just one more scary moment of my childhood years. I had just reached the age of nine, when my father took me for a swim and as usual we were enjoying another weekend together, but on this particular occasion the waves became unusually rough around the Yacht Club where I almost drowned; but being a strong swimmer he saved me.

From that day onward, the foreboding feeling still lingers on and, as a result, I prefer to be on the cricket field with both feet firmly on the ground; thus enabling me to express more pleasant and enjoyable events, which my Dad opened for me through his love, dedication, enthusiasm and motivation for the game of cricket.

It all started around the age of 11, when he took me to watch the West Indies practice one Sunday afternoon at the Wanderer's Cricket Ground on the Bayland, where many of today's cricketers learnt their cricket and reached their illustrious careers.

I was very impressed and intrigued as he pointed out the names of some of the individual players who were involved at the time. It was the sound of their names which created such an impression on my memory even up to the present time of writing. I am convinced it was on this particular occasion when the seed was indelibly sown. Such names as Rupert Tangchoon (Trinidad), Leary Constantine (Trinidad), Ganesh Persaud (B'G.), Peter Bailey (B'G.), George Headley (Jamaica), Gladdie Waithe (B'dos), Manny Martindale (B'dos), Teddy Head (B'dos), George Challenor (B'dos), George "Cudjoe" Francis (B'dos) and many others who have long passed away.

Soon after this, I started to play cricket on the Bay pasture with a tennis

ball, which we referred to as "HOPPING BALL CRICKET", thus making the majority of West Indian cricketers compulsive hookers of the bouncer.

Between the age of 12 to 13, I represented my elementary school, The Roebuck Boys, where Mr. "Shell" Harris was my Games Master. Matches were arranged to play other schools such as St. Giles Boys, Wesley Hall Boys and Bay Street Boys on a weekly basis. During these formative years, my mother played a great part in my life. She always made sure that I

Dad and Mum sent this photograph from Barbados to me in 1961 at Halesworth Road, Lewisham SE13.
Mum died in 1965 aged 65. Dad died 16 years after at the age of 86

appeared looking presentable for each match I played. Ever since then, those pleasant and encouraging memories have always remained with me.

Within the next two years, I was transferred to Combermere's Secondary School, where the game was played regularly, under the supervision of my two games masters, Mr. Harold Brewster and Mr. Ronnie Hughes. They were excellent coaches and also played in the first and second eleven teams for the School Team in the Barbados Cricket Association.

So in 1943, I started to play my first official match and continued playing for the next fifty years before retirement.

COMMENCING MY FIFTY YEAR SPAN
FROM THE AGE OF 15

At the tender age of 15, I played my first representative match against the Barbados Constabulary C.C. in the Barbados Cricket Association, Combermere's Secondary School, where Frank Worrell and Wesley Hall, to name but a few, started what was to become their illustrious cricketing careers.

Fresh in my memory that occasion of being undefeated in both innings with 10 and 21 respectively, as most of my runs came from delicate deflections, because I had not the strength to force the ball through the covers against such strong opposition, but determination and patience stood me in good stead.

After leaving school, I taught several subjects at The Illustrious Junior School and also took games and athletics for another ten years, and also played for a local team in the Barbados Cricket League organised by Mr. Mitchie Hewitt in the fifties.

I always wanted to be a cricket coach, so I commenced at the age of 20 and was pleased to have two promising youngsters in the school team. They were young Wesley Hall and Garfield Sobers, who were about eleven and twelve years old respectively. The latter showed remarkable ability as he was able to play pace bowling by matured opposition with exceptional ease, and his movements in the field were extraordinary, while the former – who had broken his ankles while riding a horse – started as a wicket-keeper batsman but eventually became one of the world's most feared fast bowlers. His book, *Pace Like Fire*, sums it up comprehensively. As they grew older and stronger they became more confident and fully aware of their talents, and as a result have improved beyond recognition. I am sure their success depended mainly on those early years of dedicated practice, concentration and watching great players of the calibre of Worrell, Weekes and Clyde Walcott, who is now chairman of the International Cricket Council.

Sir Frank Worrell died in 1965, while Sir Clyde Walcott and Sir Everton

Weekes have also been knighted.

Before leaving Combermere's Secondary School in the fourth form in 1946, my shorthand tutor was Mrs. Ruby Barrow, who was an extremely good teacher. My favourite subjects were English, Latin and Geography.

Within a year's tuition with Mrs. Barrow, I gained my Pitman's Shorthand Certificate from the Incorporated Phonographic Society in London on 26th May 1945.

Soon after this, I was able to achieve speeds of 120 words per minute and as a result, I became a part-time sports reporter for the *Barbados Times* in Cheapside Bridgetown just before coming to England to work with London Transport.

The photograph shows Mr. Richard Suttle with a group of his pupils from the Illustrious Junior School, Chelston Avenue, Culloden Road, St. Michael, Bridgetown, Barbados, West Indies. The photo was taken by Mr. Cecil Marshall of the *Barbados Advocate*, three days before Mr. Suttle's resignation. On 3rd January 1947 Mr. Suttle started as Founder and Headmaster at the age ol 19, and resigned on 29th January, 1960, after which he came to England on 17th July, 1960, to take up employment with London Transport.

During his thirteen year period, he met with a measure of success. Seventy-five of his pupils passed their examinations, which included Scholarship winners and Entrance examinations at First and Second Grade schools in the island. Scholarship winners were Winston Nicholls and Desmond Garnes both gaining (3 years each) at Combermere's Secondary, Neville Rowans (5 years) at Modern High School and Beverley Foster (5 years) at Lynch's Secondary, while overseas pupils who attended the school were Remy Lesmond and Michael Roberts (St. Lucia), Philip Henry

9

(Guiana), Neville Rowans and David Worrell (Trinidad) and Hulet Benjamin (New York).

Those who assisted Mr. Suttle were Messrs. Clifford Gittens, Eroll Gay, Caroll Morris, Trevor Maynard, Eroll Rock, Ruben Harding, Eroll Goodridge, Hugh Worrell, Hugh Walcott, Rudolph Gill, Harold Hall and Tyrone Rock who took over from Mr. Suttle after gaining qualifications in Greek, French, Latin, Mathematics and Scripture at Ordinary Level. Successful candidates in Pitman's Shorthand were:- Alice Hunte, Holly Redman, Ena Blackman and Monica Lucas.

The Illustrious Most Successful School Year 1958

These twelve students from the Illustrious School have been successful in gaining entrances to Secondary Schools for the year 1958. There are nine more, who are not in the picture.

Michael Griffith (Combermere) Learie Hampden, John Bayley (Federal

High school) Mr. Richard Suttle (Headmaster of the Illustrious School) Keith Roberts (Ch. Ch. Boys') Winston Gittens and Charles Allamby (Comb).

Jean Best (M.H.S.) Betty Adams (F.H.S.) Annette Garnes (Mc.Donald. H.S.) Esther Bayley (F.H.S.) Ovella Lashley (S.D.A.) and Malta Worrell (F.H.S). those out of the picture are:

Rosemary Redman, Jeffrey Dottin and John Redman (Regent M.S.) Jeffrey

10

Farrell (M.H.S.) Avolyn Clarke, George Gibson, Michael Elliot amd Emelda Woods, (Federal H.S.) Anthony Ellie (Arlington H.S.).

YEAR	NAME OF CANDIDATE	EXAM	SCHOOL
1949	Edward Bushell	Entrance	Combermere
1950	Winston Nicholls	2nd Grade	Combermere
1950	Desmond Garnes	2nd Grade	Combermere
1950	Earl Clarke	Entrance	Combermere
1950	Tyrone Simmonds	Entrance	Combermere
1951	Edmund Hall	Entrance	Combermere
1951	Erskine Belgrave	Entrance	Combermere
1952	Esther Browne	Entrance	M.H.S.
1952	Denize Clarke	Entrance	M.H.S.
1952	Ralph Trotman	Entrance	M.H.S.
1952	Charles Jordan	Entrance	M.H.S.
1952	Edmund Hall	Entrance	Har. College
1952	Cecil Wood	Entrance	Har. College
1952	John Lashley	Entrance	Lodge School
1952	Mark Lashley	Entrance	B'dos Academy
1953	David Gittens	Entrance	B'dos Academy
1953	Peter Gittens	Entrance	B'dos Academy
1953	Ena Blackman	Shorthand	Inc. Phon. Society
1953	Timothy Gittens	Entrance	S.D.A.
1953	Othelles Innis	Entrance	Combermere
1953	Bertam Nicholls	Entrance	Combermere
1953	Arlington Dottin	Entrance	Coleridge-Parry
1953	Arlington Dottin	Entrance	Combermere
1953	Denise Mills	Entrance	Foundation Girls'
1954	Verlyn Blackman	Entrance	S.D.A.
1954	Grace Forde	Entrance	S.D.A.
1954	Lisle Walters	Entrance	Malvern Academy
1954	Sydney Thomas	Entrance	S.D.A.
1954	Erskine Belgrave	Entrance	Har. College
1954	Henderson Jordan	Entrance	Comm. H.S.
1954	Charles Evelyn	Entrance	Comm. H.S.
1954	William Jarvis	Entrance	Comm. H.S.
1955	Randolph Walrond	Entrance	Combermere
1955	Leonard Lashley	Entrance	M.H.S.S.
1955	Addison Cadogan	Entrance	M.H.S.S.
1955	Neville Rowans	5 year schol.	M.H.S.S.

ILLUSTRIOUS SCHOOL
A RECORD OF SUCCESSFUL CANDIDATES

ILLUSTRIOUS SCHOOL
A RECORD OF SUCCESSFUL CANDIDATES

YEAR	NAME OF CANDIDATE	EXAM	SCHOOL
1956	Charles Alleyne	Entrance	Combermere's Sec.
1956	Keith Babb	Entrance	M.H.S.
1956	Winston Downes	Entrance	Combermere's Sec.
1956	Bertram Straker	Entrance	B'dos Academy
1956	Colin Redman	Entrance	S.D.A.
1956	June Gill	Entrance	M.H.S.
1957	Desmond Braithwaite	Entrance	Combermere's Sec.
1957	William Cadogan	Entrance	S.D.A.
1957	Dorothy Worrell	Entrance	Regent H.S.
1957	Hamilton Williams	Entrance	Lynch's Sec.
1057	Gresson Moore	Entrance	MacDonald's H.S.
1957	Stacy Straker	Entrance	S.D.A.
1957	Alice Hunte	Shorthand	Inc. Phono. Society
1957	Cameron Campbell	Entrance	Lynch's Sec.
1957	Holly Redman	Shorthand	Inc. Phono. Society
1958	Michael Griffith	Entrance	Combermere's Sec.
1958	Winston Gittens	Entrance	Combermere's Sec.
1958	Charles Allanby	Entrance	Combermere's Sec.
1958	Learie Hampden	Entrance	Federal H.S.
1958	John Bayley	Entrance	Federal H.S.
1958	Betty Adams	Entrance	Federal H.S.
1958	Esther Bayley	Entrance	Federal H.S.
1958	Malta Worrell	Entrance	Federal H.S.
1958	Avolyn Clarke	Entrance	Federal H.S.
1958	George Gibson	Entrance	Federal H.S.
1958	Michael Elliott	Entrance	Federal H.S.
1958	Emelda Woods	Entrance	Federal H.S.
1958	Keith Roberts	Entrance	CH. CH. H. S.
1958	Jean Best	Entrance	M.H.S.
1958	Jeffrey Farrell	Entrance	M.H.S.
1958	Ovella Lashley	Entrance	S.D.A.
1958	Rosemary Redman	Entrance	Regent H. S.
1958	Jeffrey Dottin	Entrance	Regent H. S.
1958	John Redman	Entrance	Regent H. S.
1958	Annette Garnes	Entrance	MacDonald's H. S.
1958	Anthony Ellie	Entrance	Arlington H. S.
1959	Beverley Foster	5 Yr. Schol.	Lynch's Sec.
1959	Winston Mottley	Entrance	M.H.S.
1959	Linda Livingstone	Entrance	Broomes Sec.
1959	Cecilia Livingstone	Entrance	Broomes Sec.
1959	Eureka Worrell	Entrance	Fereal H. S.
1959	Gordon Hutchinson	Entrance	Fereal H. S.

This picture portrays one of the Illustrious Sons of the soil. We are proud to know that Mr. Sobers has represented the Illustrious School, on several occasions. During that period he was a lad of 12 to 14 years of age with extra-ordinary ability, which could not be so easily hidden. These were the years when the Illustrious possessed their own playing field, which was known as "Brisbane", Chelston Gap, Culloden Road. Many of his beautiful innings will be long remembered by those who were ardent supporters of the "Illustrious".

Mr Garfield Sobers (August 1953)

Some of the most outstanding players who opposed and represented the Illustrious School Team during those years were as follows:-

Wesley Hall (W.I. Fast Bowler), Otho Hinkson, Otho Waithe, Cecil Harewood, Merlin Jones, Percival Bowen, Eammon Hope, Arnold Alleyne, Harold Hall, Michael Simmonds, Frank Grant, Ralph Moore, Colin Hope, The Daniel Brothers, Lionel, Darnley, Feddie and Charlie, Walter Codrington, Cammie Smith, Fredrick Phillips, Waldo Humphry, Keith Kelly, The Sobers Brothers, George, Cecil, Gerald and Garfield, Jim Garvey, Keth Greenidge, Frank Walcott, Richard "Prof" Edwards, Hugh Worrell, Anthony Blackman, Seymour Nurse, Gerald Ifill, Edward King, The Barker Brothers, Horace, Douglas and Justin, George Pinder, Ralph Brerton, Martin Haynes, Hubert Neblett, Cortez Sargeant, Hartley Doyle, Archie Boyce, Alston Fergusson, Trevor Inniss, Fergusson Flemming, Parsons, Martin Braithwaite, Reuben Harding, D'arcy McCollin, Hugh Walcott, Richard McChlery and Richard Suttle (Founder of the Illustrious C.C.) So Good Luck and Best Wishes for their future cricket.

David Newton 1958 Victor Ludorum
at Illustrious Sports

David Newton was Victor Ludorum of the Illustrious Sports Meeting, which was held at the Mental Hospital on Saturday 29th. Nov. 1958. Newton won the 100yds. and 220yds. He came 2nd in the 440yds. Most outstanding event of the day was the mile flat which was open to Men. The winner was Ben Straughn of the Garrison with Denis Tull of the Barbados Constabulary second and Anthony Phillips third. The 100 yds. event for ladies was won by Junior Jones of the St. Matthias Girl's School with Evedney Willoughby second and Shirley Prescod third, of the River Road Church. Eight year-old Cortland Hooper won the 80 yds. event from A. Green of Combermere, and M. Inniss of St. Giles Boys, in that order. Fifteen-year-old Keith Best of Illustrious (B Team) was winner of the Boy's 100 Yds. and 440 Yds. (under 16) events.

At the end of the meeting Mr. Rawle Garner of the Highways and Transport addressed the spectators, and Mr. C. R. W. Suttle introduced Mrs. A.E. Justice who willingly presented the prizes. A vote of thanks was moved by Rev. A. E. Justice.

The Illustrious School Team 1958

Back Row L to R:- *A. Clarke (Capt), J. Redman, Avolyn Clarke, Mr. R. Suttle (Headmaster), O. Johnson, L. Hooper, Mr. R. Harding (Asst. Master).*
Middle Row L to R:- *H. Blades, M, Elliot, A. Ellie, L. Hampden, C. Hutchinson, J. Dottin.*
Sitting L to R:- *Stc. Searles, A. Small, G. Sargeant, D. Cadogan, G. Hutchinson, G. Downes and T. Cadogan.*

Bertram Marville (left), and Richard Suttle, opening the innings for the Illustrious C.C. at Friendship Sports Club in Barbados 1959 against the local Glamorgan Sports Club

The Lodge School's Team 1959
Standing L to R:- *Cramer, Holden, Evelyn, Lowe, Agard, Goddard.*
Squatting L to R:- *Gittens, Tempro, Williams (Capt), Goddard, Black. Roy Marshall of Hampshire and Laurie Johnson formerly of Derbyshire were also pupils of the Lodge School, St. John, Barbados, West Indies*

15

Orbits v. Illustrious, August Bank Holiday, 1958

In a one-day friendly match at the Old Colridge Grounds, Orbits won the toss under the captaincy of Allen Clarke who batted first on an easy-paced wicket with ideal conditions prevailing. After nearly 3 hours batting, skipper Clarke declared with the score at 204 for 8.

O. Broome was top scorer with an aggressive 55 retired. Other useful supporting innings were contributed by F. Cadogan 52, G. Russell 42 and A. Clarke 29 not out.

Bowling for Illustrious T. Edwards took 4 for 49, while Victor Brewster took 2 for 13.

Due to poor fielding by the Illustrious, Orbits batsmen took full advantage of the situation. No fewer than eight catches were dropped.

In their turn at the wicket, the Illustrious were all out for 50 in just under two hours as their innings came to a close 15 minutes before stumps. Their elegant number 3 batsman, Bertram Marville, was the only player to reach double figures as he played a splendid innings for 21, before he was trapped leg before wicket to Todd who bowled accurately. Charlie Griffith, the Orbits paceman, ended with a sensational bowling analysis of 5 wickets for 5 runs. His last victim was skipper Suttle, who defended stubbornly with an injured right hand for 45 minutes for 8. Todd took 5 for 13 as Orbits won the match convincingly by 154 runs.

Lodge School XI v. Illustrious School XI
at Garrison Savannah, Bridgetown

On Saturday, 25th October 1958 Lodge defeated Illustrious School boys by 127 runs. On the previous Saturday, Lodge won the toss and batted first on a softish wicket, which was affected by overnight showers. They were all out for 46.

Skipper Felix Redmill top scored with 15. Grafton Williams took 5 for 19 and Ron Clements 3 for 27. Illustrious ran into trouble and could only raise 25. Paceman Noel Goddard in a hostile spell captured 7 for 10 in 7 overs.

Batting a second time, Lodge's batting showed considerable improvement and at the drawing of stumps had scored 110 for 8. Continuing on the second and final day, the remaining wickets added 13 runs to their over-week score, which brought it to 123. F. Redmill top scored with a brilliant 21, while other good scores, were contributed by I. Pierce, Goffie Edward and D. Hill who scored 20, 20 and 11 respectively.

Bowling for the Illustrious, Skipper Ron Clements took 4 for 43 and Winston Downes 2 for 29.

With nearly three hours left for play and 145 runs required for victory, the Illustrious failed miserably as they found the Lodge attack difficult as they were all out for 18 in exactly one hour. They concentrated too much on defence and were beaten by the flight and direction of Goddard's and Agard's fastish deliveries. The only batsman that showed any resistance was 12 year old Keith Redman who opened the innings and was dismissed almost at the close of the innings to a beautiful catch by Redmill at silly mid-off, off the bowling of Noel Goddard who took 3 for 8 as the match ended in an overwhelming victory for the (under 15) Lodge team.

Match Ends in a Tie

An interesting tie resulted from a friendly one-day cricket match between Illustrious and Barrows XI at the Garrison Savannah, Bridgetown, Barbados on Saturday, 1st November 1958, when both teams scored 46 runs each.

Winning the toss on a lively wicket and batting first. Illustrious could only muster 46 runs of which opening batsman Darrell Gill top scored with 11.

Bowling for Barrow's XI Braithwaite took 5 for 16 and L. White 5 for 14.

Barrow's XI in their turn at the wicket reached 45 for 6 wickets, but the Illustrious captain Richard Suttle came on from the Grand Stand end and in a sensational spell of bowling, he captured the 4 remaining wickets for one run in 1.2 overs which brought the total to 46 also.

Sharing the bowling honours was pace bowler Bertram Marville who captured 5 for 12 in 8 overs as the match ended in a dramatic tie.

Modern High School v. Illustrious at Hamilton, Barbados

On the first day of their two-day inter-school friendly cricket match between M.H.S. and Illustrious ended in a drawn match as the game was abandoned.

Skipper Errol Rock of the Illustrious won the toss on an easy paced wicket and elected to bat and after two hours of entertaining batting, Illustrious scored 248 runs. Mainly responsible for this total was a good opening stand of 45 runs between Darrell Gill and Richard Suttle who laid the foundation of the innings for the incoming batsmen. Gill was first to go when he was adjudged l.b.w. to skipper Neville Greaves for a well played 25. R. Watkins at No. 3 did not last long. He was beautifully caught in the slips off Greaves for 4. In came skipper Rock who played a fine innings of 25 before he was well caught in the covers by Greaves off Griffith's bowling. Then in came the hard hitting Rudolph Gill, who attacked the bowling savagely from the first ball. He made 46 in just under half an hour. During this period of run getting the restraint Suttle reached his individual half century with a delicate leg glance for 2. He was well applauded by the spectators for this chanceless performance. The score board read 156 for 4 as R. Gill was caught at deep square leg just 4 short of his half century. Twelve runs later, Suttle attempting a big hit off Greaves was caught on the deep long leg boundary for an invaluable 56. In came Carl Watkins at number 6. He also played very attacking strokes which enabled him to score a splendid 48 before he was caught in the slips off Manifold's bowling. The other double figure batsmen were, Glenfille Best 15 not out and I. Chase was bowled by Roach for 10.

Bowling for Modern High School, Williams took 3 for 20. skipper Greaves 3 for 63, Manifold 2 for 45 while Roach and Griffith took one each for 41 and 46 respectively.

With 40 minutes remaining for play, M.H.S. replied with 44 for 3. Opening batsman Marshall was bowled by Chase for a brilliant 23, while his partner Griffith was caught by R. Watkins off R. Gill for 8. Skipper Greaves was the last wicket of the day to fall when he snicked an outswinger from R. Gill into the slips for E. Rock to bring off a magnificent catch. At the close of the first day's play M.H.S. were left with 7 wickets in hand and 204 runs to reach the Illustrious total of 248.

Bowling for Illustrious R. Gill and I. Chase took 2 for 15 and 1 for 25 respectively.

Lodge V. Illustrious at Lodge School, St. John, Barbados

In a one-day friendly fixture at Lodge in November 1958, the home team won the toss on a shirt front wicket with ideal conditions prevailing and scored 109 for 3 declared in exactly 100 minutes. There was an opening stand of 21 runs between Nicholls and H. D. McD. Symmonds. Nicholls was beaten and bowled by Suttle for 17. Symmonds retired at 28. G. Mayers at number 3 was top scorer with an aggresive 31 before he was deceived with a well flighted leg-break by Devere Marville who bowled him. D. Goddard was next to go, when he was run out before he had opened his account. Hall who came in at number 5 was undefeated with 10. At this stage skipper Taitt made his declaration and gave Illustrious 109 runs to make in 65 minutes.

Bowling for Illustrious R. Suttle and D. Marville took one each for 23 and 12 respectively.

At the close of play, Illustrious had scored 88 for 9. Opening Batsman, Arley Crichlow was first to go, l.b.w. to Mayers the then up and coming Barbados paceman, for 4. His partner Victor Brewster was caught by Weekes off Holders bowling for 8.

Illustrious were now in trouble as pace bowler Mayers made inroads through the middle order batsmen; but skipper Suttle came to his team's rescue and played one of the best innings of his career by scoring a chanceless 50, before he was bowled by Mayers with the last ball of the day, with the score at 66 for 8. There was great excitement during that closing over by Mayers as Suttle struck him for a 6 and 4 fours, but time robbed both teams of achieving a decision. Bowling for Lodge School, C. Mayers took 4 for 26 in 10 overs. Holder and Symmonds 2 wickets each for 16 and 25 respectively while E. Goddard took the other wicket for 1 run.

Standing L to R:- *Prince Leekes (Capt.) Devere Marville, Leroy Burnette, Rudolph Johnson and Winston Stafford*
Squatting L to R:- *Richard Suttle, Cameron Livingstone, Silvan Wood, and Bertram Marville*
Those out of the picture are:- *Arley Crichlow and Coleridge Sinkler*

Illustrious Gained First Innings Lead in Drawn Game with Lodge School

On the first day of their two-day friendly fixture at Lodge School on Saturday 5th December 1959, skipper Peter Willems of Lodge won the toss on a perfect wicket, and batted first. After two hours they were all out for 97 runs. Willems top scored with 15, while Evelyn, Blades and Cramer made useful scores of 14,14 and 12 respectively. Special mention must be made of the dismissal of Blades at number 4. This attacking batsman appeared to be set for a big innings, but his innings came to an end when the agile Prince Weekes, who was fielding at mid off brought off a miraculous catch off a full blooded drive off Streats bowling. This was Streats fifth victim. Bowling for Illustrious, slow-left-arm leg-breaker, Clyde Streat took 6 for 18 in 10.2 overs while pace bowlers B. Marville and R. Johnson took 3 for 7 and 1 for 18 respectively.

With half an hour's play remaining on the first day Illustrious made 32 for 2. Continuing on the second and final day, Illustrious added 82 for an additional 4 wickets, which brought the score to 114 for 6 declared. Skipper Weekes helped the Illustrious to secure first innings honours when he retired with a graceful 26, while N. Kinch, N. Goddard and B. Marville scored 25, 19 and 14 respectively. Bowling for Lodge, Agard, Holder. Evelyn and Cramer took 2 wickets for 40, 1 for 7, 1 for 12 and 1 for 17 respectively.

Batting a second time, Lodge scored 101 for 2 at stumps. Blades was top scorer with 27. Willems and Evelyn scored 25 and 11 respectively. Bertram Marville took 1 for 16 as the game ended in first innings honours for Illustrious.

I did nothing spectacular in this match but its memories of 47 years ago, still linger, because it was my final cricket match in my native land before I came to England to take up employment with London Transport.

PRIZE DAY

On Sunday, December 13, the Illustrious School held it's Annual Speech and Prize Giving Day at the School Hall, Deighton's Road, St. Michael. Mrs. Linton, Principal of the St Maria Academy, opened the function with a short prayer, after which Mr. Suttle, the Headmaster, introduced Mr. Lawson Hooper as the Chairman. He spoke in glowing terms of Mr. Suttle the Headmaster and of the keen interest which he takes in his pupils.

During the Headmaster's report, he made special mention of nine-year-old Greta Alleyne who was the most outstanding pupil for the year 1959. She also gained first place in

Presentation 1959. Mrs. Albertha Suttle presents a prize to nine-year-old Greta Alleyne

her form (2B) with 84%. She was presented with a special prize from Messrs. William Fogarty Ltd. After the Headmaster's address, the prizes were presented by Mrs. Albertha Suttle, mother of the Headmaster.

At the conclusion, the vote of thanks was moved by Mr. William Cadogan Snr. Mr. Suttle then wished the audience the season's greetings and finally Mr. Bertie Harewood, Layman of the S.D.A., dismissed in prayer, expressing the desire that the children will not only fit themselves for a place in this world but for the world to come.

FORM 2B

Subjects	Position	Results
Scripture	1st	83%
Spelling	1st	74%
Dictation	1st	86%
Arithmetic	1st	87%
English	1st	90%
Total		420
		500

Total 84%   1st
Number of days absent during this term   26

Miss Greta Alleyne of the Illustrious School was the most outstanding scholar for the year 1959. Much is expected of this 9 year-old student who is very intelligent. On account of her splendid achievement, I must wish her a successful educational career and may God bless her in all her activities.

The 1958 Victorious Lodge Team against the Illustrious School Team at Garrison Savannah, Barbados

Back Row:- *D. Roett, K. Agard, F. Redmill (Capt,), R. Webster, T. Pierce*
Middle Row:- *R. Beale, J. Beale, I. Newton, J. Ishmeal, N. Goddard*
Front Row:- *C. Edwards and D. Hill*
Noel Goddard, fast medium pace bowler was presented with a size 6" bat by Mr. C.R.W. Suttle, Headmaster of Illustrious School for a match performance of 140. 7M. 18R. 10W.

21

Illustrious Juniors at Cricket on 18th December 1959
Standing L to R:- C. Hutchinson, A. Best, A. Small, Mr. R. Suttle (Coach), A Forde,
K. Hutchinson, V. Gill.
Squatting L to R:- G. Downes (Capt), D. Cadogan, J. Cadogan, S. Watkins and
G. Hutchinson

Richard Walker

This picture portrays 16 year-old Richard Walker (Captain) of the Illustrious Intermediate who scored 105 runs against Bascombe's XI at the Bay Grounds on Christmas Eve 1959. His innings included 19 fours and two sixes. He was finally trapped leg before wicket to R. Suttle.

Notice   Barbados Advocate 9-2-1960

Due to the resignation of Mr. Richard Suttle of the Illustrious School which was situated at the corner of Deighton's Road, St. Michael, the school has now been removed to the Priest Hall, Deighton's Road under the leadership of Mr. O.T. Rock formerly of Harrison College with certificates in Greek, French, Latin, Maths and Scripture at Ordinary Level. NB pupils are admitted as from today.

Signed by Mr. O.T. Rock (Headmaster of the Illustrious School)

M.C.C. WEST INDIES   TOUR 1959-1960

CAPTAIN—P. B. H. May (*Surrey*)

VICE-CAPTAIN—M. C. Cowdrey (*Kent*)

D. A. Allen (*Gloucestershire*)

K. V. Andrew (*Northamptonshire*)

K. F. Barrington (*Surrey*)

E. R. Dexter (*Sussex*)

T. Greenhough (*Lancashire*)

R. Illingworth (*Yorkshire*)

A. E. Moss (*Middlesex*)

G. Pullar (*Lancashire*)

M. J. K. Smith (*Warwickshire*)

J. B. Statham (*Lancashire*)

R. Subba Row (*Northamptonshire*)

R. Swetman (*Surrey*)

F. S. Trueman (*Yorkshire*)

MANAGER—R. W. V. Robins

P.S. After bowling in the nets at Kensington Oval, Fontebelle, Barbados at the M.C.C. team for long periods, I was presented with the team autographs by the Manager, R.W.V. Robins.

This has been highly treasured by me over the years.

23

Ten-Year-Old Stephen Watkins Emerged Victor Ludorum
at Illustrious Schools Sports

On Friday, 8th April, 1960, the Illustrious School held its annual athletic sports meeting at Old Combermere, Roebuck Street under the supervision of their former Headmaster, Mr. Richard Suttle.

In a day of keenly contested sport, with ideal conditions prevailing, Stephen Watkins emerged Victor Ludorum, by winning the 220 yards in a gruelling finish from Carlton Hutchinson.

In division IV, Anthony Lee and Sandra Sealy of (St. Maria Academy) won the 80 yds. for boys and girls (under 10), respectively. In the intermediate division, Carlton Marsh (Unique H.S.) won the 80 yds. boys (under 12) while Wendy Jones (St. Pauls Girls') won the 80 yds. (under 12).

David Hill (Lodge) won the 80 yds. boys (under 14), while Judy Miller (Co-operative H.S.) won the (80 yds. girls (under 14). The 100 yds. for boys (under 16) was won by Ernest Forde (M.H.S.), while Carmeta Hercules (S.D.A.) was the winner of the 100 yds. girls (under 16).

In the Senior Division, Basil Bailey (M.H.S.) won the 100 yds. boys (over 16), while Lenita Thompson (Lynch's Secondary) was the winner of the 100 yds. girls (over 16).

David Newton (M.H.S.) won the 100 yds. (men.) in ten seconds and also the 440 yds. in 51 seconds.

The highest jump of the day was 5 ft. 3 inches by Grantley Riley in Division 1, while David Hill of Lodge and Carmeta Hercules of (S.D.A.) were champions in Divisions 11 and 111 respectively.

The Girls' cycle race was won by Marva Gamble (St. M.O. Acd.), while Ben Straughn won the 1 mile flat, which was the final event of the day most convincingly.

At the conclusion of the events, Mr. E.A.V. Williams, Government Sports Officer, presented the prizes, through a background of vociferous shouts and ironical cheers.

Signed: *C.R.W. Suttle*.

(Sports Correspondent)
of the Barbados Times, Cheapside

Arriving in London on Saturday 17th July 1960

In 1960, I emigrated to England to work for the London Transport at Catford Depot in South East London. It was there where I carried on playing cricket with many of my Barbadian colleagues. We had one of the strongest teams in the entire transport network, and every year we won a major trophy in the Transport League. Before leaving in 1963, I was recommended by former Kent and England cricketer, Colin Cowdrey for a trial with Catford Wanderers, but due to the difficulty in getting time off work, I was prevented from accepting the offer and perhaps the opportunity of having a trial for Kent. This I have regretted dearly.

At the age of 31 and still hoping to become a great cricketer one day. I soon discovered how competitive a field this was for one to reach county standard. At that time I was unable to devote the time and practise which the occasion demanded so I had to settle for the Village Green standards.

About 10 years before coming to these shores I used to spend hours listening to that great poetic and cricket commentator Mr. John Arlott as he described players and places where Test and county matches were played. This helped to broaden my vague geographical knowledge of England and also built a mental picture of the atmospheric conditions under which the grand old summer game was played. So here I am, to play my first cup match at Northolt, Middlesex against Uxbridge 1961.

Catford Defeated Uxbridge by 71 Runs on 7th May 1961

Scores : Catford 95. Uxbridge 24.
(Fitz Skinner of Catford took 9 wickets for 1 run).

The first cup match between Catford and Uxbridge ended in an outright victory for Catford. Skipper Christopher Harvey of Catford won the toss on a softish wicket which was impaired by overnight showers, batted first and within two hours, Catford were all out for 95 runs.

Cecil Hope was top scorer with a sound 29, and was ably assisted by Stevenson Lynch who scored 23 arid Bryan Collins a useful 16.

Barcombe the Uxbridge's medium pacer took 4 for 21, Hales 4 for 25 and Litten 1 for 22.

In reply, Uxbridge were all out for a meagre 24. The only double figure batsman was Hales, he scored 10. Mainly responsible for their collapse, was some devastating medium pace bowling by Fitz Skinner who finished with the incredible analysis of 9 wickets for 1 run in 8 overs. This performance included the hat-trick. The other wicket was taken by R. Suttle for 10 runs as Catford won their first cup match convincingly.

Matches leading up to the Cup Final
Catford Defeated Plumstead by 104 runs

As the third league game started at Langley Park on Thursday 25th. May, between Catford and Plumstead, the former won by 104 runs. Skipper Harvey of Catford won the toss on a perfect wicket, with the sky slightly overcast, elected to bat and Catford scored 149 for 2 declared. Suttle and Lynch again dominated play as their opening stand yielded 90 runs. Lynch was first to go when he attempted a big hit and was bowled for 49. His innings included nine fours. At tea the score was 110 for 1. Suttle not out 50 and Hope not out 3.

On resumption the batsmen increased the rate of scoring and with the score at 130, Suttle was also bowled for 62. He struck eleven fours. His partner Hope batted well to score an undefeated 31, which enabled skipper Harvey to make the declaration at 149 tor 2. Bowling for Plumstead Tuersley took 1 for 46 while Russell took the other wicket for 59 runs.

With ninety minutes remaining and 150 runs required to win, the Plumstead batsmen failed, to negotiate the varied pace and direction of Skinner and were all out for 45 runs. Skinner again bowled his team to victory by taking 7 for 24. This performance included the hat trick. The only Plumstead batsman to reach double figures was Smoker. He scored 12. The other wickets were taken by Lewis 2 for 5 and Gordon 1 for 8. Thus the match ended in a victory for Catford. They have so far played three league games and two cup matches and have won them all.

Catford Defeated Streatham by 54 Runs

On Wednesday 14th June Streatham suffered their first defeat in their league match with Catford, who won by 54 runs. Skipper Mahoney of Streatham, won the toss on an easy-paced wicket with ideal conditions prevailing and sent in Catford, who found runs difficult to get. At tea they were 56 for 4. On resumption Austin and Yarde increased the rate of scoring as they became associated in a fifth wicket partnership which yielded 35 runs, thus enabling their team to score 113. Lynch topscored with 22 while other good contributions were made by Austin 21, Harvey 19, Yarde 16 and Skinner 15.

The most successful bowler for Streatham was skipper Mahoney who in a fine spell of medium pace bowling captured four wickets for 18 runs. Tipler and Porter took two each for 39 and 55 respectively. Osbourne took the other wicket for no runs.

With ninety minutes left for play and 114 runs required to win, the Streatham batsmen failed to overcome the Catford shock attack, which was spearheaded by Gordon and Skinner, and as a result they were all out for 59. Gridley topscored with an aggressive 17, while skipper Mahoney batted attractively to score 16. For the fifth time Gordon and Skinner have bowled Catford to victory as they took four each for 24 and 31 respectively. Suttle took the other wicket for two runs.

N.B. The next Cup match will be played on Sunday 18th June at Langley Park between Catford and North Street. Play commences at 11.30 a.m. Players are asked to be punctual.

C.R.W.S.

Catford Defeated North Street by Ninety-Two Runs
Scores: Catford 183 North Street 91

Catford marches on as they defeated their opponents, North Street by 92 runs in their third cup game, which was played at Langley Park on 18th June, thus enhancing their unbroken series of victories, Skipper Twyman of North Street won the toss on an easy paced wicket with ideal conditions prevailing and sent in Catford, who scored 183 in three hours. Richard Suttle batted well and topscored with 66, while other good contributions were made by skipper Harvey 30, Yarde 22, Reid 21, Lynch 19 and Austin 14 not out.

Bowling for North Street, Shepherdson took 4 for 56 in 20 overs, while skipper Twyman and Gouge took two each for 65 and 35 respectively. The other wicket was taken by Alexander for 19.

Set with the task of 184 runs to win the match and three and a half hours left for play, the North Street batsmen were only able to score 91 runs. Their left-handed opening batsman Seaman topscored with 18, while Shepherdson made 17 not out, while Twyman and Mizen scored 15 and 13 respectively.

Bowling for Catford, George Gordon and Fitz Skinner shared the bowling honours as they took four each for 33 and 50 respectively, while Keith Austin took the other wicket for no runs.

C.R.W. Suttle.
(Reporter.)

Catford V. Elmers End at Langley Park
Match Ends in a Draw. Scores: Catford 147 for 3 (Dec.)
Elmers End 101 for Three Wickets at Close of Play

On Thursday 22nd. Elmers End held Catford to a draw at Langley Park, as both teams played entertaining cricket. Skipper Harvey of Catford won the toss on, what can only be described as a batsman's paradise, batted first and scored 147 for 3 (Dec.) Mainly responsible for this respectable total was a good opening partnership between Suttle and Lewis, who took the score to 30, before Suttle was brilliantly caught at the wicket by Anthony Forde for

46 off Breakfield's bowling. Lewis who topscored with 47 was out lbw. to the same bowler. Hope at no.3, batted aggressively and scored 25, while his partner Reid was undefeated with 18 when skipper Harvey made his declaration with the score at 147 for the loss of three wickets*

Bowling for Elmers End skipper Brakefield took 2 for 44, while Huxley took one for 37. Pace bowler Clarke, who bowled well, was unfortunate not to have taken a wicket. His figures were 13 overs 6 maidens, 51 runs.

Set with a task of 148 runs to make for victory and one hundred minutes left for play, the Elmers End opening pair, Workington and Walker defended stubbornly and kept the Catford shock attack at bay. Unfortunately, Walker who seemed set for big things, attempted a sharp single and as a result Richard Yarde with a beautiful throw from backward short leg, struck the wicket with Walker well out of his ground. His individual score was 10, and Elmers End had lost their first wicket with the score at 40. Keith Crichlow who filled the breach, batted attractively and remained until close of play with an undefeated 40, while his partner Workington was caught and bowled by Richard Suttle for a well played 20. Skipper Brakefield was the last wicket to fall when he was bowled by Gordon for naught.

Bowling for Catford, Suttle and Gordon took one each for 18 and 30 respectively. Skinner who has been Catford's match winning bowler on previous occasions, failed to take a wicket, but conceded 32 runs in 14 overs, eight of which were maidens. His bowling figures up to date are 84 overs. 34 maidens. 210 runs. 42 wickets.

Richard Suttle.
(Reporter.)

Catford defeated Rye Lane by 52 runs at Langley Park
Scores Catford 132 for 7 (Dec) Rye Lane 80.
Match ends in a very thrilling victory for Catford

Catford continues their march as they defeated Rye Lane in their League match at Langley Park on Thursday 29th. Skipper Harvey of Catford, won the toss on a perfect wicket, under a cloudless sky, elected to bat and, after one hundred minutes batting he declared Catford's innings close with the score at 132 for the loss of seven wickets. Lynch topscored with 38, while Hope made 33 not out. Other useful scores were made by R. Suttle 25, Reid 13 and Collins 11. Bowling for Rye Lane, Skeete took 2 for 42 St. Croix 1 for 22 and Lewis 1 for 30.

With ninety-five minutes left for play and 133 runs needed to win the match, Rye Lane showed great resistance, but with the score at 60 for 4, and half-an-hour's play remaining, skipper Harvey brought on Lynch, who in a sensational spell of slow leg breaks, dismissed 5 for 7 in five overs, while Gordon took 2 for 25 runs and Skinner 3 for 31 runs.

Smith who defended stubbornly, did well to topscore with 24, while other useful contributions were made by Killick 14 Skeete and Palethorpe scored 10 runs each. Thus the match ended in a very thrilling victory for Catford. Congratulations to Lynch who has given a fine all-round performance by topscoring with 38 runs and also bowling his team to victory by capturing five wickets for seven runs.

Catford's next match is on Wednesday July 5th. against Streatham at Langley Park at 3.30pm sharp.

C.R.W.S.

Catford consolidated their position as leaders by defeating their opponents Streatham by ten wickets on Wednesday 5th July 1961
Scores: Streatham 47. Catford 55 for no wickets

Catford defeated Streatham a second time as they met in their return fixture at Langley Park, Skipper Tipler of Streatham won the toss on a perfect wicket in brilliant sunshine, elected to bat and within seventy-five minutes they were all out for 47 runs. At one period the score was 16 for four, with Catford's pace attack though weakened by the absence of Gordon, still demanded the respect from the Streatham openers as the left-handed Lewis with his dangerous inswingers helped his partner, Skinner to remove the four front line batsmen, but Streatham quickly recovered and half-an-hour before the tea interval they were 46 without further loss. At this period, skipper Skinner, who was deputising for Harvey made a bowling change and brought on leg-spinner Stephenson Lynch in place of himself and within a short period Lynch in another devastating spell of bowling took four wickets for no runs. Suggit was the only Streatham batsman to reach double figures. He scored 17. Also bowling for Catford, Skinner took 3 for 13 and Lewis 2 for 18.

With two hours left for play and 48 runs required to win the match, Catford's opening pair Lynch and Suttle attacked the hostile pace attack of Streatham and in twenty two minutes they had scored 55 without loss. Lynch 37 not out and Suttle 17 not out. They struck twelve fours. Lynch eight and Suttle four.

Brixton V. Catford
Match ends in an interesting draw at Langley Park
Scores: Brixton 168 (for 9 Dec.) Catford 87 for 6 at close of play

Brixton held Catford to a keen draw in their return league game at Langley Park on July 20th 1961. Skipper Allen of Brixton won the toss on a perfect wicket with ideal conditions prevailing, elected to bat and after two hours of delightful batting, he declared Brixton's innings close at 168 for the loss of nine wickets. Beckles, who topscored, was undefeated for a well-played 49, while Bennett at No.11, was also undefeated with 20. Other good supporting innings were played by Bent 25, Garner 35, Gordon (formerly of Catford) 17. Skipper Allen 12 and Taylor 11. Bowling for Catford Skipper Skinner and Stephenson Lynch took four wickets each for 69 and 68 respectively.

Set with the task of 169 runs to make in ninety minutes, Catford batsmen did not accept the challenge and at the close of play they had scored 87 for the loss of six wickets. Lynch again topscored with 31, while Holder played a sheet anchor's innings and was undefeated with 23 to his credit, while Richard Yarde scored a painstaking 11.

Within the last twenty-five minutes of play, the Brixton pacemen tried to force a win but they failed to upset the concentration of Holder, Yarde or Austin who held on doggedly and as a result the match ended in an interesting draw. Bowling for Brixton Gordon took 2 for 39, while Taylor and Clarke took one each for naught and twenty-five respectively.

Richard Suttle
(Reporter)

The semi-final is over, Merton is defeated by 65 runs and Catford become eligible to participate in the final at Walthamstow against Willesden on August 20th
Scores: Catford 158 Merton 93

It was a fine day for cricket as a keenly contested semi-final got underway at Langley Park between Catford and Merton on 30th July 1961. Both teams fought well, but at the finish Catford emerged victors over their opponents by 65 runs.

Skipper Skinner of Catford won the toss on a perfect wicket; he elected to bat and after one-hundred-and-seventy-five minutes of delightful batting, Catford were all out for a total of 158. Chiefly responsible for this total was a purely defensive innings of 42 by their opening batsman Richard Suttle. He was ably assisted by Cecil Hope with a sound 27 after the early dismissal of his partner Stephenson Lynch who was caught at second slip off Blackman for 5. Skinner joined Suttle and within ten minutes he had made 19 in aggreasive style, while C. Harvey, Richard Yarde and Reid batted well and scored 15, 14 (not out) and 13 respectively. Boxill was Merton's most successful Bowler. He captured 4 for 11 in 9 overs, while Jordan and Blackman, who bowled intelligently took three each for 22 and 28 respectively.

With four hours left for play and 159 runs needed for victory, Merton were all out for 93 runs scored in two hours. A. Blackman, who batted aggresaively, topscored with 35, while Lucas and Wiltshire contributed 13 and 11 respectively. Mainly responsible for their downfall was an immaculate spell of pace bowling by Skipper Skinner who so often in the season has enabled Catford to achieve their victories. On this occasion the fielding was brilliant, Skinner's figures were 17 overs, 2 maidens, 50 runs, 7 wickets. Holder at the other end, kept a steady length and took 3 for 18 in ten overs, thus helping his team to gain their well-earned victory. Skinner has now taken 65 wickets for 432 runs in 153 overs; 47 of them were maidens.

Richard Suttle
(Reporter)

At Walthamstow London – August 1961 Cup Final
Willesden emerged Champioms

A large and enthusiastic crowd, the majority of whom were Willesden supporters, witnessed a keen and evenly contested London Transport Cup Final which ended in a two wicket victory for Willesdon at Walthamstow. The game commenced at 11.45 a.m. in brilliant sunshine as skipper Webster of Willesden won the toss on a perfect wicket and sent Catford in to bat. They batted just over two hours and scored 106. Their bespectacled opening batsman Richard Suttle played a flawless and sheet anchor innings to top score with 43 and was ably assisted by Hannie Reid in a fifth wicket partnership which yielded 75 runs amidst a hostile opening spell of bowling by Dehany. Reid was out l.b.w. to LaLa for 30 in a face saving innings, while S. Lynch who opened the innings scored an aggressive 16 and Devere Holder at number 8 scored a useful 10.

Dehaney the Willesden paceman bowled to an immaculate length and swung the ball disconcertingly to finish with the splendid analysis of 7 for 40 in 15 overs while LaLa and Birch took 2 for 30 and 1 for 34 respectively.

With 5 hours left for play and 107 runs required for victory, the Willesden batsmen held on doggedly, while Catford under the captaincy of Fitz Skinner, kept on the attack. At one period Willesden had lost 3 for 31. This tense battle continued as both teams struggled for supremacy and with the score at 93 for 8 Catford were still on the aggressive as tension mounted; but to their dismay two more catches went abegging and as a result the Willesden batsmen made use of those opportunities and placed the issue beyond doubt. They scored 110 for 8.

Top scoring for Willesden, George in a very aggressive mood contributed an undefeated 34, while good supporting innings were played by De

Bernard 22, Birch 19 and Elwin 13.

Stephenson Lynch of Catford took 5 for 41 in 13 overs with his slow leg breaks, while Fitz Skinner took 2 for 38 in 18 overs as Willesden emerged 1961 champion.

Catford's XI at Walthamstow on August 20th, 1961. They were presented with a cup immediately after the Cup-Final for being runners-up
Standing L to R:- *A. Burke, K. Austin, D. Holder, S. Lynch, B. Collins, R. Yarde*
Sitting L to R:- *C. Hope, H. Reid, F. Skinner (Capt), C. Harvey (Vice-Capt) R. Suttle*

Catford defeated Walworth by 7 runs in League Final 1961

The game started at five minutes past twelve, under a cloudless sky and ended in a most sensational victory for Catford at Langley Park.

Skipper Freeman of Walworth, won the toss on a wicket which appeared to be perfect, but with just enough moisture to enable the pacemen to get that occasional nip which kept the batsmen guessing. However, skipper Freeman, sent in Catford. Their opening pair, S. Lynch and R. Suttle, were soon in trouble and before 10 runs were on the board the latter was beaten and bowled by Richards for 1, while his partner was also bowled in the next over for 6.

At this period things looked gloomy for Catford as skipper F. Skinner and

6-28, Blackheath Road, Greenwich, S.E.10

Catford Merton
Langley Park
Catford .... C.C. won by AN INNING .... WICKETS .... 6.5 RUNS ...... on Sunday 30th July 6
(delete w^xcessary)   Semi - Final

INSERT BELOW INDIVIDUAL SCORES OF 10 RU)R MORE, AND THREE WICKETS AND OVER.
Any additional information or special feat should be attached on a separate sheet.

Catford ...... Team.   Merton ...... Team.

BATSMAN.			RUNS.	BATSMAN.		RUNS.
S. Mc.	R.	ct. Benn b. Brill	42	Benn	bowled Skinner	4
Lynch	B.	ct. Blackman b. Blackman	5	Wiltshire	ct Harvey b Skinner	11
Hope	C.	ct. Benn b. Blackman	27	Blackman V.	ct Harvey b. Skinner	6
Shipman	F.	ct. Benn b. Blackman	1	Blackman L.	bowled Skinner	35
Harvey	B.	ct. Blackman b. Brill	13	Lucas	ct Skinner Holder	13
Walden	De.	bowled Bovill	0	Webb	bowled Skinner	1
Reid	H.	ct Blackman b. Jenkins	13	Jones	bowled Skinner	6
Marsh	B.	not out	14	Harper	ct Harvey b. Holder	2
Smith	A.	bowled Bovill	0	Fitzus	H. W. Holder	3
Jenkins	B.	ct Blackman b. Jackson	0	Jackson	not out	2
Austin	K.	b. c. w. Jackson	4	Bovill	bowled Skinner	0
		Extras	19		Extras	7
		Total	158		Total	93

BOWLERS.		WICKETS.	RUNS.	BOWLERS.	WICKETS.	RUNS.
Skinner		1	50	Blackman V.	3	28
Holder		3	19	Brill	4	11
				Jackson	3	22

33

At ....
Salford
Walkdenxlaw
Willesden .... on .... 20 / 8 / 01.

Willesden .... C.C. won by ~~AN INNS~~ 12 WICKETS/ .... ~~RUNS~~
(defensif)

INSERT BELOW INDIVIDUAL SCORES OF 10 ᵌ MORE, AND THREE WICKETS AND OVER.
Any additional information or special ~~could~~ should be attached on a separate sheet.

Salford Team.   Bup Stone Willesden Team.

BATSMAN		RUNS
Richard Suttle	clought Dehomarde Delaney	4.3
Johnston Lynch	b F.W. Delaney	16
Cecil Hope	bowled Delaney	0
Fitz Skinner	stumped Delaney	1
Chris Harvey	bowled Delaney	0
Hammie Bird	J.F.W. Lalla	3.0
Richard Gargle	bowled Lalla	0
Owen Holder	caught Chris Birch	10
Brian Gatling	caught Maynard Dehaney	0
Ashton Burke	F.W. Delaney	0
Keith Austin	not out	0
	Extras - - - - -	6
	Total - - - - -	106

BATSMAN		RUNS
Richard BeBernard	ct Ayonde L. Stewart	22
Williams	ct Harvey b Lynch	7
Birch	ct Austin b Lynch	19
Charley	ct Robins b Lynch	2
Webster	run out	3
Edwin	ct Burke Lynch	13
Lalla	bowled Lynch	4
George	not out	34
Nicholls	bowled Skinner	5
Bailey	not out	1
Maynard	did not bat	0
	Extras - - - - -	1
	Total - - - - -	110

BOWLERS.	RUNS.	WICKETS.
Fitz Skinner	38	2
Keith Hursley	13	1
Desire Holder	11	—
Keyshonben Lynch	41	5

BOWLERS.	RUNS.	WICKETS.
Dehaggey	40	7
Lalla	30	2
Burch	34	1

34

C. Harvey tried to stem the tide, but soon after, Skinner fell a victim to Waterman when he was brilliantly caught at second slip for 4. Harvey continued to bat well as five more wickets tumbled. Then Keith Austin, who came in at number 11, batted aggressively and carried the score to 47 before he was bowled by Richards for 10, while Harvey was undefeated with 14. Catford took 105 minutes to score 47 runs. This has been the lowest score for the season. Richards other victims were: Yarde for 1, Holder for 0. Hope who sustained a knee injury was bowled for 0, while Frank Small was Waterman's second victim. He had contributed 9.

Richards' analysis read 12·5 overs, 6 maidens, 12 runs, 6 wickets.

Waterman's analysis read 12 overs, 2 maidens, 35 runs, 2 wickets.

With 5 hours left for play and only 48 runs required for victory, Walworth batsmen found runs difficult to get and within an hour they were all out for 40 runs. The only double figure batsman was Waterman who came in at number 5 and scored 16 runs in aggressive style. Fitz Skinner was very destructive and claimed the wickets of: Jackman for 0, Richards for 2, Moore for 0, Greenidge for 1, skipper Freeman for 0 and Spooner for 0, while Devere Holder bowled Hargraves for 4. Small had Packer caught by Richard Yarde for 1. S. Lynch had Waterman l.b.w. for 16, while Hall was not out 4.

Skinner took 7 for 17 in 7 overs, while Holder, Small and Lynch took one each for 0, 1 and 13 respectively as the game ended in a breath-taking league final.

Magazine and Press Extracts

The 1962 cricket season for Catford is one of the most interesting for a long time. Several teams have the opportunity to win the league and as a result every match is a needle contest.

We were held to a draw by a strong Peckham side. Catford scored 160 for 4 declared in an hour and three-quarters, leaving Peckham the same time to get the runs required. They were unable to do so and at the close of play, they had reached 119 for 6, which gave us a moral victory.

Our next match was against our old rivals Walworth. It ended in a defeat by 22 runs. Walworth batted first and our captain. Skinner, soon had them in trouble as they were tumbled out for 86. Catford had an off day so far as batting was concerned. All the prolific scoring batsmen failed and we were hustled out for 64.

In the cup game at Langley Park, Catford had a fairly easy win against Harrow Weald. Batting first, we scored 245 for 6 declared, thanks to a splendid innings of 102 by St C. Gittens who was well supported by C. Harvey and F. Skinner.

Harrow Weald were soon in difficulties as Skinner and Guy Minto ripped their batting apart. Skinner took 6 for 41.

We won a thrilling match against Bromley by 4 runs with only minutes to spare. Catford batted first to amass 113 runs – most of these coming from Cecil Hope who hit 62. Steadily Bromley progressed towards this meagre target. They seemed assured of victory needing only 5 runs with 2 wickets to fall. Then Les Young was given the ball and he took the last 2 wickets in 4 balls.

The return match against New Cross proved even more exciting than the first encounter. Catford batted first and scored 145 for 2 declared. Richard Suttle, playing one of his best innings scored 71 not out.

New Cross started disastrously, losing 6 wickets for 11 runs. In spite of a spirited seventh wicket partnership by Bruce Callender and Samuel Weeks which yielded 78 runs. New Cross were eventually defeated by 50 runs.

Skinner was the main architect of victory taking 5 for 39 and Frank Small 3 for 6.

From *London Transport Magazine*, August 1962

University College Hospital C.C. 1964 V. St George's C.C. at Dulwich

St. George's Cricket Team at Woodmansterne, Surrey, August 1964

36

Coming to Chesterfield in 1967

After living in London for 6¹/₂ years, the opportunity came in February 1967, to be re-located to Loundsley Green, Chesterfield with the Accountant General's Department as part of their re-organisation to the Pension and Allowance Department where I was employed as a Clerical Assistant. As I arrived in Chesterfield, it was one of the mildest Februarys on record. I was very pleased that I had accepted the offer, because of the difficult housing situation in London. With a growing family it was just the answer to my immediate problem as better facilities gave way to a three-bedroomed house at 26 Southdown Avenue, with a front lawn and back garden. Just a quarter-of-a-mile away was the Loundsley Green Recreation ground where the A.G.D. Junior Cricket Club was formed in 1968.

L to R:- *Ian, Marva and Roger working in the garden*

Disastrous Beginning

My first match in Chesterfield was against Hundall at Hundall in April 1967. I opened the innings for A.G.D. 1st XI in the North Derbyshire League. I will never forget being out for a duck caught by Frank Tann at second slip off the 3rd ball of John Dawson's first over. The ball stuck in Frank's long pullover.

Hundall Cricket Club
Back Row:- B. Colgrave, R. Brown, G. Ede, J. Dawson, R. Hinchliffe, K. Chetwyn
From Row:- F. Tann, J. Hardy, I. Swift (Capt), G, Fearn, B. Joyce
Division 1 champions 3 times. Runners-up 4 times
Baily Shield winners 2 times. Runners-up 2 times
Cantrell Cup wiiners 1 time.Runners-up 2 times
Spriggs Cup winners 1 time. (Six-a-side)

Wicket Keeper George Fearn is recognised as the No. 1 Wicket Keeper in local cricket and has represented the League Xl on several occasions. He has also represented the Army Combined Services for which he was awarded the Corps Colours. He has played for Chesterfield C.C. on several occasions and turned down the chance to play for them in preference for Hundall C.C.

Most victims in one innings 8 for the Army against Calcutta in Singapore.

His ambitions for the future are (1) To see Hundall C.C. in the Bassetlaw League and (2) To score a century.

A.G.D. player hits first century of his career at Dronfield, Sheffield, 14th July 1967

Skipper Bob Foster of A.G.D. won the toss on an easy paced wicket and batted first. After two hours of entertaining batting, A.G.D. were all out for 180. Chiefly responsible for this total was R. Suttle who scored 103 in 95 minutes. His innings included 6 sixes and 10 fours. Useful scores were made by skipper Foster 25, Paul Haffenden 13 and Keith Lugg 12.

Bowling for Coal Aston, Bownes and Cooper took 3 each for 23 and 67 respectively, while Huss took 2 for 33 and Thorpe 1 for 31. With over two hours left for play and 181 runs needed to win. Coal Aston batsmen defended stubbornly, but were all out for 77. Young Thorpe at number 6 was undefeated with a sound innings of 37, while Cooper made 12.

Mainly responsible for Coal Aston's dismissal, was some very accurate left arm medium-pace bowling by 17 year old Philip Ward of A.G.D., who took 7 for 40 in 12 overs, and was ably assisted by Barry Drew who bowled unchanged from the southern end and took 2 for 27 in 16 overs to give their team a convincing victory by 103 runs.

This match I shall always remember. Not because it was my first 100 but it was an opportunity which my Dad welcomed. He had travelled some 3,456 miles to spend a month's holiday with my family.

Being an ardent lover of cricket, he came along to watch the match. With my individual score at 97, I could hear Dad's voice as he shouted the words "three more". As the bowler ambled in, he delivered a half-volley which I welcomed and straight drove for 6 which landed into the street. The next ball, I attempted a similar stroke, but this time I missed it completely as my stumps were spread-eagled as I returned to the pavilion to a standing ovation and 103 to my credit.

I had completed my first century after being in the nervous nineties on four previous occasions. I also had the misfortune to be bowled at 99 only a month before in a friendly match at Loundsley Green against a Methodist XI.

Since then, I have scored another century in friendly cricket and have continued to score half centuries from season to season, but I shall never be able to express in words the wonderful feeling I got when I scored those centuries. I can only hope whenever I play my last innings that it will be one of lasting memory.

I have two sons Ian (5) and Roger (3). They show interest in playing cricket. I shall do my best to encourage them to play one of the best games of a life-time.

All-rounder Foster highlighted day's play for A.G.D.

On Saturday, 4th August 1967, A.G.D. won their return match at Loundsley Green by 48 runs against a powerful Coalite team, and so gained sweet revenge for their defeat in their first encounter.

Having won the toss on a batsman's paradise, skipper 'Bob' Foster of A.G.D., elected to bat and was able to declare with the score at 194 for 1. thanks to a sound opening stand of 43 by G. Shrewsbury and M. Roberts who scored 21 and 29 respectively.

After Tim Crossley had made a quick 13, Richard Suttle at number 4 and

A.G.D. cricket team on 25th May 1968,
about to celebrate the opening of their pavilion at Loundsley Green, Chesterfield

skipper Foster at number 7 came together in an eighth wicket partnership which boosted A.G.D.'s score to a match winning total as they struck 22 boundaries between them. R. Suttle scored 60 and R. Foster 46.

Paceman Ken Scott who spearheaded Coalite's attack ended with 3 for 72 in 20 overs while Jarvis and Crooks two each for 6 and 40 respectively.

With $2^{1}/_{2}$ hours left for play and 195 runs required for victory. Coalite fought back well but were all out for 146. Longden at number 3 top scored with a workmanlike, innings of 49 which included 9 boundaries. Dunham scored 22. Two left-handers Jarvis and Marsden were associated in a last wicket partnership which yielded 46 runs. Jarvis was finally out for 18 while Marsden was undefeated with a splendid 22.

Skipper Foster once again proved his all-round ability for A.G D by taking 5 for 37 in 11 overs. P. Ward and D. Cocker 2 each for 17 and 32 respectively and B. Drew 1 for 24.

In September 1978, Hasland Village Cricket Team made it to the top. Mr. Geoff Holden secretary of the club told them that they would have to play hard to stop in that section as the opposition next season would include

The opening of the Hasland Cricket Club pavilion at Eastwood Park 10th July 1968

Chesterfield, Retford and Worksop The winning team that year included Derek Smith (Capt), David Hooper, Reg Barker, Steve Dolby, Trevor Jackson, Nick Johnson, Terry Phillips, Alan Rhodes, Mick Barnet, Graham Hartshorn and Cliff Smith.

Whirlwind knock by West Indian

Barbados born cricketer Richard Suttle hit 64 runs in 30 minutes when playing for the A.G.D. Cricket team at Chesterfield last night.

The A.G.D. team was playing Sheffield Telephone Manager's Officers in the Post Office North Eastern Region Cricket Competition.

The game was drawn after rain had held up play for nearly 50 minutes.

Batting first the Telephone Manager's Officers scored 133. A.G.D. reached 127 for 7 in reply.

From *Sheffield Star* 11th July 1968

The commencement of the A.G.D. Junior Cricket Club at Loundsley Green,
Chesterfield in June 1968
Photograph was taken by Mr. Alex Marwood of the Post Office *Courier* N.E. Leeds

1 Birth of Accountants General's Department Junior Cricket Club

At last my long awaited dream came true as I came face to face with the responsibility of organising and coaching lads between the ages of 10-16 for the above mentioned club.

It all started in May 1968 when 11 year only Nigel Rees of 2 Southdown Avenue spoke to me about being interested in playing cricket. This immediately triggered off my then dormant enthusiasm for junior cricket. The next week he started to practice and of course the following week half a dozen other lads came along to the Loundsley Green Pavilion which was recently erected for the A.G.D. senior team.

2 Stepping through its infancy

Within a month of Nigel's enrolment, I was able to form the A.G.D. Junior Cricket Club, which is now affiliated with the senior club.

I was very impressed when 42 boys reported at the Loundsley Green Pavilion for their first organised practice.

After two weeks of hard and regular practice, I was able to divide them into three teams, namely A, B and C. A tournament was started from 6th July to 10th August 1968.

This tournament is now known as the Accountant General's Department Junior Triangular Tournament for boys between the ages of (11-17).

The results from year to year have been quite encouraging.

3 On the road to success

Much of our recognition during the first year was due to press reports and photographs which appeared in the *Derbyshire Times*, *The Sheffield Star*, *The Loundsley Green Magazine*, *Poste Haste* and also the Post Office *Courier*. To these editors, I owe a debt of gratitude.

At the end of the season, H. L Brown and Son Limited, Jewellers of Chesterfield, donated a silver cup to the victorious 'B' team which was then captained by Dennis Heath of 32 Southdown Avenue, Loundsley Green and the Presentation was held on Saturday, 17th August by Mr. E. J. Walton (Chairman of the A.G.D.C.C.). He spoke in glowing terms and hoped that this youthful organisation would go from strength to strength.

4 Help, friendship and co-operation

As the first presentation finished, I shall never forget, as I can still hear those very kind, sincere and encouraging words from Mr. Ron Lovegrove of Quantock Way, Loundsley Green.

Ever since then he has stood to his words to give help with the coaching of the Junior Cricket Club. Today I can say that our Junior Club is now an established and thriving organisation. To him and his wife the club owes a debt of gratitude. They have devoted much of their time and effort towards the lads for the past two years and I am sure without their help, friendship and co-operation the club might have died a sudden death.

Boys trounce Chesterfield women cricketers

A women's cricket team, formed at the Accountant General's Department, Chesterfield, several weeks ago, were beaten by 8 wickets when they played their first match at Loundsley Green, last night.

Victors were a team of boys, aged under 14, who like the women, are receiving cricket coaching from West Indian born cricketer, Mr. Richard Suttle, of the A.G.D men's cricket team.

In the picture, the boys give the opening pair, Joan Allison and Fiona McColough a warm welcome.'

The women's team scored 82 runs with Christine Lewis, their captain, top scorer with 14.

The boys scored 86 for 2, with Brendan Wall, their top scorer with 37 not out.

A newly formed women's cricket team went into action at Chesterfield

The newly-formed A.G.D. Ladies' Cricket Team reported at Loundsley Green Pavilion in June 1968 for their first coaching session from their coach Richard Suttle

last night for the first time, and won.

The team, formed at the works of Robinson and Sons Ltd., scored a 5 wicket win over the women's team from the Accountant General's Department, Chesterfield.

Only three members of the Robinson team, which skittled the A.G.D. batting in an hour for 30 runs, had ever played cricket before.

The A.G.D. women's team has been practising regularly. The Robinson players hit the runs needed for victory in 45 minutes.

Said Miss Jean Elliott, 27 year old skipper of Robinson side "I decided to form a team after hearing the A.G.D. had a team, and were looking for opponents. I now have about 18 players."

Commenting on last night's match she added: "I think the A.G.D. underestimated us. If the members continue to show interest, I think we have the potential of a pretty good side."

From the *Sheffield Star* August 1968.

Postmaster's Account Section I
emerged 1968 Inter-Branch Champions
Scores: P.A.S. I 108 for 5 in 20 overs. M.O.B. 59 in 20 overs.

On Tuesday, 30th July, a large and enthusiastic crowd turned out to watch the inter-branch final between P.A.S. I and M.O.B. at Loundsley Green.

Skippe 'Bob' Murray of M.O.B. won the toss on a perfect wicket and sent in P.A.S. who took full advantage of this opportunity and after 20 overs were bowlec they scored 108 for 5. Thanks to skipper Richard Suttle who top scored with 53 which included 2 sixes and 6 fours, while Alan Lee and Philip Ward contributec useful scores of 14 and 11 respectively.

Bowling for M.O.B. Jeff Chambers who bowled with hostility took 3 for 41 in 10 overs, while 'Bob' Murray who bowled unchanged from the 'Nursery End' took 2 for 48 in 10 overs.

In reply, M.O.B. were all out for 59 in 20 overs. All-rounder, Jeff Chambers at number 4 top scored with a well played 24, before he was bowled by Martin Fairs while Roy Diamond made a useful 16.

Bowling for P.A.S. I Martin Fairs who kept a steady length, took 5 for 19 in 9 overs. A. Lee took 4 for 37 in 10 overs and skipper Suttle who took a diving return catch to dismiss Sweething for 4, took 1 for 1 while the agile Danny Symmonds took a spectacular catch to dismiss the impetuous Fielding off Lee's bowling for 3.

As P.A.S. I returned to the pavilion there was a standing ovation as skipper Murray congratulated the champions.

Mr. Jones presented the 1968 Inter-Branch Trophy to skipper Suttle with further congratulatory remarks to which the skipper accepted and thankfully responded to on behalf of his team.

Teams were:-

P.A.S.I: R. Suttle (Captain), M. Fairs, P. Ward, H. Roberts, E. Broome, P. Platts, D. Symmonds, K. Needham, B. Fulleylove, A. Lee, J. Mayer, M. Taylor.

M.O.B.: R. N. Murray (Captain), W. Fielding, J. Chambers, P. Sweething, F. Buddry, D. Blore, R. Samuels, F. Church, C. Swedgwick, R. Walters and R. Diamond.

A.G.D. won first round of Inter-Regional Competition
Scores: A.G.D. 201. Sheffield H. P.O. 192.

Skipper Ron Horner of A.G.D. won the toss on a perfect Loundsley Green wicket with ideal conditions prevailing elected to bat and after 35·2 overs, A.G.D. were all out for 201. At one period the score was 30 for 5, but sound batting by the middle order batsmen saved a total collapse, J. Witham at number 5, top scored with 56, which included 11 fours. He was ably assisted first by M. Fairs who scored 42, of which he struck 9 fours and then Dave Crawley 52 which included 10 fours while David Noble who opened the innings scored 10.

Bowling for Sheffield, Haley took 3 for 33 in 8 overs, Beaman 3 for 35 in 7·4 overs. Wade 2 for 41 in 10 overs. Gray 1 for 20 in 2 overs and Atkinson 1 for 37 in 6 overs.

In reply, Sheffield were all out for 192 in exactly 40 overs. With the score at 20 for 2, Gordon Greaves came in and played a splendid innings to score a century which included 17 fours before he was caught by D. Crawley off Horner with the score at 188 for 9. Neil Atkinson, Pratt, Hatley and Beaman contributed useful scores of 24, 14, 13, and 10 respective.

Bowling for A.G.D. skipper Horner took 4 for 69 in 14 overs, A. Lee 3 for 67 in 15 overs. M. Fairs 1 for 10 in 2 overs and B. Drew 1 for 55 in 9 overs.

A.G.D.'s fielding reached a high standard which helped to stop the flow of runs. Beaman at number 11 was run out for 1 off the last ball of the match while Wade was undefeated with 9, as the game ended in a thrilling victory for the home team.

Eleventh win for A.G.D.

As the North Derbyshire cricket season ended on Saturday, A.G.D. defeated Staveley Y.C. by 23 at Middlecroft. Skipper Malsbury of Staveley won the toss on a rough wicket which made batting an undesirable occupation. He sent in A.G.D. to bat and after ninety minutes they were all out for 75 runs. Tim Crossley played a workmanlike innings of 31 at number 3, while J. Hodgson contributed a useful 13.

Skipper Malsbury, who varied his deliveries cleverly, took 6 for 20 in 10 overs while Lacey and Gregory took two each for 18 and 21 respectively.

With over two hours left for play and 76 runs needed for victory, Staveley Y.C. were all out for 52 runs in an hour. T. Gregory at number 6, chanced his arm when the score was 28 for 8. In one over he added another 23 runs and brought his individual score to 27 not out, which included one six and four fours, before Barry Drew bowled Bennett for 4 to bring his total number of league wickets to 52 for the season.

Some hostile and accurate pace bowling by Dave Cocker and Barry Drew made inroads in Staveley's batting as they took four wickets each for 4 and 17 respectively. A.G.D.'s fielding reached a high standard as the agile Dave Crowley at first slip took a spectacular catch to dismiss Lacey off Drew for 4; while the ever-ready Fairs, broke the wicket at the bowler's end with a "Blandish" throw to run out the unfortunate Jacques before he had scored.

Gregory Cup Final 1968
Scores: A.G.D. 73 in 23 overs. Rolls Royce 76 for 3 in 24 overs.

Skipper Roger Varley of Rolls Royce won the toss and sent in A.G.D. to bat on an easy paced wicket at Tube Works. They started disastrously as John Witham was run out for 0. Next to go was Mick Roberts l.b.w. to Varley for 2. Jim Crossley the incoming batsman was bowled by Ball for 0. Thanks to a fourth wicket partnership of 28 between Philip Ward and Richard Suttle

The latter was first to go caught by wicket keeper Allen off Varley for 21. Ward was bowled by Varley for 6.

At this stage, there was a 2 hour stoppage because of rain. The score board then read 42 for 5, with Dave Crawley not out 11 and Martin Fairs not out 0.

During this period the tea interval was taken. On resumption, Crawley was first to go caught by Bayley at deep mid-wicket off the untiring Ball for a useful 16 while Fairs also fell victim to Ball when he was given out leg before wicket for 1. Alan Lee who came in at number 8 played an aggressive innings, before he was caught by Shaw off Ball for 18 which included three boundaries. Barry Drew was also bowled by Ball for 0. Dave Cocker was run out for 2 while skipper Ron Horner was undefeated with 2.

Rolls Royce's most successful bowler was J. Ball who bowled unchanged from the pavilion end and finished with 5 for 36 in 12 overs while the untiring Roger Varley took 3 for 32 in 11.2 overs.

With 74 runs required for victory. Rolls Royce opened the innings with Rickus and E. Grattage to the bowling of Drew and Cocker.

With the score at 18, skipper Horner made a bowling change and brought on himself in place of Cocker. This proved successful as Dave Crawley at first slip brought off a magnificent catch to dismiss the dogged Rickus for 9, E. Shaw joined the left-handed Grattage who was playing well. Allan Lee who replaced the bespectacled Drew from the pavilion end, bowled Shaw for 8. The score board now read 43 for 2. Griffith the incoming batsman was short lived. He was l.b.w. to Drew for 4.

With Grattage now in full cry and all-rounder Ball looking for runs they began to unleash scorching drives and well-timed hooks.

With the score at 72 for 3, the hard hitting Ball lifted Crawley's second delivery to the long-off boundary for 4 to give his team a well earned victory.

E. Grattage was undefeated with 38 and J. Ball was also undefeated with 13.

Bowling for A.G.D., B. Drew, R. Horner and A. Lee took one each for 17, 19 and 23 respectively as Rolls Royce emerged Champions of the 1968 Gregory Cup.

Pensions and Allowances Section II
emerged 1969 Inter-branch champions
Score: P.A.S. II 130 for 7 in 20 overs. P.S. I 70 in 16.3 overs.

On Tuesday, 22nd July, skipper Paul Clarke of P.A.S. XI won the toss on a moisture laden wicket in brilliant sunshine elected to bat and after 20 overs they scored 130 for 7. Of these Richard Suttle scored an undefeated 48 which included 2 sixes and 7 fours. Don Bush who scored an attacking 45, struck 9 fours while Ron Horner contributed a useful 17 and Mick Pritchard was undefeated with 10. Norman Menzies and John Witham took spectacular catches which got rid of Horner and Pidgeon respectively.

Bowling for P.S. I, Stuart Woodhouse took 4 for 53 in 10 overs while J. Witham took 2 for 73 in 10 overs.

In reply P.S. I were all out for 70 in 16.3 overs. Opening batsman J. Millward top scored with a well played 37 which included a six and 3 fours while S. Woodhouse was undefeated with 11.

Bowling for P.A.S. XI Don Bush finished with the fine analysis of 6 for 7 in 8 overs while the veteran Ron Horner who varied his attack took 4 for 30 in 8.3 overs and enabled their team to emerge Inter-Branch Champions.

Teams were:-
P.A.S. II: P. Clark (Captain), R. Horner, D. Bush, R. Suttle, J. Slaughter, B. Clayton, G. Pidgeon, S. Goggins, M. Pritchard, W. Kelly, J. Eden.

P.S. I: J. Witham (Captain), J. Millward, G. Shrewsbury, J. Proffitt, D. Brooks, C. Ward, S. Woodhouse, J. Sylvester, N. Menzies, J. Cotterill, D. Beastall.

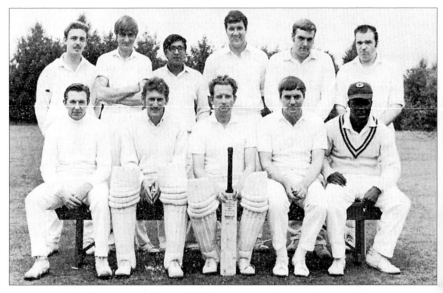

Cantril Cup Winners 1969
Coalite team: T. Marsden, J. Marshall, P. Dasgupta, G. Burton, H. Longden, H. Longden
F. Chappell, D. Cropper (capt.), H. Milnes (sec.), D. Andrews, H. Scott

Boys's Cricket Contest at Chesterfield

About 70 Chesterfield and District schoolboys are to take part in a new cricket tournament at Chesterfield during the summer holidays.

The boys turned up at the pavilion of the A.G.D. Cricket Club at Loundsley Green, Chesterfield.

Their attendance was in response to a call from Chesterfield Cricket Lovers' Society, who are organising the venture in co-operation with the A.G.D. Club.

The move is being made because it is felt that there has been a gradual decline in the opportunities for boys to play organised cricket.

Enrolled

Cricket Lovers' Secretary, Mr. F. G. Robinson said "Less and less cricket is being played in schools. We believe that if something is not attempted to fill this gap, the playing of the game by juniors will eventually disappear."

The boys who turned up at Loundsley Green came from Dronfield, Tibshelf, Grassmoor, Danesmoor and Clay Cross in addition to Chesterfield. They were enrolled for the tournament and also took part in practice. There will be four teams in the tournament, each playing the other twice.

Previous to the tournament beginning, there will be two practice evenings at Loundsley Green.

Mr. Robinson believes the fact that the summer term is short, and that examinations come into the term, may be factors in the game not being played so extensively at schools.

He adds "In the tournament which is being arranged every boy will be engaged in a match. The intention is that the society will provide some sort of a trophy and then some individual award for members of the winning team."

From the *Sheffield Star* 19th July 1969

Schoolboy reporters tackle cricket

Two schoolboys are keeping residents at Loundsley Green, Chesterfield in the know about local cricket matches. They are Colin Fielding, age 16, and Robin Ellis, 15, who have been chosen by Mr. Richard Suttle (cricket coach) to write for the Loundsley Green magazine as junior reporters.

And with these two eager reporters, when one boy is playing cricket the other is sitting on the side lines busily jotting down notes.

Colin of Cleveland Way, Loundsley Green, has already submitted several reports. A pupil at Manor School, he has just taken his G.C.E. 'O' Levels and intends studying for 'A' Levels. His ambition is to become a school teacher. "I volunteered to do these reports and I am finding it very interesting," he said.

Robin of Wenlock Cresent, Loundsley Green is a pupil of Edwin Swale School. His ambition is to become a journalist specialising in sport.

"I have wanted to write for the past five years and I am enjoying reporting on cricket – although I find it very difficult to begin my report at the moment," he said.

From the Sheffield Star, Tuesday August 5th 1969

5 Standard of play improves in 1969

This was a successful season. The 'A' team under the captaincy of Brendan Wall of 23 Wenlock Crescent emerged Champions.

During this season we joined forces with the Chesterfield Cricket Lovers under the capable supervision of Mr. Frank Robinson. It was in the month of August (summer holidays) when we formed and organised a Vacational Cricket Tournament which proved a success in finding individual talent and also extended our cricket horizon, which included youngsters from all over Chesterfield. Unfortunately this was not done in 1970 but Mr. Lovegrove and I managed to organise nine friendly fixtures and as a result of these matches 1,370 runs were scored and 116 wickets were taken. It was encouraging to see teams like Hasland, Eckington, Cutthorpe, Creswell and Newbold participating.

6 Vandalism wrecked A.G.D. Pavilion at Loundsley Green

At the end of the 1970 Tournament the 'A' Team under the able leadership of John Corden of 36 Green Bank Drive, Ashgate, became Champions for the second year running, but this nearly did not happen, because before the beginning of the season, the pavilion was badly wrecked by vandalism during the 1969 winter. It took great fortitude for me to press on at this stage, but once again thanks to the Lovegroves for their persuasion and help which enabled me to carry on, during those trying times. It was only at the end of this tournament that I was convinced that the effort was worthwhile as the boys received individual awards for outstanding performances and other achievements during the tournament. These treasured awards were donated by the A.G.D.C.C., Mr. Cliff Gladwin ex-Derbyshire player, H. H. B. Sugg Sports Shop and Mr. Les Jackson a member of the Chesterfield Cricket Lovers and once again Mr. E. J. Walton (Chairman of the A.G.D.C.C.) kindly presented the individual trophies for the third time.

To round off this eventful season we held our first coach trip to Scarborough on Saturday, 5th September. It was a fine day and we all enjoyed the trip. If the response is good in the future, we shall make it an annual trip to Scarborough for the Junior Cricket Club.

7 Capped players, ages and performances

During the past three years we have produced 12 capped players and some of them have played in the Derbyshire Junior Team.

I take this opportunity to congratulate Roy Cox who scored the first century in the history of the Club. Here is a list cf the capped players and their outstanding performances:

		Age	
1968	Roy Cox	14	54 not out and 5 for 20
1968	Peter Rose	14	9 for 36
1969	John Lovegrove	14	67 not out
1969	Paul Beard	15	53
1969	Roy Beddows	11	51
1969	Brendan Wall	13	56 not out
1970	Stephen Caddywould	15	53
1970	David Corden	11	8 for 22
1970	Roy Cox	16	100 not out
1970	Neil Edney	16	53 not out
1970	Anthony Hession	15	60 not out
1970	Norman Graham	17	5 for 13 in 6 overs which included the hat trick

Chesterfield boy hits century in cricket contest on Saturday, 11th July 1970
A 16 year old boy has become the first to hit a century in a tournament for young cricketers at Chesterfield, now in its third year. The boy who has scored the century in the tournament organised by two cricket enthusiasts at the Accountant General's Department, Chesterfield is Roy Cox, of Mendip Crescent, Loundsley Green.

The organisers are Mr. Ron Lovegrove and Mr. Richard Suttle and the boys taking part are divided into A, B and C teams.

Roy was playing for the 'C' team against the 'A' team when he hit the century which included 3 sixes and 11 fours. He stood undefeated at 100 when his side declared at 142 for 7.

In reply the 'A' team were all out for 56 in just over an hour. A trophy will be presented to the team winning the tournament which is conducted on a league basis which is aimed at stimulating interest in cricket among the boys.

8 Thanks to helpers

Before dealing with yearly statistics which follow this chapter, I am sure they would not have been written, had it not been for the help and dedication of some gentlemen who were prepared to sacrifice their leisurely hours on Saturday mornings as well as other evenings in the week to umpire the matches and help to instruct the boys on the game and maintain a high standard of discipline which is so important to the rearing of young cricketers.

Such names should be mentioned in the modern cricket books in this country because they have done and are doing a great and invaluable service to cricket. Unfortunately, such devoted men are unheard of, that is why I take this opportunity to mention their names which mean so much to me. They are as follows:-

Messrs. R. Lovegrove, R. Horner, W. J. Kedge, R. Murray, D. Corden, R. Worrell, J. Davies, J. W. Ellis, W. L. Ramsden, A. G. Edney, J. Andrew, E. J. Wilde and G. Osbourne.

Last, but by no means least, many thanks to the A.G.D. Cricket Club for fostering the Juniors and also the parents who have co-operated so well. Then the Parks Department for allowing us to use the cricket table and Mrs. Lovegrove, Mrs. Wall, Mrs. Ellis and other ladies for preparing the refreshments from season to season.

9 yearly statistics 1968
A.G.D. Junior Triangular Tournament – Boys (11 under 17)

Date	Scores	Scores
6th July	'C' Team – 89 runs	'A' Team – 53 runs
	R. Cox 26, S. Foster 24	B. Wall 13
	Bowling: R. Cox 6 for 17	*Bowling*: B. Wall 6 for 34
	M. Wall 2 for 1	K. Ward 3 for 26
13th July	'A' Team – 61 runs	'B' Team – 42 runs
	C. Fielding 16, K. Ward 14	R. Ellis 14
	Bowling: P. Rose 4 for 15	*Bowling*: P. Beard 5 for 7 *
	B. Wall 3 for 6	K. Menzies 2 for 5
	I. Stenhouse 2 for 21	D. Heath 2 for 16
20th July	'B' Team – 72 runs	'C' Team – 34 runs
	P. Beard 29, T. Grafton 11	A. Biggs 9 not out
	Bowling: D. Heath 5 for 16	*Bowling*: R. Cox 4 for 38
	P. Beard 3 for 2	S. Foster 2 for 2
	M. Lovie 2 for 19	
27th July	'C' Team – 81 runs	'A' Team – 69 runs
	R. Cox 23, J. Lovegrove 16 n.o.	J. Corden 26

	A. Geraghty 12, M. Walt 11	C. Fielding 19
	Bowling: R. Cox 5 for 27	*Bowling*: P. Rose 9 for 36*
3rd August	'C' Team – 64 runs	'B' Team — 69 runs for 8
	J. Lovegrove 18	P. Beard 41 n.o.*
	S. Evans 17	G. Hardy 9 n.o.
	Bowling: R. Cox 4 for 38	*Bowling*: P. Beard 5 for 31
	A. Geraghty 3 for 39	
10th August	'B' Team – 85 runs	'A' Team – 48 runs
	K. Menzies 22, R. Geraghty 19	S. Bungay 15
	R. Church 17	M. Barker 10 n.o.
	Bowling: D. Heath 6 for 15*	*Bowling*: B. Wall 5 for 24*
	P. Rose 3 for 24	

'B' Team 1st with 6 points   Presentation Match was
'C' Team 2nd with 4 points   held on 17th August 1968 at
'A' Team 3rd with 2 points   Loundsley Green at 9.30 a.m.

Yearly statistics 1969

7th June	'B' Team – 64 runs	'A' Team – 65 runs for 4
	R. Church 18, N. Rees 16	E. Wall, 15, B. Wall 15 n.o.
	H. Brown 10	K. Ward 10 n.o.
	Bowling: P. Hart 1 for 8	*Bowling*: B. Wall 4 for 16
	R. Church 1 for 9	I. Stenhouse 4 for 16
	K. Menzies 1 for 19	K. Ward 2 for 15
Date	Scores	Scores
21st June	'A' Team – 75 runs	'C' Team – 38 runs
	I. Stenhouse 23	R. Cox 22
	R. Beddows 16	
	Bowling: I. Stenhouse 4 for 5 *	*Bowling*: R. Cox 6 for 24*
	B. Wall 5 for 15*	M. Lovie 2 for 24
	J. Lovegrove 2 for 15	
28th June	'C' Team – 100 runs for 6	'B' Team – 84 runs
	R. Cox 45, S. Evans 21	P. Beard 53
	J. Lovegrove 14	
	Bowling: R. Cox 5 for 41	*Bowling*: P. Beard 4 for 50
	J. Lovegrove 3 for 28	R. Ellis 1 for 16
	P. Hart 1 for 15	

5th July	'B' Team – 113 runs	'A' Team – 70 runs
	P. Beard 56, K. Menzies 18	C. Fielding 28, P. Rose 16
	R. Ellis 13, P. Hart 11	
	Bowling: P. Beard 6 for 37*	*Bowling*: B. Wall 4 for 33
	R. Ellis 4 for 21	P. Rose 2 for 29
	I. Stenhouse 2 for 24	
	K. Beddows 1 for 0	
12th July	'C' Team – 93 runs	'B' Team – 62 runs
	J. Lovegrove 67 n.o.	N. Edney 22 n.o.
	R. Geraghty 11	
	Bowling: S. Evans 6 for 24*	*Bowling*: P. Beard 3 for 56
	J. Lovegrove 2 for 20	R. Ellis 5 for 25
	M. Wall 1 for 12	K. Menzies 1 for 0
19th July	'C' Team – 27 runs	'A' Team – 31 runs for 6
	J. Lovegrove 10	K. Ward 10 n.o.
	Bowling: S. Evans 4 for 12	*Bowling*: C. Fielding 3 for 1
	J. Lovegrove 1 for 16	I. Stenhouse 3 for 6
	B. Wall 3 for 18	

'A' Team 1st with 6 points	Presentation Match was
'C' Team 2nd with 4 points	held on 26th July 1989 at
'B' Team 3rd with 2 points	Loundsley Green at 10 a.m.

Yearly statistics 1969 (boys under 17)
A.G.D. Juniors and Chesterfield Cricket Lovers
Vacational Tournament

The above mentioned Tournament started on 21st July and finished on 25th August. Roy Cox (Captain of Mr. Robinson's XI) scored 125 runs in four innings which included 31, 33, 30 and 31 not out respectively.

Ledley Scott of Mr. Murray's XI was the most successful bowler He took 15 wickets for 32 runs. Best individual bowling performance went to Peter Smith of Mr. Homer's XI. He took 5 for 3 against Mr. Robinson's XI at Sheepbridge on 25th August. Stephen Evans of Mr. Lovegrove's XI took the highest number of wickets in the Tournament. He finished with 16 for 75 runs. During this Tournament 1,048 runs were scored and 113 wickets were taken.

Mr. Murray's XI	Scored 304 runs and took 30 wickets
Mr. Horner's XI	Scored 261 runs and took 24 wickets
Mr. Lovegrove's XI	Scored 244 runs and took 32 wickets
Mr. Robinson's XI	Scored 239 runs and took 27 wickets

Final Positions were as follows:

Teams	Positions	Games Played	Won	Lost	Drawn	Aban.	Points
Mr. Murray's XI	(1st	4	3	-	1	2	9
Mr. Homer's XI	(	4	3	-	1	2	9
Mr. Lovegrove's XI	3rd	5	1	3	1	1	4
Mr. Robinson's XI	4th	5	-	4	1	1	2

Other outstanding players who participated in the Vacational Tournament were as follows:-
R. Whitlock, P. Hart and G. Hardy (*Robinson's XI*).
P. Rose, R. Ellis, P. Derbyshire, C. Broughton, R. Geraghty and N. Edney (*Murray's XI*).
J. Lovegrove, B Wall, I. Stenhouse, G. Elliott and N. Graham (*Lovegrove's XI*).
P. Beard, C. Fielding, P. Matthews, J. Corden and R. Church (*Homer's XI*).

THE BARBADOS CRICKET TEAM

CLARENDON COURT HOTEL, MAIDAVALE. LONDON W.9.

MANAGER/PLAYER: RAWLE C. BRANCKER.   CAPTAIN: SEYMOUR Mc. D. NURSE

Manager :- John Griffiths
(Jamaica)

Two wicket victory
for Chesterfield Cricket Lovers' Junior Team against Creswell Juniors
Scores: Creswell (Juniors) 60. Chesterfield C.L. (Juniors) 61 for 8.

Creswell Juniors entertained Chesterfield Cricket Lovers' Juniors at Creswell on Tuesday, 9th September 1969 in their final friendly fixture which ended in a two wicket victory for the visitors in their limited 20 over game.

Skipper Robert Nash of Creswell won the toss on an easy-paced wicket, elected to bat and after 19·2 overs, Creswell were all out for 60 runs. The only batsman to reach double figures, was skipper Nash who was run out for a well played 15.

Bowling for the Cricket Lovers, Ledley Scott took 5 for 13, Peter Rose 3 for 11 and P. Hart 1 for 5.

In reply. Chesterfield Cricket Lovers' Juniors scored 61 for 8 in 20 overs. J. Lovegrove scored 18. R. Beddows 13 and skipper Cox 10.

Bowling for Creswell R. Nash took 3 for 14. C. Woolf 3 for 17. R. Plant 1 for 6 and S. Avory 1 for 10 as the game ended in a thrilling victory for the visitors. Creswell (Juniors): R. Nash (Captain), C. France, P. Limb, C. Woolf, N. Snape, S. Avory, B. Warren, M. Trenam, J. Heath, S. Scroffroan, R. Plant and D. Haddan. Chesterfield Cricket Lovers' (Juniors): R. Cox (Captain), P. Beard, J. Lovegrove, R. Beddows, N. Edney, P. Rose, J. Corden, P. Derbyshire, S. Evans, P. Hart, L. Scott and R. Worrell.

Dave Crowley of A.G.D. highlighted the day's play with 151
Scores: A.G.D. 274. Methodist C.C. 107.

In the annual friendly fixture between A.G.D. and Methodist C.C. at Loundsley Green on Saturday, 9th August 1969 the former won by 167 runs.

Skipper Crowley won the toss in ideal conditions, batted first and after two hours of scintillating cricket, his team was all out for 274. Skipper Crowley who came in at No. 6, played a hurricane innings which lasted ninety minutes and scored 151 runs which included eight sixes and nineteen fours. Johnny Witham who opened the innings with Jim Andrew, was run out for 76 as he struck three sizes and ten fours while Tim Crossley and Roy Cox scored 10 and 10 not out respectively.

Bowling for the Methodist C.C., H. Gosling captured 3 for 54 in 11 overs, D. Newbury 2 for 26 in 5 overs while Kelly, T. Ford, A. Green and A. Whitehouse took one each for 0, 22, 31 and 68 respectively.

In reply Methodist C.C. were all out for 107 in ninety minutes. D. Newbury who opened the innings with Watson, top scorer with 21. Other useful scores were made by D. Church 17, T. Baygin 17, T. Ford 14 and A. Whitehouse 10.

Bowling for A.G.D. M. Fairs took 3 for 14, R. Cox 2 for 6. P. Ward 2 for 7,

J. Witham 2 for 13 and J. Andrew 1 for 28.

Teams were:-

Methodist C.C.: A. Owen (Captain), M. Watson, D. Newbury, D. Church. A. Whitehouse, A. Green H. Gosling, T. Ford, J. Baygin, G. Owen, G. Kelly. *A.G.D.*: D. Crowley (Captain), J. Witham, J. Andrew, T. Crossley, P. Ward. M. Fairs, J. Maher, R. Clayton, J. Eden, S. Foster, R. Cox.

Brockley Internationals gained a 4-wicket victory over A.G.D. at Warren Sports Field, London
Scores: A.G.D. 84. Brockley Internationals 91 for 6 wickets.

Brockley Internationals entertained A.G.D. at Warren Sports Field on 31st August 1969 in their final friendly fixture which ended in a four-wicket victory for the home side.

Skipper Richard Suttle of A.G.D. won the toss on an easy-paced wicket in glorious sunshine, batted first and after two hours of keenly contested cricket A.G.D. were all out for 84 runs. Opening batsmen John Martin and R. Suttle took the score to 21 before Suttle was bowled by Hilcock for 8 runs while Martin was bowled by Watson for a splendid innings of 26. The only other batsman to reach double figures was Philip Ward who contributed a useful 10 runs before being bowled by Skipper Ellis. Other scores were: Chambers 0, Fairs 4, Graham 8, Lovegrove 7, Rose 8, Corden 1, West 0 and May 4 not out.

Bowling for the home team H. Campbell, who flighted his deliveries well, took 3 for 9 and was well assisted by Skipper Ellis who took 3 for 12, L. Hilcock 2 for 26 while A. Thomas and S. Watson took 1 each for 6 and 17 respectively.

With two hours left for play and 85 runs required for victory, the Internationals scored 91 for 6. Thanks to Ellis and L. Jordan who gave their team an opening stand of 31, before Peter Rose bowled Ellis for 11. His partner soon followed as he was caught by May at square leg off Chambers for 21. Skipper Suttle continued to make bowling changes which proved successful as Fairs took a splendid return catch to dismiss the impetuous Campbell for 18. Chambers then struck again trapping Trotman leg before wicket before he had scored. The Internationals were now 71 for 4. During this period the left-handed Cole kept the score moving as he remained undefeated with 17, Chambers got Hilcock leg before wicket for 0, while Norman Graham had Thomas caught by Martin for 6. The score was then 83 for 6, A.G.D. having dropped two catches in this vital period. C. Johnson who was also undefeated with 8, despatched Graham's last two deliveries to the deep mid-wicket boundary to give the Internationals a well-earned victory.

Bowling for A.G.D., Chambers took 3 for 24, Fairs, Rose and Graham took one each for 10, 10 and 11 respectively. May took none for 20. There were 10 extras.

Teams were:-

Brockley Internationals: N. Ellis (Captain), L. Jorden, H. Campbell, J. Trotam, B. Cole, N. Freeman, C. Johnson. L Hilcock, G. Watson, O. Thomas, J. Morris.

A.G.D.: R. Suttle (Captain), J. Martin, G. Chambers, M. Fairs, N. Graham, P. Ward, J. Lovegrove, P. Rose, J. Corden, P. May, M. West.

Whittington player, Michael Booker, hits first century of his career

First century of the 1969 Season was scored by Michael Booker for Old Whittington against A.G.D. at Loundsley Green.

A record total of 404 runs was scored in five hours.

Scores were:-

Old Whittington 213. M. Booker 122, A. Derbyshire 38.

A.G.D. 189. J. Witham 73, D. Crawley 30, R. Homer 20.

Bowling for Old Whittington: 18 year-old Chris Burgess took 5 for 40.

Yearly statistics 1970 (boys 11-17)

Date	Scores	Scores
6th June	'A' Team – 137 runs	'C' Team – 26 runs
	R. Beddows 52, M. Watson 39	S. Wilde 8, S. Parkes 8
	Bowling: M. Watson 4 for 3 *	*Bowling*: D. Corden 8 for 22*
	R. Beddows 4 for 22	S. Parkes 2 for 58
	A. Marshall 1 for 0	
	D. Green 1 for 1	
13th June	'A' Team – 129 runs	'B' Team – 82 runs
	R. Worrell 45 n.o.	S. Caddywould 36 n.o.
	A. Marshall 13, E. Wall 11	
	R. O'Doherty 10	
	Bowling: R. Beddows 3 for 20	*Bowling*: P. Derbyshire 5 for 42
	M. Watson 3 for 23	R. Church 2 for 34
	A Hession 3 for 28	P. Roper 1 for 24
		D. Harding 1 for 28
27th June	'C' Team	'B' Team
	MATCH ABANDONED BECAUSE OF RAIN	
4th July	'A' Team – 121 for 8 dec.	'B' Team – 43 runs
	J. Corden 28 A. Marshall 21	P. Hart 16 n.o.
	M. Watson 20, R. Worrell 19 n.o.	P. Needham 15
	Bowling: A. Hession 7 for 21	*Bowling*: P. Derbyshire 5 for 43
	M. Watson 2 for 16	P. Hart 3 for 21

11th July	'C' Team – 142 runs for 7 dec.	'A' Team – 56 runs
	R. Cox 100 n.o.*	B. Wall 11, R. O'Doherty 10
	N. Edney 15, S. Eyre 8 n.o.	
	Bowling: N. Edney 4 for 15	*Bowling*: B. Wall 3 for 35
	S. Parkes 2 for 4	A. Hession 3 for 54
	R. Cox 2 for 26	R. Beddows 1 for 44
	M. Wall 1 for 3	
18th July	'B' Team – 131 runs	'C' Team – 134 runs for 6
	S. Caddywould 53, G. Hardy 23	N. Edney 53 n.o.
	R. Church 17, K. Clarke 13	S. Parkes 21, G. Cartwright 20
		J. Lovegrove 19
	Bowling: M. West 3 for 57	*Bowling*: M. Wall 2 for 16
	R. Church 2 for 19	S. Parkes 2 for 20
	P. Derbyshire 1 for 19	D. Corden 2 for 25
		J. Lovegrove 2 for 28
		N. Edney 2 for 33

'A' Team 1st with 12 points
'C' Team 2nd with 9 points
'B' Team 3rd with 1 point

Presentation Match was
held on 25th July 1970 at
9.30 a.m. at Loundsley Green

A.G.D. Loundsley Green Junior Cricket Club 1970

Some of the boys whom Mr. Lovegrove and I are coaching at Loundsley Green, Chesterfield, have the potential and could achieve world fame: but they must be prepared to meet the conditions, which are not easy.

To succeed, they must approach the game with the right application, dedication enthusiasm, as well as the ability to accept failure and must be

60

willing to put in many hours of practice and also the desire to learn more as they improve.

I must emphasise that all matches should be played on well prepared wickets. These lads need a great deal of help from those who are in authority to spot talent. These enthusiastic youngsters should be given chances at the trials to use their talents. Otherwise we could be denied the pleasure of seeing yet another world class player from the village green, as cricket can ill afford to lose such players at this crucial stage.

Presentation Match ended in draw
Scores: 'A' Team 124 for 7 dec. Combined XI 76 for 8 (at close of play)

With icy winds prevailing on a dull grey day at Loundsley Green on Saturday, 25th July 1970, John Corden (Captain of this year's victorious 'A' Team of the A.G.D. Junior Triangular Tournament) won the toss on a rain-affected wicket and elected to bat.

After one hour and forty-five minutes of entertaining batting, he declared with his team's score at 124 for 7. Of these, Anthony Hession at No. 6, scored an aggressive and undefeated 60, which included eight fours; while Roy Beddows scored an attractive 31 at No. 4.

Bowling for the Combined XI, Stephen Parkes took 3 for 24 in 7 overs and Neil Edney 2 for 32 in 11 overs.

In reply, the Combined Xl scored 76 for 8 by close of play. Stephen Parkes was top-scorer with 18. Glen Cartwright 14 not out. Skipper J. Lovegrove 12 and R. Church 11.

Roy Cox, formerly of the 'C' Team, strengthened the 'A' Team's attack. He proved to be their most successful bowler as he finished with the splendid analysis of 6 for 18 in 9 overs while A. Hession took 1 for 17 in 5 overs.

After the match Mr. E. J. Walton (Chairman of the A.G.D.C.C.) presented John Corden with the trophy and also individual awards went to other players.

P.A.S. II defeated P.S. II in 1970 Inter-Branch Final
Scores: P.S. II 65. P.A.S. II 68 for 8.

In a keenly contested Inter-Branch Final at Loundsley Green on Thursday, 30th July, P.A.S. II won by 2 wickets as it ended in a nerve tingling finish.

Skipper 'Bob' Foster of P.S. II won the toss on an easy paced wicket with the skies heavily overcast, batted first and were all out for 65. Skipper Foster was top scorer with 19, F. Haigh 13 and Charlie Gillham was undefeated with 12.

Bowling for P.A.S. II skipper Ron Horner bowled well and finished with the splendid analysis of 7 for 28 while Don Bush took 3 for 35.

P.A.S. II replied with 68 for 8. With the score at 38 for 2 and looking well on the way to victory, the middle order batting collapsed as Foster and Bird made great inroads in P.A.S. II's batting as they slumped to 48 for 7, but thanks to a bold and undefeated 8 by that bespectacled vetern J. Kedge, who was well supported by E. Hudd until he was run out for 6. The incoming batsman, Geoff Pidgeon struck the winning run as he executed a delicate late-cut for 4. Other useful scores were made by D. Bush 22 and R. Suttle 12. Bowling for P.S. II, R. Foster took 4 for 29 and D. Bird 3 for 34.

After the match, Mr. E. J. Walton (Chairman of A.G.D.C.C.) congratulated both teams for the standard of play and then presented the Inter-Branch Trophy to Mr. R. Horner (Captain of P.A.S. II) as they emerged Champions for the second year running.

A.G.D. Junior Cricket Tournament

The A.G.D. Junior Cricket Tournament, which has been played on the Loundsley Green recreation ground, ended on Saturday with a friendly match and the presentation of the cup donated by Messrs. H. L Brown and Son Limited of Chesterfield.

The competition was one of the ways in which Mr. R. Suttle has been working hard for two years among the children of Loundsley Green to encourage a love of the game. Three teams were selected for the tournament, which was won by 'A' team, captained by Brendan Wall. Mr. Suttle thanked all who had helped in the tournament and said that he hoped to see another team in the tournament next year. He congratulated John Lovegrove, who captained 'C' team, the runners-up, and Robin Ellis, who captained the 'B' team, who were the only ones to beat the winning team during the tournament, even though they did not gain the highest number of points. The cup was presented by the Chairman of the A.G.D. Cricket Club (Mr. E. J. Walton), who said that he had been impressed by the standard of cricket among the Juniors this year, which reflected not only the hard work done by the coaches (Messrs. R. Horner and R. Lovegrove) and Mr. Suttle who had started the whole thing, but also the enthusiasm of the boys. Membership had grown from over 50 last year to over 70 this year, so that next year would see a 'D' team in the competition.

He was pleased that parents had rallied round, appreciating no doubt the value of the game as character forming pursuit and a means of fostering the team spirit.

The cup was received by Brendan Wall, and a group photograph of the 'A' team was given to each member of the winning team, C. Fielding (Vice-Captain). P. Rose, K. Ward, M. Barker, R. Worrell, E. Moulton, E. Wall, M. Church, P. Lamb, J. Corden, A. Derry, P. Hatherley, I. Stenhouse, S. Elcock,

R. O'Doherty and R. Beddows. Roy Cox was also presented with a pair of batting gloves donated by Mr. Suttle for, scoring the highest number of runs and taking the most wickets at last year's presentation match, and John Lovegrove received a gift for the highest individual score in the tournament.

The President of the Junior teams (Mr. R. Horner) congratulated the boys on playing some very good cricket and said that he was sure many of them would grow up to be very good cricketers. Brendan Wall responded and said it had been very hard to win the cup and he paid credit to the boys in the other teams.

In the presentation match 'A' team scored 90 for 8. Roy Beddows 51 not out. Cox took 3 for 50. Evans 3 for 13. Combined Xl 87. J. Lovegrove 32. D. Corden 12. Fielding 3 for 13 and Rose 2 for 13.

From *The Derbyshire Times*, Friday, 1st August 1969.

Thrilling victory for 'C' team on Saturday, 18th July 1970
Scores: 'B' team 131. 'C' team 134 for 6.

On Saturday, 18th July 1970 at Loundsley Green, the 'C' team gained a 4 wicket win over 'B' team. Having won the toss on a placid wicket with the skies heavily overcast skipper Robert Church of 'B' team elected to bat and after an hour and fifty-five minutes, his team were all out for 131. Stephen Caddywould, their opening batsman scored a brilliant 53 which included 6 fours; other useful scores were contributed by Glen Hardy 23, Robert Church 17 and Kim Clarke 13.

Bowling for the 'C' team, M. Wall, S. Parkes, D. Corden, J. Lovegrove and N. Edney took 2 wickets each for 16, 20, 28 and 33 respectively.

With eighty-five minutes left for play and 132 runs required for victory the 'C' team batsmen accepted the challenge despite the number of bowling changes which were made by skipper Church. He was unable to check the flow of runs and as a result the 'C' team scored 134 for 6 in seventy-five minutes. Thanks to an invaluable and undefeated innings of 53 by Neil Edney. It included 8 fours. He was well supported by S. Parkes, G. Cartwright and skipper John Lovegrove who scored 21, 20 and 19 respectively.

Bowling for the 'B' team, Michael West took 3 for 57, R. Church 2 for 19 and Peter Derbyshire 1 for 19.

Final positions in the 1970 Triangular Tournament were 'A' team 1st with 12 points, 'C' team 2nd with 9 points and 'B' team 3rd with one point.

The following Saturday, Mr. E. J. Walton (Chairman of the A.G.D.C.C.) presented the 'A' team which was captained by John Corden, with a trophy which was donated by H. L. Brown and Son Limited of Chesterfield.

Scores: A.G.D. Selected XI 53 and 96. A.G.D. Junior XI 99 and 54 for 2
The annual friendly match got under way at Loundsley Green on Bank Holiday Monday, 31st August 1970 at 12.40 p.m. in brilliant sunshine.

Skipper Dave Crawley, of the Selected XI, won the toss on a perfect wicket and elected to bat. The Selected XI were all out for a meagre 53 in 70 minutes. The only batsman to reach double figures was their opener David Tarlton who scored 27.

Bowling for the Junior team, Norman Graham took 5 for 13 in 6 overs. He performed his first hat-trick by taking the wickets of D. Crawley, W. Bird and J. Bird. Skipper Anthony Hession took 4 for 14 and R. Suttle 1 for 1.

In reply the Junior XI scored 99 in 105 minutes. A. Hession scored 31, R. Suttle 25 and Stephen Wilde 13.

Bowling for the Selected XI Skipper Dave Crawley took 4 for 35 in 12·4 overs, with his slow leg breaks. Derek Harding 3 for 25 in 9 overs and D. Tarlton 1 for 12 in 6 overs.

Batting a second time the Selected XI were all out for 96 in two hours. Jim Bird was top scorer with 25, D. Tarlton 21, Keith Menzies 19 and W. Bird 14.

Yearly statistics 1970

Summary of Junior Friendly fixtures played during the months of July, August and September.

Dates	Teams	Venue	Scores
31 7 70	A.G.D. v Hasland	Loundsley Green	A.G.D. 123 for 5 dec. Hasland 122 for 6 at close
7.8.70	A.G.D. v Eckington	Loundsley Green	A.G.D. 37 for 8 in 20 overs Eckington 40 for 5 in 11 overs
11 8.70	Eckington v A.G.D.	Eckington	Eckington 78 for 5 in 20 overs A.G.D. 76 for 7 in 20 overs
14 8 70	Hasland v A.G.D.	Loundsley Green	Hasland 101 A.G.D. 104 for 1
178.70	Newbold v A.G.D.	Loundsley Green	A.G.D. 73 Newbold 74 for 3
19 8.70	Cutthorpe v A.G.D.	Cutthorpe	Cutthorpe 40 A.G.D. 45 for 2
28 8 70	A.G.D. v Creswell	Loundsley Green	Creswell 54 A.G.D. 55 for 6
29 9 70	A.G.D. v Cutthorpe	Loundsley Green	Cutthorpe 56 A.G.D. 60 for 8
3 9.70	Creswell v A.G.D.	Creswell	A.G.D. 116 for 5 in 70 minutes Creswell 116 for 5 in 70 minutes

NOTE: In the above-mentioned games 1,370 runs were scored and 116 wickets were taken.

Scores: A.G.D. Juniors 116 for 5 in 70 minutes
Cresswell Juniors 116 for 5 in 70 minutes

Creswell Juniors under the captaincy of David Cuckson, entertained A.G.D. in the final friendly fixture of the season at Creswell on a sun drenched Thursday evening on 3rd September 1970.

Skipper Roy Cox of A.G.D. won the toss on a perfect wicket and elected to bat. After 70 minutes of delightful batting the visitors scored 116 for 5. Roy Cox was top scorer with 49 and the bespectacled Brendan Wall who opened the innings with Cox, scored an invaluable 41 while John Lovegrove scored 10.

Bowling for the home team, Howard Mellish took 3 for 4 in 2 overs and Terry Rushton 2 for 16 in 3 overs.

With 70 minutes left for play and 117 runs required for victory, Cresswell lost their first 3 wickets for 25 runs, but thanks to an invaluable fourth wicket partnership of 86 runs between Robert Nash and Christopher Wolf, before the former was out for 30 when the score-board read 111 for 4.

With one over left, 6 runs needed to win and 6 wickets still intact, Creswell were only able to score an additional 5 runs for the loss of another wicket.

This brought the scores level as 15 year old Christopher Wolf returned to the pavilion with a splendid and undefeated 56 to a standing ovation, Ian Mellish and Terry Rushton had scored 11 and 10 respectively.

Bowling for A.G.D. Juniors Neil Edney took 3 for 11 in 9 overs and R. Cox 1 for 24 in 5 overs as the match ended with a breath taking tie.

Teams were:-

Creswell: D. Cuckson (Captain), C. Wolf, I. Mellish, A. Trott, R. Nash, A. Wood, T. Rushton, P. Osbourne, H. Mellish, M. Turner and A. Thatcher.

A.G.D.: R. Cox (Captain). N. Edney, J. Lovegrove, S. Caddywould, A. Hession, M. West, S. Wilde, B. Wall, D. Harding, G. Cartwright and A. Marshall.

A.G.D. Junior Cricket Committee for 1971

The following officers were elected on Wednesday, 12th August 1970. They are as follows:-

Mr. William Ramsden	*President*
Mr. John Kedge	*Chairman*
Mr. John Lovegrove	*Secretary*
Mr. Ron Lovegrove	*Treasurer*
Mr. Roy Cox	*Junior Representative*
Mr. Keith Menzies	*Asst Junior Representative*
Mr. Richard Suttle	*Coach and Sports Writer*

Mr. Andrew Marshall   *Junior Reporter*
Mr. Stephen Wilde   *Asst Junior Reporter*
Mr. David Edney   *Junior Statistician*
Grounds Committee: Messrs. R. Church, M. West, G. Cartwright, A. Hession. R. O'Doherty and R. Worrell.
Selection Committee: Messrs. R. Cox, J. Lovegrove, R. Lovegrove. J. Kedge and R. Suttle.

PLANS FOR 1971

We have succeeded in introducing our first Quadrangular Junior Tournament which commenced on 15th May and concluded on 31st July.

During this period twelve matches were played among teams 'A', 'B', 'C' and 'D'. Each team was given 17 players from which the Captains and Vice-Captains selected their teams every week for the Tournament. They were as follows:-

'A' Team:
A. Hession (Captain), A. Marshall (Vice-Captain), R. O'Doherty, E. Wall, B. Wall, M. Barker, P. Smith, P. Tennant, J. Finn, J. Siveaney, A. Derry, D. Green, M. Spracklen, R. Beddows, R. Young, H. Brown and S. Dolby.

'B' Team:
R. Worrall (Captain), M. West (Vice-Captain), D. Edney, G. Hardy, P. Hart, G. Elliott, S. Willis, C. Beach, S. Wilde, N. Rees, N. Kelly, M. Holmes, S. Holden, I. Corden, P. Derbyshire, P. Milbourn and I. Corden.

'C' Team;
J. Lovegrove (Captain), M.Wall (Vice-Captain), D. Corden, S. Parkes, G. Cartwright S. Eyre, D. Wagstaff, N. Edney, J. Hancock, A. Willis, M. Crook, K. Swift, P. Gallagher, N. Fox, D. Foster, J. Murray and D. Lester.

'D' Team:
D. Harding (Captain), S. Evans (Vice-Captain), S. Caddywould, S. Gosling, P. Best, A. Davis, C. Whitehead, A. Dawson, M. Brocklehurst, P. Lamb, T. Buffery, P. Needham, P. Roberts, D. Bird, J. Beddows, S. Smith and R. Cox.

We are pleased that the A.G.D. Junior Club are entering a team in the Sheffield and District Junior League. The teams which participated were as follows:-

1. Eckington   represented by Mr. D. Woodhead
2. Frecheville   represented by Mr. B. Hobson
3. Hundall   represented by Mr. D. Billington
4. Norton Oakes   represented by Mr. D. Salt
5. Staveley   represented by Mr. B. Jones
6. A.G.D.   represented by Mr. R. Lovegrove
(Age limit — Under 18).

A most timely gesture
by R. N. 'Bob' Murray

That anyone should want to sacrifice valuable time, either leisure or otherwise, devoting it instead to coaching boys at cricket, may well be regarded by many as the height of folly. Yet, this is exactly what Dick Suttle and Ron Lovegrove (and to no lesser extent, Mrs. Lovegrove – fetching, carrying, tea-making, baking, fund-raising, indeed, the list is endless) have been doing for some three years now.

Encouraged by a very tiny band of cricket enthusiasts, amongst them being Mr. Frank Robinson and Bill Ramsden of the Chesterfield Cricket Lovers' Society and Mr. E. J. Walton of the A.G.D. Cricket Club, Dick and Ron have soldiered on in sickness or in health, in good weather or in bad whilst the vast majority make promises and pay lip service.

There is no doubt about it. To do this kind of thing, to take youngsters, most of whom were 'raw' cricket-wise and to knock them into shape so that they begin to look like cricketers calls for devotion and dedication above and beyond the call of duty. Few will ever have any idea of the amount of man hours or, indeed, human endeavour expended by these two in this most worthwhile cause; worth while, because playing cricket not only keeps the lads out of mischief, but will help to imbue them with a certain amount of self-discipline and character which, it is hoped, will remain permanently with them.

No one – particularly those of us having the interest of the game at heart – can deny that such help and guidance to young would-be cricketers is a most timely gesture. Year after year as veterans all over the country hang up their boots the gap left by their departure gets wider and wider. We see ominous signs of the great soccer take over. Each year the soccer season stretches its tentacles further and further, slowly – almost imperceptibly squeezing out this wonderful summer game of ours. Games masters of schools, colleges and even universities seem indifferent to this impending doom, devoting less and less time to cricket, more and more time to soccer and rugger. Thanks largely to the deification and glamorization of soccer by the mass media, more and more youngsters are forsaking cricket for soccer. This is why the gesture by Suttle and Lovegrove is very timely.

Cricket is fighting a desperate battle for its very existence; and if it is not to become defunct in the next few years we need our Suttles and Lovegroves throughout the length and breadth of the country. And so, let us say, carry on Dick and Ron, and when, perhaps, in the not so distant future, one of your lads steps into an England Test Side, it might truly be said: This is your finest hour.

Final friendly match ends in a draw
Scores: Cutthorpe 149. Chesterfield 129 for 8 wickets

Cutthorpe, under the captaincy of Michael Jolley, entertained Chesterfield Friendly XI in their return fixture of the season at Cutthorpe on a heavily overcast Saturday afternoon on 19th September 1970.

Skipper Jolley won the toss on an easy-paced wicket and elected to bat. Within two hours, Cutthorpe were all out for 149. Useful contributions were made by R. Suttle 27, E. Davidson 27, B. Croft 16, A. Millington 15, M. Jolley 15, whilst A. Treece and J. Armstrong scored 10 each.

Bowling for Chesterfield. R. Mayfield took 4 for 41, B. Harding 4 for 44 and I. Vardy 2 for 39.

With two hours' left for play and 150 runs required for victory. Chesterfield scored 129 for the loss of eight wickets by close of play. G. Briggs was top scorer with 29, the other major contributors being J. Revill 19, L. Davies 19, and R. Mayfield 17, while R. Horner was undefeated with 16.

Bowling for the home team, A. Treece took 4 for 26 while S. Whitworth, J. Armstrong and R. Smedley took one each for 26, 31 and 32 respectively as the match petered out in a draw and the players returned to the pavilion for the last time this summer.

Teams were:-

Cutthorpe: M. Jolley (Captain), B. Croft, A. Millington, R. Suttle, E. Davidson, J. Armstrong, A. Treece, R. Smedley, S. Whitworth, C. Millington and R. White.

Chesterfield: D. Mason (Captain), I. Vardy, G. Briggs, N. Edney, J. Lovegrove, B. Harding, R. Mayfield, L. Davies, J. Revill, A. Wright and R. Horner.

A word of warning to all cricketers especially juniors
by R. Suttle

No one should play cricket on rough wickets. This encourages bad stroke-play and involves a great risk of physical danger. It also helps to flatter the bowler who is successful under such deplorable conditions.

It is just not cricket

The main reason why many youngsters give up cricket and are no longer interested, is because as a result of playing on rough wickets, their confidence has been ruined from the start. Then it takes a really dedicated youngster to continue.

It will not hurt you to prepare your own wickets with the right instructions. From experience, there is great satisfaction when you prepare a good wicket and you are able to bat with confidence and assurance.

The bowler will appreciate his success then, because the rewards of his labour would have been well earned.

In brief, many authorities on cricket do not realise the danger of playing on rough wickets. They usually wait until someone is badly injured and then abandon the game, but it is too late to repair the damage which could have been easily avoided in the first place.

For the interest of all concerned, all players should refuse to play on rough wickets and then those in authority, will wake up and make sure that proper wickets are provided so that those who participate can enjoy the grand old summer game and also give the spectators the necessary entertainment which the game seems to lack nowadays.

Cricket with a poetical touch
by D. Tarlton

Suppose you've heard Dick's batting again,
Smiting blows to the count of ten
Cover drives, shots off his legs,
Down to third man, over slips' heads,
Any loose ball without a doubt,
Rockets to the boundary with a hefty clout.
Lofted fours and a towering six,
Consist of just a few of his tricks.
This man can turn the spectators on,
Relentless, dauntless, till the game is won.
No bowler survives Dick's flashing bat,
Pausing only to the cry – "How's that?"

Chesterfield Boys raise £3 for Derbyshire C.C.

A group of boy cricket enthusiasts at Chesterfield have collected £3 from their pocket money to send to Derbyshire County Cricket Club centenary appeal.

The boys, who have collected the money, take part in a tournament organised during the school summer holidays by two adult cricket enthusiasts, Mr. Richard Suttle and Mr. Ron Lovegrove.

The tournament is played at Loundsley Green, Chesterfield, and after the tournament teams drawn from the boys played against other teams of boys in Chesterfield area.

Said Mr. Suttle "The boys who have subscribed are between 10 years of age and 16. This money represents some of their pocket money and shows their enthusiasm for the game."

After hearing the money had been collected by the boys Major D J Carr

Secretary of the County Club, said "I think it is absolutely marvellous that the boys wanted to do this."

The Derbyshire Centenary Appeal aimed at raising £100,000 but said Major Carr, the Club had not by any means raised what they had hoped.

From *Sheffield Star* Wednesday, 2nd September 1970

POETRY IN HIS CRICKET

As an enthusiastic cricketer 41 year old West Indian born Mr. Richard Suttle loves hitting a good innings. But there is another side to the character of Richard, father of three, of Southdown Avenue, Loundsley Green, Chesterfield. He also composes poetry.

Richard, a prolific scorer in cricket with two centuries, a 99, and a number of 50's to his credit while playing for A.G.D. team at Chesterfield, is nothing like prolific with his poetry.

Since 1961 he has written only 16 poems which he hopes eventually to compile an anthology which can be published.

Richard, who came to England 10 years ago, says he likes to write when everything is peaceful, sometimes in the early hours of the morning.

From *Sheffield Star* Thursday, 1st October 1970

My Greatest Desire
While resting in the peaceful morn.
I thought of the place where Christ was born,
Good Lord to Thee I prayerfully look
For guidance from Thy matchless book.

Procrastination, still a thief of time
Has truly caused a change of mind,
But with another effort tried,
I hope to gain my spiritual stride.

Tis my desire to live for Thee
Amidst my past adversity,
Please grant me just humility
To help my frail ability.

In dreadful hours of dark despair
I'm certain of Thy presence there;
So once again. I ask of Thee
To bless me with humility.

When such a virtue is bestowed,
My gladdened heart with praises glowed
Lord help me to be reconciled
And be Thy faithful Christlike Child.

God's Great Grace, Grip and Glory

Securely by His Grace we're kept
Through danger's hours we calmly slept;
Grace clears away that fearful thought
Which evil thoughts so forcefully brought.

Upon God's Grip we need to hold
Like lost sheep from a shepherd's fold,
His presence with us now must dwell
To save us from the snares of hell.

Triumphantly His Glory shines,
Upon your heart as well as mine,
So daily we must ask for more
To reach God's bright celestial shore.

Grace, Grip and Glory God possess,
To help mankind to face life's tests;
So prayerfully now we all must be
To dwell with God eternally.

Richard Suttle

The Cricketing Cavalier of Chesterfield
By Glyn Williams – Staff Reporter *Chesterfield Star*

Dick Suttle and Tony Hession are about to open the A.G.D. innings at Loundsley Green on August 1970

Richard Suttle, he's the man,
Who loves the game of cricket.
As far as he's concerned,
It's a joy to bat on a perfect wicket.

He finds it most exciting,
On village green or Lords,
And loves to see the leather ball,
Go hurtling to the wall.

He also worships deadly spin,
And bowling, too, that's fast,
The sight of agile fieldsmen
As they go streaking past.

Pavilion banter, chattering crowds,
Also fill him with glee,
For surely sparkling cricket,
Is the ultimate ecstasy.

His exploits for the A.G.D.,
And Catford Bus Depot,
Have made him an opponent feared.
By many a cricketing foe.

A legend in his lifetime,
And for centuries ahead,
This dynamic all-rounder,
A swash-buckling life has led.

Sheffield and District Junior League Fixtures 1971

Days	Dates	Teams	Venue
Tuesday	4th May	A.G.D. v Hundall	Loundsley Green
Tuesday	11th May	Hundall v A.G.D.	Hundall
Tuesday	18th May	Staveley v A.G.D.	Staveley
Tuesday	25th May	A.G.D. v Eckington	Loundsley Green
Tuesday	8th June	Eckington v A.G.D.	Eckington
Tuesday	15th June	A.G.D. v Norton Oakes	Loundsley Green

Tuesday	22nd June	Frecheville v A.G.D.	Precheville
Tuesday	29th June	A.G.D. v Frecheville	Loundsley Green
Tuesday	6th July	A.G.D. v Staveley	Loundsley Green
Tuesday	13th July	Norton Oakes v A.G.D.	Norton Oakes

Parramore Cup

Thursday	6th May	A.G.D. v Birdwell	Loundsley Green

All matches start at 6.30 p.m.

Signed: R. LOVEGROVE Representative

R. SUTTLE

11th May 1971

A.G.D. (Juniors) 53 off 25 Overs
N. Edney 21, S. Evans 10
Bowling: R. Cox 6 for 8, S. Evans 2 for 3

Hundall (Juniors) 27off 15·4 Overs
R. Kealey 10
Bowling: I. Hall 4 for 11, I. Webb 1 for 14

(Parramore Cup)
13th May 1971

(Record)
Birdwell (Juniors) 141 for 2 off 20 Overs
A. Scott 70 not out, M. Higginbottom 38 not out
Bowling: R. Jasker 3 for 39, M. Drijaca 2 for 36, S. Wood 2 for 0, R. Walker 1 for 1

A.G.D. (Juniors) 81 off 19 Overs
R. Cox 36, A. Hession 18
Bowling: A. Hession 2 for 23

18th May 1971

A.G.D. (Juniors) 92 for 4 off 20 Overs
Roy Cox 57 not out, A. Hession 16
Bowling: N. Edney 3 for 19, S. Evans 2 for 25, S. Parkes 1 for 0

Staveley (Juniors) 47 off 14·2 overs
Brian Alien 18, S. Jones 11
Bowling: G. Rowding 2 for 28

25th May 1971
Eckington (Juniors) 91 for 5 off 20 Overs
R. Nightingale 62, P. Gledhill 16
Bowling: R. Nightingale 3 for 19, P. Gledhill 2 for 23

A.G.D. (Juniors) 57 for 5 off 20 Overs
J. Lovegrove 17. N. Edney 12. R. Cox 10, R. Beddows 10 not out
Bowling: S. Evans 4 for 37, N. Edney 1 for 8

15th June 1971
Norton Oakes (Juniors) 74 for 9 off 20 Overs
S. Kerrigan 24, J. Broughton 17, V. Silcock 14 not out
Bowling: S. Akbar 3 for 21, P. Higginbottom 2 for 29

A.G.D; (Juniors) 64 for 8 off 20 Overs
R. Cox 29, N. Edney 22
Bowling: N. Edney 4 for 26, A. Hession 2 for 9, S. Evans 1 for 36

29th June 1971
Frecheville (Juniors) 71 off 19.5 Overs
S. Copley 31. G. Oxiey 11
Bowling: S. Cantrell 5 for 39, A. Grocock 2 for 27

A.G.D. (Juniors) 72 for 7 off 18.5 Overs
J. Lovegrove 41, N. Edney 16
Bowling: S. Evans 5 for 36, N. Edney 4 for 27

6th July 1971
Staveley (Juniors) 114 off 24.5 Overs
A. Mosley 43, R. Hewitt 25, J. Hodgkinson 22
Bowling: A. Mosley 5 for 54, R. Hewitt 2 for 15

A.G.D. (Juniors) 97 off 24.2 Overs
A. Hession 32, S. Evans 25 not out, A. Parums 17
Bowling: S. Evans 5 for 42, N. Edney 3 for 16, P. Derbyshire 1 for 7, A. Parums 1 for 13

13th July 1971
A.G.D. (Juniors) 83 for 7 off 25 Overs
B. Wall 27, R. Cox 10
Bowling: S. Evans 2 for 22, R. Cox 1 for 23, N. Edney 1 for 34

Norton Oakes (Juniors) 84 for 5 off 22·4 Overs
J. Clarke 36 not out, S. Akbar 16, J. Kirkby 16
Bowling: S. Akbar 2 for U.S. Jemmott 2 for 17, P. Higginbottom 2 for 23

19th July 1971
A.G.D. (Juniors) 64 off 19.2 Overs
R. Cox 23, S. Evans 14, J. Lovegrove 10
Bowling: A. Hession 3 for 29, S. Evans 2 for 10

Eckington (Juniors) 66 for 5 off 17.4 Overs
A. Grieves 28, P. Clegg 15 not out
Bowling: R. Nightingale 3 for 26, E. Hilton 2 for 0, G. Wilson 2 for 1, P. Gledhilt 2 for 33

CONCLUSION

Finally, I would like to express my sincere thanks to all those who have contributed to this book.

I must say how much I appreciated the cup which was presented to me by Mr. T. Cocker (President of the A.G.D.C.C.) at our Annual Stag Party for the outstanding member for 1970.

Of all the trophies I have won, I treasure this more than any other because it constantly reminds me of the time and effort which had been put in to help Junior Cricket to which I am so closely attached.

Taverners C.C. at Loundsley Green

Taverners Cricket team at Loundsley Green on 29th May 1971 in North Derbyshire League against A.G.D. Taverners won by ten wickets.
Scores: A.G.D. 42. R. Suttle 15.
Taverners 44 for 0. K. Randall 28 not out. D. Pugh 18 not out.
Bowling for Taverners: B. Shaw 4 for 6. D. Smith 5 for 25.

Most successful seasons

The 1972 cricket season has been the most successful one for the A.G.D. Cricket Club. after being in North Derbyshire League for the past 8 years. The above-mentioned Club achieved the double by winning League Division II as unbeaten Champions and Winners of the Gregory Cup and also 6-a-side. Division III as well Runners-Up in Divisions I and III of the North Derbyshirp League 1973.

To add to this success, our Junior team, of which Mr. Lovegrove and I are proud to be their coaches, emerged Champions of the Southern Division of the Sheffield and District Junior League and also runners-up in the Leslie

The Old Sun, Alresford, Hampshire. *Alresford 2197*

7th September 1971

Dear Mr. Suttle,

Many thanks for your letter, and for the copy of "The Impact of Junior and Senior Cricket". Congratulations on getting it published and I will certainly notice it in the review of cricket books 1971 in the next issue of Wisden. Will you, though, let me know from what address it can be bought and what the price is - the readers usually that.

Kindest wishes,

Yours sincerely,

[signature]

Fletcher Cup and in 1973 have completed the Triple by winning the league, the Parramore Cup and the 6-a-side and our under 21 team won the league cup competition in the Chesterfield and District Youth League and also 6-a-side champions of the same league.

Many of our ardent followers and supporters will be pleased to know that because of the fine results achieved during the past 2 seasons, players and their individual performances have been recorded in an article by Mr. Les McCulloch, a member of our senior cricket team.

I was very fortunate the last 2 seasons to see some of the best Junior cricket talent in action on our local village greens. This has given me some assurance that cricket will be restored to its former glory in the not too distant future.

I was convinced that quite a lot can be done to help this youthful potential, and have to disagree with many critics who would have us to believe that cricket is a dying game*

What we need now are experienced players who are willing to devote and dedicate more of their time and try to help mould and reshape the ability of these enthusiastic youngsters who within the next decade, could give the game a new lease of life and once again give us the opportunity of seeing players of the calibre of Bradman, George, Headley, Hutton, Constantine, May, Sobers, Hazare, Worrell, Hammond, Cowdrey, Weekes, Walcott, Compton, Lloyd, Pollock, Richards, Boycott and Kanhai as well as Lindwall, Miller, Grimmett, Trueman, Hall, Laker, Lock, Gibbs, Ames, Evans, Grout, Knott and our local hero Bob Taylor (Derbyshire and England wicket keeper) to name but a few of the stars over the past 3 decades. Incidentally, Mr. Taylor's testimonial is this season and he is very grateful to the people of Chesterfield for their loyal support.

I shall be pleaded to see more organised Leagues and facilities given to these keen youngsters to improve their skills, and also more publicity through the medium of press, radio and television. Even posters with vital information that people from all walks of life will be aware of what is happening in their mjdst. This could be a way in which many of us could see the stars of the future.

To sum it all up, I was fortunate to have my first book entitled *The Impact of Junior and Senior Cricket* reviewed in *Wisden* 1972 and as a result, it made quite an impact in local circles as well as other parts of the country. I received many congratulatory letters from various parts of the world and take this opportunity to thank all those who have read and purchased my previous book. Its appeal has encouraged me to write a second, now entitled *Junior Cricket Reborn in the Seventies*.

I hope its contents will be enjoyed by all its readers and many thanks to all the secretaries and players who have included articles and statistics from the various clubs for entry as well as all the companies, firms and individuals who have contributed advertisements to help to pay for its publication.

Finally, I hope that I will be able to continue to help in the administration of cricket even when my playing days are o'er and also be able to inject a new lease of life in the grand old summer game, which to me is a way of life.

The reason for the above-mentioned title, is because during the past 3 years Junior cricket has truly sprung to life more than ever before, and it is pleasing to see many senior teams doing their utmost to foster and encourage youngsters to play competitive cricket which will prove a great asset to all concerned.

Messrs. Taylor and Hendrick of Derbyshire have been selected for the tour of the West Indies 1974. I must join with all the members of my junior cricket club in wishing them a successful tour and congratulations to them for being selected.

Will the real Mr. Suttle stand up

This story concerns a gentleman who above all can be classed as everybody's friend, especially if the gentleman requires a favour.

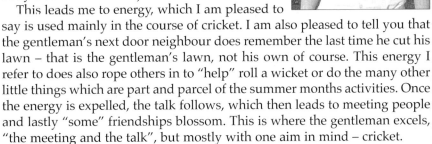

The gentleman is a mixture of energy – no one can deny this – guile, persuasion and downright cunning. He is a past master in the art of getting into cars – of course not his own – or of borrowing bicycles, sometimes without the owners consent. Coupled with these the gentleman rarely can find a pen when commencing to write a "cricket report" or if he does manage to locate one, somebody else has no doubt just lost one.

This leads me to energy, which I am pleased to say is used mainly in the course of cricket. I am also pleased to tell you that the gentleman's next door neighbour does remember the last time he cut his lawn – that is the gentleman's lawn, not his own of course. This energy I refer to does also rope others in to "help" roll a wicket or do the many other little things which are part and parcel of the summer months activities. Once the energy is expelled, the talk follows, which then leads to meeting people and lastly "some" friendships blossom. This is where the gentleman excels, "the meeting and the talk", but mostly with one aim in mind – cricket.

Through this mixture of a man he has created much happiness and joy for many people – some frustration as well I must add, but his heart is in the right place and I can only conclude by saying that if we all had the opportunity not many of us would change him. The gentleman is much better on our side than against us.

Keep up the good work and may the future hold as many pleasant memories as the past.

Ron Lovegrove

Family's Christmas Present – Their Little Girl
By a staff reporter

The Suttle family of Southdown Avenue, Chesterfield, have already had their Christmas gift – and a super one at that.

When nine-year-old Marva Suttle went into hospital in Sheffield for a hole-in-the-heart operation carried out on Novmber 20, the family wondered whether she would be home in time for Christmas.

But now Marva. daughter of Mr. Richard Suttle and his wife Lettice. is back home already.

Mr. Suttle, a member of The Cross Street Baptist Church, Chesterfield, said: "She has surprised us by the speed at which she has recovered. It was beyond our wildest dreams."

Skill

"It was due to the skill of the surgeons and good nursing that she made such a rapid recovery."

Marva's eight-hour operation was carried out at the Northern General Hospital. Mr. and Mrs. Suttle were at the hospital to be near their daughter and wait for news.

It was discovered at birth that Marva had a heart murmur. It was not until August this year that Mr. and Mrs. Suttle were told she should have an operation.

Mr. Suttle, a well-known Chesterfield cricket enthusiast added: "Marva has done everything any other child would do, including physical education."

Breathless

"It was only when she did excessive exercise that we noticed she appeared more breathless than other children."

While in hospital, Marva received gifts of a doll, nightdress and slippers from colleagues of her father at the A.G.D. Chesterfield.

She also received a letter from her class at the Brampton Primary School.

Mr. and Mrs. Suttle have three other children, Ian aged seven, Roger aged ive, and Steven aged two months.

A.G.D. Cricket Club 1972
Step by Step to the Championship and the Cup Double
North Derbyshire League by Les McCulloch
Record Number of Points 72

The season opened with an easy win over Kennings Remoulds by 88 runs. Kennings being dismissed for only 14 runs. D. Cocker taking 7 wickets for 6 runs.

Hundall were beaten by 9 wickets after being all out for 34 runs, Tube Works lost by 71 runs, Clowne Nalgo by 103 runs and Padley and Venables easily by 9 wickets.

The Spital game stopped because of rain, but Kennings Remoulds were quickly dismissed for 31 runs leaving the A.G.D. with a good win of 126 runs. A. Hession hit a fine 66, in this game.

Clowne Nalgo faced the highest score of the season 192-6, J. Sims 74, J. Witham 42, R. Suttle 32 and failed by 170 runs, being all out for only 22 runs. This was the biggest win of the season.

Rain stopped the Sheepbridge game, but the sun shone brightly against Tube Works who lost by 128 runs, the main feature of this game was the highest opening stand, of the season between L. McCulloch and J. Sims, 82 runs, who scored 47 and 59 respectively.

Hundall were beaten by 37 runs, Scarcliffe twice by 31 and 54 runs. In the first game A.G.D. were all out for 147 with L McCulloch 54 and J. Sims 33 scoring 87 of the total. In the second game a fine knock of controlled agression by D. Crowley 58 saved the A.G.D. from collapse after being 3 wickets down for only 2 runs.

At this stage of the season the result were 13 games 11 wins 2 rained off. Padley and Venables held A.G.D. to a draw. A.G.D. scored 168-7. L. McCulloch 54, D. Crowley 35, Padley reached 81-6 off the 40 overs. Seven bowlers were tried to obtain the break, through but were unable to do so.

Back on the winning trail. Spital beaten by 37 runs with A.G.D. all out for 118, another fine opening stand of 74 from L. McCulloch and J. Sims.

To retain their unbeaten record A.G.D. held S. & J. Kitchins to a draw Kitchins scoring 167-7. A.G.D. only 41-3 by dour defensive batting. A.G.D. fielded a very depleted team which lacked the opening bowling attack of Sims and Cocker.

In the Gregory Cup, Remoulds were beaten by 63 runs and Spital by 93 runs S & J Kitchins in the Semi-Final by only 26 runs and an easy win in the final by 9 wickets over Sheepbridge ended a fine season.

Outstanding performances by J. Sims 54 wickets, D. Cocker 32 and N. Graham 17 did the damage with the ball, whilst J. Sims 284 runs, L. McCulloch 349, J. Witham 206. R. Suttle 167 and D. Crowley 142 making the vital runs which ensured so many fine victories.

Pen Portraits of 1973/74 Players

N. Edney
Neil Edney, Captain of the A.G.D. Junior C.C. Age 18. An enthusiastic all-rounder. Useful right handed batsman and right arm pace bowler. Can be hostile at times. Best performance this season was 8 for 23 against Aston Hall. Played for Chesterfield 2nd XI in the Bassetlaw League on a number of occasions and has taken 109 wickets this season.

Roy Cox
Captain of A.G.D. Youth C.C., Roy Cox, Age 18. Dependable right handed opening batsman. Has scored two centuries. Slow right arm bowler and safe fielder. Has represented Derbyshire Colts 1971 and 1972. Much is expected of this dedicated youngster for future seasons. Has led A.G.D. Youth team 1973 to League Cup Champions.

J. Lovegrove
John Lovegrove, (Vice-Capt.) of the A.G.D. Jnr. C.C. Age 16. An attacking right handed batsman and promising wicket-keeper who has scored many

half-centuries. Has also represented Chesterfield 2nd XI Bassetlaw League. Has been invited to attend Final trial for Derbyshire Colts on 20/7/72, and was chosen for the Colts team to play his first match on 1/8/72. Has scored 1,090 runs last season and has the distinction of being captain of the triple crown Champions 1973.

S. Evans

Stephen Evans. Age 17. A talented right arm swing bowler and useful right handed batsman and brilliant fielder. Captured 33 wickets for 138 runs in last years A.G.D. Junior Quadrangular Tournament. Represents A.G.D. in the N.D. League. Recent performances 8 for 22 in the final against "C" including the hat-trick on 14/7/72 and 8 for 33 in semi-final of the Gregory Cup against S & J Kitchin and to crown it all, he took 4 for 27 in 9 overs in the Cup Final against Bradfield Jnrs. as three of them were taken in one over without a run being scored.

D. Harding

Derek Harding. Age 16. A promising right arm medium pacer. Useful right-handed batsman. Good fielder and improves with every game. Should develop into a fine captain. Has also represented Robinson's first XI N.D. League 1972.

A. Hession

Anthony Hession. Age 16. An aggresive right handed batsman and right arm medium-pacer. Best performance so far was 61 against Eckington. Outstanding fielder in any position. Performed his first hat-trick against Creswell when he took 3 for 38. Has also played for A.G.D. in the Bassetlaw League 1971 and was a regular player in the unbeaten A.G.D. 2nd Division of the A.G.D. League 1972.

D. Corden

David Corden. Age 14. Promising right handed batsman and slow right arm off-break bowler. Best bowling performance was 8 for 22 in 1970 in the A.G.D. triangular tournament against the "A" team who had scored 137. Should develop into a fine allrounder. At present he plays for the Chesterfield Friendly XI.

N. Graham

Norman Graham. Age 20. A hard hitting right handed batsman and right arm medium pacer with variation of pace. Performed his first hat-trick on 31st Aug. 1970 and took 5 for 13. Best performance recently was 8 for 13 against Tube Works in the North Derbyshire League at Duckmanton Lodge, 1972. Has also won the 1973 bowling average. He bowled 58·1 overs, 11 maidens, 179 runs, 22 wickets, average 8·13.

P. Milbum

Paul Milburn. Age 15. Impressive left-handed batsman with flowing cover drives. Room for improvement in fielding. Should develop into a useful player. Represented Chesterfield friendly XI during the current season and played a major innings against Bradfield juniors in the Leslie Fletcher Cup Final at Stannington on 3/9/72. Has improved during the current season.

B. Wall

Brendan Wall. Age 16. A defensive bespectacled right-handed opening batsman and slow medium right arm bowler and useful fielder. Should develop into a dependable allrounder. Represented A.G.D. in the Bassetlaw League 1971 and also played for St. Cassians College in Berkshire and was a regular player in the unbeaten 2nd Division team of the N.D. League 1972 and has just had a prolific season with the bat. He scored 1,856 runs in 52 innings.

P. M. Smith

Peter Smith. Age 16. A promising allrounder with some hidden potential. Right handed attacking batsman, and fast right arm medium pacer. Useful fielder and a good trier. Has also represented S & J Kitchin in the N. D. League 1972. Now plays for Staveley Works Youth Team. Could be selected for Derbyshire Colts next year.

R. Worrall

Richard Worrall. Age 15. A defensive opening right handed batsman with an array of strokes. Useful right arm medium pace bowler. Good fielder with an accurate throw from the boundary. Has also represented Chesterfield Friendly team and was a regular member of the A.G.D. Junior C.C.

Robin Ellis

Robin Ellis. Age 19. A right handed batsman who could develop into a fine stroke player. A slow right-arm off-break bowler with deceptive flight and a brilliant close-to-the-wicket fielder.

J. Shackleton

John Shackleton. Age 19. A right handed batsman and medium pace left arm bowler. Has the ability to develop into a useful all-rounder. Played for A.G.D. in the Bassetlaw League and North Derbyshire League. Made some respectable scores during the current season.

S. Wilde
Stephen Wilde. Age 15. A very enthusiastic cricketer. An attacking right-handed batsman and a safe fielder in any position. Has played this year in the Sheffield and District Junior League, should be a regular player next season. Has finally emigrated to Canada July 1973.

M. Brownett
Mick Brownett. Age 20. A right handed defensive batsman who is capable of scoring many runs; quick runner between the wickets. Good fielder, who excells at cover-point. Played for A.G.D. in the Bassetlaw League 1971. A regular member of the second team 1973.

D. Lester
David Lester. Age 14. A right handed batsman with some potential which can be greatly developed. Useful fielder and winner of the 1971 Junior Match Award in the Final of the Quadrangular Tournament. Played for Chesterfield friendly XI on many occasions and is a regular player in the Sheffield and District Junior League.

S. Cadywould
Stephen Cadywould. Aged 16. A stylish right handed opening batsman with a repertoire of strokes. Reserve wicket-keeper. With more concentration should develop into a fine cricketer. Has represented Robinsons and A.G.D. Senior Teams in 1971. Has finally joined the Army at the end of the 1972 season.

A. Horton
Andrew Horton. Age 16. Fast-medium right arm bowler and attacking middle-order right handed batsman and brilliant fielder. Has represented the Chesterfield Barbarians where his cricketing career began, and is now a regular member of the A.G.D. Jnrs. Has taken over a hundred wickets this season. Could develop into a good county cricketer.

A. Marshall
Andrew Marshall. Age 14. A promising allrounder who is very dedicated. An attacking right handed batsman and right handed medium pace bowler with low trajectory and brilliant fielder. Youngest member to represent A.G.D. Jnrs. in the Sheffield & District League.

M. Hollindale

Mick Hollindale. Age 17. A sound attacking right-handed batsman with a repetoire of strokes. Reserve wicket-keeper who was selected for Derbyshire Colts in 1972. Plays for Tube Works in the Bassetlaw League and the Chesterfield Youth Council C.C. of which he is captain. This year he played for A.G.D. Jnrs. and scored 1,450 in 51 innings with nine not outs.

L. Kerss

Logan Kerss. Age 17. A fast medium right arm bowler and a hard hitting right-handed batsman. Played for Spital in the North Derbyshire League. Useful fielder. Plays for A.G.D. Jnrs. and has had many fine spells of bowling.

S. Baker

Stephen Baker. Age 16. Another fast-medium right arm bowler who bowls with some hostility. Should develop into a good fast bowler. Must try to command a better length. Capable of becoming a useful middle order batsman and a useful fielder.

M. Barnett

Mick Barnett. Age 15. A promising allrounder with much potential. A right handed batsman and a useful bowler. Has taken many brilliant catches during his first season.

A. Llanwarne

Anthony Llanwarne. Age 15. Like "Mick" is a right handed batsman and right arm slow bowler. Has done well during the recent season. Should develop into a useful allrounder.

Individual Quotations
D. Crowley
(Founder of AGDCC, 1961)

In addition to wishing Richard the best of success with his latest publication, I should also like to congratulate the A.G.D. Juniors on their remarkable successes during the 1973 season. In saying this I am fully aware that the key factor to these successes can be attributed to the outstanding efforts of Mr. R. Lovegrove and Mr. R. Suttle and the Committee of the A.G.D. Junior C.C. I must

also make a special mention of Mrs. Lovegrove's untiring efforts of assistance to the juniors. Catering, first aid, scorer, supporter, this lady must be one of the clubs greatest assets.

From the senior clubs point of view I am extremely pleased with the influx of younger players into the senior teams, and speaking from the veteran stage I look forward to seeing these youngsters playing an important role in the future of the A.G.D. Cricket Club.

Mr. Dave Crowley, (Founder of the A.G.D. C.C.) and his willing workers pose for a photograph after erecting the new score box at the Civil Service Ground. Duckmanton Lodge, Calow, Chesterfield, 18/8/72

Most of my endeavours to break into the literary world have ended in the receipt of a rejection slip. This I hope will be published because it is in praise and bears also my best wishes for my friend, Dick Suttle. This man lives cricket and but for Fate could have been representing the West Indies in the Test Series just ended. He is not only a cricketer in all its aspects, he is a Crusader for the game. He may have his little foibles but few men would have the nerve to take the youth of a locality and mould them into a team of exceptionally good players. I know him also to be a Christian of some enduring faith. May he for ever go with Christ.

C. Drabble

Dick Suttle is not only to be congratulated on the fine work he is doing in promoting junior cricket but also in producing this book which I am sure has involved many hours of 'burning the midnight oil'.

It is very comforting to know that in Chesterfield there is such a thriving and enthusiastic bunch of juniors who are keen to play cricket and this I am sure is a fact that augurs well for the future. Without enthusiastic youngsters the future of our beloved game would be in dire straits and if Dick Suttle and his juniors continue to progress as they have done over the past three seasons I am confident there will be no shortage of competent young cricketers in the area for the future.

In conclusion I would like to wish him every success in the sale of this book, which I have very much enjoyed reading, and to thank him for all the excellent work he has done fctfljunioricricket so far and to wish him, his willing band of helpers and juniors every success for the future. To look forward to the day when I learn that a player who started his work at

Loundsley Green has been selected to play for a first-class county, or better still, for England. Judging by the enthusiasm shown by these lads this could not be beyond the realms of possibility.

Mr. David Mason, ex-President, from previous book.
Bassetlaw Cricket League

Selected for tour of West Indies

Chesterfield cricketer Geoffrey Miller has been selected for the England Young Cricketers team which will tour the West Indies for six weeks later this year.

Nineteen year-old Geoff, who lives at 2, Enfield Road, Highbury, Chesterfield, heard last week that he had been named as one of the 15 players, all aged 20 and under, to make the trip.

A right-hand batsman and off-break bowler, he clinched his selection in trials at Edgbaston, Birmingham a month ago. The tour lasts from July 29 September 10.

Geoff plays with Chesterfield C.C. at Queens Park, and has played regularly in the Derbyshire under-25 and 2nd XI this season. Last week he acted as 12th man for the full Derbyshire side on the second day of their match against the Australians at Chesterfield.

Last year he was 12th man for the county side when they played Pakistan, and he hopes to become a professional cricketer with Derbyshire.

Meanwhile, he is working at Thornton Firkin and Partners, Quantity Surveyors Chesterfield, and dreaming of the land of the Calypsos. Eighteen months ago, Geoff toured India with the English Schools Cricket Association.

No Wes Halls – but watch out for this spinner!

Future England batsmen can feel easy about playing Test matches against the West Indies – there are no up-and-coming Wes Halls or Charlie Griffiths. But a young leg-spinner called Imtiaz Ali could cause a few problems.

So says Geoffrey Miller, Derbyshire's 20 year-old all-rounder, who returned home to Chesterfield this week after a six week tour of the West Indies with the Young England cricket team.

Geoff, who had an outstanding tour said: "We were all surprised at the lack of true fast bowlers. We did not come across one young bowler who was as quick as our own."

However he was full of praise for the 19 year old Imtiaz Ali – "a really great bowler who could well be playing Test cricket 3 years from now."

There seems no shortage of promising batsmen either, with one called Bacchus and another named Johnson topping Geoff's list of men to watch.

Ten Matches

The tour, taking in several different islands, included 10 matches against young sides!. One was won, one lost and the rest ended in draws.

Geoff, who plays Second XI and Under 25 cricket for Derbyshire and for Chesterfield in the Bassetlaw League, was one of the individual successes. He played 8 games, finishing second in the batting averages with 43, and second in the bowling, taking 29 wickets at 16 runs each with his right arm off-spin.

He had four scores in the 60's with a top score of 68 against Barbados, and produced the best bowling haul of 7 for 32, including a hat-trick, against the Leeward Isles.

His first victim was leg before, his second bowled and his third caught.

The bowling successes gave Geoff the most satisfaction. "The wickets were so good over there that batting was comparitively easy. Bowling was more of a challenge.

"It was difficult to bowl a side out – often only 5 wickets or so went down in an innings. That was why I was pleased to take 29 wickets in my 8 matches.

"The quality of the wickets was one reason why so many of the matches ended in draws. They often looked dry and cracked, but usually played perfectly.

"We had only 2 bad wickets and it was on these that the two positive results were reached."

Playing in the monsoon season – well out of the main West Indian cricket season – produced more problems for the Young England team.

Playing sessions had to be reduced because of strength-sapping temperatures in the 90's, while heavy rain frequently interrupted proceedings.

Geoff loved the islands – "I would recommend them to anybody for a holiday" – and was thoroughly impressed with the hospitality shown towards the team. But the trip was anything but a rest for the touring party.

Of 42 days spent there 30 were taken up by cricket and another 7 by exhausting travel.

"I think the travel, with many hours spent waiting at airports, was more tiring than the cricket," Geoff commented "but there was a tremendous team spirit and that helped us through the difficult moments, as well as helping in the actual cricket."

Now back at his job as trainee quantity surveyor in Chesterfield, Geoff admits to being "very tired" after the tour. But he will soon be in training, attending indoor coaching and playing table tennis in readiness for next spring.

He said "I hope that this tour, plus my performances in the Second XI this year, will help me on in cricket."

"It is my ambition to be taken on to the ground staff by Derbyshire and play County Championship Cricket."

Article by Mark Sharman taken from *The Derby Evening Telegraph*

The Green (Eternal)

Part of the Account General Department in London was being dispersed to Chesterfield, so one week-end in August 1960, a party of us paid a visit to what in the near future would be our home.

We arrived at the Town Hall, and after being welcomed by the Mayor, we were escorted by a Corporation Official to the proposed site of the new estate on which (he vast majority of the A.G.D. staff would be housed – a site conveniently situated to the West of and about a mile from, the Town Centre. "This is Loundsley Green," the official said, and proceeded to explain in some detail everything we wanted to know, patiently answering each question. We stood at the end of Green Bank which, at that time, enjoyed an unenviable position on the edge of the 'Green Belt'. Folks who knew the area well said that years ago, it used to be a farm, but now there was no sign that – only wild, wild desolation. As I gazed mesmerically upon acres and acres of fallow land with tall trees, high grass, unbiquitous weeds, and, here and there, rugged undulating ground. I found it difficult to comprehend how anything habitable could come out of all this. My simple, unimaginative mind could visualize nothing orderly or symmetrical emerging from such chaos. It all seemed so impossible. Yet, two years later, on a subsequent visit, with all the resources of modern building techniques at command, the whole confused mass of tangled vegetation had given way to drains, roads and houses in the making. The transformation was amazing. By the end of 1963 when I finally moved from London, building on the estate was almost complete and most dispersees well settled in. In what appeared to be a short time all that wild vegetation had been replaced by a thriving community with roads, shops, schools churches and houses – rows and rows of beautiful houses of every type and description that must certainly make Loundsley Green one of the finest estates in the country.

And in the centre of the estate is the recreation ground or playing field, but always referred to simply as The Green. In the early years of 1964 and 1965, grass had to be sown and the square laid. Even so, it had to be pressed into service long before it was ready because of lack of alternative playing facilities. Much hard work had to be done to bring it up to the standard required. A small band of enthusiasts – not least of all Dave Crowley – laboured tirelessly to ensure that cricket was played on the Green. The Local Corporation gave what assistance they could so far as the ground was concerned but other amenities were badly lacking. One of the most pressing needs was some kind of shelter for scorers, spectators and even players in the event of inclement weather; somewhere to sit and enjoy a cup of tea and to entertain visiting teams; a place in which to store gear. It was again largely through the influence of D. Crowley that an old prefabricated building was acquired. This was to be our own pavilion and most of the initial work on it after its erection fell on Dave and other cricketers of the day. We all bore the work cheerfully knowing that we now had a pavilion of our own.

Of course, the up rooting of whole families from London to Chesterfield inevitably caused problems. The leaving of friends and relatives behind left a great void. Children – and boys in particular – seemed to have an abundance of time on their hands and were apt to get up to mischief. So, perhaps, it was rather fortunate that there appeared to be a breath of spring sunshine amongst our midst one Richard (Dick) Suttle. Dick, himself a fine all-round cricketer, but known primarily as a murderous striker of the ball, brought a flair, enthusiasm and passion for the game that seemed to have infected most and have certainly affected all. Alas, such qualities have often been mistaken for egotism and self aggrandisement. When Dick first mentioned his idea of coaching on the Green, some laughed derisively, but others saw it as a blessing in disguise. Indeed, the idea could not have come at a more propitious moment for cricket during the long summer holidays might help to keep the lads out of trouble. So Dick made a start. Boys who, with so much time on their hands, might have taken to the streets took to the bats a far more gainful occupation.

The Green was now becoming popular. Every summer it became a hive of activity. Boys came from far and wide to be put through their paces. The thing was becoming too big for Dick alone to handle, so Ron Lovegrove joined forces with him. Occasionally others have helped but over the years these two have shouldered the task of guiding literally dozens of youngsters through the intricacies of the cover drive, the on drive, the square cut, the hook, the run up. the delivery stride, the follow through, the techniques of wicket keeping – the lot.

And yet, the secret of their success laid, not so much in open coaching but rather in subtle advice and correction. Their recipe for perfection rested in practice and competition – particularly the latter. Each boy has his own talent which – with a little bit of guidance here and there – must be developed, not tampered with. This important maxim is constantly being borne in mind.

Each youngster is placed into a team which is the responsibility of its captain. Each team is identified by a name of letter, example, A Team, B Team, C Team etc. The teams compete against each other and at the end of the season the winning team is presented with a trophy and other prizes. But the losing teams are never entirely forgotten and all kinds of other awards are made for meritorious performance during the season. The Green has seen many of these presentations to which many friends and relatives always give their full support. These domestic or internal competitions – held on Saturday mornings – are only a very minute part of the cricket played by the youngsters during the summer seasons. They are entered in several Junior Leagues and hardly a day goes by without some important game being played on the Green. In addition several of the juniors also play in Senior Leagues. Both the domestic and League competitions give the lads their basic training both in technique and in temperament, giving them valuable experience, teaching them how to win as well as how to lose. They gradually transform boys into men – build their characters.

Much as the actual cricket claims a very large part of their time Dick and Ron can always be found busily engaged in other sphere. Largely through their endeavours the Green now boasts one of the finest local pitches for miles around, it is Dick's firm belief that nothing could daunt a young, budding cricketer's spirit more than to receive a blow from a ball when playing on a bad or unprepared wicket. And so, though the out-field is no great shakes, the square and wicket due to long hours of assiduous preparation is a joy to play on. Then there is the protection of the square after each match. When others tend to forget, these two never fail to see the wires are replaced around it – a simple enough operation, nevertheless, essential if the square is to be preserved. These two can be seen at all junior matches, Ron inevitably umpiring, Dick shouting words of encouragement from the boundary lines. There is gear to be sorted and stored, equipment to be repaired or replaced. They fetch, carry, run, jump. There is not a blade of grass on the Green not known to them. It is a long, hard, sometimes frustrating business, but they enjoy every minute of it.

And joining Dick and Ron to complete the triumvirate is Mrs. Lovegrove. An ardent supporter of the youngsters, she lias been an indispensable part of the Green ever since Ron joined Dick. One finds it difficult to remember a match on the Green (or, indeed, anywhere else) involving the lads at which she was not present – cheering, waving, roaring encouragement. Her interest is limitless.

Like all other communities these days the Green has not been immune from vandalism. There were times (thank goodness, not very often) when our treasured pavilion, suffering from the malevolent visitations of vandals, looked very much the worse for wear, forcing us, after each act of sacrilege, to move in with implements of repair. Amazingly, the thing still stands, and long may it continue to stand, for it is part of the Green

The Green has bristled with excitement when the youngsters, playing a shield or cup match, are within sight of victory, or even when playing amongst themselves, or in a league game, or in the annual Fathers v Sons match. And girls – yes girls too – thanks again to Dick, could look back nostalgically on the Green as the place where they first donned gloves and pads, bat in hand, executing all the strokes with the wizardry and panache of a Cowdrey or a Worrell; fielding with the brilliance of a Bland or a Lloyd; and exploring the mysteries of the 'Googly', the 'Chinaman', the 'Cutter', comprehending the true meaning of bowling a 'Maiden Over'.

This, then is the Green – the stage on which all the great dramas have been played. The stage managers are Dick, Ron and Mrs. Lovegrove; and the characters, the lads – some of whom are now young men – are widely ventilated in this book and need no elaboration here. What is worthy of mention is that this year, 1973, the lads won no fewer than seven major trophies in junior cricket. This is a most wonderful achievement which must have given Ron and Dick a great sense of satisfaction and fulfilment – some small recompense for all the hard work done and time spent on the Green.

To us whose feet have tread over the 'sacred' turf scores of times, the Green is not only a symbol of the game we worship, but a place of happy retreat. As I said before, there is nothing ostentatious about the Green, but to the lads it is the place of their very first venture, their initial, tentative overtures into the world of cricket, it holds the memories of success and failure, of victories and of defeats, of joy and of sorrow – something with which they could identify. To them, its the Green!

Bob Murray

A.G.D.C.C. on the map
By Dave Cocker

Following a disappointing 1971 season in which we ran two teams for the first time, perhaps a little prematurely, the summer of '72 came as a refreshing experience. Reverting to one side competing in the 2nd Division of the North Derbyshire League, and operating with a pool of fifteen players we achieved a memorable "double". The league was taken with a record number of points, without a single defeat, and the Gregory Cup was lifted to boot in the last game of the season.

Captaining the side was a real pleasure as the team was well balanced with "talent" in every department. Veterans Dave Crowley, Les "Whippet" McCulloch, Dick "Tiger" Suttle, John Sims and John Witham (sorry John) provided great experience and up and coming youngsters Brendan Wall, Steve Evans and Tony Hession from the successful Junior XI were bursting in on the scene to produce the perfect blend.

This successful season definitely put the A.G.D.C.C. on the map but more important it aroused additional enthusiasm for our return to the first division. The interest was carried through the winter and the abundance of good players made the running of two teams in the North Derbyshire League for the 73 season, a necessity.

The 1st Xl was strengthened by newcomers Ian Turner, Dave Houseley, John Lovegrove (yet another A.G.D. Junior) and the return of Martin Fairs.

Despite being warned that we had no chance amongst the "big guns" of the first division we enjoyed another successful summer clinching the runners up spot in the last game of the season. With a slice of luck or call it what you will we could have done even better. However, there is always next year and at this stage we look like having an even stronger line-up. Yes. I have just that sneaking feeling that 1974 will be our year.

One of the major reasons for the recent success of the club is the development of the A.G.D. Junior XI. The time and effort expended by Dick Suttle and Ron Lovegrove cannot be measured and the club is certainly beginning to reap the benefits as their lads graduate into the senior teams.

Another most pleasing feature of the 73 season has been the way in which Ron Lovegrove has moulded the 2nd XI into an extremely effective force. The team gradually improved throughout the summer, as the side became more settled, eventually pipping Hundall 2nd XI for the runners-up honour in their division.

This strength in depth must stand us in good stead next season and I am sure the clubs will continue to flourish.

A.G.D. celebrate first major honours with a 'double'

Operating on a squad of only 15 registered players, A.G.D.C.C. made a mockery of their League placings last year and carried off the North Derbyshire League Division II title for the first time in the club's history. In fact it was the club's first major award since it's foundation. In doing this, the club obtained a record number of 72 points and remained undefeated throughout the season.

The club's supporters were rewarded for the valuable support, by some highly imaginative cricket and with scores of 150 plus every week, were almost certainly assured of victory. Some of the best cricket was played in the Gregory Cup, with A.G.D. reaching the final and defeating Sheepbridge easily by 9 wickets.

Perhaps the most memorable match of the season was in the semi-final of the North Derbyshire League, Division II Six-a-side tournament, against Scarcliffe. This was played at Hundall before a crowd of well over 500. A.G.D. needed 13 runs off the last over. John Witham hit 2 consecutive fours before being bowled going for an almighty hit. D. Tarlton and D. Cocker were run out in successive balls before Mick Brownett ran 3 off the last ball to force a replay. Unfortunately, Scarcliffe emerged victors after a further 2 overs, in what proved to be the outstanding game of the competition, and went on to beat S. & J. Kitchin in the final.

Publicity played a large part in the success of the A.G.D., instilling confidence and pride, particularly among the junior members. It was not unusual to find half of the local sports page of the *Derbyshire Times* inundated with A.G.D. match reports and pen pictures. Chiefly responsible for this was the club's Sports columnist and unofficial public relations officer, Richard Suttle whose descriptive anecdotes were awaited eagerly by keen young sports fans throughout the country.

Dave Tarlton October 1972

"Why I enjoy coaching cricket to juniors"
By the Author

As far as I am concerned, coaching junior boys cricket is a hobby rather than a job. First of all I enjoy doing this because it is a means of helping the youngsters to enjoy one of the finest games in the world. Then there is an opportunity of passing on instructions to someone who is young and needs to be disciplined in this particular field of sport, because if the right approach is not passed on to the youngster in the early stage he becomes bored and disinterested but to the contrary when he approaches it correctly he soon becomes enthusiastic and dedicated with the determination to do better.

I am convinced that the best way to encourage youngsters is to get them playing against each other as soon as the fundamentals are taught and they soon begin to develop their skills which must be watched carefully and corrected as soon as they are going wrong. This takes time and one must be patient as they will eventually improve within a few years.

Now comes the time for the coach to enjoy the fruits of his labour as he begins to watch them play in junior leagues. The competition becomes tougher and from this he can judge the youngsters potential from match to match.

The danger which is usually lurking around the corner is limited over cricket in evening games for the youngsters, who might be selected for six games and only bats or bowls on one or two occasions. It normally makes him feel inadequate or makes him think "I am not good enough otherwise I would have played more innings or bowled more overs," but as a coach you have got to organise friendly matches and include that youngster in your first three or four batsman or bowlers and prove to him that he is good enough. When he overcomes this difficulty, immediately he regains confidence and therefore he is happy and ready to play the game again and more often than not he becomes an established member of the league team That's why encouragement is the vital factor.

While all this is happening there are other things which must be taken care of. For example, deportment, discipline and the ability to accept failure.

This might appear boastful. But during my twenty-five years of coaching and organising cricket I have helped to contribute to the success of some world class players of the calibre of Gary Sobers, Wesley Hall and in present local circles, Roy Cox, John Lovegrove, Brendan Wall, Stephen Evans and many others who no doubt will one day be able to enjoy some of the wonderful activities which the good old summer game has never lacked.

In short, cricket is a way of life to me and I must end on a very important note. To rear good cricketers they must play on well prepared wickets, otherwise you are defeating your own object, because IT IS NOT CRICKET to play on rough wickets. I have been fortunate to have one of the most hard working and dedicated men to help with Junior Cricket in the person of Mr. Ron Lovegrove of Quantock Way, Loundsley Green, the father of John, who was selected for Derbyshire Colts in 1972 and also his colleague Roy Cox who represented the Colts in 1971 and 1972.

I can only hope that these youngsters from Loundsley Green, Chesterfield will do their best and continue to enjoy many years of cricket.

Finally, after five years of devotion and dedication, we have seen the fruits of our labour as the youngsters emerged "Triple Crown Champions" in the Sheffield and District Junior League and League Cup Winners in the Chesterfield and District Youth League and also champions of the Six-a-side tournament of the Chesterfield and District Youth Council.

Slowly falls the curtain
by the Author

At the ripe age of 44, and constantly troubled with regular and severe twinges of fibrositis, retirement from cricket is not far away. Hence, within the next few years I shall be making room for, an up and coming youngster in the league. One soon senses the inability to move with the agility of a tiger, when compared with 20 years ago. At times I still experience flashes of brilliance when emotionally awakened; but time soon tells as this can only be done in short spasmodic bursts. However, when my playing days are o'er I shall still be there to help, foster and encourage youngsters to enjoy the game of glorious uncertainties to which I have devoted most of my time and effort. Given the opportunity I would do it all over again.

Finally I would like to express my sincere thanks to all those who have contributed to this book in any way, and on behalf of the junior team I join with them in extending our thanks to Garry Sobers and Harvey Walker for their gift to our Club.

I must say how much I appreciated the cup which was presented to me by Mr. T. Cocker (President of the A.G.D.C.C.) at our Annual Stag Party for the outstanding member for 1970; but of all the trophies I have won, the one which was presented to me in 1971 by Mr. E. Walton (Chairman of the A.G.D.C.C.) I treasure most. On the plaque, the following inscription:-

PRESENTED TO MR. DICK SUTTLE
FOR HIS SERVICES
TO
YOUTH CRICKET
1971

This constantly reminds me of the time and effort which I have put in to help and encourage Youth Cricket to which I am so closely attached or better still the reward to a life's ambition and I sincerely hope that the youngsters of Chesterfield will continue to enjoy their cricket for many, many years to come.

Tube Works Beat West Indies

On Sunday, Tube Works entertained the United Social C.C. from Northampton in their annual friendly 35 over match, which the home team won by 3 wickets

Skipper Horace Hogg of the visiting team won the toss and took first knock, and after 35 overs of entertaining cricket, the West Indians were 121

1971 United Social C.C. West Indian team from Northampton

96

for 7. Of these skipper Hogg's contribution was 37, S. Bates scored an undefeated 27 and Len Barnett a useful 26.

Bowling for Tube Works, Reg Barker took 2 for 17, Tony Swift 2 for 39, skipper Trevor Jones 1 for 23 and Harold Pashley 1 for 33.

With 122 runs required for victory. Tube Works scored 123 tor 7 off 32 overs. Reg Barker, their left handed opening batsman, batted soundly for a well-played 60 which included six boundaries. Other useful scores were contributed by Tony Swift 18, Les McCulloch 13 and Trevor Jones 11 not out.

Despite a fine display of fielding by these fleet-footed West Indians, they lost by three wickets. C. McFarlane took 2 for 17, Hogg 2 for 17 and L. Barnett and L. McFarlane one each for 20 and 55 respectively.

Martin Forte
Record Hit in Junior League

Martin Forte, Frecheville's 16 year-old batting prospect, equalled the Sheffield and District Junior Cricket League's individual scoring record this week when he hit 98 of his side's 136-6 against Hundall.

League secretary Ivan Priestley says: This is terrific scoring from a junior cricketer in an evening match and equals the League record which has stood since 1964.

Not content with his fine innings Martin, a Hurlfield Comprehensive schoolboy went on to crack 65 of Frecheville's 101 in the Paramore Cup semi-final win over Norton Oakes.

Other innings were 138 against East Dene, 92 against White Lane, 62 against Dronfield and 47 not out in the return fixture, 61 against Staveley. Martin scored 399 in 11 Junior Matches, twice not out for an average of 44.3.

The Green Un 24/6/72

Martin (see photo on colour page 1) who is now 39 years old, has a cricket career which spans nearly 30 years and so far has included 44 centuries and two double centuries. His first century was made at the age of 10 for St. Augustines Primary School in St. George, Barbados in an Inter-School match.

His first double century was 201 not out against Old Walcountians in Surrey in 1989, in the Surrey Slazenger League. His second double century was 207 not out in 45 overs against Eynsford in the Kent Metropolitan League and his last century was 110 against Christ Church Institute on 29th July 1995.

In final trial for Colts Team

Seventeen-year old John Lovegrove of 46 Quantock Way, Loundsley Green, was due to take part in the final trial to select the Derbyshire Colts team at

Derby yesterday.

A batsmen/wicket-keeper, John plays for A.G.D. Juniors in the Sheffield Junior and Chesterfield Youth Leagues. He is captain of the C team, which won the A.G.D. Triangular Tournament.

Having made a number of half centuries, John keeps wicket for Chesterfield second team in the Bassetlaw League.

Team selected for Country Trials at Derby on Thursday, 20th July, 1972
Standing L to R:- *D. Walters (Burton-on-Trent), P. Cork (Derby), P. Chambers (Derby) I. Akers (Derby), M. Hollindale (Chesterfield), J. Sissons (Derby), R. Abbott (Derby), A. Acton (Allestree).*

Squatting L to R:- *P. Thompson (Long Eaton, Notts), I. Sadler (Whitwell. Notts), C. Roe (Derby), R. Ireland (Derby), J. Lovegrove (Chesterfield), K. Butler (Sandiacre, Notts).*

A.G.D. Cricket
A cricket season to remember

This cricket season has been one to remember for the A.G.D. Club, Chesterfield.

Their senior side are leaders of Div. 2 of the North Derbyshire League with 47 points. So far they are undefeated and have won eight out of 13 games, most of them convincingly. Their last win was by 128 runs over the Tube Works.

Star of the side is all-rounder John Sims of Calow. John has taken 3 wickets for 155 runs which include figures of 8 for 9, 7-22, 6-13, 6-14, 6-19, and 5-7. He knocked 237 runs in seven innings, two of them not out, and has a highest score of 74.

With six matches left the club hope to stay out in front and so capture the title for the first time. And they are in line for a double triumph as on Sunday. September 10 they take on Sheepbridge in the Gregory Cup Final, at Sheepbridge.

Success story number two for the club is that their Junior Team has won the Sheffield and District League Division "A". After winning nine out of ten games they gain the title after a play off against Frecheville.

The Star 17/8/72

A.G.D. crawl for a point
S. & J. Kitchin 168-7
A.G.D. 41-3

In the last match of the season A.G.D. retained their unbeaten record by forcing a draw against S. & J. Kitchin.

Batting first Kitchins declared at 168 for seven after an opening stand of 50. G. Vine (27). M. Potter (32). M. Robinson (48) and J. Austin (29 n.o.) were the main scorers and Evans took four for 53.

A.G.D. made no attempt to reach this target, refusing to run between the wickets until the closing overs.

They batted for a draw/losing three wickets for 41 runs. An indication of the scoring rate is given by the fact that out of 40 over, 30 were maidens.

Derbyshire Times 22/9/72

Chesterfield Y.C.C. beat A.G.D.

An undefeated 44 by opening batsman David Hooper backed by the medium-pace bowling of Neville Holmes (6 for 14) led the way to Chesterfield Y.C.C's. victory over A.G.D. in the return fixture in the Chesterfield and District Youth League at Loundsley Green on Wednesday week.

Skipper Michael Hollindale of C.Y.C.C. won the toss on a rain-affected wicket, batted first and after 20 overs the visitors were 55 for 6. David Hooper was top scorer with an undefeated 44, while Hollindale and Ian Turner scored ten and 13 respectively.

Stephen Evans was A.G.D's most successful bowler. He took three for 15 in three overs. Norman Graham took two for 24 in seven overs and John Storer one for 15 in four overs.

In reply A.G.D. were all out for 46 in 17·3 overs. No batsman reached double figures as 19-year-old Neville Holmes destroyed his opponents' front line batting and was amply rewarded with the splendid analysis of 6 for 14 in nine overs while Ian Turner took 2 for 18 in 6·3 overs.

A.G.D. complete the double

Although they have one match left to play, A.G.D. Sports gained their first honour since joining the league by taking the Division Two championship, and on Sunday they completed the double by winning the Gregory Cup with a nine wickets margin with man of the match J. Sims hitting 34 not out and with a 5-25 bowling return against Sheepbridge.

A.G.D. win title after play-off

Frecheville joint leaders of Division 'A' in the Sheffield Junior League, suffered their first defeat of the season when A.G.D. Juniors beat them at Eckington in a play-off on Monday.

A large crowd travelled to Eckington and skipper Neil Edney, winning the toss, sent in Frecheville to bat.

The Sheffield team were soon in trouble when Stephen Evans, with the last ball of his first over, had Martin Forte magnificently caught by Stephen Cadywould at mid-on before he had scored. Two more wickets fell cheaply before Paul Milburn took a running catch on the boundary to dismiss skipper Cantrell for a well played 15. With the score at 22 for 3, 20 more runs were added before Copley was trapped l.b.w. to Edney for eight.

Evans struck again when the score was 48, Haugue was caught by Hession at mid-on for 17. The only other batsman to reach double figures was Grocock who was run out for 11.

Frecheville never recovered and as a result the score was 68 for 9 after 18 overs Stephen Evans was their most successful bowler with 5 for 28 in nine overs. Neil Edney took 2 for 35 in nine overs.

With 69 required for victory and the opportunity to meet the champions of Division B in the cup final, A.G.D. batsmen accepted the challenge and after 15·2 overs were 70 for 6 and will now meet either Bradfield or Rockingham in the final, probably on September 3.

With only three runs on the board, Brendan Wall was run out for one. Next to go was Anthony Hession for 14 after hitting a towering six the ball before.

Another 36 runs were added before Frecheville took another wicket, when John Lovegrove was caught by Jackson off Forte for 25. The score was 56 for 3 and Stephen Cadywould who went in at number three continued to play a graceful innings and was undefeated with 20 while the wickets of Edney, Evans and Milburn fell for ten runs before Cadywould executed a lofted off drive in the gathering gloom off Forte to put the issue beyond doubt. For Frecheville, Winspear took 2 for 3, M. Forte 2 for 18 and S. Cantrell 1 for 14.

The Derbyshire Times 14/8/72

Final League Match

On Wednesday A.G.D. played their final league match against last year's champions, Clay Cross at Loundsley Green in a return fixture of the Chesterfield and Dist. Youth League and won by 21 runs.

Skipper Roy Cox of A.G.D. decided to bat and after 20 overs the home team were 85 for 8. Fifteen year-old Richard Worrall came in at number ten and top scored with an undefeated and face-saving innings of 20 which included one six and two fours. Peter Smith (15 n.o.) and Cox (15) gave their team a respectable total.

David Flavell, who spearheaded the Clay Cross attack, took 5 for 26 in ten overs, while David Scoffings at the other end took 3 for 55 in ten overs.

With 86 runs required for victory, hope of retaining their leadership were shattered when Stephen Evans struck a vital blow by bowling the impetuous skipper Roger Bowler for ten when the score was 14. The champions never recovered and after 19·2 overs were all out for 64. Max Bailey (13) and D. Scoffings (11) were the only other batsmen to reach double figures. Neil Edney took 3 wickets in four balls in his ninth over and finished with 4 for 28 and Stephen Evans 4 for 34.

Soundly Beaten

On Tuesday, Frecheville Juniors entertained A.G.D. Juniors at Frecheville in the Sheffield Junior League.

The home team won by ten wickets after their opponents had battled for a meagre 45 off 18 overs. Roy Cox, who was undefeated, top-scored with a sound 23. Andrew Grocock who captured 4 for 10 in nine overs bowled accurately and was well backed by skipper Stephen Cantrell who took 4 for 32 in nine overs.

In their turn at the wicket Frecheville Jrs. won convincingly by scoring 46 for 0 as Martin Forte struck an undefeated 33 while his partner, S. Cantrell was also undefeated with 13 as A.G.D. met their first defeat of the season in the Sheffield League while Frecheville remain top of the table.

The following team will, represent A.G.D. Juniors against Treeton Jnrs. at Loundsley Green on Tuesday at 6.30 p.m. Players are asked to meet at the pavilion at 6 p.m. Team: N. Edney (Capt.), R. Cox, A. Hession, J. Lovegrove, D. Harding, S. Evans, P. Smith, P. Milburn, D. Lester, R. Worrall, S. Cadywould, 12th man S. Wilde.

The Derbyshire Times 13/6/72

North Derbyshire Cricket League

The runners-up awards in Division Two should go to Scarcliffe, unless S. and J. Kitchins can beat A.G.D. Sports in their final game and collect five points. Already a sell-out is the league's annual presentation and dance arranged for Friday, November 10 with A.G.D. Sports Club as hosts. Semi-finals and final of the postponed six-a-side contest are arranged for next Sunday at Sheepbridge Sports ground, Newbold Road. starting 10.30 a.m. The N.D. League XI, featured in a drawn game on Sunday versus Derby and District League XI.

Results

Gregory Cup (30 overs knock-out), final, played at Sheepbridge Sports ground on Sunday: Sheepbridge 58 (C. Cooke 20. J. Sims 5-25, D. Cocker 4-29), A.G.D. Sports 60-1 (J. Sims 34 not out).

Division Two. S. and J. Kitchins 162 (M. Rowbotham 33. N. Whitworth 25, G. Vine 23, B. Boulter 6-60). Remoulds 39 (F. Moseley 18, K. Potter 4-10, M. Rowbotham 3-19).

Representative match: Played on Sunday at Robinson's ground: N.D. League XI, 117-8 (M. Sullivan 29, H. Longden 25, B. Monks 20, B. Shaw 4-40). Derby and District League XI, 161-6 in 40 overs (D. Carr 48 n.o., D. Shaw 34 n.o., M. Boden 4-50).

The Derbyshire Times 15/9/72

A.G.D. cricketers beat rivals to clinch first championship

The A.G.D. senior cricket team at Chesterfield have clinched their first ever championship title.

They are Division II champions of the North Derbyshire League after a win over nearest rivals Scarcliffe.

A.G.D. lost the toss and were put in to bat by Scarcliffe skipper Tony Field. The move was successful at first as three of the main A.G.D. batsmen were back in the pavilion with only four runs scored.

Fine innings

But veteran Dave Crowley, coming in at number 5 made 58 – an innings of controlled aggression which included nine fours.

His was the top score and he was helped by Philip Ward (20) and John Witham (13). A.G.D. were 119 all out off 39 overs. Tony Field took four for 48.

When Scarcliffe batted, it was their turn to struggle with four wickets down for five runs. A.G.D. were without their opening bowlers John Sims, and Stephen Evans, but it was captain Dave Cocker who did the damage with six for 25.

Mr. Richard Suttle, club coach and committee member of A.G.D. said of his side's championship win: "It's been an all round performance by the team helped by consistent batting and bowling.

"I wouldn't like to single out any one in particular."

The club has been in existence for eight years.

A.G.D. C.C. unbeaten champions Div.2 North Derbyshire League
Standing L to R:- E. Gadsby (Umpire), S. Evans, D. Crowley (Vice-Capt.), D. Cocker
(Capt.), D. Tarlton. A. Hession, N. Graham. F, Webster (Umpire) and P. Ward.
Kneeling L to R:- B. Wall, J. Sims, J. Witham, L, McCulloch and R. Suttle (Club Coach).

Young Stephen had a good day

The A.G.D. Chesterfield, junior cricket side were defeated by 21 runs in the Sheffield and District Junior League's Championship the Leslie Fletcher Cup at Stannington.

Victors, were Bradfield Juniors, who scored 124-8 off 25 overs, with A.G.D. totalling 103-8 off 25 overs.

Bradfield won the toss and batted first. Stephen Evans aged 16, who swung the ball well for A.G.D. in the heavy atmosphere, was their most successful bowler.

His final figures were 4-27 in nine over. In one over Stephen took three wickets for no runs.

Skipper Neil Edney took two for 39 and Anthony Hession 1-19.

When A.G.D. batted. Wall scored a splendid 32 before being caught at backward point. At one stage they were 61-5 with five overs left but the partnership of Paul Milburn and Neil Edney led to some attacking batting and 30 runs.

However this did not prove enough and at the close of the innings Edney was undefeated with 17.

It was Bradfield's third consecutive championship.

The Sheffield Star 7/9/72

A.G.D. 128 for 8
H.P.O. Chesterfield 88

On a sun-drenched afternoon at Duckmanton Lodge, on Thursday week Calow A.G.D. entertained H.P.O. Chesterfield and won the first round of the North Eastern Region Competition by 40 runs.

Skipper Dave Cocker, of the A.G.D., elected to bat, A.G.D. were soon in trouble as their first three wickets fell for six runs.

But Richard Suttle and Austin Corcoran made 76 in a fourth-wicket partnership before the former was caught by Conroy at backward point for 33.

Two more wickets fell cheaply before Corcoran was run out for a superb 65, which included five boundaries. Dave Tarlton at number eight scored a quick 15 before the score reached 128 for eight off 40 overs.

Skipper Conroy finished with four for 60 in 20 overs while Eyre took two for 33 in nine overs.

With 129 runs required for victory HPO started disastrously as Neil Edney clean bowled Tim Crossley with the second ball of his first over without a run on the board.

Worse was still to come as skipper Cocker had Goucher brilliantly caught in the slips by Corcoran with the score at four and when Gray was caught by wicket-keeper Lovegrove off Cocker the score was nine for three.

Edney struck again as Lovegrove took his second catch to dismiss Reddish with the score at 15. In came Terry Conroy at number five to play a skipper's innings and restore his team's score to a respectable total before he was stumped by Lovegrove off Cocker for a splendid 52 which included one six and five fours. The only other batsman to reach double figures was Gosling who scored 11 before being bowled by Edney.

A.G.D.'s fielding looked vulnerable as no fewer than six catches went down, but some fine pace bowling by Cocker and Edney enabled A.G.D. to dismiss their opponents for 88. Cocker took five for 33 in 18 overs, while Edney also took five for 47 in 18·1 overs.

Derbyshire Times 21/7/72

A.G.D. 168-7
Padley & Venables 81-6

Padley and Venables, under the leadership of Colin Tanser, entertained A.G.D. at Dronfield on Sunday and held A.G.D. to draw.

After winning the toss, Dave Cocker, captain of the visiting team, took first knock, and after 40 overs, A.G.D. were 168 for seven.

Les McCulloch, their opening batsman, scored a splendid 54 which included eight fours. Other useful contributions came from D. Crowley (35), B. Wall (28), R. Suttle (22). and P. Ward (15n.o.).

P. Harrison was P. & V's most successful bowler, with three for 56, while skipper Tanser took two for 30 and G. Barker one for 29.

With 169 runs needed for victory, P. & V, batsmen batted defensively and made no effort to chase the runs and after 40 overs, they were 81 for six. A. Wainwright was top scorer with 19 while D. Bown, K. Weston and K. Gill contributed 17, 13 and 10 respectively.

For A.G.D. Philip Ward took three for 16, Cocker two for 15 and D. Crowley one for 16.

A.G.D. 104 for 9, Scunthorpe 105 for 5
by C. W. R. Suttle

On a dull day at Scunthorpe on Wednesday week, Scunthorpe entertained A.G.D. (Chesterfield) in the second round of the North East Region competition and won by five wickets.

After winning the toss Dave Cocker of the visiting team took first knock. Runs came at a brisk pace as John Lovegrove and Neil Edney took the score to 25 before the latter was trapped lbw for nine.

Witham joined Lovegrove but with the score at 49, Lovegrove was also lbw for 32.

The only other batsmen to reach double figures were Alan Eyre (12 not out) and Richard Suttle (ten). Four batsmen were run out.

For Scunthorpe R. Hitchin took two for nine.

In reply Scunthorpe scored 105 for five off 27.3 overs. Of these R. Hitchin, who was dropped before he had scored, made 43 and was assisted by T. Clarke (33) and P. Wilson (10).

For A.G.D. Philip Ward took two for 22.

Fletcher Cup Final
Bradfield Jnrs. 124 for 8 off 25 overs
A. G. D. Jnrs. 103 for 8 off 25 overs

A large and enthusiastic crowd witnessed a keenly contested cup final which ended in a 21 run victory for Bradfield Jnrs. over A.G.D. Jnrs. at

Stannington on Sunday week.

After 25 overs of entertaining cricket the Sheffield team were 124 for eight of which skipper G. Powell top scored with a valuable 29, which included two sixes and three fours. Opening batsmen Furniss and Scorah scored 24 and 18 respectively whilst J. White at No. 4 scored a useful 15 to boost the total to 111 for four after 16 overs were bowled but a devastating spell of bowling by Stephen Evans took three wickets in his next over without a run being scored and at the end of the 25th over Bradfield were 124 for eight.

Sixteen year-old Evans was A.G.D.'s most successful bowler. He took four for 27 in nine overs whilst skipper Neil Edney took two for 39 in nine overs and Anthony Hession one for 19 in four overs.

With 125 runs required for victory and the opportunity to win the Leslie Fletcher Cup for the first time, the Chesterfield team failed by 22 runs as the match ended in a dramatic finish. Wall and Hession opened the innings to the bowling of Ludlam and Barker, and took the score to 23, before the latter was bowled by Ludlam for four. In came Cadywould who was bowled with Ludlam's next delivery. Lovegrove came in on a hat-trick: but survived to score a useful 17 before he was caught by Scorah off Ludlam.

At this stage, 16 overs were bowled and A.G.D. were 51 for three. Skipper Edney partnered Wall who was batting well, but with another 10 runs added. Wall was caught by White at backward point for a splendid 32, Evans joined his skipper but was short-lived as he was bowled with Barker's second delivery in his tenth over. With the score at 61 for five and five overs left A.G.D.'s chances looked very remote but with the arrival of Paul Milburn with Edney they attacked Ludlam's bowling with savage onslaught before the former was bowled by Barker for 18 invaluable runs which took their partnership to 30 and the score to 91 for six. Skipper Edney continued to push the score along and with 11 balls left and 34 runs needed. Smith and Harding were both run out for 4 and 2 respectively leaving Edney with an undefeated 17 and the score to 103 for eight.

R. Ludlam who bowled unchanged took four for 60 in 13 overs and D. Barker two for 34 in 12 overs to help Bradfield to their third consecutive championship.

Another fine bowling feat came from John Lovegrove who took 3 for 7 against Treeton, followed by David Lester with 2 for 0 and Derek Harding 2 for 8, while Anthony Caunt took 3 for 37 against Aston Hall.

Two more startling performances came from Andrew Horton who claimed 3 for 15 against Norton Oakes and 4 for 4 against Frecheville, while Evans took 4 for 39 and Logan Kerss 2 for 28 to round off a most successful season in the Sheffield and District Junior League.

Many thanks to our secretary Mr. Ron Lovegrove for all the hard work he has done in helping our junior cricket team to 2 major achievements. First as League Champions of Division "A" and also as Parramore Cup Finalists against our old rivals "Frecheville" at Norton Oaks on Thursday 19th July at 6.30 p.m. All outstanding performances will be recorded in a booklet at the end of the season and a full report of the cup final will be published in the local press.

A.G.D. (Jnrs) defeat Frecheville (Jnrs) by 22 runs to win the Parramore Cup at Norton Oaks

By C. R. W. Suttle

Scores: A.G.D. (Jnrs) 109 for 5 off 20 overs

Frecheville (Jnrs) 87 for 5 off 20 overs

On Thursday, 19th July, 1972 A.G.D. (Jnrs) of Chesterfield met Frecheville (Jnrs) of Sheffield in the Parramore Cup Final at Norton Oakes on a rain-soaked wicket and won the match by 22 runs. Skipper John Lovegrove of the A.G.D. (Jnrs) won the toss and elected to bat and after 20 overs they were 109 for 5.

Play started at 6.30 p.m. with the skies heavily overcast as Mick Hollindale and Brendan Wall opened the innings to the bowling of Christopher Winspear and skipper Martin Forte. Runs came at a fair rate as the openers laid a steady foundation and after the tenth over they were still together with 60 runs on the board but at 71, Hollindale attempted a big hit and was bowled by Peter Vernon for a splendid 43 which included three sixes and two fours Stephen Evans the incoming batsman was short-lived. He was caught and bowled by Peter Vernon for 3. Andy Horton filled the breach but was soon caught by Bentley at short third man off Mark Hannah for 1. Skipper Lovegrove joined Wall who was batting well but with the score at 88, Wall was run out for a well played 30 and Frecheville were back in the game; but with the arrival of David Lester who chanced his arm in the last two overs brought his individual score to 18 not out while Lovegrove was stumped off the last ball of the innings by wicket keeper Stephen Copley off Vernon for 6 which brought the team's total to 109 for 5.

Bowling for Frecheville P. Vernon took 3 for 22 in 5 overs and M. Hannah for 24 in 5 overs.

With 110 runs required for victory and the opportunity to win the Parramore Cup for the third time, Frecheville failed by 23 runs in an innings which delighted the large and enthusiastic crowd despite the inclement weather as skipper Forte and the left-handed Richard Hague opened the innings to the bowling of Logan Kerss and Stephen Evans. They batted well and took the score to 71 after the thirteenth over. With Barbados-born Forte now in full cry and his team needing 39 runs off 7 overs, Lovegrove made a tactical decision by bringing on Andy Horton in place of Evans from the pavilion end and in the fourth ball of his third over he struck the vital blow by bowling the aggressive Forte for a splendid 38 which included two towering sixes and two fours as he returned to the pavilion to a standing ovation. After this Frecheville never recovered. Copley joined Jague who was batting well but with the score at 73 the latter was run out for a sound 29. Philip Jackson partnered Copley but the former was bowled by Kerss for 1.

With 5 overs left and 37 runs needed Peter Burke was bowled by Kerss for the dreaded cipher. Bentley then joined Copley who decided to force the pace as the fleet-footed youngsters from Chesterfield continued to pile on the pressure and as a result Copley was caught at deep mid-off by Hollindale for 2 off Kerss. With only two overs left, Vernon and Bentley required 32 runs to win the match but they were only able to add another 10 runs which brought their individual scores to 7 and 3 not out, respectively and the total to 87 for 5. Bowling for AGD L. Kerss took 3 for 30 in 10 overs and A. Horton 1 for 23 in 6 overs.

Umpires were Messrs. R. Lovegrove and B. Moule.

After the match; Mr. Ben Jessop, President of the Sheffield and District

Junior League thanked the officials of the Norton Oakes Cricket Club for the use of the ground. He then congratulated both teams on the splendid performances which they displayed before the large crowd. He also thanked Mr. Ron Lovegrove and Richard Suttle for their time and effort spent on junior cricket. He then presented the Parramore Cup to skipper John Lovegrove of the A.G.D. Junior Cricket Club who are also League Champions. Lovegrove thankfully responded with a short speech on behalf of his team to a background of vociferous shouts and delightful cheers.

At the Civil Service Sports Club, Duckmanton Lodge, Calow the popular Geoff Miller once again presented the "Winners" and "Runners Up" awards at the A.G.D. Triangular Tournament to Ian Drayner, (Vice-Captain) of the "A" Team and Mark Calvert of the "C" team respectively. Others looking on are a small group of the teams who participated in the tournament which started eight years ago.

Club officials include Left to Right:-

R. Suttle (Coach),

R. Lovegrove (Secretary)

and E. J. Walton, Chairman of the

Account Generals Department, Chesterfield.

The Cup was donated by H. L. Brown & Son Ltd., while the Shield was donated by Mr. Dennis Harding formerly of Robinson & Sons Limited.

A.G.D. (Jnrs.) Triple Crown Champions defeated in Leslie Fletcher Cup Final by Bradfield (Jnrs.)

Scores A.G.D. 57 off 23 overs   Bradfield 59 for 6 off 24 overs

On Sunday, 5th August, A.G.D. (Jnrs.) this season's Triple Crown Champions entertained, Bradfield (Jnrs.) under the captaincy of David Furness at the Civil Service Sports Ground, Duckmanton Lodge, Chesterfield in a limited 25 over match before a large crowd.

The game ended iin a breath-taking finish as the visitors won by 4 wickets off the last ball of the 24th over, to give them the Leslie Fletcher Cup or the second consecutive season and a bat donated by Gray Nicholls.

Skipper John Lovegrove of the home team won the toss on a softish wicket, which was affected by overnight showers. He elected to bat as Hollindale and Wall opened the innings and took the score to 31 off 13 overs before the former was out to a brilliant catch by Burnett off Ludlam for 25. Evans joined Wall, but with another 14 runs added, the latter was bowled by Ludlam for 15. After this, A.G.D.'s middle-order batting collapsed. Evans was run out for 5, followed by Lester, Harding, Milburn and Baker all victims to Ludlam's bowling. Then skipper Lovegrove was run out for 3. Barker then took the wickets of Kerss and Marshall while Barnett was undefeated for 1 and the team total to 57 off 23·5 overs.

Bowling for Bradfield, Richard Ludlam took 6 for 23 in 11.5 overs and D. Barker 2 for 29 in 12 overs.

In reply Bradfield (Jnrs.) scored 59 for 6 off 24 overs. Of these, skipper Furness, who opened the innings, piloted his team to victory with an undefeated 30, which included 4 fours. Hilton, his partner was caught by the wicket keeper Lovegrove off Kerss for 2. Sanderson was bowled by Kerss before he had scored while Stephen Evans had Ludlam trapped leg-before-wicket for 13. At this stage Bradfield were 23 for 3. With another 2 runs added, Evans bowled Barker for 1. With 10 overs left and 35 runs needed for victory, A.G.D. were on the attack as Furness and Baldwin became associated in a fifth wicket partnership which yielded an invaluable 30 runs before Evans bowled Baldwin for 10. With 2 runs needed Burnett was run out for 0. With 7 balls left and 2 runs still required, Bradfield got 2 leg byes and won the match by 4 wickets with an hour to spare. Bowling for A.G.D. S. Evans took 3 for 18 in 12 overs and L. Kerss 2 for 31 in 9 overs.

A.G.D. Junior Cricket Club emerged 1973 League Champions

The Sheffield and District Junior League ended on Tuesday, 10th July, in Division "A". The A.G.D. Junior Cricket Team under the astute captaincy of John Lovegrove emerged league champions for the second consecutive year.

With 8 matches played, 7 ended in victories over their opponents. Teams which they defeated were:-

Eckington by 7 wickets.
Norton Oakes by 43 runs.
Staveley by 4 wickets.
Aston Hall by 5 runs.
Treeton by 57 runs.
Norton Oakes in a return fixture by 7 wickets.
and Frecheville in their final league match by 19 runs.

Their only defeat of the season was against Frecheville who won by the narrow margin of 2 runs in a keenly contested match in their first league encounter.

In the Parramore Cup competition the A.G.D. Junior team defeated Beighton by 10 wickets and in the next round Staveley lost by 9 wickets and on Thursday 21st June, Thorncliffe were beaten in the semi-final by 64 runs. Outstanding performances were contributed by Brendan Wall who scored 21,17 not out, 35, 32 not out, 45 not out, 25 and 53 not out. Michael Hollingdale scored 21 not out, 25, 53, 26 and 33. Paul Milburn 20 not out, 20 and 18 while John Lovegrove and Anthony Hession scored 30 not out and

23 respectively.

In the bowling department, Stephen Evans took 5 for 18 including (the hat-trick) against Beighton and Andrew Horton 3 for 4 in the same match.

Stephen Baker 3 for 11 against Frecheville in their first encounter then 4 for 25 against Staveley and was well backed up by Horton with 5 for 22.

Stephen Evans was in his best form against Thorncliffe in the semi-final. He took 4 for 2 while Horton took 4 for 12 at the other end.

The presentation was made by Mr. J. Bland of the management committee of the Sheffield and District Junior League. Before the presentation he was introduced by Mr. C. Scholey (Chairman of the League). Mr. Bland then congratulated both teams for their entertaining cricket after which he presented the Leslie Fletcher Cup to David Furness, captain of the Bradfield team and also a Gray Nicholls bat and finally the cup to John Lovegrove, captain of the A.G.D. team for being Champions of the Southern Division, also Parramore Cup Winners and Winners of the Derek Hitchen Memorial Trophy to round off a most memorable season in the Sheffield and District Junior League. Umpires were Messrs. B. Barker and R. Lovegrove.

Mr. T. Cocker, President of the A.G.D. Cricket Club presents members of the Junior Club with the trophies, after becoming Triple Crown Champions in 1973 at the Civil Service Club, Duckmanton Lodge, Calow, Chesterfield

A.G.D. Youth Cricket Club (under 21) emerged
1973 League Cup Champions

The Chesterfield and District Youth League ended on 9th August A.G.D. C.C. under the shrewd captaincy of Roy Cox, emerged league cup champions

With 12 matches played; 8 ended with victories over our opponents. We were defeated first by Calow by 20 runs, then Blackwell by 9 wickets, Chesterfield Youth Council by 8 wickets and we also had a tied result with the same team.

We defeated the following teams:-

Morton (Cup) by 8 wickets
Brimington (League) by 46 runs
Calow (League) by 63 runs
Staveley Works (League) by 55 runs.
Clay Cross (Cup) by 18 runs
Matlock (Cup) by 6 wickets
Morton (Cup) by 20 runs

The matches against Staveley Works and Brimington Methodist, were abandoned because of rain on 30th May and the 6th June respectively.

P.S. Mr. Lovegrove and I would like to take this opportunity to thank all the Clubs who have played against us in this year's competition. So on behalf of all our players, we would like to express our appreciation to the officials of the Chesterfield and District League for their services to cricket and cricketers and long may this interest continue.

Blackwell emerged League Champions of the
Chesterfield & District Youth Council League

Blackwell 89 for 5 off 20 overs
Chesterfield Y.C.   74 off 18·2 overs.

On Sunday last, Chesterfield Youth team under the captaincy of Mick Hollindale, met Blackwell Y.C. under the leadership of Julian Riley in the play off for the league championship at Chesterfield Tube Works and as a result Blackwell won by 15 runs.

Having won the toss on a sun-drenched afternoon and a perfect wicket skipper Riley of Blackwell elected to bat.

Williams and Gascoine. opened the innings to the bowling of Holmes and Turner. Runs came slowly but at 16, Holmes bowled the former for 7. With only 3 runs added Turner had Riley caught by Hooper before he opened his account. Skipper J. Riley joined Gascoine as runs came at a faster rate. With the score at 41, Gascoine was caught. Johnson bowled Holmes for 22

Hopkinson joined Riley but at 46, Holmes caught Riley off Turner for 4. Forbes was next in as runs came steadily but at 54, wicket keeper Hollindale caught Hopkinson off Turner for 6.

Parkin partnered Forbes when they became associated in an unbroken sixth wicket partnership which yielded-35 invaluable runs and at the end of the 20th over, the total was 89 for 5 with Mark Forbes 33 not out and Trevor Parkin 13 not out.

Bowling for the Chesterfield team Ian Turner took 3 for 34 in 10 overs and Holmes took 2 for 40 in 8 overs (before he twisted his ankle and had to retire.)

With 90 runs required for victory and the opportunity to regain the League championship, the Chesterfield team failed by 15 runs. Turner and Hooper opened the innings to the bowling of Julian Riley the Derby Colt and Mark Forbes. They started disastrously as J. Riley bowled Turner for 4. In came Jackson with the score at 10. Only another 8 runs were added off 6 overs before Hooper was bowled by Forbes for 10. Skipper Hollindale joined Jackson who attempted a big hit and was out to a well judged catch by Graham Riley at deep long on for 5 off J. Riley. The score was 28 for 3 off 8.2 overs. Bradley Joined Hollindale and at this stage they neede 59 off 11 overs. Bradley was run out by Forbes for 2. The score board now read 37 for 4 off 10 overs. The bespectacled Constantine partnered the aggressive Hollindale who continued to attack the bowling but Riley bowled intelligently and as a result Hollindale was caught at the wicket off Riley for 14. The lelt handed Johnson joined Constantine as the rate of scoring died down. The former was caught by wicket keeper Hopkinson off Riley for 1.

Paul Beard came in to bat when 50 runs were needed off 8 overs. Riley struck again and Beard was bowled for the dreaded cipher. Richardson another bespectaled player joined the patient Constantine as the tempo increased but the latter was run out for 7. Logan Kerss joined Richardson with the score at 49 for 8 and 5 overs left. The aggressive Richardson lifted Forbes for 6 in front of the pavilion but Forbes had the last word as Riley brought off yet another fine catch on the long-on boundary to dismiss Richardson for 17. The score was now 70 for 9 as the injured Holmes joined Kerss; but with another 4 runs added the latter was run out for 9 to give Blackwell victory by 15 runs and the championship.

Bowling for Blackwell, Riley took 4 for 28 in 9·2 overs while Forbes took 3 for 43 in 9 overs. Umpires Mr. H. Bedford and Mr. A. Martin.

Result of the six-a-side tournament
By E. Wall (Junior Sports Writer)

A.G.D. "A" team emerged Champions of the six-a-side tournament

Geoff Miller presenting the six-a-side trophy to Andy Horton (Capt.) of the A.G.D. Cricket Club, 1973.
L to R:- A. Horton, I. Drayner, K. Swift, W. Scott, T. Hession, E. Wall

organised by the Chesterfield and District Youth Council League.

Twelve teams participated. The teams defeated by the Champions were as follows:-

Matlock "A" in first round
A.G.D. "B" in Quarter Final
Darley Dale "A" in Semi-Final
Matlock "B" in Final

Mr. Harold Bradford (Chairman of the Chesterfield and District Youth Cricket Council) introduced Mr. Cliff Gladwin, Ex-Derbyshire and England player who presented the trophies and individual awards.

Mr. Bradford spoke about a most successful season and thanked first of all the Blackwell Committee for their co-operation last Sunday for the use of their ground for the six-a-side tournament and also the Chesterfield Tube Works Co. Ltd. for the use of their ground for the league final and also the

114

semi-final and final of the six-a-side which had to be stopped because of bad light the previous Sunday.

He also thanked the helpers, the clubs' umpires and scorers and ground staff who participated. After this Mr. Gladwin thanked him and presented the awards to the following team captains:-

M. Hollindale	Chesterfield YC (Northern League Winners)
J. Riley	Blackwell YC (Southern League Winners)
R. Cox	A.G.D. YC (League Cup Champions) .
J. Riley	Blackwell YC (League Champions)
R. Cox	A.G.D. YC (Six-a-side Champions)

Individual prizes were donated by the Derbyshire Youth Cricket Council and the Chesterfield Cricket Lovers' Society.

Officials for the tournament were Messrs. R. Margaresson, B. Cox, H. Riley, W. Bush and W. Parr.

Team Stewards: Messrs. T. Brocklehurst and R. Hooper.

Umpire Steward: Mr. C. Gladwin.

Prize Numbers drawn: 782 : 24 : 843 : 1656 : 1679 : 2158 : 1980

Brimington Methodist Church Cricket Club
(Members of North Derbyshire League)

Brimington Methodists Youth XI have enjoyed their first season in the Chesterfield League. Under the captaincy of D. Hingley there have been plenty of moments to cherish. Mark Taylor scored his most runs in his very first match.

Keith Burton performed a memorable hat-trick, clean bowling them all, and in that match finished with 4 for 1. Glyn Jones scored 15 and Alan Orwin 13 runs in the same game.

Glyn Jones had his best bowling figures against Chesterfield taking 6 for 20 and Keith Burton scored 13 runs against the same team.

Stephen Elcock, who kept wicket very well throughout the season claimed three victims against Calow, and in the same match D. Hingley took 4 for 33 and scored 38 glorious runs. Ian Francis scored 15 runs and Martin Ward not out in the game also.

The most creditable victory was against Staveley Works by seven wickets. Staveley could never master the bowling of D. Hingley (4 for 12) and Glyn Jones (5 for 16), and were all out for 31, Brimington Methodists scoring 32 for 3. The game against Darley Dale was played in the rain, and ironically this was one of the most consistent batting performances, Keith Burton 15; Glyn Jones 16; Richard Mallender (an extremely promising all-rounder) 20 runs.

David Hingley scored 24 runs (mostly in boundaries) in the match against Chesterfield, and another good victory was against the League Leaders Calow, Chris Dart scoring a very quick 19 runs. Calow were dismissed for only 30, Barry Whitehead and, David Hingley each taking 3 wickets for 13.

When Blackwell were the visitors to Brimington, Richard Mallender was the most successful bowler taking 3 for 31, and in the same match opening batsman Andrew Heelin was still not out at the close of Brimington's innings.

When Brimington Methodists played at Morton, the, chief scorers were Chris Dart (18), Glyn Jones (13 n.o. (including a six), Dave Hingley (11) and Steve Fuller (10). Probably the most memorable victory was in a friendly game at Clowne, when Brimington could only muster 41 runs thanks chiefly to captain Andrew Heelin (13). Kevin Madin only 12 years of age, hit a boundary, which proved to be the winner, because Clowne were dismissed for 38 runs after once being 28 for 2; a sure example of a game never being lost until the last ball has been bowled. Roger Barfoot claimed 7 for 18 in this match.

Against Clay Cross, Brimington Methodists had their finest opening partnership of the season, when Dave Hingley (42) and Stephen Elcock (16) put on 49, Chris Dart scored 16 out of a total of 90 for 3 off 20 overs. A formidable total which Clay Cross failed to reach by 10 runs. Barry Whitehead taking 4 for 28.

At Matlock, in the League Cup the best perfomances were Dave Hingley (17 runs and 4 for 45), Stephen Elcock 18 not out, Glyn Jones 8 and Ian Francis 8 not out.

All the Youth Team Participants in the season were:-

David Hingley – Forceful right-hand bat, medium pace bowler. A very able and respected captain who has now made his mark in the 1st XI.

Stephen Elcock – Left-handed opening batsman and wicket-keeper. Regular 2nd Xl wicket-keeper.

Andrew Heelin – Right-hand stylish opening batsman and specialist slip fielder. Several 1st XI games.

Keith Burton – Forceful right-hand batsman, medium right-arm bowler and stand-in wicket-keeper. Some 2nd XI games.

Glyn Jones – Right-handed batsman, medium pace bowler. Has played some 1st XI matches.

Andrew Hickin – Right-handed batsman.

Mark Taylor – Right-handed batsman, right-arm bowler.

Alan Orwin – Right-handed batsman. Several 2nd XI appearances.

Ian Francis – Right-handed batsman.

Barry Whitehead – Pace bowler and forceful right-handed batsman.

Played several 1st XI games.

Chris Dart – Quick-scoring right-handed batsman. A few 2nd XI appearances.

Stephen Fuller – Promising right-handed batsman. Regular 2nd XI appearances.

Martin Ward – Right-handed batsman and right-arm bowler. Performed hat-trick in 2nd XI game v. A.G.D.

Richard Mallender – Right-handed batsman and very promising left-arm and medium pace bowler.

Michael Rowbotham – Right-handed batsman, right-arm bowler.

Gary Abbott – Right-handed batsman, right-arm bowler.

Chris Norton – Forceful right-handed batsman.

Michael Wilkinson – Right-handed batsman and right-arm bowler. A few 2nd XI appearances.

Richard O'Doherty – Right-handed batsman and right-arm bowler.

Kevin Madin – Left-handed batsman and left-arm spin bowler.

Nigel Bale – Right-handed batsman.

Michael Cantrill – Right-handed batsman, right-arm bowler.

David Tipping – Right-handed batsman, right-arm bowler.

And many more young, enthusiastic cricketers will be joining the ranks of Brimington Methodists in the years ahead.

Spital Diamond Jubilee

Spital C.C. 1972

117

This year Spital St. Leonard's cricket club celebrates its Diamond Jubilee. Formed to satisfy a village need it continues to enjoy the use of a local playing area for its matches, although this year of all years, it is without a pavilion; this having recently been razed by fire.

It is with pride that it boasts an enthusiasm that throughout its history it has never failed to field a side. The records show many sons have followed fathers as members and great encouragement is found in the number of past members who support the two teams.

Spital St. Leonards Sports Club
General Secretary: Bryn Jones

Spital Cricket Club was founded in 1913 and is certainly one of the pioneers of cricket in the North Derbyshire area. Our club can boast that, war years apart, we have never failed to field two sides during the whole of our existance and have always produced cricketers of a very high calibre.

I myself have been secretary of our club since 1969 and during that brief time have found life very eventful. In 1970 our cricket club amalgamated with Spital St. Leonards F.C. to form Spital St. Leonards Sports Club which has added another dimension to organised sport in our small village.

In 1973 our cricket section celebrated its Diamond Jubilee year, yes 60 years in existence, which over the years has seen the coming and going of some very good local sportsmen and indeed some wonderful personalities also.

Our cricket club is at present a member of The North Derbyshire Cricket League and although in season 1976 we were involved in rebuilding our first eleven, we still enjoyed a respectable league position which is a very encouraging sign for future years.

In conclusion I would like to say what a privilege it has been to have been connected with Spital Sports Club over the years and can only applaud the enthusiasm and sheer hardwork of a committee that has made a chosen pastime in the village of Spital very worthwhile.

Bryn Jones

Robinsons CC Emerge Cantrill Cup Winners
Skipper Keith Middleton of Robinsons won the toss with the skies heavily overcast on Sunday last and sent in Coalite to bat on an easy-paced wicket at Sheepbridge Sports Ground, Newbold.

Kevin Longden and Colin Holmes opened the innings to the bowling of Brian Harding and Tony Swift. With the score at 20, Swift bowled Holmes for 5. Don Cropper joined Longden and at 29, Cropper was caught and bowled by Swift for 1. The left-handed Barry Prestley entered the arena and

118

immediately opened his account with a 6 to deep mid-on and then 2 more sixes followed by a four which brought the score to 51 for 2 off 12 overs; but at 66, Longden was bowled by Boden for 28. Albert Revill partnered Prestley who was now in full cry, as the score accelerated to 93 for 4 off 19 overs, before Prestley was caught by Drury at deep fine leg off Swift for a well-played 48. Longden was next in with Revill who seemed to play second fiddle to the other batsmen. Up came the hundred in the twentieth over with a single through the slips off Swift, but at 117, Longden chanced his arm once too often and was brilliantly caught at deep mid-off by Harding off Drury for 16.

With 8 overs left and 5 wickets standing Robinsons appeared to be back in the game. Chappel joined the sheet anchored Revill as another 26 runs were added. Both batsmen were undefeated at the end of the 30th over. Revill 26 not out Chappel 13 not out. Bowling for Robinsons, T. Swift took 3 for 56 in 14 overs, M. Boden 1 for 27 in 3 overs and P. Drury 1 for 33 in 8 overs.

Goodwin and Boden opened the innings for Robinsons to the bowling of Trevor Marsden and Ken Scott. Scott struck the first blow for Coalite when he bowled Goodwin for 5. Sullivan partnered Boden as runs came slowly but with the score at 22 off 7 overs, Sullivan was bowled by Marsden for 4. Swift was next in as the opening bowlers continued to keep the run rate down. It was not long before both batsmen increased the tempo and 10 overs were bowled the score was 41 for 2. At this stage, Robinsons needed 104 to win off 20 overs with 8 wickets standing.

With the score at 61 for 2 Boden was bowled by Scott for 35. Skipper Middleton partnered Swift who was batting well but with another 21 runs added. Swift was caught by Presley off Scott for 30. Foster who joined Middleton, was unfortunate to be struck in the face and had to retire hurt with his score at 1. Hodby filled the breach and at 96 Middleton was l.b.w. to Longden for 14. Drury joined Hodby and they took the score to 114 before the latter was bowled by Marsden for 9. In came Donaldson and scored a quick 19 before he was bowled by Marsden. McDermott and Donaldson became associated in an unbroken seventh wicket partnership which yielded 23 invaluable runs which took their teams total to 145 for 7 and their individual score to 8 and 15 not out respectively as Robinsons emerged winners of the Cantrill Cup. Bowling for Coalite, Scott took 3 for 57 in 13·2 overs, T. Marsden 3 for 59 in 11 overs and H. Longden 1 for 18 in 3 overs.

Umpires: Mr. C. Gladwin and Mr. H. Bedford.

Coalite C.C. Winners of the Bayley Shield and Runners-Up Cantrill Cup 1973, Division I, North Derbyshire League.

Quotations

In addition to wishing Richard the best of success with his latest publication, I should also like to congratulate the A.G.D. Juniors on their remarkable successes during the 1973 season. In saying this I am fully aware that the key factor to these successes can be attributed to the outstanding efforts of Mr. R. Lovegrove and Mr. R. Suttle and the Committee of the A.G.D. Junior C.C. I must also make a special mention of Mrs. Lovegrove's un-tiring efforts of assistance to the juniors. Catering, first aid, scorer, supporter, this lady must be one of the clubs greatest assets.

From the senior clubs point of view I am extremely pleased with the influx of

D. Crowley
(Founder of AGDCC, 1961)

120

younger players into the senior teams, and speaking from the veteran stage I look forward to seeing these youngsters playing an important role in the future of the A.G.D. Cricket Club.

A.G.D. Junior Triangular Presentation

The 1973 season for the A.G.D. Junior Cricket Club came to an end on Saturday 21st July with the presentation of trophies and individual awards by Mr. E. J. Walton (Chairman of the Club) on the Loundsley Green Recreation Ground at 12 noon.

The main awards were for the Champions and best performances in the triangular tournament in June and July.

The cup donated by Messrs H. L. Brown and Son was won by the "A" team under the captaincy of 15 year old Andrew Marshall of 218 Ashgate Road. His team won two of the four matches, lost one, and the other ended in a tie with the "B" team, while the "C" team under the leadership of Michael Wall of 23 Wenlock Crescent, were Runners-up and were presented with a shield donated by Mr. Dennis Harding of Robinsons.

In addition to the above mentioned tournament the club completed the double in the Sheffield and District Junior League by winning the South Division of the League and then the Parramore Cup Final by 22 runs against Frecheville at Norton Oakes last Thursday.

Mr. Walton congratulated the parents for their co-operation and effort made over the past six years thus enabling the club to improve from year to year. He also spoke about the fine work which Messrs. Derek Billington, Ron Lovegrove and Richard Suttle have done to make this occasion a success and hoped that better facilities will be available for the youngsters in the not too distant future.

Individual awards went to David Lester of the "C" team for the best batting average for which he received a pair of batting cloves. Other awards were made to the following:

Michael Barnette (B) a cap for best bowling average.

Anthony Llanwarne (C) a gift token for most outstanding fielder.

David Lester (C) a shield for the highest individual score.

Paul Greatbatch (A) a plaque/abdominal protector for the most wickets taken in tournament.

Richard O'Doherty (C) a plaque for the best individual bowling performance.

Andrew Marshall (A) a pen for an outstanding bowling performance.

Colin Haw (B) a pair of batting gloves for the best allround performance in the same match.

Nicholas Fishwick (A) a cap for the most promising wicket-keeper batsman.

Many firms in Chesterfield contributed to the presentation as well as Messrs. Ramsden, Clayton, Walton and Lovegrove. Mr. Robert Murray (Secretary of the North Derbyshire Umpires Association) thanked the crowd for their support despite the inclement weather, he also thanked the A.G.D. C.C. for their help and Mr. Walton for his keen interest in the junior cricket Club, after which the youngsters celebrated their success in the pavilion.

The following teams participated in the 1973 A.G.D. Tournament.

Champions were the "A" team: A. Marshall (Capt.), P. Smith, E. Wilde (Canada), J. Corden. M. White. D. White, E. Wall. P. Greatbatch, N. Fishwick. D. Hayes. R. Penton. P. Weller, M. Beresford, P. Friend, W. McAdam, M. Stone.

Runners up were the "C" team: M. Wall (Capt.), D. Corden. D. Wagstaff, P. Gallagher. D. Lester. K. Lester. R. O'Doherty, A. Thorpe, J. McCulloch, J. Patterson, C. Pollard. S. Collins. R. Hoskin, A. Llanwarne. J. Drayner, P. Curbban, I. Suttle, S. Gibbons.

Wooden Spoonists were the "B" team: S. Wilde (Capt.), emigrated to Canada, A. Dawson, D. Edney, S. Gosling, M. Barnett, A. Genn, D. Bird, P. Best. D. Beddingham, S. Hussain. S. Smith. N. Corden. A. George, C. Bell, P. Drayner. C. Haw, D. Stone, J. Jones, A. Wilde (Canada), S. Higginbottom.

Richard Suttle hits 103 not out

West Indian Cricketer Richard Suttle reached another milestone in his eventful career by scoring 103 not out for A.G.D. against Kirkby Wyvern at Kirkby-in-Ashfield on Sunday June 17th. His innings consisted of four sixes and nine fours which were struck to all parts of the spacious Kirkby ground. This equalled his previous highest score for the club. Needless to say, A.G.D. easily won this friendly fixture by 89 runs with Dave Cocker taking 5 wickets for 29 runs. Scores were:-

A.G.D. 204 for 6 declared   Kirkby Wyvern 115 all out.

The first division of the North Derbyshire League already shows signs of developing into a tight contest and A.G.D. 1st XI are at present among the pace-setters, having won 3 drawn 1 lost 2 of their 6 league games. By beating Taverners on May 26th the 1st XI have also reached the semi-final of the Cantrill Cup.

The 2nd XI, playing in the newly formed third division of the North Derbyshire League have now won 3, lost 3 of their 6 league games to date.

The Bayley Shield competition as always, provided an upset when A.G.D. 2nd XI defeated first division opposition Scarcliffe by 13 runs in a thriller played at Loundsley Green on Monday June 11th. A.G.D. batted first and scored 102 runs for the loss of 9 wickets. Roy Cox and Andy Horton making his debut for the senior side) scoring 28 runs each. Scarcliffe replied with 89 for 8 wickets off the allotted 20 overs. Andy Horton captured 5 wickets for 50 runs while Peter May took 3 for 39. A feature of this match was the brilliant wicket-keeping of Alan Eyre, emphasized by the fact that not one extra was conceded. However, in the 2nd round of the competition A.G.D. 2nd XI lost to Bolsover Coalite by 9 wickets while the 1st XI defeated Glassworks by the same margin*

D. M. Tarlton. Secretary A.G.D. C.C.

Chetwynd Post August 1973

*Edward Wall (Vice-Capt.) of A.G.D. C.C. receives the Sheffield and District Trophy from Geoff Miller, the Derbyshire and England Cricketer, 1973
Others looking on are members of the successful team*

The bespectacled 16 year-old Brendan Wall has been A.G.D. Juniors' most prolific run-getter this season. I can only wish him further success in the future and hope that he will get the opportunity to represent the Derbyshire Colts team next year. He has achieved the distinction of being the Senior Club's first single-wicket Champion.

Season to remember for John

Compulsory retiring as skipper of a Chesterfield Boys' Cricket team, John Lovegrove has the satisfaction of knowing he has led the team in its most successful year in its short history. John, of Quantock Way, Chesterfield, has

WEST INDIES TOUR TO U.K.
1973

CAPTAIN—R. Kanhai (*Guyana*)

K. D. Boyce (*Barbados*)

G. S. Camacho (*Guyana*)

M. L. C. Foster (*Jamaica*)

R. C. Fredericks (*Guyana*)

L. R. Gibbs (*Guyana*)

V. A. Holder (*Barbados*)

Inshan Ali (*Trinidad*)

B. D. Julien (*Trinidad*)

A. I. Kallicharran (*Guyana*)

C. H. Lloyd (*Guyana*)

David Murray (*Barbados*)

Deryck L. Murray (*Trinidad*)

L. G. Rowe (*Jamaica*)

G. C. Shillingford (*Windward Islands*)

E. Willett (*Leeward Islands*)

MANAGER—E. S. M. Kentish (*Jamaica*)

ASSISTANT MANAGER—G. Gibbs (*Guyana*)

to retire because at the age of 18 he is too old to compete with the A.G.D. Junior team in the Sheffield and District Junior Cricket League next season.

During the past season, the team's third in the league, the A.G.D. side has won three of the possible four trophies and came runner-up in the competition for the fourth. They have won the Paramore Cup, a knock-out contest for all the teams in the league, the trophy for winning the southern section of the league and Derek Hitchen Memorial Trophy for winning the league's six-a-side contest.

They were runners-up in the play-off between the winners if the Northern and Southern sections of the league for the Leslie Fletcher Cup being beaten by Bradfield Juniors.

Last year with John as vice-captain the team won the Southern section of the league.

John, a postal assistant at the A.G.D., took up cricket at training sessions held by enthusiast Mr. Richard Suttle at Loundsley Green, Chesterfield. Of the past season John says "It has been a great season for the team and it's a pity we couldn't gain all four trophies."

John's cricket is continuing with the A.G.D. senior cricket team in the North Derbyshire League on Saturdays and with another A.G.D. team in an under-21 league on Wednesdays.

The Star 9/8/73

Robinsons C.C. Champions list Division Six-a-side
North Derbyshire League 1973

Teams which were defeated as follows:- Taverners (A & B) A.G.D. and Spital "A" in the Final by one run. (See colour page 1.)

Incidentally, a fine gesture was made by Mr. R. B. Nightingale to Robinsons Cricket Club in memory of his late son, Paul, a former member of the club.

His donation of a memorial shield and an annual individual trophy plus a monetary gift to the most outstanding (under 25) cricketer of the club, should encourage the development of up-and-coming talent.

Honours List

Division One – Winners, Spital 1st; runners-up, Robinson's Works. Cantrill Cup – Winners, Robinson's Works; runners-up, Spital 1st. Division Two – Winners, A.G.D. Sports; runners-up, Scarcliffe. Gregory Cup – Winners, A.G.D. Sports; runners-up, Sheepbridge, Bailey Shield – Winners. Spital 1st; runners-up, S. & J. Kitchins. Six-a-side (Division Two) – Winners. Scarcliffe; runners-up. S & J Kitchins; single wicket competition. Winner, Gerry Clarke (Taverners); runner-up. Dave Crowley (A.G.D. Sports.)

Six-a-side Knock-out (Division One) was completed on Sunday at the Sheepbridge Sports ground and featured a thrilling last-ball-of-the-last-over hit by John Lumsden to gain the Spriggs Cup for Taverners who beat Hundall in the final.

Semi-final wins were by Taverners over Robinson and Hundall over Ridgeway.

Division Two – S. & J. Kitchins 168-7 dec. (M. Potter 32, M. Robinson 48, G. Vine 27. J. Austin 29 n.o.), A.G.D, Sports 43-3. Kitchins, requiring five points for a win to finish runners-up, got only three points for a winning draw, and A.G.D. one point for a losing draw. and the runners-up are now Scarclffe.

Division Two
Final Two

	P	W	L	D	P
A.G.D. Sports	18	12	0	6	72
Scarcliffe	18	10	6	2	54
S. & J Kitchin	18	8	4	6	53
Sheepbridge	18	8	4	6	50
Spital 2nd	18	8	6	4	48
Hundall 2nd	18	8	8	2	44
Tube Works	18	7	8	3	41
Padley/Venables	18	4	10	4	27
Clowne Nalgo	18	3	12	3	22
Remoulds	18	2	12	4	16

Cricketers and Markham Pit Fund

Proceeds of a sponsored cricket match played at Loundsley Green onAugust 28 will go to the Markham Disaster Fund.

Orgamsed by Ron Lovegrove and Richard Suttle between a senior A.G.D. XI and a junior A.G.D. XI (this year's triple-crown champions of Sheffield and District Junior League), the match raised a sum of £97.69 which was donated to the Markham Fund,

Scores:- A.G.D. juniors, 125 for 9 off 18 overs. S. Evans 51 n.o., M. Hollindale 45, R. Cox 18. Bowling for the senior XI, D. Cocker I for 42, D. Houseley 2 for 30 and R. Suttle one for 27. D. Crowley 3 for 28.

A.G.D. seniors, 115 for 3 off 18 overs. D. Crowley 44. N. Lester 40 R. Suttle 18 n.o. Bowling for the juniors, S. Evans 2 for 37, A. Horton one for 46.

A.G.D.'s Junior & Senior XI's pose for photograph before the start of the sponsored cricket match held at Loundsley Green on Tuesday 28th August 1973 in aid of the Markham Disaster Fund. The proceeds of £100 was donated to the fund.
Organisers were: Messrs. Ron Lovegrove and Richard Suttle.
Scores:- A.G.D. (Jnrs) 125 for 9 off 18 overs. A.G.D. (Snrs) 115 for 3 off 18 overs.

A.G.D. (Jnrs.) defeat Cromford (Jnrs.) by 67 runs

In final match of the season (by R. Suttle at Cromford Meadows)
Scores; A.G.D. (Jnrs.) 143 for 7 off 30 overs
Cromford (Jnrs.) 76 off 22·4 overs

On Sunday 16 September, Cromford (Jnrs.) under the captaincy of Michael Barling, entertained A.G.D. (Jnrs.) at Cromford Meadows in their first friendly fixture at the end of the season and lost by 67 runs.

Roy Cox, captain of the visiting team, won the toss on a greenish wicket with the skies slightly overcast. He batted first and after 30 overs the A.G.D. Jnrs. were 143 for 7. Of these, J. Lovegrove and B. Wall scored 40 runs each while M. Hollindale arid K. Wilde scored 36 and 11 respectively.

Bowling for Cromford, J. Eshelby took 3 for 19, A. Pearson 2 for 26. Atkin and Barley took one each for 35 and 57 respectively.

In reply Cromford scored 76 off 22·4 overs. Top Scorer was Niel Hartley with 17 and Robert Atkin 14.

Chiefly responsible for their dismissal, was a fine spell of bowling by Norman Graham who took 5 for 26. R. Cox 2 for 7 while D. Harding, P. Milburn and E. Wall took one each for 4, 10 and 13 respectively as their team won convincingly to round off a most. successful season in the six year old history of the club.

Umpires: Messrs T. Gilman and R. Lovegrove.

127

The author relaxes with his family after a very hectic but successful season in 1973.
L to R:- Marva (10), Dad, Roger (5), Baby Steven (1), with Lettitia and Ian (9).
My wife and I are very grateful to the Doctors and Nursing staff of the Northern General
Hospital, Sheffield, where our daughter "Marva" underwent a most successful hole-in-the-
heart operation eleven months ago.

All cricket lovers know of the contribution made to the game by the West Indies and one immediately thinks of the great names – Worrell, Weekes, Walcott, Constantine, Sobers and many more.

I would suggest that, in a much less glamorous way, Richard Suttle's enthusiasm and effort in the cause of Junior Cricket deserves our applause.

He would be the first to admit that he has had some equally hard-working colleagues and the evidence of their devotion is there for all to see.

F. G. Robinson
Hon. Sec. Chesterfield Cricket Lovers Society

During my first 2 week visit to Barbados after fifteen years in the United Kingdom, I narrowly escaped serious injury. After visiting my youngest son, Steven, who was 2 years-old, developed breathing difficulties and had to be admitted to the Queen Elizabeth's Hospital, Bridgetown. On my return to the Cadogan's residence I stepped off the pavement to catch a bus, but was hit by a 30-ton bus and ended up with just broken ribs.

Personal achievements involve a changed life style

On the 15th October, 1974, I received "The Service to Cricket Award" from Mr. S. C. Carter, President of Chesterfield Cricket Lovers Society. He also presented me with two autographed cricket books by Messrs. Brian Johnston and E. W. Swanton entitled *It's Been a Lot of Fun* and *Sort of a Cricket Person* respectively.

Chesterfield Cricket Lovers' Society

SERVICE TO CRICKET AWARD

1974

Presented to

Mr. Richard Suttle

in recognition of his outstanding service to the game, and particularly in the sphere of Junior Cricket

J. C. Carter
President

15ᵗʰ October, 1974

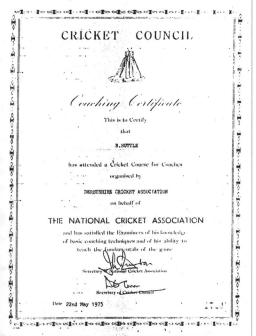

Shortly after this, I decided to further my studies by taking a full-time Business Course for matured students at the Chesterfield College of Technology, where I found some of the best lecturers in the country.

Within a year, I achieved a measure of success by passing examinations which included Royal Society of Arts in English (Stages 1 and 2) and Mathematics (Stage 1). During this period I also gained my National Cricket Association Award Certificate at the above-mentioned College under the supervision of Mr. Bob Deardon (N.C.A. Advanced Coach from Derbyshire C.C.C.

The Daily Telegraph and Morning Post

From
E. W. Swanton, O.B.E.

At ....Fleet.Street........

Reply to ....

25th October 1974

Dear Mr.Suttle,

I am so glad you have enjoyed Sort of a
Cricket Person.

I hasten to thank you for your book Junior Cricket
Reborn in the Seventies which I found quite fascinating. Cricket depends on people, and is a reflection
of those who play and administer and work for the game;
and it is clear that Chesterfield and **district** are
lucky in your presence there, and in the work you do.

I see we have in common having taken teams to
Barbados. My wife and I are shortly off to Australia,
and it may be we cannot get to Barbados this year –
in which case it will be the first we have missed
since 1591

All good luck to you in your efforts to help the
young.

With kind regards.

Yours sincerely,

Jim Swanton

---

98 HAMILTON TERRACE
ST. JOHNS WOOD
LONDON, N.W.8
01-286 2991

24th October 1974

Dear Mr. Suttle,

Thank you so much for
sending me your booklet which I
found extremely interesting
particularly as I'm very keen
on encouraging young cricketers.

I'm also delighted that you
enjoyed my book and congratulate
you on winning the award.

Many more thanks.

Yours sincerely,

Brian Johnston

(Brian Johnston)

Amsterdam

Within a few weeks, I was offered a six month coaching contract with the Amsterdam Cricket Club, Holland. I accepted the offer and arrived there to a great welcome from the Officials of Amsterdam C.C. in April 1975.

New opportunities in a foreign country brought new and exciting challenges, which I thoroughly enjoyed. However, before my contract ended, I was given a week's leave to attend an interview at Matlock College, Derbyshire where I have applied for a 2-year course in Community Studies, six months before I was offered my post in Amsterdam. Fortunately I passed the interview, but some weeks later I received a letter which informed me that after careful consideration and bearing in mind the demands of the course, it was decided not to accept me.

Surprisingly, my coaching certificate arrived at No. 8 Tintoretta Street, Amsterdam on the 6th June, 1975 after accepting the contract. Following this chapter, is a series of cricketing activities, which were successfully achieved and gratefully appreciated by the Club Officials as my contract concluded on 31st August, 1975, On the next page are examples of me coaching the Amsterdam Juniors, with whom I had to use an interpreter for the first month, until they got used to the English language, which made communication easier between us. It was not long before I started to learn the Dutch language, which presented a new and wonderful challenge for me and helped me to cope with the domestic side of life during my six month stay.

42e jaargang, nr. 4   12 mei 1975
RICHARD SUTTLE EN ACC

To the President, Officials and Members of the Amsterdam Cricket Club

After almost two weeks with your club, I would like to take this opportunity to express my sincere thanks through the medium of your weekly magazine how much I am enjoying coaching your enthusiastic cricketers.

First, I must thank your President, Mr. Max de Bruin, and members of the Club who gave me a warm welcome at Schipol airport. This was followed by a short reception at Mr. Nauta's home, where the hospitality and friendiness made me to feel at home.

In addition, we ended our celebration at the Preanger Restaurant, which is about a mile from the picturesque cricket ground where our home matches are played and is better known as the A.B.N. Sports field which Mr. Nauta kindly took me to see before I went to his home.

A word of thanks goes for Mr. Jan Prent who obligingly offered his home to the Club in order that I could have adequate lodgings and last but by no means least Mr. Jan Hendriks, president of the pupils and junior teams to whom much of his time and arduous work is devoted, also the help given by Mr. Rene Lapierre to take me to away matches by car in order to see the potential of our youths under match conditions.

Finally, I hope that within the next decade, the A.C.C. can look back and enjoy the rewards for what is done now for our up and coming youngsters, who one day will not only grace the cricket fields of Amsterdam, but be true ambassadors for their country wherever the grand old summer game is played.

Thanks once again for all that the committee, players and parents have done in order to make my four month stay a happy and enjoyable one and I sincerely hope that from these initial efforts, that Holland will become a force to be reckoned with in "World Cup Series" in the not too distant future.

C.W.R. Suttle

Amsterdamsche Cricket Club

Opgericht 5 maart 1921

*

Verzonden door:

M.M.de Bruin
Achterberglaan 117
Uithoorn

Uithoorn, september 22nd 1975.

To whom it may concern.

We hereby certify that Mr.Richard Suttle has been employed by our club as coach during the period 1.5.75 - 31.8.75.

He has been rendering his services to our club as a full time club coach and we have found him to be an accurate and enthousiastic clubcoach with special dedication for junior cricketers.

For our club he had about 80 youngsters to attend to and we have found his dedicated coaching to this group to be very useful.

We certainly do wish Mr.Suttle every bit of good luck on his future road of professional coaching.

Yours Sincerely
Amsterdam Cricket Club

A typical demonstration of close catching by Max de Bruin (Jnr) WK catches the ball with an outstretched left hand. (Two hands if possible, is safer.) Others taking part are Marc Polders and Dennis Steggink with their coach in the foreground.

A demonstration in the art of batting by Theo Wiegel. He is using more top hand than bottom hand in order to avoid being "caught out" by close-fielders as the coach throws the ball from a short range with varying bounce.

A demonstration of how to use the slip-catcher. These youngsters make use of this opportunity as their coach instructs how to catch the ball as it skids off the cradle.

Officials and a small section of players of the Amsterdam Cricket Club with their overseas Cricket Coach, Richard Suttle, formerly of the A.G.D. (Jnr. C. C.), Chesterfield, Derbyshire, England.

Skipper Karel van Osch leads out the A.C.C. in the opening friendly fixture against Bloemandaal on 4.5.75 at A.B.N. Sports. A year later this team won the National Championship.

International Fixture

Buitenlandse Coaches XI take the field at The Hague C.C. Holland against the Dutch International Team, who won by 73 runs.

A very memorable date for all cricket lovers, because on this date, Australia played West Indies at M.C.C. Lords in the first ever Cricket World Cup, which the West Indies won by 17 runs.

21st June, 1975 The Hague
K.N.C.B. XI – Buitenlandse Coaches XI.
1st Innings KNCB XI

1.	M.Flohil	l.b.w. B. Allum	0
2.	G.v. Laer	bowed B. Allum	25
3.	C.v. Schouwenburg	retired hurt	0
4.	A Bakker	bowled B. Allum	0
5.	S. Lubbers	c. Hartigan R. Ambler	48
6.	R. Schoonheim	bowled R. Ambler	40
7.	E. Abendanon	c. Rajak R. Hartigan	17
8.	R. Derogee	not out	37
9.	R. Onstein	c. Rishworth R. Hartingan	6
10.	R.v.Weeldc	not out	12
11.	Brouwer	d.n.b.	–
		Extras (b; Ib; w; nb	17
		(for 7 wickets) declared	202

1.	D.Gibson	16 - 6 - 35 - 0
2.	B. Allum	15 - 5 - 52 - 3
3.	R. Ambler	13 - 0 - 57 - 2
4.	K. Khan	6 - 1 - 11 - 0
5.	R. Hartigan	6 - 1 - 30 - 2

Buitenlandse Coaches Innings

1.	R. Goodacre	c.R. Schoonheim	b.E. Abendanon	25
2.	D. Brigden	bowled	R.v. Weelde	4
3.	R. Hartigan	retired hurt		8
4.	R. Suttle	c.Substitute	b.E. Abendanon	6
5.	D. Gibson	not out		54
6.	K. Khan	bowled	R. Derogee	16
7.	H. Rajak	c.A. Bakker	R. Onstein	3
8.	R. Rishworth	bowled	R. Derogee	0
9.	D. Branson	not out		3
10.	B. Allum	d.n.b.		–
11.	R. Ambler	d.n.b.		–
		Extras		10
		Total (voor 6 wickets)		129

1.	Rob v. Weelde	8 - 4 - 20 - 1
2.	R. Derogee	9 - 3 - 17 - 2
3.	R. Onstein	10 - 3 - 19 - 1
4.	E. Abendanon	11 - 3 - 37 - 2
5.	A. Bakker	6 - 0 - 26 - 0

A.C.C. v H.M.S. "MATAPAN"
Sunday, 29.6.75

Signatures:*
1. Lieutenant H. Wylie
2. Lieutenant B. Shackleton
3. Rees
4. French
5. Lord
6. Mitchell
7. Maddams
8. Leader
9. Hurne
10. McCarthy
11. Webb
12. Sub Lieutenant Hermans
13. Mullen

Scores:- A.C.C. 263 for 3 dec. Hab Van de Heydel 128, K. Mulder 100 not out, K.V.Osch (Capt.) 15.

Bowling for H.M.S. Matapan:- L Hum 2 for 80, D. McCarthy 1 for 56.

H.M.S. Matapan 145. Webb 34 not out. Hum 24, Shackleton 19, Leader 19, Rees 15, Herman 12.

Bowling:- M. Kis de Barre, de Hann and Lapierre took 2 each for 19, 10, 56 and 19 respectively.

UNFORGETABLE
Memories at A.B.N. Sports Ground, Amsterdam

A Trans-Avion passes overhead as play stops momentarily. A slight hazard to a cricketer's concentration, while on its way to the near by Schiphol Airport. At times the noise is incredible from larger planes. After a few weeks of constant repetition, they pass almost un-noticed with habitual regularity.

Scaitcliffe School
Englefield Green, Surrey
Thursday 24.7.75

1. Simon Pardoe (Capt.)
2. Harry Cator
3. David Bagnall
4. Gavin Phillips
5. Mark Milliken-Smith
6. Ian Hossack
7. Charles Harris
8. Peter Edwards
9. Stephen Fordham
10. Richard Moore
11. Mark Cunningham-Reid
12. James Denham
13. Richard McKerrow
14. Paul Walsh
15. Tim Baker
16. Riley Smith

Bristol University C.C. at the Amsterdam Cricket Club

Bristol University XI
Thursday 26.6.75

Signatures:-
1. Jim Jamison (Capt.)
2. Bob Reeves
3. Graham Cripps
4. Mark Day
5. Brian Joseph
6. Phil Davy
7. Mark Winter
8. Bob Nicol
9. Kevin Brown
10. Jim Gowling
11. Steve Smith
12. Dave Dance
13. Nick Birchall
14. Mark Travis
15. Andy Leech

Scores:- Bristol University 196 for 8, B. Birchall 89, Joseph 22, Jamison 18 n.o., Winter 16, Davy 15 and Dat 12 n.o.
Bowling for A.C.C.:- R. Suttle 3 for 43 while Schoonerveldt, Ostia, Hinnen and De Heyde took one each for 32, 26, 27 and 11 respectively.
A.C.C.:- 102. Ostra 28, Mulder 18, "Rob" Dukker 15, Suttle 14, De Heyde 12. Bowling:- Leech 3 for 21, Winter 2 for 24.

Extract from the Derbyhire Times 27.6.75

A local cricket coach who emigrated as a "Missionary" to give the game wider appeal in Holland, is to tour Southern England with a team of youngsters in July and August. Mr. Richard Suttle flew over to join the Dutch recently to take a summer job as a coach – and it will be in that capacity that he accompanies an (under 18) touring party.

Most of the teams matches will be played against Middlesex junior teams he hopes to make a full coverage of the tour in his third book, entitled *Stimulating The C.A.D.A. of Cricket.*

(Under 18) Amsterdam C.C.
On Tour To England – 27th July, 1975

A party comprising of 16 boys and 5 adults left for England on July 27th and returned to Amsterdam on August 3rd. They played four matches and visited the Lord's Cricket Ground.

They were accommodated by the East Cote C.C., North West London. The itenerary was as follows:–

Monday	28th July	Harrow C.C.
Tuesday	29th July	Harefield C.C.
Wednesday	30th July	Ealing C.C.
Thursday	31st July	Visit to Lords (2nd Test)
Friday	1st August	East Cote C.C.

after which a party will be held by the East Cote C.C. at the Sir Winston Churchill Hall in the form of a "Summer Hop".

N.B. Many thanks to the President of the A.C.C. Mr. Max de Bruin (Snr.) who organised the tour.

From all the members of the A.C.C. I join with them in wishing (16 year-old) Arne Van Teunenbrock and his team every success from this tour and I also hope that the experience which he gained as captain of the Dutch Youth team which toured England under his leadership a month before will be an asset to him.

Many thanks to Mr. C. R. E. Lapierre who organised the 8 match series which commenced on June 28th and included such fixtures as:-

Sussex Youth Cricket Festival
1. Western Area.
2. Eastern Area.
3. Eastbourne College.
4. Sussex School Cricket Association at Hove.
5. Christ Hospital in Horsham.
6. Kent Cricket Schools.
7. Essex Schools in Dagenham.
8. Three Bridges Club.

Amsterdam C.C. off to a good start
By C. R. W. Suttle (Eastcote, Middlesex)

On Monday, 28th July the A.C.C. touring party under the astute leadership of Mr. Rob Dukker, deputising for Mr. Max de Bruin, President and Manager of the touring team, organised net practice at their host Club, Eastcote, for a period of two hours as the sun shone brilliantly.

All the players looked extremely fit as they were put through their paces by their two coaches R. Lapierre and R. Suttle, two hours before the start of their first match against Harrow C.C.

Harrow defeated A.C.C. by 7 wickets
Scores: A.C.C. 145 off 49 overs
H.C.C. 148 for 3 off 32.3 overs

Play commenced at 2 p.m. with ideal conditions prevailing as A. van Teunenbroek, captain of the A.C.C. Junior team, won the toss and elected to bat and after 49 overs. the tourists were all out for 145

Skipper Teunenbroek topscored with a well played 32 and was ably assisted by Viddeleer with 28, Hinnen 18, de Bruin 13. Zeegers 12, Balk 11 and R. Dukker 18 not out.

Bowling for Harrow C.C. M. Rigby took 5 for 35 in 5 overs, while Newby Bregi, Regali and Buyrne took one each for 1, 28, 11 and 7 respectively.

In reply, Harrow scored 148 for 3 off 32.3 overs. Mainly responsible for this total was a splendid undefeated innings of 89 by the left handed Newby, who was well supported by Somersall with 24 and Bradman 18.

Bowling for the tourists, skipper Teunenbroek took 2 for 34 in 11 overs, Hinnen 1 for 29 in 7 overs as Harrow won by 7 wickets.

Scores: Harefield (jnrs) 197 for 9 off 40.5 overs
A.C.C. (Jnrs) 120 all out of 27 overs

The second fixture got underway for the tourists at Harefield C.C., Middlesex under a cloudless sky as the temperature soared into the eighties, but at stumps the home team won by 77 runs.

Skipper Evans of H.C.C. won the toss on a batsman's paradise, took first knock and after 40·5 overs, he declared the innings closed with the score at 197 for 9 and a personal contribution of 99 before being trapped L.B.W. by his opposite number, Teunenbroek. Other useful scores came from West with 33, Papworth 23 n.o., Sherritt 17 and Knife 14 after being at one period 98 for 8.

The tourists standard of fielding was very poor and once again proved their undoing in this important department of the game as no fewer than eight catches were dropped.

Bowling for A.C.C. Teunenbroek took 3 for 73, Hinnen 2 for 71, Allema 2 for 12, Zeegers 1 for 12 and Heyblorn 1 for 5.

In reply, the tourists scored 120. Thanks to a fine innings of controlled egression of 55 by all-rounder Hinnen. It included three lusty sixes and nine fours while opening batsman Balk scored a fine 34 and Viddeleer a useful 13

Bowling for H.C.C. Singleton took 4 for 49, Papworth 3 for 15, while

Doorker and Ingleton took one each for 19 and 18 respectively and enabled their team to win by 77 runs. After the match a friendly exchange of gifts between the two captains Arne van Teunenbroek of A.C.C. and Philip Evans of Harefield C.C.

Tourists register their first victory

Scores: A.C.C. (jnrs) 115 off 39.5 overs
Ealing (Colts) 100 for 9 off 40 overs
In an evenly contested combat, the touring team under the astute captaincy of H. Dukker won by 15 runs in a nail-biting finish against Ealing (Colts) on Wednesday, 30th July.

H. Dukker, having won the toss on a placid wicket on a sundrenched afternoon, the A.C.C. were all out for 115 after a disastrous start. But once again all-rounder Hinnen, following up his previous day's score with a sound 54 which included one six and six fours.

The only other batsman to reach double figures was Schuurmans with an invaluable 24 at number 9. Bowling for E.C.C., skipper Hughes took 6 for 8 in 7·5. overs three of which were maidens, to emphasize his immaculate length and line while Wilson. Pull and Newton took 2. 1 and 1 for 21,10 and 21 respectively.

With 116 runs required for victory, Ealing (Colts) made a gallant effort as they needed 19 to win off the last over with one wicket to fall, but at the end of the 40th over they were still 16 runs short. Top scorer was all-rounder Hughes with 26. Other contributions came from Fanklin 16 and Pull with an undefeated 17.

All-rounder Hinnen took 3 for 14, van Leeuwen 2 for 9 while Teunenbroek, Heyblom and Schuurmans took one each for 20, 13 and 24 respectively to win their first match of the tour by the narrow margin of 15 runs.

Eastcote C.C. wins final match of tour by nine wickets

Scores: A.C.C. 107 of 37 overs
E.C.C. 110 for 1 off 20 overs
Friday 1st August, saw the end of the Amsterdam Junior Cricket Tour of the U.K. and also the arrival of their President Mr. Max de Bruin who was unable to attend earlier during the tour.

Neil Stevens, who ably captained the Eastcote C.C. won the toss on a rain affected wicket with dark overhanging clouds, hovering over the picturesque ground as the tourists were sent in to bat.

With little experience against the rising ball and unfavourable conditions, the youngsters of Amsterdam started their innings disasterously. as two wickets fell before a run was scored.

However, skipper Teunenbrock and Hinnen came to their rescue with a partnership of 27 runs to give some respectability to the score, but when the consistent Hinnen departed with 12, wickets began to tumble, while Teunenbrock counter attacked at the other end with a classical 39. The only other batsman to reach double figures was Gosewehr with 11, before the team was all out for 107 off 37 overs.

Bowling for the home team, Stevens took 2 for 18, Rice 2 for 15, Kirkham 3 for 31, Thorn 2 for 18 and Caple 1 for 1.

With 108 runs needed for victory, the Eastcote batsmen went for the runs on a pitch, less responsive to lift, as the sun came out and at the end of the 20th over, the home team had lost one wicket for 110 runs. Of these, Dane scored an undefeated 56 which included nine boundaries while his partner Ingram also carried his bat for 39 to give their team a well-earned nine wicket victory over the tourists, who won their only victory of the series against Ealing C.C.

They lost to Harrow C.C., Harefield C.C. and finally Eastcote C.C. as the tour ended on an enjoyable note.

Plans are now on the way to organise a tour of the Midlands next season.

Mr. Ben Jessop

Harefield Junior C.C. 1975

Standing Left to Right:- *Mr. C. Woodward, (Secretary), M. Birch, M. Woodward, D. Singleton, N. Skerviett, R. Ingleton, A. Hollis, Mr. C. Kempster, (Manager/Coach).*
Seated Left to Right:- *B. Knife, S. Papworth. P. Evans. (Capt.), M. West and J. Dunbar*

Resume of The Sheffield & District Junior League's Tour of Holland 1975

Our Sheffield and District Junior League was established in 1950, toured Holland in 1975 in July and August. Our party included 16 junior and 5 officials.

We played matches against Kampong, Hilversum, Hercules and Amersfoort and ended the tour without conceding a defeat.

We enjoyed the tour immensely. We were well accommodated by the Kampong C.C. at their Headquarters, Jeugdherberg Rhijnauwen Bunnik (U), Netherlands.

Finally, on behalf of the committee of the Sheffield & District Junior Cricket League, I must join them in thanking the following firms and individual sponsors for their generous support for the tour. They are as follows:-

A.G.D.C.C., George Basset & Co. Ltd., Batchelors Foods Ltd., J. Beck Esq., British Tissues, G. Burdett Esq., Croda Int. Ltd., E. Dixon Esq., Gray Nicholls Ltd., S. Grayson Esq., & Mrs. Grayson, F. Harrison Esq., Izal Ltd., B. Jessop Esq., National Cricket Association, P. Parramore & Sons (1924) Ltd., Sheffield United, Sheffield United C.C., Stanley Tools Ltd., Viners Ltd., Whitbread East Pennines Ltd., Thorncliffe Printers Ltd.

The party included the Officials:-

Eric Dixon (Party Leader), Ben Jessop, Dennis McDonald, Arthur Noble and Eric Pearson, while the Junior Cricketers and were chosen from:– Shaun Beck (Frecheville C.C.), David Brailsford (Staveley C.C.), Andrew Brown (Shiregreen C.C.), Steven Childs (Mortomley C.C.), Nicholas Fishwick (A.G.D.C.C.), Stephen Foster (Whitley Hall C.C.), Peter Frost (Beighton C.C.), Mark Johnson (Sheffield United C.C.), Glyn Jones (Brimington C.C.), David Lester (A.G.D.C.C.), Michael Lomas (Aston Hall C.C.), Philip Marsden (Stocksbridge C.C.), Keith Martift (Treeton C.C.), David Pearson (Thorncliffe C.C.), Patrick Piearcy (Bradfield C.C.), Tony Walton (Stocksbridge Old C.C.)

Scores:-
SHEFFIELD v. KAMPONG
Sheffield 103.
D. Brailsford 27, M. Johnson 23, D. Lester 16. P. Engehart 5 for 20.
Kampong 66.
R. VanderWeile 24, H. Hendriks 15. S. Foster 3 for 21, A. Brown 3 for 15, D. Pearson 4 for 16.

SHEFFIELD v. HILVERSUM

Hilversum 132 for 7.

R. Lifmann 51, N. Atkins 28. C. Boonen 29 not out.

Sheffield 134 for 5.

G. Jones 39, K. Martin 21, D. Pearson 28 not out. F. Smit 2 for 23.

SHEFFIELD v. HERCULES

Hercules 96

G. Melkert 27, H. Daudery 15, S. Foster 3 for 10, M. Johnson 2 for 12, K. Martin 2 for 4.

Sheffield 97 for 4

D. Brailsford 49 not out, S. Beck 33, N. Atkins 2 for 13.

SHEFFIELD v. AMERSFOORT

Amersfoort 147

E. Snoek 20, H. Zwart 32, N. Atkins 44, A. Brown 3 for 49, S. Childs 3 for 34.

Sheffield 145 for 7

D. Brailsford 58, T. Walton 12, D. Lester 12, H. Zwart 2 for 24, N. Atkins 2 for 22.

SHEEFIELD v. KAMPONG

G. Jones 19, D. Brailsford 24, M. Johnson 32, S. Beck 29, D. Pearson 33, N. Atkins 3 for 31, F. Smit 2 for 35.

Kampong 98

H. Hendriks 14, T. Wallinger 37, A. Brown 7 for 27.

Brimington Cricket Club performances of 1976 and Tour of Belgium & Amsterdam
By John Buxton

The highlight of our 1976 season was the club tour of Belgium and Holland, where we were received amidst great hospitality. 1977 will see us touring Sussex, where 7 matches have been arranged. (See colour page 3.)

Our Second Eleven won the Third and Second Division Six-a-Sides, and our Youth Team won the Sheffield League Six-a-Side at Treeton during 1976.

The lads who did us proud in the North Derbyshire League Six-a-Side were 1. Alan Jones (Capt.) 2. Geoff Bradley. 3. Geoff Wragg. 4. Nick Russell. 6. Richard Mallender and 7. Neil Collings, whilst our under 18's Six-a-Side winners were 1. Austin Globe (Capt.) 2. David Key. 3. Peter Bagnall. 4. Nick Russell. 5. Richard Mallender and Neil Collings.

We have attractive Sunday Friendly matches arranged, and our Captain Ernie Fidler has won tremendous respect from all our players, particulary the Youth Team members. of whom many will be involved in our various activities during 1977.

Chesterfield Accountant Generals Cricket Club chairman, Mr. Edward Walton presents the Chesterfield Youth Council knock-out cup and six-a-side trophies to junior vice-captain Eddie Wall at Duckmanton Lodge last night. Looking on are (from left) coach Richard Suttle and club secretary Ron Lovegrove.

Morning Telegraph Saturday 10/10/75

Unable to face another long spell of unemployment, I enrolled in the Autumn of 1975 and took G.C.E. 'O' Levels in Mathematics, English, English Literature, Geography, Sociology and Biology at Chesterfield College of Technology and at the same time coached professionally in the Sports Hall with two Derbyshire and England players Messrs. Cliff Gladwin and Geoff Miller when time permitted at weekends. These coaching sessions were organised by Mr. Harold Bradford, Chairman of the Chesterfield and District Youth Council and Mr. Frank Robinson (Secretary of the Chesterfield Cricket Lovers' Society, with the occasional visit from another Ex-Derbyshire and England Cricketer, George Pope.

A.G.D. Cricket News 1976
By Dave Tarlton (Secretary)
First and Second Elevens
In his first season as 1st XI Captain, Dave Housely, ably assisted by vice-captain Dave Cocker, guided his team to a respectable third position in

145

Geoff Miller (Derbyshire and England Cricketer) explains to Matthew Joy, how to play a defensive forward stroke at the indoor nets at the Chesterfield College of Technology in October 1976. Others in the photograph are:-
L to R:- *R. Suttle (N.C.A. Coach), Steven Thompson, Peter May, Andrew Cooper and Nazir Latif*

Division One with a notable victory over League Champions, Robinsons Works in their last match of the season at Walton Dam. The 2nd XI too, in their last match avoided finishing at the bottom of Division Three by defeating Brimington Methodist II at Duckmanton Lodge.

The complete record of both teams in league and cup games reads as follows:-

	Played	Won	Drawn	Lost	C'cld.	Points
1st Xl Division 1	16	7	4	4	1	45
2nd Xl Divisions	14	4	2	8	–	24
1st Xl Cantrill Cup	1	0	0	1	–	–
2nd Xl Minor Cup	7	3	1	2	1	20
1 st Xl Bayley Shield	3	2	0	1	–	–
2nd Xl Bayley Shield	1	0	0	1	–	–

Derbyshire Minor Cup games played on a League basis.

1st XI: *Batting*, N. Lester (35 – 29). *Bowling*, D. Cocker (10-71)
Fielding, J. Lovegrove (17 catches).
2nd XI: *Batting*, C. Haw (19 – 29). *Bowling*, N. Edney (9-62).
Fielding, D. Tarlton and J. Shackleton (13 catches).
Friendly XI: *Batting*, N. Lester (34 – 90). *Bowling*, P. May (11-61).
Fielding, N. Lester and N. Graham (8 catches).

Mention must also be made of the AGD 'A' team, captained by Neil Edney, who battled through to the final of the Division Three Six-a-side Competition at Hundall only to be defeated by a very fine Brimington Methodist side.

A special award of an engraved tankard was presented to Mr. E. J. Walton, now Chairman of the Club for 40 years continuous membership for the A.G.D. Cricket Club (1936-1976). He has also been Chairman of the Club since the A.G.D. came to Chesterfield in 1963.

Friendly Fixtures

On 5th September, Duckmanton Lodge had a taste of international cricket when A.G.D. played host to the West Indians of Derby Carribbean Cricket Club. The home team did well to restrict the skilful visitors to 135 all out, Peter May taking 4 wickets for 43 runs. In reply A.G.D. were all out for 94 runs including some big hitting by Norman Graham who scored 26 before being trapped lbw by McDonald. Sewell, a 15 stone, 6 feet plus, off spinner, played havoc with the home team's batting, taking 6 wickets for 38 runs off 15 overs for Derby Carribbean who, although playing well within themselves, were easily the better team on the day. Of the other 17 friendly fixtures arranged, 7 resulted in victories for A.G.D., 4 were defeats and the rest drawn with 2 matches having to be cancelled. By far the highest number of runs recorded in a season by any A.G.D. players were the 843 scored by Norman Lester in League, Cup and Friendly cricket to become one of only 9 players to have attained 1,000 runs for the Club; the others being R. Suttle (over 2,000), D. Crowley, J. Witham. L. McCulloch, J. Lovegrove, A. Hession, D. Tarlton and D. Houseley, (McCulloch and Hession have since left the Club). In the friendly against the Coding Section of Sheffield H.P.O. on Sunday 16th May. 1976, Norman hit 110 and combined with J. Lovegrove to put on 172 runs for the first wicket. Both scores were A.G.D. Club records. Indeed Norman had quite a season, proving that as well as being a prolific runmaker, he is no mean bowler too and with a total of 36 wickets costing 556 runs wasn't too far behind winning one of the bowling awards. He also chipped in with 14 catches to emphasise just what an asset he is to the Club.

1976 North Derbyshire Cricket League

Presentation Division I at The Goldwell Rooms, Ashgate Road, Chesterfield

Winners are:
Back Row L to R:- *Derek Harding (Robinsons C.C.), Keith Rockliffe (Brimington C.C.),*
Brian Harding (Robinsons C.C.)
Front Row L to R:- *Roy Guest (Taverners C.C.), Mick Sullivan (Rcbinsons C.C.),*
Gerry Clark (Taverners C.C.), Berry Leatherday, (Taverners C.C.)

At the end of the 1976 Cricket Season, I applied for several coaching posts which were advertised in the *Cricketer International*. These posts were from Schools and Clubs throughout the United Kingdom. Unfortunately, my applications were not immediately successful, therefore, I made further applications as far afield as Australia and New Zealand as well as Holland and Denmark.

Then out of the blue, I was offered a six month contract at Prestwick C.C. Ayrshire, Scotland. Surprisingly, I did not apply for the job at Prestwick C.C., but through a mere coincidence, I had sent an application to Mr. James Hill, Secretary of Kilmarnock C.C., with a copy of my second book, entitled *Junior Cricket Reborn In the Seventies*. He was so impressed with its contents that he passed it on to Mr. Douglas Haggo (Secretary) of Prestwick C.C., because Mr. Hill had just given a six month coaching contract to an Indian Test player at his club.

Within a month, an interview was arranged at Prestwick C.C. and, as a result, I accepted the contract and within a few days, I returned to Prestwick on a cold but sunny April afternoon, to become their first Professional Coach, Cricketer and Part-time Groundsman, assisting Mr. Arthur Vincent, who gave me many useful tips in groundsmanship. Next day, my first job was to clean 16 pairs of batting pads and tidy the cricket equipment.

Within a month, I started to settle down as well as could be expected and began to enjoy my coaching, as most weeks I coached between (50 – 70) youngsters in addition to the 1st and 2nd XI adults.

Prestwick Cricket Club

(FOUNDED 1955)

Tel.: Prestwick 77720

Secretary:

11 AYR ROAD
PRESTWICK
KA9 1SX

28th. February, 1977.

Dear Richard,

On behalf of Prestwick Cricket Club I hereby offer you the appointment of Player/ Coach/ Groundsman and enclose for your attention two copies of the proposed contract of employment which we have in mind.

If after reading this you find it acceptable, I would be obliged if you would sign one copy and return it to me as soon as possible.

Yours faithfully,
Ian M'Kinnell
Secretary.

Twelve young cricketers on London trip on 18/3/77 to Alf Gover's Cricket School at 172 East Hill, Wandsworth, London SW18 2HD

From L to R:- R. Suttle (club-Coach), H. Bradford (Chairman & Organiser of the Chesterfield & District Youth Cricket Council) A. Gaunt (Assistant-Coach)
Back row:- A. Margerison, D. White, N. Beckingham, S. Collins, J. Jones & D. Duroe
Front row:- P. Steele, M. Joy, I. Suttle, D. Wall & A. Robson.
Missing from the photograph is G. Cook. After the trip, the boys; recommended for the Derbyshire County Colts (under 16) trials were Paul Steele (left handed batsman & medium pace left arm bowler) Jameison Jones (right handed batsman & right arm pace bowler) & Dale White (left handed batsman & right arm slow medium pacer)

Four Junior Members of Prestwick C.C. received Trophies at their Annual Presentation of Prizes in the Clubhouse on 29th April 1977. They are. Front Row- *Andrew Tennent David Haggo Gordon Webster, Ian Farquharson.* Back Row- *Mr. P. McSherry (Past Convener), F. Pirrie (Junior Convener), D. Y. Haggo (Club President.)*

One of my first jobs, was to clean 16 pairs of pads on Tuesday 12th April 1977 and then help Mr. Vincent to prepare a wicket for a mid-week fixture

Richard Suttle practising at Prestwick Cricket Club

Richard is settling in well as cricket club's first 'pro'

A man who coached some of the world's best-known cricketers and rubbed shoulders with many big names in the sport, was this week rolling the wicket at Prestwick Cricket Club.

West Indian Richard Suttle who helped the great Gary Sobers on the road to fame, is making history as the first full-time professional to be appointed by the ambitious local club.

He is going about his duties at the trim little ground, thankful of the employment and deeply confident that he can repay the faith of the Prestwick committee. He has set his sights high.

"I want to see a number of boys so well equipped cricket-wise," he says thoughtfully, "that they will play for the Prestwick senior team and then one day may even play at national level. That is my target."

From Barbados

Richard Suttle is 48 and comes from Bridgetown, Barbados. He first held a cricket bat at the age of eight and even then, felt "something about the game thrilled me."

Since that day, he has devoted his life to coaching, yet he never had the opportunity to make his mark as a test player himself. He has written books on the sport, published a booklet of poetry, worked as a London bus conductor and sampled the hardships of being unemployed.

"It was soul-destroying being out of work," he confided. "I applied for a number of posts without success. Then I went after a position at Kilmarnock Cricket Club. I didn't get the job but their secretary James Hill wrote to Prestwick recommending me. And, fortunately, I am now installed here."

Winter Job

Mr Suttle is on a 20-week contract with Prestwick but he is looking for a winter job and hopes to remain attached to the club for many years.

He spends his time helping the club groundsman during the day, then training the juniors and seniors in the evening. At the weekend he plays for the Prestwick XI.

Richard Suttle has promoted junior cricket all over the world – in places such as Bridgetown, London, Chesterfield and Amsterdam. It was fitting that in his first published book – *The Impact of Junior and Senior Cricket* – Sobers himself should write a foreword.

Sobers wrote: "Richard Suttle has never played test cricket but his wealth of experience in club and league cricket has helped many youngsters to benefit from his coaching."

Suttle, who first became interested in the sport after hearing the commentaries of John Arlott and noting them meticulously in shorthand, says simply of Sobers; "Gary was just 12 when I first saw him but I said to myself, "this lad has something exceptional. At that age he would face fast bowling, I knew he would become a test cricketer."

Mr Suttle keeps an album – "my *This Is Your Life* book," he says – containing photographs of himself taken with the game's top stars and letters of recommendation and thanks from people in all walks of the sport."

As Conductor

It was in 1960 at the age of 32, that he came to England and worked as a bus conductor at Catford Garage, London. He met former England test captain Colin Cowdrey, who recommended him for a trial with Catford Wanderers but lack of time off work prevented him from joining the club and perhaps entering county cricket.

In 1967, Mr Suttle moved to Chesterfield, where he played in the North Derbyshire League, but again with the accent on coaching. Eight years later, he gained his treasured national coaching certificate.

After four months as coach to Amsterdam Cricket Club in Holland, who later won the national championships, Suttle, now fully devoted to cricket, returned to England and continued coaching, spending much time with the successful Chesterfield District Youth Cricket Council.

Persuasion

In his book, Suttle is described as 'everybody's friend,' a man of energy and persuasion, who himself writes, "This might appear boastful. But during my 25 years of coaching and organising cricket, I have helped contribute to the success of some world class players of the calibre of Gary Sobers, and Wesley Hall. Cricket is a way of life to me."

The infectious enthusiasm of Richard Suttle, married with four children, is already rubbing off on some lucky young Prestwick cricketers.

Troon and Prestwick Times 29/4/77

A test of character

At this particular juncture in my life, the domestic side began to fall apart as my marriage began to break up, and being 300 miles away did not help, although fortnightly visits were made throughout my six-month contract. During this period, it took what I can only describe as intestinal fortitude and God's guidance to overcome some very mischievous propaganda which almost took its toll. What follows in the form of a sporting article on 6th June 1977 is reproduced for you to draw your own conclusions.

Postman Dick takes a big knock

A town's cricket fans were bowled over when their team signed West Indian professional Dick Suttle.

And Dick certainly looked the part as he strode out confidently to the wicket in his first game of the season.

But he was back in the pavilion in double-quick time after scoring only four.

Hopes started to fade as Dick's next five innings yielded just ten runs.

Which isn't surprising, really. For Dick has never played for a first class club. In fact he faced most of his deliveries playing for a Post Office team.

Dick, 48, said of his £70 a week summer job for Prestwick, Ayrshire: "I wrote to clubs all over the world before I was appointed here as a player-coach and groundsman.

"Altough I haven't scored too many runs I believe I've been carrying out my other duties satisfactorily."

But his former colleagues at the Post Office finance HQ in Chesterfield, Derbyshire, said they were amazed when they heard that cricket-crazy Dick had landed the job.

A source said: "There's a big difference in the cricket he was involved with here and professional cricket."

At Prestwick, club captain Johnny Hubbard said: "We signed Dick principally as a coach and groundsman. Any runs were to be regarded as a bonus."

Prestwick's 2nd XI 1977
Back row:- J. Enos, M. Sweeney, J. Morrison, J. Docherty, T. Graham, G. Webster
Front row:- I. Davey (Capt.), D. Haggo (President), G. Vincent, R. Suttle (Coach),
G. Dinwoodie (Scorer)

Unfortunately, as you continue to read the forthcoming pages, you will discover the less glamorous side of a professional sportsman, especially when the media is being misguided by people who seem to enjoy passing on incorrect information, which can sometimes embarrass and completely decimate an individual's career. A typical example of the book's title, which deals with the vicissitudes of life.

For the record, I have also reproduced my letter, which I wrote to the editor just over 29 years ago; but so far there is no reply.
The Editor

Dear Sir,
After reading the cricket article on page 3 of last Sunday's edition (12/6/77) I would like to express my personal disapproval of its contents.

First of all the report is inaccurate. You will find enclosed an up-to-date and correct record of all my scores and bowling performances for the club to which I am now engaged as a professional coach and groundsman.

Secondly, it would appear as though your reporter used some misguided

154

information which could be harmful to my career as well as the club's organisation.

Due to the inaccuracy of the above-mentioned report, I would be very grateful if those concerned with such reports would be more careful in future to obtain the correct information before presenting it for publication.

As I await your reply, I thank you.

Yours faithfully

C.R.W. Suttle (N.C.A.) (Cricket-Coach)

Batting and bowling performances from 19/4/77 to 5/6/77

Fixture	Team	Scores	Bowling	Dates
1. Against Poloc	2nd XI	5	1 for 10	(17/4/77)
2. Against Redbrae	3rd Xl	18 (not out)	3 tbr 8	(5/5/77)
3. Against Kelburne	1st XI	0	1 for 8	(8/5/77)
4. Against Brechin	1st Xl	9	Did not bowl	(15/5/77)
5. Against Poloc	lst XI	0	- ditto -	(22/5/77)
6. Against Wier Sports	2nd XI	0	- ditto -	(29/5/77)
7. Against Westminster Bank	lst XI	12	1 for 12	(1/6/77)
8. Against Babcock & Wilcox	2nd XI	13	Did not howl	(5/6/77)

8 innings - 57 and took 6 for 38
From 17/4/77 to 5/6/77

N.B. I finished the season with over 300 runs and took 18 wickets. I also finished with a fine coaching record for the Club, which ended the season as Triple Crown Champions for the first time in its 22-year-old history.

PRESTWICK'S FINE TROPHY WIN AT BRECHIN

Prestwick travelled to Brechin on Sunday to meet last year's runners-up in the Strathmore Union in the first round of the Shish Mahal Trophy.

On a drying wicket, Brechin batted first and were soon in trouble, when Appleby bowled Smith with the first delivery of the innings. Only Panchasara, the Brechin professional, batted with any confidence and, after his dismissal to a brilliant catch by McKinnell, Brechin were in trouble.

Outstanding among the Prestwick bowlers was Alan Appleby, who took three wickets for ten runs in his nine overs.

Apart from Bankhead, who had an intelligent innings of 52 not out, the Prestwick batsmen failed to master the bowling of Panchasara – the home professional took six wickets for 13 runs. But Bankhead and Appleby

155

survived to get the necessary runs to see Prestwick to viciory.

Prestwick now meet Carleton at home in the next round on June 12.

Chesterfield & District Youth C.C.
Leaves for Holland on Sunday 31st July 9 1977
By C.R.W. Suttle

On a slightly overcast day, a number of parents, relatives and friends saw the departure of 20 enthusiastic junior cricketers (under 19) from Chesterfield Town Hall at 1.15 p.m. on Sunday 31st July by coach under the supervision of Messrs. David Cook (Manager) and Richard Suttle (Coach) for the first time to participate in four 40 over matches against Stichste Cricket Bond, Kampong (The Host Club), Hercules and V.O.C. (Rotterdam).

Also arranged were two matches played under 7-A-Side rules for the (under 15's).

Mr. Harold Bradford (the Chairman of Chesterfield Y.C.C.) was unable to make the trip because of business commitments, organised the tour with Mr. Verheyen (Chairman of Kampong C.C.).

Mr. W.B. Robson who assisted Mr. Bradford with tour plans was also unable to make the trip. The touring team included:-

1. Ian Thacker (Capt.)	12, Chris Ironside
2. Roger Varley (Vice Capt.)	13. Andrew Cooper
3. Garry Cook	14. David Duroe
4. Chris Marples	15. John Cupitt
5. David Bamford	16. Robert Elliott
6. Jameison Jones	17. Paul Durward
7. Paul Steele	18. David Wall
8. Alistair Robson	19. Steven Knight
9. Kou Setch	20. Andrew Margerison
10. Dale White	
11. Neil Beckingham	

Touring Activities

After reaching Harwich about 8p.m. on Sunday 31st July, 1977, we boarded the Juliana which set sail for the Hook-of-Holland and departed at 10 p.m.

The voyage was unusually rough but everyone disembarked safely, fit and well about 7 a.m. on Monday. We then boarded a train and arrived at Utrecht Station about 10.30 a.m. At 11a.m. Messrs. Verheyen and Andriesser of Kampong C.C. met us at the Station and directed us to the Youth Hostel "RHIJ-MAI-WEN" RHIJNAUWENSELAAN, 14 BUNNIK, after which we travelled to Kampong C.C. where Mrs. Jansen, wife of the Ex-President of the club, prepared us a delicious lunch.

Following this, our manager Mr. David Cook made a short speech on behalf of the tourists in extending thanks for the invitation and hospitality shown on our arrival. To this Mr. Verheyen ably responded. Mr. Suttle then conveyed greetings from Mr. Harold Bradford who was unable to make the trip.

After lunch, an exhilarating net practice followed, under the supervision of Ian Thacker (Captain) and Richard Suttle (Coach) and lasted $2^1/2$ hours. After this, tea was taken and an announcement of the teams to play on Tuesday was made. Finally, the team returned to the Hostel for an evening meal to round off the first day's activities.

On Tuesday before the commencement of the 40 over match against Stichste-Cricket-Bond XI, Messrs, Thacker and Suttle presented Mr. Verheyen with gifts which were sent by Mr. Bradford. Mr. Verheyen accepted the gifts and thankfully responded.

The tour then officially got underway with a defeat by 8 wickets but on Friday we defeated V.O.C. the Champions at Rotterdam in a dramatic last wicket victory which ended a hectic but memorable and enjoyable tour of the Netherlands.

Last but by no means least, many thanks to Mr. Cook and all the Umpires who did a splendid job during the tour.

Brief Summary of Tour To The Netherlands

Six matches were played. The first three were won by the Dutch teams, Kampong & District C.C. The Stichte Cricket Bond and Hercules C.C. respectively, but the last three were won by the Tourists against Kampong (Snrs.) Kampong Juniors and the final match against the present Champions "V.O.C." Rotterdam. It ended on a high note as the last wicket partnership which was unbroken yielded 36 runs with Roger Varley undefeated with 20 and his partner Dale White also undefeated with 16 to square the well contested series.

Outstanding performances on the tour from the tourists came from:- D. White, 40 not out; A. Margerison, 30 not out; N. Beckingham 23; A. Robson, 14 not out and C. Marples 2 for 6 for the (under 15's).

For the (over 16's) Skipper Ian Thacker, 38 not out; D. Bamford 36; P. Durward 18; D. Duroe 14 not out; S. Knight 23; A. Cooper 20 and C. Ironside 13, while R. Varley and D. Bamford took 11 wickets each in the series for 85 and 107 respectively to end a very hectic memorable and enjoyable tour to Holland.

Kampong and District team won first match of tour in 7-A-Side fixture
Scores: Chesterfield Y.C.C. 73 for 4 off 21 Overs
Kampong and District 77 for 2 off 16·3 Overs

On Tuesday 2nd August, Chesterfield and District Youth Cricket Council opened their tour against a Kampong and District team of Utrecht.

Having won the toss with the skies heavily overcast, skipper Martin Wallinga sent in the tourists to bat and at one stage, they were 13 for 4; but a fine recovery came, when Dale White and Alistair Robson became associated in an unbroken fifth wicket partnership which yielded 60 runs from which White was undefeated with 40, while Robson was also undefeated with 14, as they took the score to 73 for 4 off 21 overs.

Bowling for the home team. Mark Reisen took 2 for 18 and S. d'Hont 1 for 9.

In reply, the home team made 77 for 2 off, 16·3 overs. Mainly responsible for this total was a topscore of 26 by Van Esveld, while Meyer scored 24 and Wallinga was undefeated with 16.

Bowling for the Tourists, David Duroe took 1 for 16 and G. Cook 1 for 19 as the game ended in a fine win for the home team.

Teams were:-

Chesterfield: A. Margerison (Capt.), G. Cook, A. Robson, D. Wall. C. Marples, D. Duroe and D. White.

Kampong and District: M. Wallinga (Capt.), R. Vrolijks, D. Meyer, M. Reisen, R. Lub, S. d'Hont and J. Koreneef.

Stichtse Cricket Bond defeat Chesterfield Y.C.C.
by 8 wickets in first fixture
Scores: Chesterfield Y.C.C. 61 off 34·2 Overs.
S.C.D.C.C. 62 for 2 off 13·2 Overs.

The Tourists under the captaincy of Ian Thacker, opened their first official match at Kampong, Utrecht, Holland on Tuesday 2nd August against the Stichtse Cricket Bond Team.

Having won the toss with the skies slightly overcast, skipper Thacker elected to bat and after 34·2 overs, his team's score was 61.

Chief contributions came from Thacker with 16 and 13 by Christopher Ironside who came in at no. 3 and was the last wicket to fall as the remaining batsmen failed to negotiate with the spin of the opposition.

Bowling for the home team, Hessias took 2 for 0. Boone 2 for 8, Boesehoot 2 for 8 while Sellink, Andriessen and Floberg took one each for 5, 1 and 1? respectively.

In reply, S.C.D. made 62 for 2 off 13·2 overs, as Verhoef and skipper Floberg were both undefeated with 30 and 20 respectively.

The only wicket-taker for the tourists, was Roger Varley who took 2 for 1?

in 7 overs as the match ended in an eight wicket victory for the Stichtse Cricket Bond XI.

Hercules C.C. defeat tourists by 37 runs
Scores: Hercules 141 for 8 off 39·5 Overs
Chesterfield 104 off 38·4 Overs

On Wednesday 3rd August, Hercules entertained the visitors at their picturesque ground in Utrecht under the leadership of K. Buryze, who won the toss in brilliant sunshine, batted first and after a poor start they were 2 for 2. However, his team made a splended recovery and finally scored 141 for 8 off 39·5 Overs. Thanks to a resolute innings of 44 by N. Verhoeff, followed by consistent contributions of 20 not out by P. Schriek while Andriessen, Heshusesius, Meyer and K. Buryze scored 13, 13, 11 and 11 respectively.

Roger Varley was the Tourists' most successful bowler. He took 3 for 41 in 15 overs. David Bamford 2 for 38 in 8 overs while fourteen year old Paul Steele took 1 for 17 in 7 overs with his left arm medium pacers. Many lapses in the field gave the opposition a firmer grip on the game thus enabling them to place themselves in a winning position.

With 142 runs required for victory off 40 overs, the tourists made a slow but encouraging start but with the score at 23, Ironside fell to Heshuseuis for 4 while his partner David Bamford went on to topscore with 36. Again the middle order batsmen failed to negotiate the Hercules spin attack from which they press home their advantage; but not before David Duroe and Paul Steele at no. 11 brought some respectability to the score as the tourists ended up with 104, with Steele run out for 9 and Duroe with an undefeated 14.

Bowling for Hercules, J. Meyer in a splendid spell of bowling took 3 for 5 and was ably assisted by Heshuseius 3 for 21, W. Sellink 2 for 12 and Schriek 1 for 13 to give them victory by 37 runs.

Chesterfield touring team wins 8 a-side match over Kampong C.C.
Scores: Kampong 84 off 21 overs
Chesterfield 85 for 5 off 20·3 overs

On Thursday, 4th August at Kampong Utrecht, Chesterfield touring team, under the captaincy of Andrew Margerison, defeated their host's team by the narrow margin of one wicket with three balls left, to gain sweet revenge after being beaten two days before by a combined Utrecht team.

Having won the toss on a sundrenched morning, Margerison sent in the home team to bat and after the allotted 21 overs, Kampong were all out for 84. Prolykn topscored with a valuable 36 while Koneiveif batted well for 21 and Wallinga was left undefeated with 5.

Bowling for the Tourists, C. Marples took 2 for 6 while D. Wall, N. Beckingham and K. Setch took one each for 0, 10 and 15 respectively.

In reply. Chesterfield batted well as skipper Margerison carried his bat for a well played 30. Neil Beckingham scored a useful 23 while R. Elliott scored 8 not out and G. Cook 6.

Bowling for the home team, Reisen took 3 for 8 and was ably supported by Vrolyks with 2 for 13 in a nail-biting finish to square the (under 16's) competition.

Chesterfield Y.C.C. defeat Kampong C.C. by 5 wickets

Scores: Kampong C.C. 81 off 22·2 Overs
Chesterfield Y.C.C. 83 for 5 off 33 Overs

On a sun-drenched afternoon at Kampong C.C. Utrecht, on Thursday 4th August, skipper Verhoef of the home team won the toss and batted first, and after 22·2 overs Kampong were all out for 81 of which he made an aggressive 35 which included four lusty boundaries. Other useful scores came from Vrolyks with 11 while opening batsman Andriesen who scored 10 was brilliantly caught one handed to a diving catch by wicket-keeper Thacker off Varley, who tore the heart of the Kampong batting apart with his immaculate line and length which earned him 7 for 15 in 8·2 overs, while at the other end David Bamford with his slow left arm deliveries took 3 for 26 in 8 overs.

With 82 runs required for victory the tourists started disastrously as they lost their first five batsmen for 36 runs; but skipper Thacker at no. 5 came in and played a face-saving innings and was undefeated with 38 which included six boundaries and was well assisted by Andrew Cooper who was also undefeated with 8 to win the match with 7 overs to spare. The only other batsman to reach double figures was S. Knight with 14.

Bowling for Kampong, R. Boeschoten took 4 for 22. in a fine spell of medium pace bowling while Andriessen took the other wicket for 14.

Dramatic finish squares series
as Varley and White triumph in last wicket stand

Scores: V.O.C. 133 for 9 off 40 overs
Chesterfield Y.C.C. 139 for 9 off 36·4 overs

On Friday, 5th August, 1977 the tourists travelled from Utrecht to Rotterdam to play against a strong V.O.C. team, captained by L. Hennink, who won the toss on their picturesque ground with a very fast outfield as the sun shone brilliantly and after 40 overs, V.O.C. were 133 for 9. Skipper Hennink who batted aggressively topscored with 30 and was well supported by Blanalies with 23 not out, while other useful scores came from dc Croot, Ruiten de

*Leaving the Cadogan's residence "Se-Lah" Carlington Terrace, St.
Stephens Hill, St. Michael, Barbados, West Indies.
L to R:- Mrs. Cadogan and Mr. Cadogan, Ian, Steven,
Lettice and Marva and R. Suttle*

Martin Forte

Robinsons C.C. Champions list Division Six-a-side North Derbyshire League 1973

*Standing L to R:- Derek Harding, M. Sullivan (Capt.), Dennis Harding,
(Secretary). K. Bramall.
Squatting L to R:- T. Foster, M. Goodwin and K. Swift*

A rare moment of nostalgia, as I recollect the beautiful tulips of Amsterdam at Mrs. Sanderson's home, 53 Amstelveen, Via A.B.N. Sports Stadium

Two-year full-time course for 5 applicants at Matlock College on Monday 16/6/75 for interview in the field of Community Studies and Youth Leadership. Accompanying them are two lecturers

New indoor nets at Chesterfield College officialy opened in March 1975. Dick Suttle practicing

From the scenes of cricket to an old traditional scene, as every Wednesday morning in the streets of Amsterdam, can be seen the famous mobile organ of H. Gosling, greeting passersby, with a mixture of melodious strains

Brimington C.C. of the 1970's

Chesterfield Youth Council Team Tour of the Netherlands 1977

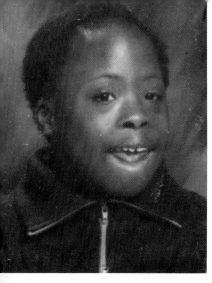

Steven Suttle

Forty-eight members of the Loundsley Green Junior Cricket Club all chipped in to buy a special trophy for Dick Suttle in recognition of 17 years' service to their association

Derbyshire N.C.A. (Un-13) Team 1981 at Gunthorpe against Notts (Un-13) on Sunday 30/8/81

*Barbados Overseas Cricket Association Team at Queen's Park, Chesterfield, 1996,
with Martin Forte (Capt.) in front row, 3rd from left*

*Foundation School Cricket Team with Bruce Cousens (games master) extreme left and
Norman Puckerin (coach) extreme right in 1996*

Chesterfield Transport cricket team at Bradford 1984
Back row L to R:- D. Devonport, K. Bown, P. Milnes, M. Norris, S. Bennett, P. Williams,
T. Ramdell, I. Beck (WK), G. Hollingshead (Team Manager)
Front row L to R:- D. Seakston, J. Hadfield, Eric Marsh (Capt), K. Nicholls, C. Colley
(12th man), S. Pike

Chesterfield Centre for the Unemployed C.C. at Tube Works against Haringey C.C. August
1987 by Carol Herring

Pictured above are a group of cricketers, 6 of whom are from the Chesterfield Centre for the Unemployed (54 Saltergate) with pupils from Highfields School, Matlock on 15/12/87 completing their National Cricket Association course at Lea Green, Matlock, Derbyshire, under the supervision of Messrs. John Brown and Les Bradbury, Advanced coaches from Derbyshire County Cricket Club. Local (N.C.A. Coach) Dick Suttle recommended them for the course, which they have successfully passed. Similar results were gained by former students of the centre of 1984 and 1985 respectively

Cricketers of the future? Maybe there are some budding Test match stars in this line-up of young cricketers from St. Peter and St. Paul School, Hasland Road, Chesterfield. Aged from six years upwards, the youngsters attend weekly coaching classes at Chesterfield Leisure Centre under the guidance of N.C.A. Coaches Dick Suttle and Gerry Nunn

Roger Suttle after being awarded
BSc. Hons. Biological Science degree by
Nottingham Trent University

Mr Ralph Ironside, who was the founder
of the Chesterfield & District Cricket
Touring Team 1988.
He designed the touring teams' emblem,
which is worn with pride by all the members
of the 1993 tour of Barbados.
He passed away on Saturday 24th July, 1988

Holme Hall School with N.C.A. coaches. L to R: Steven Lee and Dick Suttle 1995

Highfield Hall School with games masters: D. Connock and D. Richardson 1995

Back Row L to R:- M. Lomas, J. Johnson, R. Suttle, T. Kirk (Capt.), S. Lee, S. Baddeley,
R. Gratton, P. Pollard, M. Rowland (Umpire).
Front Row L to R:- A. Rogers, N. Bradbury, A. Pearce, D. Suttle (Coach) 1993

St. Peter & St. Paul cricket team
Back Row L to R:- *Matthew Hook, Jamie Squires, James Chapman, Oliver Hill.*
Middle Row L to R:- *Charles Sommut, Edward Crowther, Simon Calow,*
Christopher Merrid, Jonathan Machent, Ben Jones.
Front Row:- *Ross Sylvester (Capt.) 22nd July 1993*

Tim Kirk (Capt. of the Chesterfield & District Cricket Touring Team) presents Mark Walker
(Capt. of Wilmslow C.C.) with a plate with the insignia of the Chesterfield Crooked Spire
on Sunday 15th August 1993 at Cheshire

Budleigh Salterton C.C. at Queen's Park, Chesterfield on Sunday 19th September 1993

England Ladies 8-a-side at Sharley Park, Clay Cross 1996
Photograph was taken by Mr. John Palmer, Wendy Watson gets in some practice with 12
year old Andrew Rogers (behind the stumps) with other players left to right, Evette Burton,
Ann Woods, Jane Cheney, Gwyn Morris, Kate Scott and Kim Robertson

The Touring Team at Harrison College 1993

The wedding of Stuart Baddeley and Caroline Gregory in Barbados 9th October 1993

L to R:- *Sally, Andy, Peter, Neil, Ernie and Andrew on a sight-seeing tour 1993*

L to R:- *Peter, Neil, Roger and Andrew enjoying the scenery of the island 1993*

The 1993 Barbados Combined School's XI at Kensington Oval with their coach, Keith Boyce, 3rd from the left, back row

1993 Chesterfield & District Cricket Touring Team at Kensington Oval, Barbados

28-year-old, David Haggo, one of my 1977 protegés now keeps wicket for Scotland's National Team. On Tuesday 2nd May 1995, I had the privilege of watching him play against Yorkshire C.C. at Hamilton Crescent, exactly eighteen years after my appointment as Prestwick's first professional. That day David kept wicket to Malcolm Marshall who is at present Scotland's professional

Long-serving cricketers honoured in 1996 Three north Derbyshire cricketers have been made life members of the A.G.D. Cricket Club after chalking up 30 years' service. They are former treasurer Philip Ward, coach Dick Suttle and John Hodgson, chairman for the last eight years. Another A.G.D. trio, Ron Lovegrove, Dave Crowley and Tom Cocker, are to receive similar long-service awards from Mrs. Jane Powell (Sect of the Club)

Sir Gary Sobers met our cricket statistician, Allan Haggo at the Europa Hotel, St, James during the last week of the Chesterfield & District Cricket Touring Team's Tour in October 1993

The 1996 Chesterfield and District Touring Team and supporters stop for a rest at the Welcome Break via Gatwick Airport

Back row L to R:- Morris Rowland (Umpire) Peter Feather, Robert Dumelow, Mick Barratt, Jon Branson, Ian Smith, Steven Lee, Ian Frost, Richard Williams (Wkt.)
Front row L to R:- Martin Cheshire (Vice Capt»), John Johnson, Phil Adamson, Tim Kirk (Capt.) Phil Baker, Dave Hallam, Dick Suttle (K.C.A. Coach) Ann Wells (Sect, & Treas)
At Kensington Oval Tuesday 8th October, 1996

Roger Suttle, with his wife Rachel and their son, Isaac

Claleir-Maulo and Kruynemg who made 14, 13, 11 and 10 respectively.

The Chesterfield left arm spinner D. Bamford in a fine spell of bowling took 6 for 43 in 15 overs, while J. Cupitt took 2 for 39 in 14 overs and the tiring Varley 1 for 29 in 10 overs.

With 134 runs required for victory and the last chance to square the series, the tourists batted well as scores of 23 by S. Knight, 20 by A. Cooper, 18 by Durward and 16 by Bamford helped to boost the total to 97 for 6. Then disaster struck, as skipper Thacker was L.B.W. to Bloam for 2 and in rapid succession Steele and Cupitt were dismissed with the score at 103 for 9 with 8 overs left; but with the advent of the bespectacled Varley to partner the left handed White, they became associated in a last wicket partnership which remained unbroken as they contributed 36 runs which took the total to 139 for 9 with Varley undefeated 20 and his partner 16 not out with 3·2 overs to spare.

Bowling for V.O.C. de Moura took 3 for 24 in 9 overs, Kruyena took 4 for 30 in 9·4 overs and Bloan took 1 for 11 in five overs to end a very hectic but memorable and enjoyable tour.

Double Win

Prestwick's undcr-16 cricketers defeated a Chesterfield touring select in two friendly matches at the weekend.

Chesterfield Youth Cricket Council also challenged Ayr Cricket Club's under-18 side and won both their under-18 ties.

It is hoped to make the Prestwick-Chesterfield games an annual event and already the local lads are planning a trip down south some time next year.

In Prestwick's first game, they scored 89 for four off 20 overs.

Prestwick

Alan Haggo	20
David Haggo	17
Ronald Martin	14
Gordon Webster	11
Total for 4 wickets	89

Bowling for Chesterfield:- Andrew Margerison 2 for 16, Michael Joy 1 for 13, Dale White 1 for 13.

Chesterfield:- 63 for five wickets (Brian Robinson 27 not out).

Bowling for Prestwick:- Andrew Tennant 1 for 7, Gordon Webster 1 for 2, Alan Haggo 1 for 15, Ronald Martin 1 for 17.

In the second game, Chesterfield scored 54 for seven off 25 overs.

Bowling for Prestwick:- George Webster 2 for 8, Ronald Martin 2 for 12,

Prestwick Cricket Club's under-16 side and their opponents from Chesterfield

Michael Sweeney 2 for 12 John Hill 1 for 12.

Prestwick replied with 53 for one off 14 overs. M. Sweeney was 34 not out and A. Haggo scored 12.

Troon & Prestwick Times 18/8/78

Chesterfield & District Youth Cricket Council
leave for Scotland on Wednesday 9th August 1978

On a wet and heavily overcast morning, a number of parents and members of the Chesterfield Y.C.C. saw the departure of 21 Junior cricketers (all under 18) from the Town Hall Chesterfield at 8.40a.m. by coach, under the supervision of Messrs. Harold Bradford (Chairman & Manager), "Bill" Reddish (Assistant-Manager) and Richard Suttle (Club Coach) for the first time to participate in two, forty over matches against Ayr C.C. at Cambusdoon and two, twenty over matches against Prestwick at the Oval.

The touring teams included: (Under 18)

M. Davidson (Capt) (Old Whittington); J. Walker (V/Capt) (Wingerworth); J. Wilson (Wingerworth); T. Wilson (Wingerworth); W. Scott (A.G.D.); D. Evans (A.G.D.); D. Duroe (A.G.D.); P. Barnett (Brimington); M White (Tibshelf); P. Steele (Hundall); J. Cupitt (A.G.D.) (unable to make the trip due to illness).

(Under 16)

A. Margerison (Capt) (A.G.D.; J. Jones (V/Capt) (Brimington); B Robinson (Brimington); C. Marples (Robinsons); D. White (Tibshelf); M. Jo⁷ (Chesterfield); I. Jones (A.G.D.); R. Suttle (jnr) (A.G.D.); 1. Saich (A.G.D.) N Cook (Ches. Y.C.C.); A. Chalmers (Coal Aston)

Others accompanying the touring party were: Mr. & Mrs. R. Jones and son Ashley, Mr. & Mrs. Ryder and Rainer Schwarz.

The 260 mile Journey lasted approximately 7 hours and was enjoyed by all. We arrived at Cambusdoon, Ayrshire, Scotland at 4.40p.m. and were warmly welcomed by Mr. J. A. Bagnall (Secretary of the Ayr C.C.)

A wonderful tea was soon prepared and was enjoyed by everyone. After this, Mr. Bagnall spoke in glowing terms of his team's achievements this year and hoped that the tourists would have an enjoyable stay. To this, Mr. Bradford (Chairman of the touring side) ably responded and thanked Mr. & Mrs. Bagnall and members of the Ayr C.C. for all the arrangements made for the boys' accommodation in their homes and the hospitality shown on arrival. After this, the boys went to their various places of abode to end the first day's activities.

On Thursday, 10th August, the weather Improved sufficiently, that the start of the 20 over match at Prestwick began punctually for the under 16's while the under 18's had their first net on the County ground at Ayr under the supervision of skipper Mick Davison and (Vice-Capt) John Walker for approximately 2 hours before the commencement of their 40 over match against Ayr County Colts.

Prestwick (under 16) defeat Chesterfield Y.C.C. (under 16) by 26 runs at the Oval
by R. Suttle

Scores: Prestwick 89 for 4 off 20 overs. Chesterfiedl 63 for 5 off 20 overs.

On Thursday, 10th August, Chesterfield Y.C.C. (under 16) met Prestwick (under 16) at the Oval, Prestwick, Ayrshire, Scotland and lost by 26 runs.

Andrew Margerison, captain of the touring team, won the toss on a rain affected wicket and sent in Prestwick, led by Gordon Webster to bat.

After 20 overs, the home team were 89 for 4. Opening batsman Alan Haggo top scorer with 20 while other contributions came from David Haggo 17, Ronald Martin 14 and skipper Webster 11.

Bowling for the tourists skipper Margerison took 2 for 16, while Matthew oy and Dale White took one each for 13 and 13 respectively.

In reply Chesterfield Y.C.C. were 63 for 5 at the end of their alloted 20 overs. Brian Robinson who opened the innings was undefeated with 27 and Chris Marples contributed 15 before being run out.

Bowling for the home team, Andrew Tennant, Gordon Webster, Alan Haggo, and Ronald Martin took one each for 7, 12, 15 and 17 respectively to give their team victory by 26 runs.

Chesterfield Y.C. (under 18) defeat Ayr (under 18) by 12 runs at Cambusdoon

by R. Suttle

Scores: Chesterfield Y.C.C. 150 for 4 off 40 overs. Ayr C.C. 138 off 38 overs.

An undefeated innings of 70 by Tim Wilson of Chesterfield Y.C.C. led the way to the tourists' victory over Ayr on a placid Cambusdoon wicket, refreshed by overnight showers, as skipper Mick Davison of the touring team won the toss and elected to bat and after 40 overs his team had scored 150 for 4. Tim Wilson battled splendidly for an undefeated 70 at No. 4. His Innings included one six and six fours. John Walker contributed 24 while David Evans was not out with 19 and Jamie Wilson scored 14.

Bowling for Ayr County Colts, B. Patterson took 2 for 15, while skipper M. Craig and D. Henderson took one each for 25 and 28 respectively.

With 151 runs required for victory, the Ayr batsmen went for their shots and at the end of the thirty-eighth over, they were all out for 138 runs. A sterling innings:- A. D. Simpson threatened the tourists' attack but he was brilliantly caught by T. Wilson at short mid-wicket for 82 which was bestudded with six boundaries. Other contributions came from B. Patterson 19 and I. Penman 10.

Bowling for Chesterfield Y.C.C. J. Walker took 3 for 30. P. Barnett 2 for 23. W. Scott 1 for 17 and P. Steele 1 for 36 to win by 12 runs.

Prestwick's (under 16) wins 2nd match by 9 wickets

Scores: Chesterfield Y.C.C. 54 for 7 off 25 overs.

Prestwick (Under-16) 55 for 1 off 14.5 overs.

Prestwick Juniors shrewdly led by Gordon Webster for the second time won their match at the oval convincingly.

Having won the toss on an easy paced wicket at the Oval, skipper Margerison of the touring team, batted first and after 25 overs. Chesterfield were 54 for 7.

Brian Robinson topscored with 34 and was the only batsman to reach double figures.

Bowling for Prestwick, skipper Webster took 2 for 8; Ronald Martin 2 for 12; Michael Sweeney 2 for 12 and J. Hill 1 for 12.

In reply, Prestwick scored 55 for 1 off 14.5 overs. Of these Michael Sweeney was undefeated with 34 while his partner Alan Haggo was leg before wicket to Steele for 12 at a personal cost of 20 runs. As the match ended in a nine wicket victory for Prestwick as well as two victories in two days.

Chesterfield Y.C.C. defeat Ayr on second encounter by 15 runs

Scores: Chesterfield Y.C.C. 125 off 32·5 overs. Ayr C.C. 110 Off 33·5 overs

On Friday 11th August, Ayr C.C. ably led by A. D. Simpson, won the toss and sent in the tourists who were astutely led by Mick Davison at Cambusdoon, Ayrshire.

After 32·5 overs on an easy paced wicket, the Chesterfield team were all out for 125. Of these Wayne Scott at No. 6, scored an invaluable 19, while good supporting innings came from skipper Davidson 24, Phil Barnett 29 and Tim Wilson 12.

Bowling for the home team Patterson took 3 for 22, Craig 2 for 9, Baird 2 for 19 while Henderson and Jones took one each for 8 and 22 respectively.

With 126 runs required for victory and a chance to square the two day tournament, they started disastrously as they lost MacKay before a run was scored. They continued to struggle as another two wickets fell with the score at 25, but D. Simpson and R. Jones became associated in a fourth wicket partnership which restored some respectability to the score, before Jones was brilliantly caught by J. Wilson at short extra cover for a well played 38 and his partner soon followed with 21. Other useful contributions came from A. Simpson 21 and D. Dunlop 10; but due to accurate bowling by the visitors, Ayr were all out for 110 just 16 runs short of victory.

Bowling for Chesterfield, all-rounder Wayne Scott took 3 for 10. David Evans 2 for 24, Phil Barnett 1 for 19, Jamie Wilson 1 for 12, and John Walker 1 for 30 to win the tournament by 2 games to nil.

After the match, Mr. & Mrs. Bagnall and colleagues prepared a delicious tea before the party set off at 3.40p.m. for Chesterfield.

Mr. Bradford made a fine speech and thanked Mr. & Mrs. Bagnall and members of the Ayr C.C. for their generous hospitality which was showered on the tourists. He then presented Mr. Bagnall with a tie with an insignia of the "Crooked Spire" Mr. Bagnall ably responded and hoped that next year a tour of Chesterfield would be arranged for the Ayr C.C.

Finally, a vote of thanks was moved by Mr. Richard Suttle after which the party of 30 departed to Chesterfield and arrived at the Town Hall at 10.40p.m. to end a most memorable and enjoyable tour of Scotland.

Ayr (Juniors) defeat Prestwick (Juniors) by 48 runs

Scores: Ayr (Under 16) 142 for 8 off 40 overs
Prestwick (Under 16) 94 off 39 overs

An undefeated 70 by skipper David Simpson backed up by accurate bowling by Penniman 3 for 7 and Simpson 3 for 11 the way to Ayr's victory over the visitors in their first 40 over friendly fixture at Cambusdoon on Thursday, 18th August 1977.

Having won the toss on an easy paced wicket with the skies heavily overcast, skipper Simpson elected to bat and after 40 overs his team's score was 142 for 8, His individual score was 70 not out which included nine boundaries, while other useful scores came from J. Mitchell 24, D. Crawford 11 and S. McKay 12 not out.

Apart from a few lapses, Prestwick fielded well as their left arm medium pacer, Ronald Martin took 3 for 38 in 12 overs, while Stephen James who flighted his off-breaks well took 3 for 44 in 11 overs as one of his victims was brilliantly stumped by David Haggo. Other wicket takers were Webster and Farquahson who took one each for

Jubilant Prestwick cricketers celebrated their fourth championship win in six years in the Glasgow and District League by cracking the champagne in the clubhouse on Sunday evening In the centre of the picture is Mr Archie McCallum, League President. September 1977

18 and 19 respectively as the former was unfortunate not to have taken Simpson's wicket earlier in his innings due to a chance in the slips. Skipper Alan Haggo operated his bowlers well and at one period Ayr were 103 for 8 off 35 overs, but with the advent of the left-handed McKay another 39 runs were added off the last five overs as Simpson and McKay shared in a ninth wicket unbroken partnership which took the score to 142 for 8.

In reply, Prestwick were all out for 94 off 39 overs Michael Sweeney who opened the innings topscored with 31, while Stephen James scored an undefeated 21 and D. Haggo 14. In a fine spell of bowling, I. Penniman took 3 for 7 in 8 overs, D. Simpson 3 for 11 in 5 overs while C. Ceasure 2 for 15 in 9 overs and J, Mitchell 1 for 6 in 5 overs to give Ayr a well earned victory over Prestwick.

Ayr (under 16) wins second match by 17 Runs against Prestwick (under 16)
Scores: Ayr 152 for 6 off 40 overs.
Prestwick 135 off 39.4 overs

Having won their first 40 over fixture against Prestwick by 48 runs at Cambusdoon the day before, Ayr (under 16), astutely led by David Simpson, followed up that victory with another win by 17 runs to win the two day tournament by two games to nil.

Batting first for the second time on a placid wicket with a fast outfield and the occasional ray of sunshine, Ayr scored 152 for 6 off 40 overs. Thanks to an undefeated 93 of controlled aggression by John Mitchell at No. 5. His innings was bestudded with eleven fours and a six. The only other batsman to reach double figures was skipper Simpson with 34.

Medium pacer, Ian Farquahson was Prestwick's most successful bowler. He took 3 for 46 in 13 overs. Skipper Gordon Webster who used his bowlers well, took 2 for 27 in 12 overs while David Haggo took 1 for 15 in 2 overs.

With 153 runs required for victory and a chance to square the tournament, the Prestwick opening batsmen were off to a good start as the first wicket fell at 33 with Michael Sweeney 28 stumped off Penman off 10 overs while his partner David Haggo had to retire at 18 because he was selected to captain the (under 16's) against Clydesdale at Prestwick. After the fall of a few more wickets, Gordon Webster rose to the occasion and scored a splendid 45 before being run out while Farquahson ably assisted with 17 before another three batsmen were run out, leaving Prestwick 18 runs short of victory.

Bowling for Ayr, D. Simpson took 2 for 33 in 9 overs while D. Crawford and I. Penman took one each for 15 and 31 respectively to give their team victory by 17 runs.

**Quotation by Mr. Douglas Haggo (Junior Convenor) of
Prestwick Cricket Club in "Jubilee Souvenir" (1955-1980)**

In October, 1976, a major decision was taken by the General Committee to employ a professional player/coach. This was a vital step in the history of our Club and indicated that the Club was prepared to prove that the hopes and ambitions of the early days could now be fulfilled.

Our first professional was Richard Suttle, a native of Barbados with coaching experience In England and Holland. Richard was a "colourful" character, completely and absolutely dedicated to the game.

It was decided, however, that a change was needed for 1978 season, with the result that Australian Grant Stanley was engaged. A left-arm quick bowler and aggressive batsman. Grant is a first class cricketer whose limited coaching experience is more than compensated for by a tremendous enthusiasm. The future of any club is in youth, and we at Prestwick must ensure our junior policy continues to thrive through the support and encouragement of all members.

Cricket club in danger of falling apart
By Glyn Williams

The tenth annual presentation of awards to winners of the AGD junior cricket club triangular tournament was made by Mr. E. J. Walton, chairman of the A.G.D. club. at Loundsley Green, Chesterfield. Mr. Walton presented the H. L. Brown Cup to Wayne Scott, captain of the winning B team, and the Dennis Harding Shield to Paul Durward, captain of the C team, the runners-up.

A Jubilee Shield donated by Mr. Richard Suttle, the juniors' coach, was presented to Paul Drayner, the most improved young cricketer of the season.

A ball donated by a sports shop went to Ian Drayner, who topped the bowling averages, and a cap donated by Mr. Walton was given to Wayne Scott, who topped the batting averages.

Mr. Walton. said that if more support was not forth-coming from parents and other followers of the game, there was a great danger of the junior club falling apart.

The absence of Mr. Suttle during the season when he had been coaching Prestwick cricket club in Scotland had been greatly felt.

The burden of coaching, fixture/making, umpiring and Catering had fallen almost entirely on Mr. Ron Lovegrove, the club secretary. his wife, Nellie, and son John and three parents of boys in the club.

The A.G.D. juniors play in the Sheffield and District Junior League. The: club had a membership of about 40 boys during the past season.

The Satisfaction & Rewards For a Job Well done.

THE UNDERNOTED JUNIOR MEMBERS OF PRESTWICK CRICKET CLUB
HAVE APPRECIATED THE SERVICES OF C.R.W. SUTTLE AS COACH AND
WOULD LIKE HIM TO RETURN FOR SEASON 1978.

* David Haggo
Derek Pettigrew
Graeme Rennie
Bruce M'Donald
* Andrew Tennant
Allan Haggo
Graeme Dinwoodie
Brian Nairn
Nicholas Rigby
John May
Roy McCulloch
Ricky Bicker
Alan Farquharson
* Gavin Richmond
Ross Dumigan
Alan Richmond
Brian Tracey
Nigel Cochrane
John McLafferty
Paul Stracey
Stephen McLafferty
Iain Pettigrew
Jim McCulloch

Andrew Gibson
Ian Boyd.
Steven Cairns
Kevin Davey
Kevin Hendren
Wilson Cowan
Scott Pirie
Jim Goodwin
Stuart Rennie
Gordon Webster
D. Hill
G. Suttle
Roger Suttle
Ronald Nairn
Debbie Mill
Jacqueline Mackenzie
Drew Howie
Michael Sweeney
Elizabeth Pettigrew
Mark Hendren
Karen Anthony

John Docherty
Jim Malcolm
Arthur Robertson
Kevin Hill
Craig McNeil

* This signifies players who have
become professional cricketers during
the last eighteen years.

169

Wayne Scott, captain of B team, the winners of the A.G.D. junior cricket tournament, receives the trophy from A.G.D. chairman Mr. E. J. Walton of Loundsley Green, as other players and award winners look on

Visit to M.C.C. Lords

An enthusiastic group of Chesterfield young cricketers recently attended cricket coaching at the Indoor Cricket School at Lords under the supervision of chief coach Don Wilson (former Yorkshire & England Cricketer).

Having coached these youngsters for some years, I would like to say on behalf of the Chesterfield & District Youth Cricket Council, how much we must thank all the Headteachers who gave their pupils permission to attend the course on 8th November, 1977.

As a result, 6 of the 24 were selected by Mr. A.W.P. Fleming, Manager of the M.C.C. Indoor School for more advanced coaching. They are as follows:-

Christopher Marples	(William Rhodes)
Peter Douglas	(Chesterfield College of Technology)
David Bamford	(Chesterfield College of Technology)
Roger Varley	(Chesterfield College of Technology)
Wayne Scott	(Manor Secondary)
Philip Dickinson	(Chesterfield Grammar)

Photograph by the courtesy of *Chesterfield Star*

Eddie Barlow (Captain of Derbyshire C.C.)
Like the visiting Kampong players of the Netherlands, I came to England where I was warmly welcomed by the people of Chesterfield, Derbyshire, both from a cricketing point of view as well as socially.

Queens Park, Chesterfield, is rated as the best county ground in the country and I do agree.

I hope you will thoroughly enjoy your stay as much as I did mine when I came here; but most important, is to enjoy your game of cricket.

Welcome To Chesterfield, Derbyshire
By Ian Thacker
(Tour Captain of last year's team to the Netherlands.)

At the beginning of 1977, I was asked to captain a (under 19) touring side to Holland. I am always glad for a game of cricket so I accepted, but thought that Dick Suttle had got the wrong country. They don't play cricket in Holland?

Let me put you right about the myth that there aren't cricketers in Holland. They are, and good players at that.

On the tour to Holland, the party as a whole was given a first class reception and the Dutch hospitality was tremendous. I personally, had a wonderfully enjoyable tour, the memories of which I will cherish for a long time.

I sincerely hope that the Dutch touring party to Chesterfield will receive the same hospitality as I received (if there is any justice in this world they will), and that all the party thoroughly enjoy their cricket.

I also hope to have the chance to play against them again this year and meet some old friends.

Finally, to all the touring party. Good Luck and Best Wishes.

Queen's Park, Chesterfield
By Clive Baxter, Vice Captain and Press Secretary of Chesterfield C.C.

A Yorkshireman making any comment about any aspect of Derbyshire cricket, is a bit like the Pope discussing contraception. However, I believe that there is somewhat of an affinity between the two counties, in terms of cricketing background and pedigree.

I am a self confessed Yorkshire fanatic, but I will readily agree that we haven't anything in Yorkshire like Queen's Park.

For this and two other reasons, it gives me great pleasure to contribute to

171

Richard Suttle's magazine, the proceeds of which are going to help foster youth cricket in the area.

The two other reasons are that firstly Richard Suttle is a complete and avowed nut about cricket and in my book that is important, secondly he is providing a little cricket oasis for young cricketers, in a footballing, skate boarding and T.V. watching desert.

My association with Chesterfield Cricket Club, who play at Queen's Park, goes back only 5 years, but my love of the Park goes back many more years, possibly to when I heard John Arlott describe it as the most beautiful county ground in the Country.

Having watched very cold tourists, from very warm climates, play their opening matches of the season at the beautiful Worcester ground, I could not imagine any cricketing arena being more peaceful, but when I first saw the Queen's Park I realised that John Arlott was right.

The first time I saw the ground was when Yorkshire in happier times was murdering Derbyshire by plenty, but not only was I captivated by the ground, I was also delighted by the shrewd and humorous banter from the beer tent.

It was at the Park that I saw Tom Graveney play his last innings against Derbyshire, and in this age of battery hens, processed peas and the grading of standards down, rather than up, this was a brilliant glimpse of a cricketing master, displaying unashamedly his individualistic talents.

Who can forget the run feast laid on the cricket table by the all conquering West Indians of 1976, when they played at the Park?

I believe that of the thousands that watched that game, only eleven people did not enjoy it and they were the eleven Derbyshire players.

Finally, I must join with the other contributors, in wishing the visiting Kampong Cricket Team from the Netherlands, a very happy and enjoyable stay in Chesterfield, Derbyshire.

Dutch treat at cricket

This party of young cricketers from Kampong Club, Holland, have arrived in Chesterfield to play local representative sides.

They are on an exchange visit organised by Chesterfield Youth Cricket Council who sent a party to play in Holland last year.

They will stay in the homes of members of Chesterfield Youth Cricket Council.

The first game for members of the 17-strong party, ages ranging from 14 to 20, will be against a Chesterfield and District XI at Sheepbridge.

They also play a Staveley XI at Staveley, a further match against at Chesterfield and District XI at Calow, and a match against a Clowne XI at Clowne.

172

The party will also visit Chesterfield Aquarius Club, Middlecroft leisure centre and Chesterfield swimming baths.

They were officially received by the Mayor of Chesterfield, Coun. Patrick Kelly.

Links between the young cricket council and Kampong C.C. were established by coach Mr. Richard Suttle, of Pennine Way, Loundsley Green, Chesterfield, who coached with Amsterdam in 1975.

The Kampong club field several sides playing one-day cricket.

Our side will consist of the following persons:-

a. Jos Andriessen	18	j. Nico Verhoeff	20
b. Ronnie Elferink	16	k. Guus Vermeulen	17
c. Sebastiaan d'Hont	16	l. Fred Verziji	17
d. Floris Jansen	16	m. Gertjan Wallinga	18
e. Jan Kees Koreneef	14	n. Marten Wallinga	16
f. Vidjai Orie	20	o. Tammo Wallinga	18
g. Jan Pruschen	19	p. David Constantine (trainer)	
h. Ferry Smit	19	q. Charles Verheyen (manager)	
i. Maarten Verhoeff	20		

Dutch team on tour

A touring cricket team from Holland, Kampong C.C., of Utrecht, visited Chesterfield last week and in their matches with the Chesterfield Youth Cricket Council they shared the spoils. At the last minute the matches were switched from U-18 to U-20. The Chesterfield committee thus named greatly revised teams for the four games at Sheepbridge and Calow.

Two games at Staveley Works ground were washed out on Wednesday, but a double win by the visitors to Clowne Town Y.C. on Friday made it honours even for the contesting teams. It was a triumphant tour for South African born 16-year-old Ronnie Elferink, who can be credited with a hat-trick of "man-of-the-match" awards. His bowling record for the three 40-overs games was 40·2 overs. 13 maidens. 22 wickets for 93 runs – plus two catches. This included a 7-22 return on Tuesday, a 6-42 return, a last three wickets for none hat-trick on Thursday and a 9-29 return on Friday. In the opening game at Sheepbridge he hit eight fours and four sixes in an undefeated 101, including 27 in one over.

The Dutch visitors were given a civic reception at Chesterfield Town Hall on Monday, and 15 local families provided hospitality for the tourists. Full-time coach for the past seven months for the five teams of Kampong, has been 22-year-old David Constantine, former resident of Newbold Road, Chesterfield, and one-time cricketer with Chesterfield Parish Church, and Youth Council and Cutthorpe teams. Leading the organizing committee were Harold Bradford. (Chairman). Richard Suttle, a one-time coach with Amsterdam C.C.; and David Cook (team manaager).

Results

Tuesday (at Sheepbridge Sportsground). – Kampong C.C. 188. (R. Elferink 101 n.o.. N. Verhoef 24. F. Jansen 20. J. Orie 18) beat Chesterfield XI 130 (N. Russell 33 T. Onions 20. D. Stevenson 19. J Wilson 18. K. Hartley 10 Ronnie Elferink 7-22, .M. Verhoeff 2-26) eight-a-side. – Chesterfield Cricket Lovers' Juniors 86-5 (B. Robinson 42, D. Roberts 23). beat Kampong 85-2 (M. Verhoeff 26. F. Smith 29 including 22 in one over).

Thursday (at A.G.D. sportsground, Calow). – Chesterfield XI 132 (N. Brown 35, I. Thacker 31 I. Jones 29. R. EJferink 6-41 including hat-trick last three wickets. M. Verhoeff 2.32). beat Kampong 93 (R. Elferink 27. M Verhoeff 26. J. Orie 18, J. Wilson 4-19, P. Bagnall 2-13. R. Varley 2-28. N. Brown 2-30); eight-a-side – Chesterfield 100 (D. Duroe 77) beat Kampong 80 (T. Wallinga 38 M, Wallinga 11. I. R. Suttle 3-44).

Friday (at Clowne Town ground) – Kampong 166-9 (twin brothers Nioo Verhoeff 46 and Maarten Verhoeff n.o., R. Elferink 24, F. Jansen 15. M. Wallinga 15. Philip Baker 4-14 including hat-trick. G. Ashley 2-41). beat Clowne Youth Council 110 (P. Baker 26. G. Ashley 26, P. Blackham. 21. N. Ashley 10. R Elferink 9-29 – last nine wickets); eight-a side. – Kampong 97 (Nico Verhoef 35 F. Smith 28). beat Clowne Y.C. 62 (N. Ashley 29, F. Verzvl 5-50.

4/8/78

174

Junior Cricket

On behalf of the Chesterfield & District Y.C.C. who have organised the current visit of the Scottish Youth Team, we would like to wish them a successful series against the opposition from North of the border

The Chesterfield Cricket Lovers' Society was formed in 1963. One of its objectives was to encourage cricket among youngsters up to the age of 13 and in this the Society proved to be in the forefront in the area. Early efforts met with some success but it really prospered with the opening of the Sports Hall at the local College of Technology in 1974. Sessions were held on Saturday afternoons during the winter and as many as 100 youngsters have attended a three hour session, and to date, over 600 boys and girls have been through the Society's coaching system. Many of these have moved on to local clubs and are now giving a good account of themselves at senior league level even though still in their early-teens. A number of boys have also represented the County at under thirteen, under fifteen and under seventeen level.

The Society has entered a team in the National Cricket Association, under thirteen competition for the past five years and has won the County Championship on every occasion. Last year the team won the Midlands Regional Final and competed in the last eight for the National Championship out of an original entry of over one thousand teams.

In addition to competing in the National Championship, the Society formulated a local league in the district for under thirteens in 1977 and this has proved most popular with the result that more and more clubs are now entering teams and this can only be good for the game.

The society will again be organising coaching sessions this coming autumn for youngsters under the age of 13 on 1st September, 1980 and any who are interested should watch the local press or contact the undersigned.

W. B. Robson

Juniors reap rewards

Chesterfield and District Youth Cricket Council has presented prizes and certificates to youngsters attending coaching sessions at the Chesterfield College of Technology's sports hall.

The courses have been organised by the chairman of the council, Harold Bradford, with the assistance of National Cricket Association coaches Richard Suttle, Benita White and Alf Gaunt.

Plaques and certificates were presented to William Vermeulen, right, Richard Joy and Brian Gladwin by Frank Rasmussen, honorary secretary of Derbyshire Youth Cricket Council. Other certificates went to: A. Pierrepont, C. Kirk, P. Walker, S. Lavender, M. Joy, G. Cook, P. Yeomans, J. Bullock, R.

Waugh, M. Smith, A. Riley, N. Dunham, T. Kirk, P. Hand, A. Platts, A. Chalmers, S. Andrews, R. Hallam, M. Granger, M. Hallam, D. Calow, D. Phillips, T. Russell, J. Hardy, A. Francis, S. Bean, J. Jones and J. Peers.

The Formation of the Chesterfield & District Ladies C.C. June 1978

Chesterfield & District Ladies Cricket Club formed in June 1978
It's a wicket maiden
Women cricketers took the field at Loundsley Green, Chesterfield, to knock

for six that old joke about glances to fine leg.

The women were taking part in a practice match to make sure no slips will show in their performance against a team of women cricketers from Scotland next month.

And in the 20 overs match the team showed there was plenty of talent to array before the north of the border team when it visits Chesterfield.

The game, between the women of the Chesterfield area, and those from Scotland, had been arranged by cricket coach Mr. Richard Suttle, of Pennine Way, Loundsley Green.

He met some of the women players with the Drumpellier Cricket Club in Lanarkshire while coaching in Scotland last summer, and said he would fix up a match for them in Chesterfield.

Selection of the captain of the team has already been made – all-rounder Denise Leary, aged 19, of Sandringham Close, Calow.

Denise who has been playing cricket for two years, and has had trials for England, usually plays for Nottingham Ladies in the East Midlands.

Mr. Suttle believes cricket is a good game for women, being a test of skill but also a relaxing pastime.

But he adds: "Just as their male counterparts, they need concentration, application, dedication and the ability to overcome failure."

Chesterfield Ladies Victorious
Scores:- N. of the Border XI - 89 off 24·3 overs
Chesterfield XI:- 90 for 7 off 24 overs

On Sunday, 20th August, Davina Crawford (captain of North of the Border Team) travelled to Loundsley Green, Chesterfield to play against a Chesterfield & District Ladies XI in a friendly fixture, which is to become an annual event.

Denise Leary, who led the home team inspiringly, won the toss on a rain affected wicket and sent in the tourists to bat, and after 24·3 overs, they were all out for 89. Skipper Crawford top scored with 19 and was ably assisted with 12 from Catherine McDowell, 12 not out from Penny Green and 10 from Pat Reid.

Bowling for the local ladies XI, Elizabeth Brown with her slow off spinners, took 5 for 27 in 4·3overs. Sally Elliott 3 for 22 in 8 overs and Jane Hoskin 1 for 2 in 1 over.

In reply, Chesterfield & District Ladies scored 90 for 7 off 24 overs, skipper Denise Leary, who batted at No. 5, played an invaluable innings and was undefeated with 33 while Enid Bakewell scored a stylish 32 to place their teem in a winning position.

Bowling for North of the Border Ladies XI, Sue Smith, who bowled cleverly flighted medium paced deliveries, took 5 for 31 in 11 overs while Davina Crawford took 1 for 24 in 8 overs as the home team won by 3 wickets with one over left.

Teams were: North of the Border XI: D. Crawford (Capt.) C. McDowell (V. Capt.), H. McWhirter, E. McWhirter, P. Reid, S. Smith, C. Cormack; J. Andrews, J. Cursiter, A. Baker, S. Came and P. Green.

Chesterfield & District Ladies XI: D. Leary (Capt.) S. Charlesworth (V. Capt.), W. Watson, S. Elliott, E. Brown, J. Fox, J. Hoskin, M. Corigan, S. Menzies, C. Spracklen, P. Saich and E. Bakewell.

By R. Suttle

M.C.C. Advanced Coaching Award Course August 1978

A group of cricketers at Scalby High School, Scarborough, attending the M.C.C. Advanced Award Course from (26th July – 1st August 1978). They are:- Les Lenham (National Cricket Coach) Sussex, Ramesh Wadhawan, (India), Tony Greaves (Devon), Tony Bowes (Yorkshire), Stewart Burrows (Nottingham), Hylton Ackerman (S. Africa), Maurice Hallam (Leicester), Abud Ali (India), Ralph Middlebrook (Yorkshire), Babu Haffajee (India) John Curry (Yorkshire), Doug Ferguson (Minor Counties), Jackie Bond (Lancs & I.O.M.), Richard Suttle (Derbyshire), Alan Knott (Kent), Gregg Hayes (S.Africa).

Working for the Apperknowle Community Association as their Community Organiser

In 1979, I was employed by Mr. Mick Emmens, Chairman of the Apperknowle Community Association, as a Community Co-ordinator, to  raise money to build a Community Centre in the area,

This took the form of producing thousands of brochures for annual events in the form of Summer Fairs.

To achieve this project, I used to travel many miles on foot, collecting paid advertisements from the local stores and shops to place in the brochures. This gave the information of the location and itinerary of the kind of sporting activities displayed,

Another form of fund raising came from the sale of raffle tickets, which brought in thousands of pounds.

These funds were eventually divided between the schools, the church and the Elderly People's Club, all in Apperknowle.

Apperknowle Community Association presents
Attractions

Helicopter Joy Rides	Sweet Stall
Country Crafts 3- Produce	Tombola
Aerial Flight	Pony Rides
Balls in Buckets	Model Engines
Bottle Stall	Air Bed
Lucky Dip	Balloons
Pot Smashing	Tin Shy
Jumble	Raffle
Roll-a-2p	Test Your Strength
Soft Toys	Guessing Games
Flat Cap Throwing	Refreshments

and various other stalls and displays
PLUS
Open Fancy Dress, Fancy Bikes & Prams Competition
All Ages 0-90

L to R:- *(Gala Queen 79) Vicki Ward with udith Hall and Sarah Dawson in attendance*

Call for probe into son's death

Doctors have scotched the possibility of a meningitis scare.

But now a grieving father has called for an investigation into what he claims was a delay in doctors seeing his son, Steven.

Mr. Dick Suttle, of 16 Pennine Way, Loundsley Green, Chesterfield, has been told by the General Practitioners Committee at Derby that his complaint has been passed to the Chairman of the Medical Services Committee.

Three children at a Chesterfield school were rumoured to have been affected by the meningitis virus.

One was said to have died, another to be ill and another cleared.

All three were reported to be pupils at Ashgate Croft – a special school at Chesterfield.

But a County Council spokesman said only two children, both from Ashgate Croft, had been involved.

Concern

The first child who had shown symptoms similar to meningitis died and there was a moment of concern when a second child developed similar symptons.

But he was discharged from Chesterfield Royal Hospital after a day or two of tests and a spokesman for the Schools' Medical Officer said it was believed he had a urinary infection.

Mr. and Mrs. Suttle are divorced and Steven lived with his mother, Lettice, at 26 Southdown Avenue, Chesterfield – but he turned out to be a hole-in-the-heart boy.

"We had been told he had a heart murmur, but we didn't know he had a hole-in-the-heart until the post mortem examination," said Mrs. Suttle.

Added Mrs. Suttle, a qualified nurse: "The death certificate showed he died from congenital heart disease and meningitis."

Mrs. Suttle said that when Steven started vomiting she made several telephone calls to a doctor but was repeatedly told to ring back later.

Steven was not fit to take to a surgery but she was able to get a prescription, she said.

"Perhaps I should have insisted on a doctor coming in the first place, but I had to make five telephone calls and wait from Wednesday until Saturday before a doctor came," said Mrs. Suttle.

Steven was finally taken to Chesterfield Royal Hospital four days after Mrs. Suttle's first call and he died in a Sheffield hospital two days later.

In a letter to the General Practitioners' Council, Mr. Suttle asked for an investigation into the lapse of several days between Mrs. Suttle's first phone call and a doctor arriving at the house.

Wrote Mr. Suttle: "The time lapse could have been vital, irrespective of the patient's medical condition, and I hope that similar instances will be avoided in the future for all concerned.

The family doctor has declined to comment.

Chesterfield Cricket Lovers win 8-a-side
(Under 13) Competition by 25 runs by Dick Suttle

The 8-a-side (Under 13) Knockout Tournament organised by (N.C.A. cricket coach) Benita White, got underway at Staveley Welfare Cricket Ground on Saturday 13th September despite light intermittent showers which persisted almost throughout the event.

Seven boys' teams and a girls' team entered the competition which was well attended and keenly contested by all the teams. First round draw included:

Stretton & Stonebroom v Chesterfield (No. 3)

Chesterfield Jnr. & Young Ladies C.C. v Chesterfield (No. 2)

Chesterfield (No. 1) v Chesterfield (No. 4)

Chesterfield Cricket Lovers v Chesterfield (No. 5)

Semi-Finalists included:

Stretton & Stonebroom v Chesterfield Young Ladies C.C.

Chesterfield Cricket Lovers v Chesterfield (No. 1)

Emerging as Finalists were:

Stretton & Stonebroom v Chesterfield Cricket Lovers

In the final, David Harding (Capt. of Stretton & Stonebroom), won the toss and sent in Chesterfield Cricket Lovers under the captaincy of Ian Bullock to bat. After their 7 allotted overs, they were 67 for 3, with Bullock and Stephen Bates both undefeated with 21 and 20 respectively.

Bowling for Stretton & Stonebroom, K. Hardy took 2 for 2 and D. Hardy 1 for 6.

In reply Stretton & Stonebroom were all out for 42 of which Michael Wharton scored 16. Bowling for the Cricket Lovers, Bullock and Richard Coleman took 2 each for 7 and 4 respectively, while M. Coleman, Roger Suttle and Stephen Bates took one each for 5, 2 and 6 respectively to win the final by 25 runs.

Mrs. White presented the inscribed glass cup to Ian Bullock and a cup to David Harding (Capt. of the Runners-up) as well as trophies to Elizabeth Brown who won the Batting Award, Ian Bullock the Bowling Award and Nigel Oliver the Wicket-keeping Award, to end a most successful competition.

The Loundsley Green Junior section 1980
by Dick Suttle

The "Mini Test" series at Loundsley Green, Chesterfield, for young cricketers was won in a sixth and deciding match by the 'A' team during the long summer holidays.

At the presentation which followed the match, the Derbyshire County Cricket Club Captain, Geoff Miller presented players with ties, tankards, sports bags and plaques, donated by many local firms for their individual performances.

The best batting average for the B team was won by Ian Suttle, the best bowling for the B team by Andrew Warnes, best fielder for the A team was John Littleton, best wicket-keeper Ian Saich of B team, highest individual score of A team, Shaun Gibbions, most wickets in series, Roger Suttle of B team, most outstanding bowling performance, Nicholas Millward of B team, second best bowling performance, Robert Hoskin.

Ten year-old Alan Williams from Littleover, Derby, was given a special award for his enthusiasm while wicket keeper Pauline Saich, age 15, was presented with a box of powder for her contribution to the series, which produced some remarkable results, as 287-4 overs were bowled, 35 of which were maidens, 1090 runs were scored and 107 wickets were taken.

A Deserving Tribute to Mrs. Benita White

To add to the success of many local young cricketers, I must congratulate Mrs. Benita White who has worked extremely hard in organising and coaching the beginners to a standard whereby they can play and enjoy their cricket at competitive level. I hope she will get much more support from all those involved in the promotion of junior cricket and for the invaluable work done in the past and that which lies in the future for such a wonderful sport.

Chesterfield lady cricketer, Denise Leary, toured India in January 1981 as a member of a young England Women's team. Denise, aged 21, of Sandringham Close, Calow, helped to save the team from defeat in the five three, day test series when in the final test at Ahmedabad with Jane Powell, the Sheffield cricketer, as the last pair at the wicket, they managed to stay to bat out time.

The tour party of 15 players travelled 25,000 miles and played eleven matches in 41 days. They won a series of one day tests against the Indian women's team 3-1. These matches were broadcast on television and radio.

Denise is a medium pace left arm bowler and took a number of wickets on the tour. The standard of women's cricket in India is high and at Ahmedabad the crowd was over 30,000.

A tribute to the pioneers of Youth Cricket in Chesterfield
by Nazir Latif (Spire Sports)

As a keen and enthusiastic cricketer who enjoyed the game at Loundsley Green some ten years ago, while still at school. I often wondered why more interest is not shown by cricket authorities in this area toward the development of the present facilities as well as the budding younger players of the future.

So often there seems to be an offensive attitude taken when the word "CRICKET" is mentioned in certain circles, but thanks to people like Ron Lovegrove, Jim Brailsford, David Forbes, Ralph Ironside, Brian Holling, John Buxton, Benita White and last but by no means least, that tireless pioneer, author and cricket coach, Dick Suttle who has compiled this brochure for the Caribbean tour in October this year.

Finally, I wish the Loundsley Green Youth Cricket Club and its organisers all the best on their two week tour to the lovely island of Barbados, West Indies.

Lynne Bates won single wicket competition by 9 runs
by Dick Suttle

To round off a very hectic, but eventful cricket season at Loundsley Green, Lynne Bates won the first ever Ladies Single Wicket Competition presented by the Chesterfield and District Youth Cricket Council on Friday 5th September from a group of 20 participants.

Quarter Finals included: Pauline Saich v Heather Bourne, Francis Hooper v Lynne Bates, Tracey Walker v Alison Sadler and Debbie Griffiths or Sharon Baldry v Elizabeth Brown.

From the above mentioned, Saich, Bates, Sadler and Baldry emerged Semi-Finalists. As a result, Saich and Baldry lost to Bates and Sadler respectively.

In the Final, Bates batted first, and scored 14 not out off her allotted 2 overs, while Sadler was stumped for five of the first ball of the second over to give Bates victory by 9 runs and Winner of the Single Wicket competition.

After the Final, (N.C.A. Coach) Richard Suttle introduced Mr. Harold Bradford (Chairman of the Council) to present the trophies and awards. Mr. Bradford made a short speech and spoke on the interest and keen contests shown by the ladies and thanked Mr. Suttle for organising the event, after

L to R:- *Lynne Bates, Pauline Saich, Alison Sadler and Sharon Baldry, quarter-finalists in the 1980 Ladies Single Wicket*

which he presented the trophies to Lynne Bates (Winner) and Alison Sadler (Runner-Up), and also autographed cricket books to all the participants to rounds of applause from the spectators as the shadows of the evening lengthened to remind us of the passing of yet another summer.

Next season we hope to see a girl's team from St. Helena's School under the supervision of Miss Patricia Hooley.

Boys' summer 'Test' series

Youngster in the Loundsley Green area of Chesterfield are spending their summer Caribbean style.

Under the guidance of Barbadian junior coach Dick Suttle, they have formed two 20-strong cricket squads to play each other in a series of five games.

The teams have adopted the names of Loundsley Green Junior 'A' and 'B' and the winners will be presented with medals by former Derbyshire captain Ian Buxton on Wednesday. There will also be an award for the "Boy of the Series".

"This sort of activity goes on all the time in the West Indies," said Dick. "And over here in the summer, it keeps the kids occupied during the holidays."

The 'B' team have teken a 2-1 lead in the series with one match tied.

The 'A' teams only victory so far came in the fourth game on Monday.

They were put in to bat and scored 136·9 off 30 overs with Shaun Gibbions hitting a fine 38 which included four boundaries. Good support came from Andrew Lunn (21), Robert Hoskin (14) and John Littleton (15).

For the 'B' team, Andrew Warnes took three for 11. Malcolm Brown 2-16 and Roger Suttle 2-18.

But when it came to their innings, the 'B' team failed to get to grips and make sure of the series. Apart from the opening batsman and captain Ian Suttle, who compiled an attacking 31, the side was unable to cope with some accurate bowling in which Hoskin took four for eight, Ian Benison 2-5 and John Littleton 1-1.

The tie came in the second game with both teams ending on 83 all out.

In reply, the 'A' team were all out for 48 in 15 overs. Longmate was their top scorer with 10. The main reason for their collapse was a fine spell of medium pace bowling from Nicholas Millward who took 5-5 in three overs, including a hat-trick.

The 'B' team batted first and their innings owed a lot to the opening batsmen Andrew Warnes (25) and Roger Suttle (17 not out).

For the 'A' team, both John Littleton and Andrew Riley took two wickets for five runs while Tim Kirk took two for 21 and Robert Hoskin one for 23.

Hoskin then played a true captain's innings in reply, being run out for 39. But the only other batsman to reach double figures was Ian Gregory on 13.

Christopher Kirk took three for 13, Frankie Hanion 2-10, Nicholas Millward 2-14 and Roger Suttle 1-20.

In the second of the first two games, the 'B' team batted first and scored 129-9 off 30 overs. Ian Suttle was again the mainstay with a 53.

'Test' series decided

The sixth and deciding match in the summer 'Test' series between two groups of youngsters from the Loundsley Green area of Chesterfield was won by the 'A' team, by one run.

They scored 100-7 off their 20 overs in a rain-restricted match. Ian Benison hit an aggressive 46 which included nine boundaries and was well supported by skipper Robert Hoskin (16) and Shaun Gibbions (24).

For the 'B' team, Christopher Kirk, Roger Suttle, Paul Benison and Nicholas Millward each took a wicket.

Ian Suttle and Paul Benison then got the 'B' team reply off to a good start putting on 52 for the first wicket in 10 overs before Benison was run out for 28.

And the middle order collapsed after the dismissal of Ian Suttle to a brilliant catch at deep fine leg by John Littleton for 47, which included seven boundaries.

The score was at 99-6 when Littleton faced the last ball from Andrew Warnes. The ball beat Littleton through the air and wicket-keeper Longmate whipped off the bails to give the 'A' team victory.

I. Benison took 2 for 2 in four overs. T Kirk took 1-3 and I. Littleton 1-2.

In a presentation, the 'A' team received their trophy and the 'B' team a consolation glass bowl from Derbyshire captain, Geoff Miller. Individual awards also went to:

Best batting average – Ian Suttle; best bowling average – Andrew Warnes; best fielder – John Littleton; best wicket-keeper – Ian Saich: highest individual score for 'B' team – Ian Suttle; highest individual 'A' team score – Shaun Gibbions.

Most wickets in the series – Roger Suttle; most outstanding bowling performance – Nicholas Millward; second most outstanding bowling performance – Robert Hoskin; lady cricketer to play in five games – Pauline Saich; enthusiasm and dedication – Alan Williams; Player of the Sixth and Final Test – Ian Benison.

In all, 267·4 overs were bowled in the series. Thirty-one were maidens and 108 wickets were taken for 1090 runs.

15/8/80

Young Scots' visit a triumph

"Very friendly" cricket links have now been established between Chesterfield and Scotland.

That was the view of touring manager Mr. Jim Bagnall after the visit to

The young Scottish visitors with their Chesterfield hosts before the final game at Wingerworth

Chesterfield last week by a Scottish youth squad, mainly from Ayrshire.

The young Scots – who had among their ranks three youth internationals – spent four days in Chesterfield playing matches at both under-15 and under-19 level.

Mr. Bagnall praised Chesterfield hospitality and handed over a large shield to Mr. Harold Bradford, chairman of the Chesterfield Youth Cricket Council, for presentation in future youth competitions in Chesterfield.

The Scots, whose visit was in return for a similar one made by Chesterfield to Ayrshire in 1978, won two of the five matches played at Loundsley Green, Glapwell and Wingerworth – one at U-19 level and the final match between the two combined sides.

The Chesterfield Youth Council cricket teams were under the supervision of Dick Suttle.

Club cricket in Barbados

Richard Suttle approached me during the West Indies vs Derbyshire game at Chesterfield to write a short article for his brochure and although I was delighted to do so, there was little time at my disposal as he wanted it before we left for our next game at Leeds.

I have therefore decided to write a little about Club Cricket in Barbados.

Our club cricket has a distinct flavour about it in that the matches are played over three consecutive Saturdays in the first and intermediate divisions, with two days allocated to the second division. Needless to say, these are all two innings matches which enable young players to learn from an early age the merits in building a long innings which is an ideal training ground for the first class, and ultimately, test scene.

In addition, school teams take part in these competitions and it is therefore not uncommon to find players coming to the fore at a very early age of their cricketing careers.

The wickets are by and large very good batting strips except when the weather intervenes and then they can become very spiteful; but here again, this provides invaluable experience as it allows the young players to cope with varying type wickets in one match.

The general standard of cricket has always been of the highest quality; although of late we have suffered as a result of the exodus of players who now appear in first class county cricket and the various league competitions, especially in the North of England and Scotland.

To give some idea of the standard of club cricket, I have had the privilege of taking part in one of these games with such players of the calibre of Everton Weekes, Conrad Hunte, Charlie Griffith, Seymore Nurse, Clairmonte Depeiza, Rawle Branker on one team, and the likes of Wes Hall, Peter Lashtey, David Holford and myself on the other (all players who were members of West Indian Touring Team).

In addition, Sir Garfield Sobers, Manager Clyde Walcott and the late Sir Frank Worrell only to mention a few, have been part of cricket in Barbados.

It can readily be appreciated what there is meant by referring to club cricket of being of the highest quality.

Richard Suttle when a student at Combermere School was also part of the club cricket scene before he came to Britain and I believe he is well qualified to continue the good work which I understand he has done for the youth in Chesterfield over the past few years.

Long may he continue to do so.

Cammie Smith
(Assistant Manager West Indies Touring Team 1980)

Rush for cricket coaching

Young star under instruction – Derbyshire CCC's newly appointed chief coach Phil Russell hands out some advice on batting technique to Chesterfield youngster Chris Marples.

Chris (16) is one of a record number of promising cricket youngsters in

Cricket coaching course, Chesterfield College

Chesterfield who have enrolled for winter indoor training at the College of Technology.

Phil Russell dropped in at the first session on Saturday to assess the standard of the youngsters and was impressed.

NCA cricket coach Richard Suttle (standing left) said that far more youngsters had enrolled this year than previous years because of the success of past Chesterfield youngsters in progressing through the ranks to county and national level.

Suttle coaches for the Chesterfield Youth Cricket Council and Chesterfield Cricket Lovers Society — both of whom have supplied about 40 pupils for the coaching sessions. These groups include a number of young lady enthusiasts.

Others assisting at the sessions, organised by Youth Council chairman Harold Bradford, are Alf Gaunt and Sid Yeomans and, from the Cricket Lovers by Brian Robson, Peter Joy and John Buxton.

Most of the group will also be attending a special coaching session at the Lords indoor cricket school under the supervision of former Yorkshire and England cricketer Don Wilson in December.

Derbyshire Times October 29th 1980

Dale wins junior cricketer award

Dale White of Halcyon Approach, Wingerworth, gained the Chesterfield Cricket Club junior player of the year award at a presentation evening at

West Indies Cricket Tour
United Kingdom
1980

Manager
Clyde Walcott O.B.E.
Assistant Manager
Cammie Smith

Captain
Clive Lloyd
Vice Captain
Vivian Richards

LONDON OFFICE
2-2A GATE ST.
LINCOLNS INN FIELDS
HOLBORN, LONDON WC2
Tel: 405 5619

SPONSORED BY
SAVE SECURITIES LTD
ELECTRICAL, MECHANICAL BUILDING CONTRACTORS

REGIONAL OFFICE
Tel: RUISLIP 755 89

AUTOGRAPHS

Captain — CLIVE LLOYD	
Vice-Captain — VIVIAN RICHARDS	
DERYCK MURRAY	
ALVIN KALLICHARRAN	
ANDY ROBERTS	
DESMOND HAYNES	
DEREK PARRY	
COLLIS KING	
COLIN CROFT	
DAVID MURRAY	
JOEL GARNER	
GORDON GREENIDGE	
MICHAEL HOLDING	
MALCOLM MARSHALL	
FAOUD BACCHUS	
LAWRENCE ROWE	
Manager — CLYDE WALCOTT	
Asst. Manager — CAMMIE SMITH	
Physiotherapist — DENIS WAIGHT	

Team Headquarters: Hotel Russell, Russell Square, London WC2
Telex: WESTCRICK LONDON WC2

Elizabeth Brown receives the 1980 Batting Award from Derbyshire's captain, Geoff Miller

Hasland Village Hall.

Pace bowler Dale, aged 16, gained his success after a season in which he took 80 wickets.

During the past season, Dale played for the Chesterfield Cricket Club's junior side in the Derbyshire U-16 League and the Sheffield U-18 League,

He also played in the Chesterfield Cricket Club third eleven in the North Derbyshire League and played occasional games for the club's second team in the Bassetlaw League.

Dale is the son of National Cricket Association coach Benita White who coaches the Chesterfield Cricket Club junior players.

Awards were presented by Derbyshire captain and England player Geoff Miller.

Third class proficiency badges were presented to Jonathan Clarke, Ian Davis, Jonathan Gilthorpe, Andrew Gilthorpe, Jonathan Leighton, Chris Lomas, David Morton, John Wass, Andrew Walker, Beverley Oldman, and Elizabeth Brown.

Second and third class badges were presented to Duncan Calow, Steven Drury, Jonathan Dix, Michael Grainger, James Hardy, Richard Ironside, Timothy Kirk, Michael May, David Shannon, David Ward, Simon Wall, Alison Sadler and Sharon Baldry.

First and second class badges were presented to Neil Bradbury, Andrew Burdett, Richard Fidler, Paul Gofton, David Gray, Richard Hughes, Andrew Hiron, Richard Roddis, David Standen, Paul Stanton, David Sharp, Graham Slatcher, William Vermuelen, Paul Whitworth, Mandy Bean.

Sport

First, a second and third class badges were presented to Stephen Cantrell. Second class badges were presented to Chris Adams, David Adams, Shaun Morris, and Adam Young.

Members of the club team which won the North-east Derbyshire Sports Council Trophy at the Sport For All days at Tupton Hall School received medals.

They were: Timothy Kirk (capt.), Parley Briggs, Richard Barker, Duncan

Calow, Jonathan Denton, Stephen Drury, Chris Mitchell and Andrew Walker.

Cups presented to under 18s – Paramore Cup: batting, Ian Waring; bowling Peter Bedford.

Cups and plaques presented to u-16s – Ryaford Trophy, Chesterfield Advertiser Trophy. Cliff Gladwin Knock-Out Cup and Brailsford six-a-side competition trophy – batting Robert Carlisle; bowling Paul Simpson.

Most improved player of the year: Ian Davis.

Sheffield Star 30/10/80

Coaching at new centre

Cricket coaching has got under way at the new Sharley Park Leisure Centre at Clay Cross.

Taking part in the sessions on Monday evenings are members of the Loundsley Green junior cricket club and in charge of the course is National Cricket Association coach, Richard Suttle, of Pennine Way, Chesterfield.

About fifteen young cricketers attended the first session and Mr. Suttle says there is room for more.

He added. "Use of premises of this type on a weekday evening is some-thing for which we have been looking for a long time. The boys are getting

Eugene Grant, Mark Turner, Michael Davies, Nicholas Ratcliffe and Paul Savory receiving their trophies from national cricket coach Richard Suttle after their week's course at Sharley Park Leisure Centre, Clay Cross

The Star 17/8/81

there by public transport and lifts.

The Loundsley Green junior cricket club was formed 14 years ago.

On women in a man's world
Benita puts the boys on course
by Jon Culley

Cricket, despite the significant progress made in recent years by pioneers such as Rachel Heyhoe Flint, remains a sport dominated by men in which women perhaps do not get the opportunities they deserve.

This unsatisfactory state of affairs is one area of the game in which Benita White, well-known in Chesterfield cricket circles, takes a particular interest – but it is not the only area in which she has become influential.

Having already stood in a women's international match, Mrs. White next season becomes the Bassetlaw League's first woman umpire. But it is her role in developing cricket coaching for youngsters in which she has made the more significant strides.

Through her own perseverance, and with a little help from Derbyshire youth coach John Brown, Mrs. White has introduced to the county a high standard of cricket coaching for youngsters aged between ten and 13.

A long-time Derbyshire supporter, Mrs. White, 43, has keenly followed cricket for many years but has only recently become actively involved in the sport.

"I suppose I began my involvement because of my two sons." she said. "They wanted to play when they were quite young, but coaching programmes for juniors of their age were practically non-existent.

"Just over three years ago I got in touch with John Brown to see what could be done. He put me on to Chesterfield Cricket Lovers' Society and I've never looked back."

Mrs. White succeeded in obtaining a National Cricket Association Junior and Youth Coaching Certificate and contacted schools, further education sites and industrial concerns in search of facilities.

She has since established coaching in schools and leisure centres on a regular basis and has this year helped organise an indoor cricket league for youngsters.

Her work has gained her positions on committees of Chesterfield Cricket Lovers' Society, the Derbyshire Cricket Association and the Derbyshire Cricket Coaches' Association, and she has recently become the first woman to be appointed sports and social secretary at Chesterfield Cricket Club where she is also coach to the under-13 boys.

"My great regret is that I could not play cricket myself when I was younger," she says. "But when I was a teenager there simply were not the

The First Lady… Cricket coach Benita White during one of her coaching courses

openings for women in the sport which exist today."

Two tours of Barbados?

Plans are now going ahead in Chesterfield for two youth cricket tours of Barbados.

A meeting of the Chesterfield and District Youth Cricket Council on Friday unanimously backed an earlier decision made to postpone their proposed tour – originally scheduled for October – possibly until next Spring.

But committee member Mr. Richard Suttle – who solely opposed that earlier decision – has now resigned from the council and intends to press on with the original tour plans under the new name of the Loundsley Green Youth Cricket Club. He did not attend Friday's meeting.

The youth council have sent letters to their Barbados opponents to inform them of the decision to postpone for the meantime and have set a date for a meeting of the parents of boys who have been selected to go on their tour. It will be held at St. James Hall on Friday, April 24.

"We will decide at this meeting precisely when we are going to have our tour – although quite a few seem to favour Spring next year – and how we will go about fund-raising" said youth council chairman Mr. Harold Bradford.

Mr. Suttle, meanwhile, has invited players and parents interested in going on his Loundsley Green tour in October to report to the Sharley Park Sports Centre at Clay Cross on Monday night.

He said: "What I am dong now is nothing at all to do with the youth council. The only connection is that some boys are down to go on both tours.

"But it is entirely up to these boys to decide which tour they would like to go on. I am not pressing or forcing anyone to go in October. If the boys would prefer to go in 1982 then they must do that.

"I am doing this because I thought it would be inconvenient for many boys to go next year. I am not even bothered if I don't go. The boys come first."

Mr. Suttle intends to honour the original match dates set for October – he has received confirmation on one of these – and has started his fund-raising. Among the ideas he has is to arrange for his selected boys to be sponsored for the amount of runs they make or wickets they take during the summer.

10/4/81

This team was the one chosen to visit Barbados in October 1981, but due to the unavailability of some players, eight replacements had to be found within a few months of departure. Included in these replacements, were:-Damian D'Oliveira & Dave Banks of Worcestershire County Cricket Club

Dear Reader,

First of all, may I wish you luck with the draw and hope that this booklet has the winning number!

This brochure has been compiled for a very special reason. The money which is collected from its sale will pay for some local cricketers (under nineteens) to go to Barbados and gain invaluable experience, playing in matches against the world's best.

One of the nicest things about moving into the area, was seeing the amount of work done by people trying to encourage cricket for the youngsters. But to crown this, a tour of Barbados?!! What bigger incentive could there be? It is the type of enthusiastic attitude by the organisers which will develop youth cricket in this area so that it is unrivalled in the country. The game needs more people willing to stick their necks out and devote a lot of time to the sport.

Now's the time to say "Okay, we're not the best in the world ... but we will be soon!" It's the youngsters who hold the key to future success. We have to promote their talents and give them all the help possible.

Wouldn't it be good to see our touring team in five years' time taking on the West Indies and Australia at the highest level?... and absolutely thrashing them!!

How many English people are there out there who support the opposition? Let's support the Englishman's game! Good luck to the touring team!

S. Palframan.

Coaching and encouraging youngsters with their cricket is so important. I remember so well at school being encouraged by my history master. Jack Morris, to practice my cricket. What a great help this was to me.

Richard Suttle, with his amazing enthusiasm for the game is doing a similar job with the boys that pass through his hands. I know, that Richard and all the young players heading for Barbados will have a wonderful time and I am sure they will come back better cricketers from this experience of a lifetime.

Have a wonderful tour,
Best Wishes,
Alan Knott.

From: Clive Baxter
ex Chairman of Chesterfield Cricket Club.

I was delighted when I heard that Dick Suttle was going ahead with his planned tour to Barbados, taking with him a bunch of Chesterfield youngsters.

I do not know the "whys" and "wherefores" of this erstwhile fated tour, and I do not wish to know. But one thing is certain, "Maybe Tours" in the future are no good, and I hope everybody who has cricket at heart, and particularly young cricketers, will give Dick Suttle their support.

When I look back, (some would say way, way back), to my own junior cricketing days in South Yorkshire, the only cricket tour that we went on was a twopenny tramride to Bramall Lane to watch Yorkshire. I can't even remember knowing if Barbados even existed, never mind planning to visit it. I do remember that Chesterfield was over 'The Border', and we looked on Derbyshire as a nice place to visit on charabanc mystery outings. Derbyshire also had a friendly cricket team that used to regularly supply Yorkshire with lots of championship points.

Well Barbados does exist and its a cricket haven, and Derbyshire is still a nice place, but they no longer "give" championship points to anyone. I believe that this is due more to the time and effort that is given to developing young Derbyshire players, rather than to the importation of overseas players.

One black spot on the cricket scene is that the schools are no longer taking interest in cricket. Whatever the reasons, be they the cost of ground upkeep, the unwillingness of teachers to give up their out-of-school hours, or the bloody-mindedness of some local authorities, we cricket lovers have got to actively encourage junior cricket at club level.

Chesterfield and District, I believe, is in the fore front of youth cricket. We have leagues, competitions, cups, coaching schemes and cricket tours. A lot has been done, but if Derbyshire is to be a force in County Cricket, (one championship win in 1936 only), then people like Dick Suttle, who do so much for youth cricket, must be helped and encouraged.

I hope the tour to Barbados is a huge success and merely a fore runner to many more.

I am sick to the back teeth of people who say things can't be done; Dick Suttle tries to prove they can. Well done! and thank you Dick on behalf of a lot of cricket lovers.

C. Baxter

Hello Lads,
I was thrilled for you all when I heard about the plans for your tour to Barbados in October this year.

Already, I have had the privilege to play cricket in many parts of the world and I give you my assurance that you are about to visit what is probably the most fascinating land in the game today.

Your support and help to those responsible must be unwavering and you will find yourselves embarked on the cricket holiday of a lifetime.

I wish every one of you the very best of luck.

Yours faithfully,
Derek Randall

Nemesis

"I want you to write a piece for the brochure" said Dick Suttle.

"I don't know what to write about" said I.

"Write about how you became involved with the Loundsley Green Youth Cricket Club" said Dick.

"O.K.," said I. So here goes ...

I was strolling along, minding my own business, harming no one, when all at once I heard a voice:

"Hey Fergie, just the man I want to see."

I looked around – very carefully, because I recognised the voice. Yes it was Richard Suttle. Feverishly I searched for cover, but no, there was no welcoming doorway through which I could dive. Squaring my shoulders I turned to meet my Nemesis.

And that is how I got roped in to help with the aforesaid Club. Before I knew what was happening I found myself agreeing to join the Committee, and to help with the fund-raising for the tour of Barbados which was already in an advanced state of organisation.

If you know Dick Suttle, then you will know just how persuasive he can be. I'm sure that he could sell ice-cream to Eskimos. But to be strictly honest, he didn't need to twist my arm very much. I was already aware of the difficulties that he had faced, trying to get a tour "off the ground" under the aegis of another organisation. And I was fully in sympathy with his ambition to get a tour actually "off the ground". So I was half-sold on the idea before he started on me.

By the time you read this you will, I hope, already have made a contribution to our funds – unless, of course, you have borrowed, or pinched this brochure from someone else (in which case, shame on you,

DERBYSHIRE COUNTY CRICKET CLUB

President : HIS GRACE THE DUKE OF DEVONSHIRE, P.C., M.C.
Chairman: R. A. Palfreyman.
Chief Executive: D. A. Harrison.

County Cricket Ground, Nottingham Road, Derby DE2 6DA   Tel.: Derby 44849

Our Ref: DAH/MJH/JMC

20th May, 1981

Mr. R. Suttle,
16 Pennine Way,
Loundsley Green,
Chesterfield,
Derbyshire.

Dear Richard,

We are very pleased to hear about your tour to Barbados and
we congratulate you on the organisation which has been
responsible for it.

Our best wishes are extended to all those due to depart and
we know that they can be fully relied upon to give you their
whole-hearted support both on and off the field of play.

It is our pleasure to wish you every success on this
cricketing adventure.

Yours sincerely,

Geoff Miller

Barry Wood

Bob Taylor

Derbyshire County Cricket Club and England

200

don't be so blooming mean, buy your own!). But you can do more. We need as much help as we can get to raise money for the tour. If you can't give time, or more money, maybe you are one of these bright, imaginative characters who can think of novel (but legal!) ways of parting people from their cash in support of such a good cause. If so, we need your ideas – at once if not sooner. The main stipulation is that they should cost little or (preferably) nothing to arrange. We don't want to spend money, only collect it. The more we raise, the easier it will be for the lads who have been selected to play on the tour.

So there you have it. Largely it is up to you. And remember, any back-sliders may find that I have set Richard on their trail. And I'd hate to do that, really I would.

Come to think of it, it would keep him off mine!! Seriously though, he's a great guy (Roll on Bonfire Night).

A. Ferguson

Cricket coaching at M.C.C. Lords

A group of 46 enthusiastic cricketers, some of whom will be touring Barbados in October 1981 from the Chesterfield and District Youth Cricket Council, will attend a special course at the M.C.C. Indoor School at Lords on 26th April under the supervision of their chairman, Mr. Harold Bradford and N.C.A. coach, Mr. Richard Suttle.

The main part of the course will include the analysis of faults and the development of strengths by chief coach Don Wilson (ex-Yorkshire and England player) and a practical net session, videoed for teaching purposes.

The party leaves Chesterfield Town Hall at 8.30am to arrive at Lords at approximately 12.30pm. Nets 2 - 4pm. Playback of video 4.15 - 6.15pm to arrive in Chesterfield about 10.30pm.

Loundsley Green Tourists Win Cliffhanger
at Saville Park, Pontefract

Scores:-		
	Loundsley Green Tourists	139 for 8 off 40 overs
	Pontetract Casuals	135 all out off 39.2 overs

In a keenly contested match at Saville Park, Pontefract Casuals, captained by John Nixon, entertained Loundsley Green Tourists at their picturesque ground in a return friendly fixture on Sunday, 23rd August, as the match ended in a dramatic finish.

Andrew Margereson, who led the touring side, won the toss on a perfect wicket, and elected to bat under a cloudless sky. The innings started disastrously as their four front line batsmen failed, but thanks to a chance-less and undefeated face-saving innings of 89 by Margereson, who struck 15 fours and was ably assisted by wicket-keeper batsman Steve Alldread with 14 and Michael Davis 19.

Bowling for Pontefract, D. Hill took 4 for 26 in 8 overs while Nixon, Underwood and Ransome took one each for 7.15 and 23 respectively.

In reply, Pontefract scored 135, thanks to an opening stand of 60 between Chris Hewison and David Leigh. Wickets began to fall as Ian Wells took four quick wickets backed up by spectacular catching, and, with one over left and six runs needed and one wicket standing, Roger Suttle had Hill caught by Sylvester off his second delivery for 5. Top scoring for Pontefract, David Leigh made 39, Chris Hewison 27, Andy Clough 15, John Nixon 11 and M. Bowler 10.

Bowling for Loundsley Green Tourists, Ian Wells took 4 for 36 in 8 overs, Roger Suttle 2 for 22 in 7·2 overs, Dick Suttle 2 for 22 in 8 overs and Richard Sylvester 1 for 30 in 9 overs to win by the narrow margin of 4 runs.

Loundsley Green Tourists beaten by Old Derbyshire XI by 101 runs at Walton Dam in a fund-raising match for Caribbean visit
By R. Suttle

Scores:-   Old Derbyshire XI   169 off 39·3 overs
                  L/Green Tourists   68 off 26 overs

On Sunday, 19th July, the Loundsley Green touring team to visit Barbados this year, was led by Andrew Margereson, who won the toss on a lively wicket at Walton Dam and sent in the Old Derbyshire XI, captained by Ian Buxton, to bat. They were all out for 169 off 39·3 overs, thanks to an agressive 55 from their guest player at No, 5, Ole Mortenson of Denmark. His innings included one six and five fours, while good supporting contributions came from Edwin Smith 36 not out, Barry Gittins 32, Dale 11 and Billy Oates 10.

Dick Suttle was the tourists most successful bowler, with 3 for 34 in 8 overs. Duncan Forrest 2 for 30 in 8 overs, while Mark Hutton, David Whitworth and Mark Graves took one each for 6, 17 and 46 respectively, backed up by good wicket-keeping by Steve Alldread. In reply, Loundsley Green Tourists were all out for 68 off 26 overs. Mark Hutton, who opened the innings, topscored with 17, while Dick Suttle scored 16 and Skipper Margereson 10.

Barry Gittins, who bowled the last over of the innings, performed the hat trick with the last three balls as he dismissed Stone, Graham and Forrest and ended with the incredible analysis of 1 over, 1 maiden, 0 runs and 3 wickets, while other wickets were taken by Edwin Smith 3 for 21, Derek Morgan 3 for 30 and Les Bradbury 1 for 4 to win the match by 101 runs. The match was sponsored by G.B. Sports and each player of the touring team received a gift voucher from H.H.B. Sugg. The funds raised were £30.

Raffle results: 1st: No. 72 (Green) Football
2nd: No. 56 (Green) Bottle of Wine
3rd: No.. 23 (Pink) Basket of Fruit

John Waghorn scores century for the Loundsley Green Tourists against S. & J. Kitchin
by Dick Suttle, at Loundsley Green)

Scores:- Loundsley Green Tourists 226 for 6 off 40 overs
S. & J. Kitchin 119 all out off 33·1 overs

Highlighting the day's play was a fine knock of 108 by John Waghorn for the Loundsley Green Tourists after opening the innings with his captain Mick Davison, who won the toss on a wicket with the occasional bounce on a sun-drenched Sunday afternoon, and after 40 overs the Tourists were 226 for 6.

Waghorn's century included seventeen fours. He was ably supported by Andrew Robinson with 58, Mick Davison 21 and Dick Suttle 14.

Bowling for S. &J. Kitchin, Farndon took 2 for 28, while Roper, Campbell. Pashley and Whitworth took one each for 9, 16, 18 and 19 respectively.

In reply. S. & J. Kitchin were all out for 119 after 33·1 overs. Mainly responsible for their total was a splendid and aggressive innings of 54 by Michael Pashley who struck two sixes and seven fours, while Phil Roper made a useful 14.

Dick Suttle took 3 for 11, Roger Suttle 2 for 7, Richard Sylvester 2 for 19, while Ian Suttle, John Charter and Andrew Robinson took one each for 2. 3 and 10 respectively to give the Tourists victory by 107 runs.

Notts Evening League v Loundsley Green Tourists
Final fixture before departure to Barbados on 16/10/84

6/9/81 by Dick Suttle (Walton Dam)

Scores: Notts Evening League: 188 for 6 off 40 overs
Loundsley Green Tourists: 143 all out off 40 overs

Loundsley Green Tourists, led by Michael Davison, entertained Notts. Evening League Team skippered by Andrew Pick at Walton Dam on Sunday. Davison won the toss on a lively wicket and sent in the visitors to bat, and, after their allotted 40 overs, Notts, had scored 188 for 6. Mainly responsible for this total was a splendid innings of 39 by R. Evans, followed by consistent contributions of 31 by R. Poole, 24 by M. Newell, 22 by K. Evans. 21 not out by D. Spencer, 15 not out by A. Pick and 14 by C Miller.

Bowling for the tourists, Andrew Robinson took 2 for 29, Paul Douglas 2 or 49 while David Banks and Duncan Forrest took one each for 20 and 35 respectively.

In reply, Loundsley Green were all out for 143. Topscoring was David

Banks, the young Worcester player who struck 68 which included three sixes and six fours, while John Waghorn and Mick Davison scored 28 and 10 respectively.

Bowling for Notts. K. Evans took 3 for 16. P. Such 2 for 47. while A. Pick, R. Evans. R. Rhodes and R. Poole took one each for 12, 13, 21, and 26 respectively, to win by 45 runs. as the tourists played their last match before departing to Barbados on October 16th, 1981.

From Chesterfield, Derbyshire to Bridgetown, Barbados, West Indies
by Dick Suttle

The Loundsley Green Tourists departed from Chesterfield Town Hall, Derbyshire to Bridgetown, Barbados, on 16th October, 1 981, on a chilly but dry October morning as a number of parents, relatives and cricket enthusiasts saw the departure of 11 young cricketers at five past seven by George Holmes coach to Heathrow Airport via Coullidge Airport. Antigua at 5.55 p.m. local time, and finally to the lovely Caribbean island of my native Barbados to sunnier climes under the supervision of Messrs. Graham Ottewell (Manager), Terry Graham (Assistant Manager), Richard Suttle (Club Coach and Tour organiser). Gary Collier (Baggageman) and Mrs Maureen Ottewell completing the quintet of officials.

Also accompanying the team were two young potential professionals from Worcestershire County Cricket Club in Damian D'Oliveira and David Banks who joined the party at Watford Service Station at 8.35 a.m. (G.M T.).

The touring team participated in 5 limited over matches against the following school teams which were as follows:- Harrison College, Foundation School, Combermere Secondary School and Colridge & Parry. Included in the tourists' team were:- M. Davison (Capt. L. D. Banks (V. Capt), D. D'Oliveira, A. Robinson, J. Waghorn. S. Alldread, I. Saich, D. Forrest, I. Suttle, A. Williams, M. Graves, P. Douglas, and R. Sylvester.

Results of all the matches are carefully recorded as they took place and are in the forthcoming chapters of this well edited book. Those unable to make the trip due to family commitments were Steve Palframan (Chairman) and the Club's (Secretary & Treasurer). The latter worked tremendously hard and helped to make this unique venture possible as we finally booked with Harlequin Travel Agents of West Street, Sheffield, Yorkshire.

Congratulations to the splendid effort and support given by some parents, relatives and friends to give the youngsters the chance of a lifetime as we arrived safely at twenty to seven at Grantley Adams Airport Barbados, West Indies, to end an enjoyable $8^1/2$ hour Transatlantic Flight We were met at the airport by Mrs. Joyce Noble (Manageress) of the Fairholme Hotel, and her assistant Mrs. Weekes, who accompanied us to our destination, where we stayed for the rest of the tour.

I must join with all the lads, who expressed their thanks to our hosts, including the former West Indian Test player and schoolmate Wesley Hall. his staff at Banks Breweries, the Games Masters of the aforementioned school teams who did their best to make us feel at home.

Finally, the kindness and hospitality shown to us bv Mr. Grannum (Manager) and his staff of the Fairholme Guest House in Christchurch during our short but enjoyable tour, which could so easily have been wrecked in the early stages by some very unpleasant and embarrassing circumstances, which almost decimated the original party chosen to visit the Caribbean island of Barbados.

With three years hindsight, and many sleepless nights as a result of the prevailing circumstances, what a great difference it has made to all the lads who were just fortunate to make the trip as the results and personal experiences are so wonderfully recorded for posterity, after completing some 9,000 miles across the Atlantic and safely back to Chesterfield.

Good luck lads, may God richly bless you and use your wealth of experience advantageously, in your quest for the future in your various fields of endeavour.

P.S. Many thanks to Steve Alldread who acted as our Statistician on the Tour for which every game and tour averages have been carefully recorded.

Loundsley Green Touring Team Barbados 1981

Standing L to R:- *J. Waghorn, M. Graves, T. Graham (Asst. Manager), M. Davison (Capt.), A. Robinson, D. Forrest, S. Alldread (Wkt/keeper & Statistician). G. Collier (Baggage Man).*
Squatting L to R:- *R. Suttle (Club Coach & Tour Organiser), I. Saich, I. Suttle, R. Sylvester, A. Williams & P. Douglas.*
Missing are:- *G. Ottewell (Manager), D. D'Oliveira, D. Banks & Mrs. Ottewell*

Fixtures for tour to Barbados 1981

20th October	Harrison College	v	Loundsley Green Y.C.C.
22nd October	Foundation Secondary	v	Loundsley Green Y.C.C.
26th October	Lodge School	v	Loundsley Green Y.C.C.
27th October	Combermere's Sec.	v	Loundsley Green Y.C.C.
29th October	Colridge & Parry	v	Loundsley Green Y.C.C.

Match Results & Scenery

(Match 1) 20th October v Harrison College
Harrison College won toss
LG. Tourists

1.	M. Davison*	l.b.w.	b. Wiltshire	4
2.	M. Graves	c. Alleyne	b. Bancroft	1
3.	D. Banks	c. Bancroft	b.Burke	19
4.	D. D'Oliveira	c. Bancroft	b. Burke	8
5.	J. Waghorne		b. Griffith	5

6.	A Robinson	c. Alteyne	b. Griffith	13
7.	S. Alldread	c. Bancroft	b. John	9
8.	I. Suttle	c. Bancroft	b. Griffith	0
9.	P. Douglas		b. Bynoe	0
10.	R. Sylvester		b. Bynoe	0
11.	D. Forrest	Not Out		8
			Extras	8

Byes 3, Leg Byes 3, Wides 2.

	TOTAL	75

All Out in 33 overs

Fall of Wickets, 2 8 19 38 54 56 56 56 56 75
Bowling
Wiltshire 7-1-15-1, Bancroft 7-39 1, Cozier 4 180,
Burke 5-1-15-2. Griffith 5-1-9-3, Bynoe 4 1 5-2. John 1071

Harrison College

1.	John	l.b.w.	b. Banks	2
2.	Atteyne	c. Suttle	b. D'Oliviera	22
3.	Bethell	c. Alldread	b. Banks	4
4.	Ellis		b. D'Oliviera	8
5.	Alleyne		Not Out	18
6.	Bancroft		b. D'Oliviera	5
7.	Wiltshire		c&b D'Oliviera	7
8.	Cozier	st. Alldread	b. D'Oliviera	0
9.	Bynoe		Not Out	6
			Extras	5

Byes 4, n.b 1

	Total	77

for 7 wickets

Fall of Wickets 3 7-30 38 43 62-62.
Bowling
Banks 7-1-23-2, Forrest 4 1 11 0.
D'Oliveira 7-1-20-5. Robinson 3.1-0 18 0.
Did not Bat Burke & Griffith
Harrison College Won by 3 Wkts

(Match 2)22nd October v Foundation School
L.G.Y.C.C. won toss
L.G. tourists

1	M. Davison*		b. Harris	13
2.	M. Graves	l.b.w.	b. King	5
3	D. Banks	c.Pickerin	b. Walker	7
4.	D. D'Oliveira		c&b Applewake	11
5.	J. Waghorne	l.b.w.	b. Applewake	2
6.	A. Robinson		c&b Applewake	4
7.	S. Alldread		c&b Matthews	12
8.	D. Forrest		b. King	32
9.	I. Suttle		b.King	3
10.	P. Douglas		Not Out	0
11.	I.Saich		b. King	0
	Byes 10, Leg Byes 6, Wides 1			17
			Total	108

Fall of Wicketsl 1-24-38-40-44-44-87-99-106-108
Bowling
King 7-1-2-1 7-4, Walker 7-0-1 9-1, Applewake 7-1-22-3,
Harris 7-2-11-1, Bourne 5-1-13-0, Matthews 5-2-9-1.
in 38.1 overs

Foundation School

1.	N. Pickerin	C. Douglas	b. D'ONveira	23
2	W. Carrington	c. Suttle	b. Banks	24
3.	P. Bourne	c. Suttle	b. Banks	0
4.	C. Applewake	c. Davison	b. D'Oliveira	3
5.	J. Harris	l.b.w.	b. Banks	0
6.	M. Matthews		Not Out	26
7.	A. Drakes	c. Graves	b. Banks	7
8.	P. Small		Not Out	21
	Byes 5			5
			Total	109

for 6 Wkts in 19·3 overs
Did not bat I. Smith, R. King & C. Walker
Fall of Wickets 36-36-53-54-66-81.
Bowling Banks 8-0-59-4, Forrest 2-0-9-0, D'0liveira,7.3-1-23-2
Robinson 2-0-13-0.
Foundation won by 4 wkts

(Match 3) 26th October v Lodge School
LG.Y.C.C. won toss
Lodge School

1.	E. Seale	c. Alldread	b. Banks	4
2.	K. Seale		c&b D'Oliveira	24
3.	M. Innis		b. Banks	1
4.	R. Holder	st. Alldread	b. Robinson	13
5.	T. Agard	c. Alldread	b. D'Oliveira	11
6.	R. Wiltshire		b. Robinson	21
7.	D. Headley	c. Alldread	b. Waghorne	0
8.	D. Springer	Run Out		3
9.	J. Squires	c. Banks	b. Forrest	0
10.	P. Cook	c. Graves	b. Forrest	3
11.	A. Collins		Not Out	1
No Balls 5				5
			Total	86

all out in 35·5 overs
Fall of wickets 15-19-45-46-76-79-79-83-85-86.
Bowling
Banks 6-0-16-2, Forrest 5.5-0-15-2, D'Oliveira 8-0-25-2
Waghorne 8-2-12-1, Robinson 8-2-13-2.

L.G. Tourists

1.	M. Davison	c. K. Seale	b. Collins	2
2.	M. Graves	l.b.w.	b. Holder	23
3.	D'Oliveira	c. Collins	b. Springer	9
5	D. Banks	c. E. Seale	b. Cook	2
6.	A. Robinson	c. Agard	b. Collins	25
7.	S. Alldread	l.b.w.	b Springer	0
8.	I. Suttle		Not Out	6
9.	D. Forrest		Not Out	5
Leg Byes 1, Wides 3				4
			Total	87

for 7 wkts off 32 overs
Did not bat:- Sylvester & Saich
Fall of wickets 9-24-44 47 73-73-78.
Bowling
Squires 8-3-14-1, Collins 7-1-21 2, Springer &-1-1 7-2,
Holder 8-2-11-1, Cook 4-0-17-1.
LG. Tourists won by 3 Wickets

(Match 4) 27th October v Combermere School
LG.Y.C.C. won toss
Combermere School

1.	P. Pitt	c. Davison	b. D'Oliveira	57
2.	M. Estwick	c. Alldread	b. D'Oliveira	13
3.	A. Harrison	c. Alldread	b. Waghorne	4
4.	S. Alleyne	c. Alldread	b. Waghorne	50
5.	M. Edghill	c. Robinson	b. Forrest	22
6.	J. Annel	Run Out		2
7.	H. Springer		Not Out	37
8.	R. Holder		Not Out	6
Byes 4. No balls 1 Leg Byes 4, Wides 1				10
			Total	201

for 6 wkts of 34.2 overs
Did not bat:- D. Allerley. C. Lynch, & I. Gill
Fall of wickets 40-54-92 141 166 174.
Bowling
Banks 6.2-1-43-0. Forrest 7-0-33-1, Waghorne 7 0 50 2,
D'Oliveira 7-0-36-2. Robinson 7-0-34-0.

L.G. Tourists

1.	M. Davison	l.b.w.	b. Springer	3
2.	M. Graves	c. Estwick	b. Lynch	90
3.	D'Oliveira	c. Holder	b. Alleyne	47
4.	J. Waghorne		b. Allerley	4
5.	D. Banks	c.Annel	b. Allerley	2
6.	A. Robinson	l.b.w.	b. Allerley	13
7.	S. Alldread	l.b.w.	b. Gill	2
8.	I. Suttle		b. Alleyne	0
9.	D. Forrest	c. Estwick	b. Lynch	7
10.	R. Sylvester		b. Pitt	0
11.	I. Saich		Not Out	0
Byes 7. wides 2,leg byes 2, no balls 4				15
			Total	183

all out in 33 overs
Fall of wickets 8-86-89-102-127-136-137-171 176-183.
Bowling
Lynch 7-1-39-2, Springer 6-1-35-1, Alleyne 7-0-36-2,
Allertey 7-1-25-3, Pitt 4-1-20-1. Gill 2-0-13-1.
Combermere won by 18 runs

(Match 5) 29th October v Coleridge & Parry
L.G.Y.C.C. won toss
Coleridge & Parry

1.	Holder	l.b.w.	b. Banks	8
2.	Lynch	l.b.w.	b. Banks	10
3.	Thompson		b. Banks	16
4.	Griffith	c. Waghorne	b. Banks	0
5.	Cumberbatch	c. Alldread	b. D'Oliveira	0
6.	Wallace		Not Out	135
7.	Gaskin		Run Out	16
8.	Royce		c&b D'Oliveira	7
9.	Jackman		b. D'Oliveira	5
10.	Babb		b. Graves	1
11.	Simmons		Run Out	3
	Byes 1, leg byes 8, wides 1			10
			Total	210

all out in 30·1 overs
Fall of wickets 14-30-30-37-58-107-160-182-183-210.
Bowling
Banks 7.1-1-18-4, Forrest 5-0-27-0. D'OlJveira 8-0 56 3,
Waghorne 4-0-29-0, Robinson 2-0-34-0, Graves 4 1 35-1.

LG. Tourists

1.	J. Waghorne		Run Out	0
2.	M. Graves		b. Babb	43
3.	D. D'Oliveira	c.Babb	b Wallace	10
4.	D. Banks	c. Gaskin	b. Babb	15
5.	M. Davison	l.b.w.	b. Cumberbatch	0
6.	A.Robinson	c. sub	b. Cumberbatch	1
7.	S. Alldread	c. Gaskin	b. Cumberbatch	0
8:	I. Suttle		Not Out	11
9.	D. Forrest		Run Out	5
10.	P. Douglas	c. Cumberbatch	b. Boyce	0
11.	A. Williams		b. Boyce	0
	Leg byes 5, wides 4, no balls 1			10
			Total	95

all out in 32 overs
Fall of wickets 0-18-69-71-72-72-83-87-95-95.
Bowling
Wallace 5-0-12-1, Babb 9-2-13-2, Jackman 4-0-24-0,
Cumberbatch 8-2-20-3, Boyce 4-2-9-2, Simmons 2-0-7-0.
Coleridge and Parry Won by 115 runs

Bowler Wes at Tour match

A Loundsley Green, Chesterfield youth cricket team on a two-week tour of Barbados had a special guest at their first match – former West Indies fast bowler Wes Hall.

The Tourists lost their first match against a local college side.They scored 75 and the college team responded with 77 for seven. In a message to *Chesterfield Star* from Barbados, tour organiser Richard Suttle, Loundsley Green club coach, said: "The boys are enjoying the tour tremendously."

The Tour averages

Steven Alldread our No. 1 wicket-keeper and team statistician, arrived safely home at 5.15 p.m. after a superb fortnight in the beautiful Caribbean island of Barbados, sometimes referred to as "Little England".

Batting

	Name	M	I	R	NO	HS	AV
1.	M. Graves	5	5	162	0	90	32·4
2.	D. Forrest	5	5	57	2	32	19·0
3.	D. D'Oliveira	5	5	85	0	47	17
4.	A. Robinson	5	5	56	0	25	11·2
5.	D. Banks	5	5	45	0	19	9·0
6.	I. Suttle	5	5	20	2	11*	6·7
7.	S. Alldread	5	5	23	0	12	4·6
8.	M. Davison	5	5	22	0	13	4·4
9.	J. Waghorne	5	5	20	0	9	4·0
10.	I. Saich	4	3	0	1	0	
-	R. Sylvester	3	2	0	0	0	
-	P. Douglas	2	2	0	1	0	
-	A. Williams	1	1	0	0	0	

Bowling

	Name	O	M	R	W	AV
1.	D. D'Oliveira	37·3	2	160	14	11·43
2.	D. Banks	34·3	3	159	12	13·25
3.	J. Waghorne	19	2	91	3	30·33
4.	D. Forrest	23·5	1	95	3	31·67
5.	M. Graves	4	1	35	1	35·00
6.	A. Robinson	22·1	2	112	2	56·00

Cricket in the sunshine

Playing cricket in Barbados was certainly a great experience for all of the team members; definitely one not to be missed.

Although our results were not outstanding, we had some very good and close games against teams which were really no better than we were.

The pitches over there are very different to the ones in England. Wickets were generally very hard and good, although some of us got out to 'freak' deliveries which were totally unexpected. Fielding was difficult on rough outfields, and, to add to our problems in the field, we had the very high temperature to cope with.

We didn't hit top form with the bat, with the exception of Mark Graves who was consistent throughout the Tour, although if fielding had been tighter, our batting would have been adequate to win us more matches. The game we did win was a good match and we were all pleased with the out-come. It was the only day when we bowled, batted and fielded well and played as a team as the weather reminded us, for once, of a real English summer's day.

Finally, on behalf of the team members, I would like to thank Richard Suttle and Graham Ottewell for all the good work they have done, both in Barbados and here in England, and all the other officials for the time and effort they have put in, to enable the Tour to take place.

By Mick Davison,
(Captain of the Loundsley Green Touring Team)

Cricket Lovely Cricket 1981
by Ian Suttle

Oh Island, in the sun,
    Provided us with lots of fun,
Friendly people for us to meet
    On the bus or in the street.

The food was great and really nice
    Including dishes of peas and rice.
Enjoyment swimming in the pool
    Accompanied with a beer so cool.

The Hotel staff looked after us well,
    As we enjoyed our daily spell
They helped us out in every way
    As all of us enjoyed our stay.

We really loved our holiday
And cricket games we had to play
We ended up the losing side
But played our games with National pride.

Farewell Barbados, "Island in the Sun",
May be, another tour is due to come
So to the future, lads, we look
A cricketing venture for this book.

Reality's initiation

As a cricket tour manager, to be put down as having very little experience would possibly be paying me a compliment.

Having said that, everybody has to start somewhere and it became apparent very early on that morning of the 16th October 1981 that destiny had chosen this period of my life to enlighten me to modern technology and the ways of the world more in 24 hours than I had previously gained in 10 years.

To illustrate what I mean I shall endeavour to tell you the experience of coming in to contact with and exploring my first airplane and flight, a Boeing 747.

Well if you are going to start, start big and they don't come any bigger than a jumbo 747.

My first recollection of how big these iron birds of the sky were, came as I wandered along endless corridors in Heathrow with the other members of our party and suddenly found ourselves in what I thought was a large reception area. This reception area turned out to be the main body of the 747. At this moment of realisation was when my first myth of boarding aircraft exploded.

I had always assumed that to board an airplane you trundled along the tarmac of the runway and climbed aboard, up a flight of portable stairs. Maybe I watch too many old films.

The next traumatic experience for me came as we prepared for take off and started to taxi to lift off to speed down the runway.

Previously I had welcomed the chance to sit on the side gangway behind the emergency door and look through the windows. Now I wasn't so sure that what I was seeing was what I wanted to see.

As I looked along the wing to the huge jet slung underneath, it looked anything but safe to me.

The engine was bouncing as if it didn't belong to the plane at all and I was convinced that it was going to fall off before, or even worse just after take off.

Needless to say it didn't, but I took a stiff brandy and an explanation by an experienced air traveller (I think that he had flown round the Blackpool

Tower on a day trip once), to convince me with the explanation that the engines needed to be flexible, because if they were rigid they wouldn't absorb vibration and would fracture and eventually fall off.

My next brush with reality as opposed to fiction came approximately 3 hours and 5 brandies later by which time I was feeling a lot more relaxed and composed enough to want to know more about the technicalities of this huge machine.

Having enjoyed a splendid lunch of steak, croquettes and 3 vegetables, when the stewardess came to remove the tray I had the effrontery and enough brandies inside me to ask if it was possible to visit the flight deck, cabin, cockpit, (I wasn't sure what it was called). To see where all the action took place.

She smiled at me much to the displeasure of my better half who was sitting beside me and said "It is rather irregular sir but I will make enquiries to see what I can do."

Twenty minutes later she returned and said, "The captain welcomes you on your maiden journey sir and would be only too pleased to entertain you on the flight deck in ten minutes time."

Ten minutes later I got up from my seat and started to follow the stewardesses direction to the flight deck.

The first thing that I noticed as I meandered my way in the direction indicated was that I had entered the first class area. I knew immediately it was the first class area by the amount of lobster shells and empty chablis bottles that were around.

I proceeded further to a rather steep set of stairs which I had been told to climb and remember thinking "Ah the flight deck must be up in the loft."

I climbed the stairs to a small landing, knocked and entered the captain's flight deck.

I could not believe what I saw, the blood drained from my face and the previous brandies went straight through to my bladder. What I saw bore no resemblance to what I had imagined. There in that cabin were three very smart uniformed personnel, sat in chairs with their feet up reading books, not even looking in the direction we were travelling. I was astounded and speechless, but the captain endeavoured to put my mind at ease and reassured me that this was a perfectly normal matter of fact procedure.

He then went on to explain the various functions of the instruments and the technicalities of flying the iron bird. He told me he was flying at 550 m.p.h. at 35,000 feet and that the temperature outside at the present time was -55° C.

That was another thing I found hard to believe because we were flying above any clouds and the sun was burning down from above, yet it was -55° C!

The captain was very patient and endeavoured to explain the reason why this was so whilst I listened intently.

During the next forty five minutes I tried to absorb all this information and come to terms with reality as it really was in modern day and as I walked back to my seat after having thanked the captain and his crew for their hospitality and bubbling over with information and enthusiasm to tell the others, I couldn't help thinking of an old saying I once heard somewhere. "What a difference a day makes."

Graham Ottewell
Tour Manager

My dream tour to Barbados – island in the sun

I first met Mr. Suttle, the cricket coach, in the middle of the 1979 cricket season at Queen's Park, Chesterfield. I was waiting behind, after the match with a few of my friends for the players' autographs when he asked us if we would like to play for his Chesterfield team, Loundsley Green Youth Cricket Club. I was the only one to take up his offer and this involved me in going up to Chesterfield every Monday evening for practice. Mr. Suttle told me that the team had toured Scotland in 1978 and were hoping to tour Barbados, his birthplace, in 1981. My dream began!

Winter passed and the 1980 cricket season began. More practice and I was in the team. That season there was a series of mini-tests at Lounsley Green and I played in all six matches and became a seasoned British Rail traveller to Chesterfield at the ripe young age of ten!

That Autumn boys and their parents were invited to a film show about Barbados, and a representative of the Barbados Travel Association came to talk to us. We were told that a tour brochure would be published with a lucky number raffle draw, raffle-tickets and sponsorship sheets were to be printed for the next season. Our job was to work hard and raise as much money as we could in the next few months.

Throughout the 1981 season, special events and matches were held for fund-raising purposes. At the end of September, we were still short of the target, so in the last fortnight, an all-out effort was made. We finally made it, five days before our visit to Paradise Island was due to commence!

We left Chesterfield at 7a.m., on the 16th of October, in a temperature of 30° farenheit, and after an $8^1/_2$ hour flight in a jumbo-jet, we arrived at Grantley Adams Airport, Barbados in a temperature of 30° centigrade. After arriving at our hotel, which was run by two English ladies, we unpacked and made straight for the coral-water swimming pool. So my fortnight's dream began ...

In the Caribbean, dawn is at 3a.m. and sunset is at 6p.m. so each day began at 6a.m. for us with a dip in the pool and a game of beach cricket before breakfast. We had breakfast at 8a.m. and a glorious day lay ahead for us. Our first proper practice session was at 4p.m. (end of their school time). On the first Monday at Harrison College, where we were to play the next day. Although we lost that match, it gave us great enjoyment. We found the light much brighter and the heat much greater than we had ever experienced before. On Wednesday, we practiced at our next venue, Foundation School, where we were to play the next day. This practice was more of a game situation being run by Worcestershire Second XI players David Banks and Basil D'Oliveira's son, Damian. We lost again but it was very tense. Friday, Saturday and Sunday were free to spend as we wished – sunbathing, swimming and playing beach cricket.

On Monday we chalked-up our first victory of the tour, beating Lodge School overwhelmingly. On Tuesday, we were playing at Mr. Suttle's old school, Combermere. We lost in another tight match, although Mark Graves scored a brilliant 90.

Wednesday was the most enjoyable day of my life. We went on a sea-cruise on the 'Jolly Roger', along the calm west coast of the Island. It was a four-hour cruise, with a steak dinner and drinks (rum-punch) included in the price. We were about one hundred yards from the shore with an hour break for dinner and a swim in the forty-feet waters. Even at this depth, it was possible to see the sea-bed as the water was so clear. During the cruise it was possible to have a half-hour water-ski or a ride on a catamaran – my friend, Richard, the Manager, Mr. Ottewell and I had already had the thrill of a sail on a catamaran.

On Thursday we played our last match at Colridge and Parry School. We lost again, mainly due to Henderson Wallace, of Colridge and Parry, scoring an unbeaten 135.

Friday was our last day. with an afternoon at the Banks' Brewery with free drinks, after a tour of the works. I had left my bags packed at the hotel, ready for our midnight flight home.

On the playing point of view, we didn't do well, but the tour was a success.

By Alan Williams
(11 years-old, from Littleover, Derby)

Trans-Atlantic Flight to & from Barbados
By Paul Douglas

A British Airways Boemg 747, a magnificent aircraft, took us over 9,000 miles to Barbados and back safely.

Before the $8^1/2$ hour flight, I thought it would be tedious and boring, but I couldn't have been more wrong.

Thanks to the British Airways crew for their kindness and hospitality as time passed amazingly quickly.

There were films to watch and lots of entertainment from multi-channelled radio as we crossed the Atlantic.

The food was delicious. Our first stop was at Coullidge Airport Antigua, West Indies, on our outward journey, but on our return, we flew from Grantley Adams Airport, Barbados non-stop to Heathrow.

We disembarked at 12.40 p.m. as everyone appeared very excited as we concluded a most memorable and enjoyable tour of the Caribbean island of Barbados as a delighted number of parents and relatives came to welcome us on our homeward journey to Chesterfield, Derbyshire.

Thank You
By Andy Robinson

On behalf of myself and all the players who have just returned from the tour of Barbados with the Loundsley Green Youth Cricket Club, I would like to thank all the Sponsors and anyone who helped in any way in making the tour a success.

I would also like to thank our Manager Graham Otterwell who kept all our spirits high. Last but not least that man Dick Suttle, what a guy. He worked miracles for this unique project even when there was little hope of the tour continuing. He battled away and most of all he won triumphantly.

An Experience to be Remembered
By Mark Graves

From playing in the local West Riding League for Carlton Towers C.C. I suddenly found myself 4,500 miles away walking out in the Barbados sunshine to open the innings, looking back I can still hardly believe it.

From the results, our performances look quite poor; but apart from the last game when we came up against Henderson Wallace (135 not out and the quickest bowler I have ever faced) the games were quite tight and I think we were a little unlucky to win just the one game. Perhaps cutting down on our social activities the night before, may have had some positive effect; but what's good enough for the English cricket touring side was certainly good enough for us.

On a personal note, batting on Barbados wickets was a pleasure and fielding in the outfield, a nightmare, but with the help of Richard, Dave Banks and Damien. I think my game improved on tour, although I never expected to do quite so well as I did.

Finally, I would just like to thank Richard Suttle, who without his enthusiasm and dedication the tour would not have been possible.

What We Thought of the Tour
By Steve Alldread and Duncan Forrest

The tour in all its capacity, proved to be extremely experienced, memorable and highly enjoyable.

The results of the matches were not vitally important as four of the games were very close.

A high spot of the tour on the social side was the 'Jolly Roger' fun cruise. Finally, the players and the officials enjoyed immensely the hospitality shown by the Bajan public. The team spirit on and off the field was essential in making the tour a great success.

Welcome to one of the finest small breweries in the world

At 2.00 p.m. Wes arrived at the hotel to transport us to 'Banks' Brewery', of which he was Managing Director.

Reflections of our recent Caribbean Tour
By Terry Graham (Assistant Manager)

The tour party, from Loundsley Green that almost everybody said would not leave the country, arrived back from a most enterprising tour of fifteen days from the wonderful island of Barbados.

Although the tourists only won one game, the finishes to most of the games were very tight. One has the feeling that if our lads had more time to acclimatise, we probably would have reversed the results.

The people in Barbados were most helpful and very kind to us. Special mention must be made of the former West Indian pace bowler, Wes Hall, who helped us tremendously, nothing being too much trouble for him.

All the party had a most enjoyable and memorable time. Many thanks must be made to several people, as the club's secretary & treasurer and Steve Palframan did much work behind the scenes in promoting the tour. Graham Ottewell and his wife Maureen for keeping a guiding hand on the party and last but by no means least Dick Suttle whose constant persistance made the whole project possible through the co-operation of all the parents involved in so great a venture which a few weeks before departure seemed destined to failure.

Youngsters at Cricket Festival

Pictured are (left to right) back: *A. Dyson (Old Glossop), C. Hodgetts (Alvaston, Derby), C. Marples (Clay Cross). I. Waring (Chesterfield), A. Chalmers, (Dronfield), C. P. Marples (Chesterfield).*
Front: *A. Brown (Langley, Mill), D. Coates (Glossop), Paul Meakins (Derby), P. Bedford,(Chesterfield. capt.), A. Pierrepoint (Chesterfield), D. Hopkinson (Chesterfield).*

Our picture shows former England Test captain, Ted Dexter, giving some last minute advice to members of the Derbyshire Under-19 county team just before they played in the Commercial Union Oxford and Cambridge Festivals.

The CU Festivals of Cricket, which are now in their third year, provide a welcome opportunity to teams of young cricketers from 24 counties. Not only do they have a week of highly competitive cricket on the excellent grounds of the Universities – but some 250 players are accommodated at the various colleges where the living is good and has enabled the CU Festivals to develop a style and an atmosphere of their own.

Derbyshire Times 3/9/82

A.G.D. Cricket Club 1983

At the time of writing there are still several weeks of the season to go but even now we can reflect on a relatively successful and certainly enjoyable season for the club overall.

The second XI in particular has had a good season, easily its most successful for several years if not since the start of the club and is currently poised to win Division 3 of the Chesterfield League. The high spot of the season came against Dronfield Woodhouse when we rattled up a league record score of 283 for 3 with Neil Collings scoring 131 and Geoff Wells 111 no, again, a league and club record partnership of 268.

Other good batting performances this season have come from Mark Hutton, Neil Brown and Robert Wells who all have 50's to their credit. The most notable bowling performances have come from Neil Collings, 8-23 v.

Chesterfield, Phil Baker, 6-42 v. Ashover, and the veteran Norman Graham 6-45 v. S. & J. Kitchin. It is particularly encouraging for the future of the club that the second team contains so much obvious talent as this, and should ensure a strong club in the future. It is also nice to see so many FAD lads in the side and credit for this must go to Garry James and Darrell Roberts for their highly effective recruitment policy.

The first XI has had a rather leaner time and is trying to stave off relegation to Division 1E of the Bassetlaw League. Hopefully, by the time you receive this, we will have succeeded. There have been many close games but all too often we have been on the wrong end of the result. There have, though, been some successes; Paul Foster's 131 against Dinnington, which, in partnership with Nick Houghton (89 not out) allowed us to pass the Dinnington score of 238 for the loss of only two wickets, was a particularly fine effort. It comes to something when a partnership of 232 isn't a club record!

Foster and Houghton have been the most successful batsmen this season but newcomer, Dean Andrew, has made a number of valuable contributions and Dick Suttle continues to defy the years (as do some others in the side).

The bowling has not had the penetration of recent years but, to be fair, has not been all that well supported by the catching which has cost us results on several occasions. The best performances have come from Ian Drayner, 5-36 v. Marshalls, 6-58 v. Ashover, and Pete Williams, 7-94, in a marathon 23 over spell against Dinnington.

The club now has a lot of potential and it is to be hoped that we can build on this season to develop two string sides. Talking of the future, the club is again organising a stag night at The George in Alfreton, on 28th October, and anyone who is interested in attending this rather up-market event can obtain further details from Phil Ward.

MOTIVATING THE UNEMPLOYED

Howzat! Centre members run up £56

Robotics and body popping, the new dancing craze is finding a lot of fans among young unemployed who meet at Chesterfield's centre for the unemployed at the Goldwell Rooms.

Up to 20 young people take to the floor on Tuesday afternoons to demonstrate their skill and agility at the new dance, which can involve aerobatics and has a competitive edge to it.

"All we do is offer the facilities for people to come here and do robotics. It's very physical, they form a circle and pass a move from one to another," explained centre supervisor Doug Herring.

The centre is opened weekdays, providing sports facilities and advice to anyone interested, mostly the unemployed.

A creche is available for young mums to leave their children while they take part.

Mcanwhile, a group of nine cricketers from the centre took part in a sponsored indoor cricket competition at Sharley Park Leisure Centre and raised £56 for funds.

Below at bat is John Johnson getting some tips from National Cricket Coach Richard Suttle during a session at the Unemployed Centre while other members look on.

Batting on a jobs wicket

Three unemployed men have been bowled over by a chance to escape the dole queue.

Their talents were spotted as they whiled away their time playing cricket at Chesterfield unemployed centre.

Now Tim Wildman, 24, Paul Nixon, 2 5, and Peter Tromans, 35, hope they may find a future as professional cricket coaches after being picked for a National Cricket Association award course.

"I have been trying to get a job for two years now but each time I go for an interview I am told, I have been out of work for too long," said Mr

Tromans, a former paint-sprayer, of Tapton View Road, Chesterfield.

The trio turned to the game for something to do. All hope something may come of the opportunity and to boost them the centre is to pay half the £16 cost of the 12-week course.

"If they are good enough it may get them jobs. We hope so," said centre organiser Doug Herring. They were noticed by coach Richard Suttle, who alerted Derbyshire County Cricket Club coaches John Brown and Les Bradbury, who will supervise the course at Lady Manners School, Bakewell.

D. Suttle (N.C.A. Coach) with P. Tromans, D. Duroe, T. Wildman, B. Allen,
P. Nixon, who successfully passed their N.C.A. award.
Missing from the photograph are D. Booth and A. Platts.

Thank Your Lucky Stars

The above title could not be more appropriate as I have personally experienced the realities of such a saying which I will try to relate to the best of my ability as it occurred just over 20 years ago; but lives vividly in my memory.

With hindsight, I still ask myself a number of questions. For example, was I dreaming when the incident happened, or can I just thank my lucky stars to be at the right place at the right time. It all happened one cold and frosty January morning while helplessly standing beside the telephone in the Goldwell Rooms (Centre for the Unemployed) which was used by them for leisure and recreational activities.

I can vividly recollect picking up the receiver to phone someone about helping me to provide transport for three unemployed lads whom I had coached and recommended to the Derbyshire County Cricket Club to enrol for a twelve-week National Cricket Association Award course at Lady Manners School, Bakewell, due to start in three days. For some unknown reason I replaced the receiver without phoning anyone as a series of names clouded my thoughts as I stood mesmerised because many promises were made by so-called friends; but were all unfulfilled and time was no longer on my side. A silent prayer might have been said as I stood there in utter helplessness, amidst the encircling doom and gloom of unemployment. Seconds passed, then miraculously the phone rang. I picked up the receiver and said "Goldwell Rooms". The immediate reply came "Hello Dick! Just the man I want to see. It's Brian." "Who?" "Brian Allen." "Hello Brian, what can I do for you?" But before I could say another word he began to describe a sports report which he had seen in the *Morning Telegraph* of the 6th January, 1984. This was very aptly described by him as he mentioned a photograph of me instructing the lads from the Unemployed Centre to enrol for the above-mentioned course in three days. His conversation obviously led to enquiries about the course and his eligibility to enrol.

I informed him to get in touch with the organisers of the course at Bakewell immediately and to ring back as soon as possible and let me know if he was accepted.

Within three minutes the phone rang, it was Brian with the good news he would be accepted and best of all he would be able to use his car to take us to and from Chesterfield for the course, thus miraculously solving my problem which a few seconds ago seemed insurmountable and virtually non-existent.

As a result, all the lads completed the twelve-week course as well as successfully passing it and are now all employed in various fields of endeavour including posts as cricket coaches.

Just a year later, an added bonus came for Brian. He received a letter informing him that his exam results were very highly graded, thus enabling him to qualify for his Senior Cricket Award Course which he has just completed. If successful, he will be able to coach the talented players at County level, thus giving him the opportunity to take the highest award in coaching which is an N.C.A. Advanced Award which places him in the position for International Honours. In short, the coincidence has changed our lives, hence we can thank our lucky stars to be at the right place at the right time on that cold and frosty January morning in 1984.

9/1/84

Sponsored Indoor Cricket
by Tim Wildman (Team Captain)

Under the expert eye of Richard Suttle, N.C.A. Coach, cricket has gone from strength to strength at the Centre for the Unemployed. Indoor cricket sessions have been held throughout the winter at Sharley Park Leisure Centre, Clay Cross, from 12.30 -1.30 every Wednesday. Dick Suttle has not only helped with the obvious development of cricketing skills amongst the team, but also organised a number of fund-raising activities for the Centre. The following is a brief rundown of some of the most notable highlights and future events:-

November 30th – Sponsored Indoor Cricket Competition

After training for two months, nine centre cricketers took part in a sponsored competition to raise money for the Centre. The competition raised £56, with 335 runs being scored for the loss of 5 wickets.

January 11th – Sponsored 6-a-side indoor Cricket Match

This was a great success with over £200 being raised. For cricket enthusiasts, the 'B' team won the match by 3 wickets scoring 72 for 2 in reply to the 'A' team's 69 for 5.

March 24th – Centre 6-a-side team versus Ladies International team

This match will again be held at Sharley Park and will be followed by a presentation by Ian Buxton of Intersports.

The most notable achievement of the team so far has been the acceptance of four of its members on a twelve week National Coaching Association Coaches Award Course at Lady Manners School, Bakewell. The four players involved, Tim Wildman, Paul Nixon, Peter Tromans and Brian Allen are presently attending the course and its successful completion will certainly enchance their opportunities of finding work.

£202.50 raised in 3 weeks from 6-a-side match 11.1.84.

Looking to the future
by Richard Suttle (N.C.A. Coach)

It is with great pleasure that I take this opportunity to wish Tim Wildman, Paul Nixon, and Peter Tromans every success in their approach to the twelve-week National Coaching Association Coaches Award Course at Lady Manners School, Bakewell supervised by N.C.A. Advanced coaches Messrs. John Brown and Les Bradbury of Derbyshire County Cricket Club.

On the day of enrolment, Mr Geoff Wells (N.C.A. Coach) came to the

Goldwell Rooms and gave a brief outline of the course to the lads for which, on their behalf, I would like to thank him for his time and effort as well as all the firms and individuals who so generously sponsored and donated to our first ever Indoor Six-a-Side Competition which took place at Sharley Park Leisure Centre, Clay Cross on Wednesday 11 th January and as a result, we raised the welcome sum of £202.50, which will be used to help our activities at the centre and quite an effort will be made to organise other events in the future from other groups.

Finally, thanks for the co-operation and combined efforts of Gordon Smith, Dougie Herring, Marian Brooks and Margaret Randall as well as the splendid help from the media.

Last, but by no means least, the lads and lasses who have played their part in making the Chesterfield Centre for the Unemployed a pleasant and worthwhile organisation.

President's team defeat West Yorkshire of A.C.C.
by 14 runs at Lilleshall, Shropshire
By Dick Suttle
Scores: President's Team:- 108 for 3 off 10 overs
West Yorkshire Team:- 94 all out off 10 overs

On Sunday 19th February, the Annual Six-a-side Indoor Cricket Fixture got underway at Lilleshall National Sports Centre at 8 a.m., as Ralph

Group of N.C.A. coaches at their Annual Conference Course at Lilleshall, Shropshire, on 19/2/84. Taken by Keith Andrew N.C.A. Director of coaching.

Middlebrook (N.C.A. Staff Coach) and captain of the West Yorkshire Team, won the toss and sent in the President's team, astutely led by Mike Bore of Notts. C.C.C.

At the end of their alloted 10 overs, the President's team scored 108 for 3. Chiefly responsible for this total, were undefeated innings of 26 by Mike Speak (of Lancaster University), 25 by Richard Suttle (N.C.A. Coach of Chesterfield Centre of the Unemployed), 20 by Mike Bore (Notts) and 16 by Graham Gayton, before being bowled by Ramish.

Ramish was West Yorkshire's only successful bowler. He took 1 for 16 in his 2 overs of cleverly flighted medium to fast away swing bowling.

In reply, West Yorkshire scored 94 all out, as skipper Middlebrook made a great effort to try to win the match, as he topscored with a splendid 47, before being run out off the last ball of the match, while other useful contributions came from all-rounder Ramish with 22 and Hepworth with an undefeated 10.

Bowling for the opposition, Mike Speak took 1 for 6 in 2 overs as no fewer than three batsmen were run-out, including the confident looking Ray Collins, as the match ended in a victory for the President's team by 14 runs.

Ladies International lost by 8 wickets
By Dick Suttle
Scores:- Ladies (Int.) 60 for 5 off 15 overs.
Goldwell C.C. 67 for none off 11 overs.

With the advent of the 1984 cricket season upon us, and the desire to form a new indoor cricket league in the autumn, a ladies international team, led by Wendy Watson from Ambergate, played against a Goldwell C.C. ably led by Tim Wildman, (for the Chesterfield Centre for the Unemployed) on Saturday 24th March 1984 at Sharley Park Leisure Centre. The match ball was sponsored by Nazir Latif, manager of Spire Sports.

Play started soon after 7p.m. as Wildman won the toss and requested the ladies to take first knock.

After 15 overs, the ladies were 60 for 5, of which Enid Bakewell scored a splendid 26 and won the trophy, donated by Starr Promotions while Wendy Watson who opened the innings, was brillianty caught by Wildman off Brian Allen for 11 at mid off.

Bowling for Goldwell C.C., Brian Allen took 2 for 6 with his slow left arm spinners while Ian Suttle and Tim Wildman took one each for 5 and 10 respectively as Paul Nixon excelled in the field but wicket keeper Tromans sustained a broken finger,

In reply, Goldwell C.C. scored 67 without loss off 11 overs as Brian Allen and Peter Tromans were both undefeated with 43 and 20 respectively to win convincingly.

After the match, Ian Buxton, manager of Intersports, was introduced by Dick Suttle to make the presentation to the individual winners who included, Enid Bakewell for the Highest Individual Score for the ladies while Brian Allen for consistent batting performances and Tim Wildman for the best allrounder.

Umpires:- Messrs. Ron Lovegrove & Alf Gaunt.

Scorer:- Roger Suttle.

Results of 7 overs per side match Goldwell C.C. 67 for 2 Geoff Wells 41 (retired) Tim Wildman 13 not out.

Ladies International 68 without loss Kim Robertson 31 not out Val Twittey 17 not out.

Enid Bakewell receives the trophy

Tim Wildman receives the trophy from Ian Buxton

Suttle saves Goldwell with 52
Goldwell C.C. 164
Wilmslow C.C. 137

Goldwell were sent in to bat at the Rectory Field, Wilmslow in Cheshire and totalled 164 thanks mainly to Ian Suttle, batting number 6, who made 52 not out including a six and three fours. His father Dick made 26, Ian Saich 26, Paul Yeomans 17 and Andy Robinson 14.

Four Goldwell batsmen were run out. When the home side batted they were soon in trouble and were all out 137 despite a fine 38 from Toby Newson, who earlier took 4-37.

229

Tim Wildman took 3-7, Andy Robinson 2-13, Roger Suttle 2-18, Andy Evans 2-23 and Dick Suttle 1-27.

Foreword by Rt. Hon. Tony Benn M.P. for Chesterfield

This cricket book is the record of a highly successful cricket tour by Chesterfield youngsters to Barbados in the autumn of 1981.

But it is more than that, for it also records the committment to cricket of the organiser of the tour, and the author of the book – Dick Suttle.

Dick was born in Barbados in 1928 and he began playing cricket over forty years ago in 1942, and has been coaching since he was 18 years-old.

He carried his passion for cricket with him when he came to Britain in 1960 and always found time to play it here.

His work has taken him to many places in the United Kingdom and abroad but he is best known in Chesterfield as coach for the Youth Cricket Council and through his leadership in the Chesterfield Cricket Lovers.

It was his determination to raise the money, through sponsored swims and cricket matches, that he was able to find the £6,500 necessary to take 13 boys and 5 officials out to Barbados for two weeks in October 1981 where they played five matches, made many friendships and gave pleasure to all those who were to take part.

Dick's efforts, so well chronicled in this book, will be an encouragement to all those who believe that anything is possible if you have the energy and imagination to try, and an example of how sport can bring people of different lands together in friendship.

Tony Benn
April 15 1984

Norman bowls out ten ...

Cricketer Norman Graham was promoted from his club's second team into the first team on Saturday – and responded with the best bowling performance of his life, taking all ten wickets.

It was the first day of the new season, but soccer calls meant that A.G.D. could not find enough players for two teams.

So Norman, vice-captain of A.G.D. 2nd XI, took his place opening the 1st XI attack in their Bassetlaw League 1D match at Pilsley.

He had the opening batsman dropped at mid on by Dick Suttle...but went on to achieve the rare feat of all ten wickets with the sensational figures of 9·5 overs, 1 maiden, 10 for 34.

Norman, 31, was for 14 years groundsman at Queen's Park, responsible for preparing wickets for Derbyshire, and in 1979 won a coveted national groundsman's award. He moved to Essex in 1981 as groundsman, but is now back in Chesterfield.

He said: "My previous best performance was 8 for 13, for the second team in the North Derbyshire League. But the Bassetlaw is a higher standard."

His bowling dismissed Pilsley for 75 and A.G.D. scored 79·2 to win by eight wickets.

On Sunday, Norman was involved in another match with an amazing personal achievment.

A.G.D. 2nd XI, who won promotion from Division 3 of the North Derbyshire League last season, were up against Ridgeway and ten of their 11 batsmen failed to reach double figures.

The other man made up for it, though as Brian Woolley scored 132 out of Ridgeway's total of 162 all out

Norman managed only two wickets and then A.G.D. were dismissed for 107 to lose by 55 runs.

Chesterfield Gazette 4/5/84

Goldwell C.C. defeat Wilmslow C.C. by 27 runs
By Dick Suttle
Scores:- Goldwell C.C. 164 all out off 35 overs
Wilmslow 137 all out off 33·2 overs

On Sunday 20 May, Andrew Warner, captain of Wilmslow C.C. entertained Goldwell C.C. (Chesterfield Centre for the Unemployed), skippered by Tim Wildman at the Rectory Field, Wilmslow, Cheshire. The match ball was sponsored by Allen Blood & Co, Insurance Consultants of Saltergate, Chesterfield.

Skipper Warner won the toss and sent in the visitors to bat on an easy paced wicket, with the skies heavily overcast and after 35 overs, Goldwell were all out for 164,of which the bespectacled Ian Suttle at No. 6, topscored with an aggressive and undefeated 52, which included one six and three fours, while Dick Suttle scored 26, Ian Saich 26, Paul Yeomans 1 7, and Andy Robinson 14.

Wilmslow's most impressive bowler, was Toby Newson who took 4 for 37 n 8 overs, while Ken Manuel took 1 for 24. No fewer than four Goldwell batsmen were run out, as the Wilmslow fleet footed fielders kept the pressure on their apponents.

With 165 runs required for victory off 40 overs, the home team made a gallant effort, but failed by 27 runs, as they were all out for 137 off 33·2 overs, due to some very splendid fielding and accurate bowling by the opposition.

Allrounder, Toby Newson at No. 7, batted splendidly to topscore with 38, which included one six and six fours before being brilliantly caught by Ian Suttle at deep mid-on off Wildman's bowling. Useful contributions also came from Tim Gilchrist 18, Bill Oliver 16, Brian Vaughn 16 and Neil Thorpe 15.

Bowling for Goldwell C.C. medium pacer. Tim Wildman took 3 for 7 in 4 overs, Andy Robinson 2 for 13 in 6.2 overs, Roger Suttle 2 for 18 in 7 overs, Andy Evans 2 for 23 in 4 overs and Dick Suttle 1 for 27 in 6 overs, to give Goldwell victory by 27 runs to end an enjoyable match in gathering gloom, accompanied by persistent drizzle.

Dougie Booth N.C.A. Cricket Coach

My situation over the last few months has made it much easier to understand Dick Suttle's philosophy upon life and cricket.

Along with many other employees, I suffered the ignominy of redundancy in September 1983 at one of Sheffield's oldest and most respected companies as a result of a takeover and decimation by one of this country's busiest multinational organisations.

Like many others, I thought I understood what it was to be redundant and unemployed. This I learned, was one of the fallacies of our time. People who have not experienced it, cannot possibly comprehend the destruction it causes to the family unit. If they did understand, then redundancy and unemployment would not exist.

It was against this background that I started to attend the Chesterfield Centre for the Unemployed. One of the characters I began to take notice of, was Dick Suttle. He invariably carried a cricket bag and wore a cricket sweater that directed my attention towards him, but I soon realised that I had met a man with a burning enthusiasm towards organising the cricket side of the activities at the Centre.

I approached Dick and asked if it was in order for me to join in the cricket coaching session at the Clay Cross Leisure Centre and the reply to which I have since become accustomed. "Yes Man" was given.

I found it easy to talk to Dick, because we both had many years of playing experience and we both loved the game and therefore a bond of friendship and understanding was formed.

One week later, Dick said that he was taking some of the Unemployed lads over to Bakewell on Wednesday evenings to take their coaching awards and would I be interested in joining them.

I had no hesitation in accepting, and over the next few weeks a strong bond of friendship grew among the lads. We talked about cricket coaching in depth and discussed it in order to help one another for the forthcoming examinations. As the course went on, the lads main topic of conversation was on various methods of coaching techniques.

The examinations arrived and the worry and tension was very noticeable on the lad's faces. In the end, the fears were unfounded, because all seven lads submitted for the examinations through the Chesterfield Centre for the Unemployed, passed their coaching examinations and have gained employment.

Dick, in one of his earlier books, refers to "having the ability to overcome failure," I think the results of the coaching course at Bakewell Lady Manners School achieved just that. A group of lads brought together firstly, by the result of being unemployed, and secondly, through the caring attitude of Dick, which welded together as a unit, showing great comradeship and achieving their goal.

Junior cricket in the Chesterfield area, owes much of its success to Dick Suttle. He puts so much care and effort into arranging events for other people. The one good thing that came out of my adversity, was the meeting of a man of the calibre and integrity of Dick Suttle, and it gives me great pleasure to contribute in some small way to his book.

HITTING UNEMPLOYMENT FOR SIX... CRICKET STAR WITH A HEART
By Geoffrey Newson

The man who wants to convince the unemployed that there is a future for them in Britain is using an unusual method … cricket.

Pushing 60 now, Dick Suttle, who used to bat with Garry Sobers and once nursed dreams of Test cricket, has just completed his most successful season.

He has organised a league of indoor cricket played by lads whose only qualifications was that they were on the dole.

Promise

During the season several of the youngsters were found jobs and seven of them passed courses as N.C.A. cricket coaches.

Loundsley Green in Chesterfield, is a long way from Barbados.

It's a council estate which Dick Suttle joined in Chesterfield with his family after his personal dream of winning a place in the West Indies Test team faded.

Immediately he saw the patch of grass between the houses as a bowl of promises for kids on the estate. He organised coaching sessions, even mini Test matches against other estates.

Now he has taken on his biggest test. Motivating the unemployed youth of his adopted home town.

Through cricket

And so successful has his cricket-on-the-dole become, with bosses of local firms being encouraged to both sponsor and employ the players that Dick Suttle hopes to start up a national league this winter.

Already he has hosted a test in which a Scottish youth team took on the Chesterfield youngsters.

"So far interest has been shown in Cheshire, Shropshire and Yorkshire," said Dick Suttle, "If we can get a national league for the unemployed off the ground it could be a great shot in the arm for the out-of-work.

"Working with the Centre for the Unemployed throughout the country and the leisure centres we could bring sport and hope to many youngsters.

"We are not a job centre" says manager Doug Herring. "But we try to stimulate people through our activities, and potential employers, too, to find work and workers.

"We owe a lot to Dick Suttle and his "Jobs through cricket" scheme. He's a marvellous motivator of youngsters and bosses."

Recently Dick Suttle has taken his unemployed lads to coaching at Lord's and Lilleshall. He doesn't pretend that producing national coaches or even useful cricketers is a global solution to unemployment.

"It's a contribution" he claims modestly. "And cricket's good because it requires discipline and even though it's a team game the performance of the individual is vital.

"Most of all it's a way of showing unemployed lads that someone takes an interest in them.

So many youngsters are written off these days before they have a chance to prove themselves and its very easy for them to become lay-a-bouts.

Sincere

One of his lads, Tim Wildman, was out of work for 18 months. Now he's a national cricket coach and has a job at a printing works.

"Before I met Dick Suttle I didn't know which way my life was going," he said. "He's certainly made a big difference to the attitudes of the local youth."

It may all sound like another variation of job agency, but Dick Suttle, a sincere, unselfish man in his community, believes strongly in his new dream

We have already found that employers are more willing to take an interest in youngsters who are organising themselves in something positive than those standing on street corners," he said.

"What I'm trying to say to these youngsters is that there is always a part for them to play as long as they have the will.

"But, like the best batsmen, they need patience. They can't expect to win every time. Back in Barbados I thought I might get into the West Indian Test side.

"But they had three other useful batsmen at the time... Walcott, Weekes and Worrell."

Daily Express 24/5/84

Wilmslow C.C. defeat Loundsley Green C.C. by 56 runs
Scores:- Wilmslow C.C. 144 off 31·2 overs
Loundsley Green C.C. 88 off 32 overs
By Dick Suttle

On Sunday 8th July, Loundsley Green C.C. travelled to Wilmslow, Cheshire, under the leadership of Paul Yeomans and lost by 56 runs.

Andrew Warner who led the home team, won the toss and decided to bat at 2.45pm, under a cloudless sky, with ideal conditions prevailing on a wicket with variable bounce, but after 31·2 overs, Wilmslow were all out for 144.

Giles Newson at No 4, topscored with a splendid 43, but was unfortunate to be struck on the head from a short pitched ball from Ian Wells. Other useful scores came from J. Kelly 27, A. Vaughan 25 and B. Vaughan 11.

Bowling for Loundsley Green, off spinner Dick Suttle took 4 for 46 in 8 overs. Roger Suttle 3 for 17 in 8 overs, Ian Wells 2 for 24 in 7·2 overs and Andy Evans 1 for 12 in 3 overs. In reply, Loundsley Green were all out for 88 in 32.2 overs. Allrounder, Dick Suttle, topscored with a workmanlike 32, and was ably assisted by Ian Wells with 21 in an invaluable fifth wicket partnership, which yielded 41 runs. while skipper Yeomans, who opened the innings scored 19.

Main destroyer of the innings, was paceman Andrew Vaughan with a sensational spell of bowling as he took 4 for 4 in 3 overs, B. Burns 3 for 14 in 3 overs while J. Kelly and I. White, took 1 each for 2 and 22 respectively to give Wilmslow a convincing victory by 56 runs.

Langwith defeat Loundsley Green by 9 wickets
By Dick Suttle
Scores:- Loundsley Green 62 off 28·2 overs
Langwith 63 for 1 off 11·3 overs

As the glorious spell of fine weather continued, Langwith captain Mark Waketon won the toss on Thursday 26 July, and requested the visitors, led by Roger Suttle to bat on an easy paced wicket. Play started at 2.25pm. under a cloudless sky and after 28·2 overs Loundsley Green were all out for 62 runs.

James Carley and Stephen Dunks each scored 11 runs as none of the other batsmen reached double figures.

The Langwith bowlers gave nothing away and as a result, they ended with splendid bowling analyses, as Darren Stacey took 3 for 5 in 6 overs. Mark Binfield 3 for 7 in 6 overs. Adrian Bailey 2 for 9 in 5 overs while David Downes and Kevin Hales took one each for 9 and 18 respectively.

Wayne Levick and Kevin Hales who opened the batting for Langwith wasted no time in achieving victory for their team as the former was undefeated with 26 while his partner was bowled by James Carley for 20 leaving David Downes 5 not out as the home team scored 63 for 1 off 11·3 overs to win convincingly Carley who bowled 5·3 overs took the only wicket to fall at the cost of 26 runs.

Wilmslow C.C. Defeat Goldwell C.C. in return match by 4 wickets
By Dick Suttle
Scores:- Goldwell C.C. 81 off 31 overs
Wilmslow C.C. 82 for 6 off 30 overs

On a sundrenched afternoon, Sunday 19th August, Wilmslow C.C. of Cheshire, travelled to Chesterfield to meet Goldwell C.C. (Chesterfield Centre for the Unemployed) at Tube Works Ground in a return fixture, which the visitors won by four wickets. The match ball was sponsored by Allen Blood & Co Insurance Consultants of Chesterfield.

The Cheshire team, ably led by Andrew Warner, won the toss and sent in Goldwell C.C. captained by Peter Tromans to bat, as play started at 2.15 p.m. under a cloudless sky. After 31 overs, the home team were all out for 81 runs due to some very accurate bowling and brilliant fielding by the opposition. Dick Suttle at No.3 led the way with 22 while Tim Wildman at No.4 scored 20 and Roger Suttle undefeated with 9. Spearheading the Wilmslow's attack was Mike Partington who took 3 for 5 in 5 overs, Giles Newson 2 for 4 in 1 over, while Stan Sexton, Simon Gilchrist, Bill Oliver and Toby Newson took one each for 6, 8, 15 and 24 respectively.

In reply, Wilmslow scored 82 for 6 off 30 overs as most batsmen found runs difficult to get Andrew Vaughan who opened the innings scored 21. while other contributions came from Partington 14, Saxton 12 not out. T. Gilchrist 12 and T. Newson 10 not out. Bowling for Goldwell C.C. Dick Suttle took 2 for 17 in 8 overs. Paul Yeomans 2 for 18 in 8 overs, and Brian Allen 2 for 19 in 6 overs as Wilmslow won by four wickets, after losing their first match to Goldwell by 27 runs in May.

After the match both teams travelled to the Aquarius where they were well entertained by local artists to end a most enjoyable day's activity.

Chesterfield captain Ken Aspinall won the toss and elected to bat in their first visit to Duckmanton Lodge.

After some tight bowling from Gary James and Norman Graham. Chesterfield found runs hard to get. Opening bat M. Coleman struggled for 37 overs to score 28, P. Whitworth contributed a quick 29 and N. Bradbury made a useful 12 and looked like boosting the scoring rate until he fell to a superb catch by Brian Hawkesworth.

At 81 for 3 Chesterfield must have expected a late rally with six overs to go, but A.G.D.'s captain Graham produced a spell of six wickets for one run in 12 balls, including three wickets in four balls to kill off Chesterfield's hope.

James bowled well for 19 overs, made the initial breakthrough, and finished with 1 for 57, but deserved belter.

Graham took 8 for 26 and Andy Horton took the final wicket for one run in four balls

Wicketkeeper Mark Hutton took a superb catch in a good display of fielding from the A.G.D. side.

Metcalfe soon made the breakthrough, dismissing opener Hawkesworth in the second over, but this brought Dick Suttle to the wicket and he soon started to attack in the usual West Indian style.

Hutton was out five overs later, bringing in Pete Tromans to the wicket to join Suttle and both men settled in to carve out a match-winning partnership of 42.

Suttle ended up four short of his 50 and Tromans contributed a useful 12.

Dave Hewitt (10 not out) and A. Horton (4 not out), saw A.G.D. to victory with five wickets and 11 overs to spare.

M. Coleman bowled well for seven overs to take two for nine, A. Chance (1 for 2), Metcaffe, (1 for 10) and N. Johnson (1 for 31) were the other wicket-takers.

"A" Team the Loundsley Green 1984 Champions
lose presentation match by 94 runs
By Dick Suttle
Scores:- "B & C" Team combined XI 156 off 32·2 overs
"A" Team 62 off 11·4 overs

On Friday 31 August, the Presentation Match commenced at 2p.m. in glorious sunshine as the "Unbeaten Champions", led by Robert Wells, met their first defeat, as they lost by 94 runs to the Combined XI chosen from from the B & C teams of the Triangular Tournament, with the inclusion of Geoff Wells and Dick Suttle (N.C.A. Coaches) on either side.

Lee Beddingham, who skippered the Combined XI, won the toss on a perfect wicket, took first knock and after 32·2 overs they were all out for 156. Steven Dunks topscored with 49, Dick Suttle 45, Jane Goldstraw 18 and Lee Beddingham 10. Bowling for the "A" team. Graham Lomas took 3 for 18 in 7·2 overs, while Spalding, Geoff Wells, Robert Wells and Edwards took one each for 2, 18, 21 and 29 respectively.

In reply, the "A" team were all out for 62 in 11·4 overs. Robert Edwards topscored with 26, which included five fours, and skipper Wells 21, with two sixes and two fours.

Bowling for the Combined XI, off-spinner, Dick Suttle took 3 for 0 in 2 overs. Sean Hoole 3 for 29 in 3.4 overs and Steven Cropper 1 for 12 in 2 overs, to give their team victory by 94 runs.

After the match, Mr. Michael Beddingham (Chairman) of the Club thanked all the parents, lads and lasses who helped to make the tournament a success, under the supervision of Dick Suttle and members of the Committee. He then presented the trophies to Robert Wells, captain of the "A" team and Champions of the tournament with 16 points in 4 games, and Roger Suttle captain of the "B" team Runners-Up with 8 points, and each member of the winning team received a medal. Individual awards went to:- Robert Wells (Best Batting Avr.) Roger Suttle (Best Bowling Avr.) John Payne (Most outstanding Wkt Keeper) Robert Wells (Highest Individual Score 102 n.o.) Steven Dunks (Most Imp. Jnr. All rounder) Lee Beddingham (Most promising Wkt Keeper) Jane Goldstraw & Robert Tann (Special Awards) Messrs. Beddingham & Joynes (Gifts for Services to the Club) & Dick Suttle (Services to Cricket Award) from the lads of the Loundsley Green Cricket Club.

Finally, Mr. Beddingham presented the autographed bat, signed by the 1984 England & West Indies players to 12 year old Lee Buckley of Totley C.C. who won it at the Clubs Grand Summer Draw on Friday 24 August, when Kim Barnett, Derbyshire (Captain) drew No. 4821 at Queen's Park during the Derbyshire v Yorkshire Match. Amount of money raised £350.00

Statistics of the Triangular Tournament were:-

240·2 overs 52 maidens 936 runs 78 wickets to round off an enjoyable and successful summer's activity.

Loundsley Green B Team 170 for 7
Loundsley Green A Team 171 for 8

Loundsley Green A team led by Lee Beddingham, won the toss and sent in the B team, skippered by his father Michael Beddingham to bat.

Play started with the skies heavily overcast, as the B team batted on a placid wicket and at the end of their allotted 40 overs, they were 170 tor 7.

N.C.A. coach Peter Tromans, who opened the innings, topscored with a fine innings of 74, which included seven fours and was well assisted wtth 20 from Stan Goldstraw, his partner, while Dick Suttle scored a useful 31 and wicket-keeper batsman Ian Saich 29.

Bowling for the A team, veteran Bill Hoole took five for 19 in five overs, with well-flighted deliveries and John Littleton one for 27 in eight overs.

In reply, the A team scored 171 for eight off 37·2 overs. Thanks to a chanceless, face-saving innings of 52 by 16-year-old Roger Suttle, ably assisted with an undefeated 28 by Robert Tann and also some useful contributions from John Littleton 26, Ian Longmate 14 and Bill Hoole ten.

Bowling for the B team, Stephen Dunks took two for 21 in five overs, George Burnley two for 27 in seven overs, Tromans, Sean Hoole and Michael Beddingham took one each for 11, 13 and 24 respectively to give the A team victory by two wickets and their third win over the B team this season.

The L.G.C.C. presents a film show of Barbados on Wednesday, August 22 by Redfern Travel, Guide Hall, St. Margaret's Drive, 7.30 p.m.

A new indoor cricket league
By Dick Suttle
A.G.D. Emerged Champions of the North Derbyshire Indoor Cricket League
14th & Final Round

A.G.D. emerged champions of the first ever North Derbyshire Indoor Cricket League, which concluded at Sharley Park Leisure Centre, Clay Cross on Sunday 17th March with an aggregate of 46 points, but lost to Spital by 5 runs off the last ball of the competition, which was sponsored by Starr Promotions & Spire Sports of Chesterfield.

Results and final positions are as follows: for 17/3/85 Round 14

Team	Matches				
	P	W	L	Ab	Points
1. A.G.D.	14	10	1	3	46
2. Bolsover "A"	14	9	2	3	42
3. Bolsover "B"	14	9	2	3	42
4. Robinsons	14	5	6	3	26
5. Spital	14	5	6	3	26
5. Sharley Park I.C.C.	14	3	8	3	18
7. Cutthorpe	14	3	8	3	16
3. S. & J. Kitchin	14	0	11	3	6

The Star, Tuesday September 11, 1984
Readers' Letters

I would like to express my sincere thanks and gratitude to all the doctors, nurses and staff at the Royal Hospital, Calow, Chesterfield, for the splendid work which they perform daily.

After being struck accidentally with a cricket ball on the head while coaching at Loundsley Green, on Wednesday, August 29, I was admitted and kept in for observation until Friday, August 31, when I was discharged.

During this brief period, I realised how well equipped and dedicated the above mentioned staff have been to all the patients on the Basil Ward, where I stayed.

Finally, I would like to thank them for all their wonderful and unstinting service to us and I am sure they deserve a greater monetary reward for their dedicated service to the community.

Mr. R. Suttle (N.C.A. cricket coach). Pennine Way, Loundsley Green, Chesterfield.

Dick Suttle, displays the inscribed plaque presented by Lee Beddingham (Secretary of the L.G.C.) donated by the junior members of the club for his "Services to cricket" just five hours after being discharged from Chesterfield Royal Hospital Calow

Loundsley Green Junior Cricket Team at Tube Works Ground 9/9/84
Front row L to R:- *R. Suttle (V. Capt), M. Evans, S. Hoole (Capt), L. Holland, C. Davison, J. Procter & D. Suttle (Club-Coach).* Back row L to R:- *K. Dunks, J. Goldstraw, S. Goldstraw, S. Cropper, J. Carley S. Dunks, D. McGwyre, M. Beddingham (Chairman)*

240

Old Whittington Cricket Club
1953 – 1984
A Jotted History

Founded in 1953 by three optimistic people the following is a brief statement of an unbelievable happening.

Totally inexperienced these (3) members set about their task, but soon there were only two, one became Chairman and the other Secretary/Treasurer. A brief encounter with a tiny field with a spirit level, laid a wicket where one nearly went into the river and on the other side was a wooden fence.

A first match with borrowed equipment, 5 old pence each, a first victory aided by a Polish member, only laid the foundations of this, today's outstanding Chesterfield District Club.

A chance vacancy led to the granting of a wicket on a Public Park (Brearley Park), progress to Chesterfield League, Derbyshire League, Derbyshire Alliance, Bassetlaw League, North Derbyshire League, Chesterfield & District Youth League, North Derbyshire Youth League during this period A.W. Wilkins served on every Committee either as Secretary, Treasurer, Chairman or Committee member.

They progressed to possibly the Club's Golden Years as winners, the 1st XI won everything in sight, in the Derbyshire Alliance League, the foundation of the Under 21 XI and 2nd XI was now proving a remarkable support, an early application to the Bassetlaw League failed but several years later this was accepted and today the Club's 1st and 2nd XI's play Bassetlaw League Cricket a 3rd XI play in the North Derbyshire League. Our 14 and 16 year's XI in the North Derbyshire Junior League. The Club have its own pavilion valued around £40,000 with more projects in the pipeline.

An ambitious Club and loyalty of several Senior members have justified the work and dedication it has needed, they have proved there is no such word as "Impossible" I can speak with honesty and courage I have been with the lot all through!

A. W. Wilkins, Sec/Treasurer

Poetical Motivation
By Richard Suttle

The Treasures Of Darkness

Out of darkness, we bring to light,
Our Christian embers with delight,
But in these days of human plight,
Jesus is our guiding light.

In the darkness, we behold,
Those wondrous promises once foretold,
In wintry weather, amidst the cold,
A chance to reconcile the fold.

Out of darkness come silver and gold,
From depths beneath the terrain mould,
So let our vision. World wide be,
Embracing all Hu-man-ity.

While on this marvellous U-ni-verse,
There's need for scriptures verse by verse,
So we must thank Him for His grace,
Which guides the whole fraternal race.

NB. Sermon by Rev. Alan D. Ogle of the Loundsley Green Methodist Church, at Cross Street Baptist Church on Sunday 23rd November 1980. Text was taken from 2nd Corinthians chapter 4 (vs 6-18)

My book of poems is entitled *AWAKENED FROM THE DREADFUL GRIPS OF SLUMBER* and include such poems as:- My Initial Awakening, 2. My Greatest Desire, 3. Awaiting the End, 4. Depthless Love, 5. Life's Inevitable Crossroads, 6. A Thoughtful Prayer, 7. Life's Stages, 8. The Movement of Time, 9. Looking into Space, 10. Everlasting Assurance, 11. Cured by Faith, 12. The Misuse of Material Values, 13. Starting Again, 14. Farewell to You, 15. An Acrostic entitled "Christmas".

A group of 1985 N.C.A. award course students at Lady Manners School, Bakewell, under the supervision of Les Bradbury, N.C.A. advanced coach and assistant Dick Suttle from (9/1/85 – 27/3/85). Devon Malcolm is 3rd from left, back row

Cricket maiden bowling 'em over

Eighteen-year-old Jane Goldstraw of Matlock has become one of only a few girls to be awarded the National Cricket Association Coaching Award.

Jane, of Carlton Avenue, Darley Dale, is a keen supporter of Derbyshire Cricket Club, and she started playing the game herself last year when she met coach Dick Suttle.

Jane, of Lady Manners School, Bakewell, said: "I always used to mess about playing cricket with my dad, but I took it up seriously when I met Dick and he coached me for the exam."

Coach Dick Suttle said: "There is no reason why more girls should not take up this sport."

Lesson of the school that makes a profit
By Geoffrey Newson

In the Intermitional Year of Youth, headmaster Jim King is hoping to point a new way forward for Britain's schools.

Like many schools throughout Britain Chesterfield's Manor School, is organising special events for "Youth Year" to promote better understanding between the world's teenagers.

Manor is a remarkable council school with an equally remarkable head. For last year King made a profit, of £3.500 and ploughed it back into school funds.

"I see myself not only as a headmaster," he said. " but also as manager of a £1 million community asset.

"In these times of cost cutting I see nothing wrong with a head going into business."

Mr. King, who is 49, feels it is a year when the education system in Britain is at the crossroads.

"With today's pressures on school spending we will all have to decide which way we are going to go," he says.

With the backing of Derbyshire Education Authority, he chose his way when he transformed the Manor into a community school.

He opened his doors, between 8 a.m. and 10 p.m., including weekends and most holidays, and invited Chesterfield people to come in and share the school's facilities at a modest cost.

Worst day

Community groups use the gym, the computers, the videos, and join in music, poetry, camera, and art projects.

243

The school library is becoming accepted as the local community library, and his "pupils" range from 11-year-olds to grandparents in their eighties.

"As a headmaster, the worst day for me was always the last day of the summer term when the leavers ran out of school and said, "'Thank God that's over.'" he said.

"What we are trying to do now is create a school which nobody leaves for good. They are encouraged to keep coming back because it's their community centre.

"I have 600 schoolchildren officially, but even after they reach 16 I have a thriving sixth form. Many are working, but keep coming back to be part of the school."

A key part of Jim's new school deal is his two "Outreach Workers," an ex-teacher and a youth worker who go out and encourage people to "start up things" using the school as a base.

So far they have come up with ideas for school use ranging from coffee groups for the elderly, a newsletter for the blind to a regular "parents and teenagers" discussion group filmed on video.

"With massive assets like schools and money tight we can no longer afford to lock these places at nights and during the holidays," he says. "It is time school authorities entered into self-help.

"Apart from the money made, which can go back into books and facilities we have found that we also save on school vandalism. One reason is there is usually a lot of people around, the other is that the community regards it as its own."

As a contribution to the spirit of International Youth Year, the school has been organising fun runs and events to raise cash to send a party of cricketers to tour Barbados this autumn.

"As a spin-off we have six teams totalling 120 boys, who have been able to meet people like Sir Gary Sobers, employ a first-class national coach in Dick Suttle and provide material to study West Indian life in our community classes."

Big changes

"Our education laws simply require that each child shall receive classroom education for four and a half hours a day, but with the goodwill of both teachers and pupils those hours could be made flexible.

"Big changes will have to come in education. Already in America there is a strong 'de-schooling movement' into alternative schools, like street-corner classrooms and ordinary houses where those who can't cope with mainstream education can go.

"Myself, I prefer the community system, where school is part of our lives

244

from cradle to grave and the public share and pay for it.

"And if that means headmasters like myself having to become business-men to pay for it that can only be for the general good."

Daily Express Monday June 10, 1985

Lads club together for coach!

Young cricketers in Chesterfield clubbed together to say a special thank-you to their long-serving coach, Dick Suttle. (See colour photos page 4.)

The 48 members of the Loundsley Green Junior and Youth Cricket Club all chipped in to buy a special trophy for Mr. Suttle, in recognition of 17 years' service to their association.

The surprise award took place at the end of an evening of presentations to the boys, who have just completed a "mini test" series.

The guest of honour was Chesterfield footballer, Ernie Moss, who was standing in for his business partner, Derbyshire cricketer Geoff Miller.

Dick is pictured on colour page 3 with awards presented by the young cricketers.

Derbyshire Times 31/8/85

The Touring Party

The managers

Mr. Ralph Ironside	Ralph is Chairman of Chesterfield C.C., Vice Chairman of Manor Cricket Club. An ex-Wicket-keeper Batsman, a member of M.C.C. and a good bloke. He knows the game and demands high standards.
Mr. Richard Suttle	Manor C.C. Coach for the past two years. Received the 1974 'Service to Cricket' award in Chesterfield, gained an N.C.A. award in 1975 and gained an Advanced award in 1978. Dick has coached professionally in Holland and Scotland. His book *Caribbean Mission Accomplished* tells vividly of his previous tour to Barbados in 1981 with Loundsley Green C.C. He still plays as an exciting all rounder.
Mr. Brian Allen	Brian is Captain of Cutthorpe Cricket Club. He is a hard-hitting batsman, slow left arm bowler, young enough to keep pace with the touring players (?) and Youth Leader with Derbyshire County Council.
Mr. Paul Tonge	An ex-Manor School student. Paul is a freelance photographer who will try to capture the highlights, atmosphere and ethos of the tour.

LOUNDSLEY GREEN JUNIOR AND YOUTH CRICKET CLUB

Secretary: Lee Beddingham
31 Pennine Way·Loundsley Green
Chesterfield · Derbyshire S40 4ND
Tel: Chesterfield (0246) 74534

DEDICATION TO C.R.W. SUTTLE

There is just one more presentation to make. This particular presentation is on behalf of the Loundsley Green Cricket Club, to a certain gentleman we all know.

This certain gentleman has worked consistently hard over the past years to benefit the youngsters of Chesterfield and numerous other areas, such as Scotland and Holland, where his boundless enthusiasm has benefited many young cricketers.

Included in his many achievements are the tours to Scotland and Holland, he is soon to take his second touring party to Barbados.

It is the totally selfless devotion of this man that has enabled so many of us to enjoy so much cricket over the years.

So, for his dedication, devotion and services to the game of cricket, and the youngsters he has coached over the years, I would like to present him with this small token of our appreciation and say quite simply Dick Suttle thank you very much.

I hope this is just the beginning of many awards you so richly deserve.

The inscription reads "Presented to C.R.W. Suttle, N.C.A. Coach, for his devotion, dedication and services to the game of cricket"

Dick Suttle, thank you very much.

SEPTEMBER 1985   BY I. SAICH, I. SUTTLE & R. SUTTLE

The Players

Tim Kirk – Tour Captain
Tim Hollinshead – Tour Vice-Captain

David Shannon	Roger Suttle	Simon Wall
Chris Mitchell	Mark Pearson	John Payne
David Spolding	Anthony Holmes	David Ward
Tim Medcraft	Graham Lomas	Richard Ironside
Sean Hoole	David Gray	Neil Bradbury
Robert Edwards	Lee Marriott	Andrew Bamford
Andrew Crofts	Andrew Creasey	Paul Pollard

Spectators

Mr. and Mrs. Lack (Mr. Lack is bringing his Umpire's coat)
Mr. and Mrs. Crofts
Darren Crofts
Mr. Dave Clarke
Mr. and Mrs. Marriott
Wayne Marriott (a good cricketer in an emergency)
Mr. and Mrs. Oliver Wright

Useful addresses and telephone numbers

Rockley Resort and Beach Club: P.O. Box 35W, Worthing, Christ Church,
Barbados
Barbados Board of Tourism: Harbour Road, P.O. Box 242, Bridgtown
809-427-2623/4.
Home Link: Mr. Jim King, Headteacher, Manor School, Old Road,
Chesterfield 73083
15 Wrenpark Road, Wingerworth, Chesterfield. 32798.

Acknowledgements

Chesterfield Borough Council	The Spa, Wingerworth
The Chatsworth Estate	Pinxton Transport
The Governors of Manor School	Alan Bonsall, Chesterfield CC
The Manor School Parent-Staff Ass.	Chesterfield Cricket Club
The Manor Community Fund	Rick Boxer, Chesterfield Cricket Club
The Manor Youth Club	Caledonian Mining Co.
John Lamb (Chesterfield) Ltd.	Spire Sports
Peter Blake (Chatsworth Road) Ltd.	Geoff Newsom, Wilmslow Cricket Club
Mr C's Restaurant	Moss and Miller Sports
Spire Graphics	Chesterfield School
Brampton Print and Design	Cresskin Motors

The Aquarius
The Britannia
The Peacock
The Star
Dale (Mansfield) Ltd.
Tomlinson and White Ltd.
GlapweB Parish Council
The Bradbury Club
Derbyshire Schools Journeys Ass.
Leesons Trophies
The Chesterfield Advertiser
Cutthorpe Cricket Club
North East Derbyshire Cricket League
The Bassetlaw and District League
Saxtons
The AGD Cricket Section
Mr. W. Halliwell, Harlequin Holidays
Mrs. J. Chambers, Redfem Travel Group
Yorkshire Bank
Baskills
TNT Transport
Dennis Skinner MP
Tony Benn MP
Mr. F. A. Cookson (Builders), Notts.

Parents, Staff, Pupils & Friends of Manor
School
Chris and Joanne Ironside
Frank Hill
Chesterfield Duplicating Services
Staleys of Glapwell, Motor Dealers
Massarellas
Ernest Brocklehurst
Ma Cherie
Bolsover District Council
Dr Ryan
N.E. Derbyshire Health Authority
Senior Citizens Group (Manor School)
Chambers Cycles
Macdougall Rose (Paints)
Sharley Park Leisure Centre
Howarths Leather
Bowlers Shoe Repair
Mr. T. Wilmott
The Liu Family

At the time of going to print, help is
still being given. Our thanks to all.

Barbados has suffered from hurricanes in the past. In the 18th and 19th centuries the most severe ones occurred in 1781, 1831 and 1898.

The Manor School
Old Road
Chesterfield

Tel: Chesterfield 0246 73083

I am delighted to wish good luck to all members of the Chesterfield Manor School Cricket Club Barbados Tour 1985. This brochure gives a flavour of the hard work and organisations which has been necessary to achieve our goal. I would like to thank all those involved for their generosity, confidence and time.

Barbados is a paradise for the Cricket lover. The local enthusiasm for the game is unsurpassed anywhere in the world. The pitches are hard and fast and the climate is warm and friendly like the Bajans themselves. The island has produced so many fine cricketers and we were privileged to meet Sir Garfield Sobers while preparing for the tour.

It is a great opportunity for our young cricketers to broaden their experience. For our Cricket Club to make the tour is prestigious. I know the players, staff and spectators will carry the best cricketing traditions with them and play this fine game in a keen, sporting and spirited way.

Jim King
President of Manor Cricket Club, Headteacher, Manor School

A Foreword from Geoff Miller, Youth Leader, Parent & Friend of Manor School
Cricket in the Caribbean has been led by Barbados for quite a long time. Two great sights not to be missed are Sunday cricket on the beach and the Softball competitions. The opposition will want to 'Hit de ball, man' and bowl the ball quickly so you would be wise not to under-estimate any Barbadian side. The brightness of the light will surprise you and you will need to adjust to the conditions. I advise you to practise hard when you get out there.

Geoff Miller
Derbyshire and England

The grounds are a lot less green than our own and your opponents will insist on hitting your best balls for six. Barbados is a breeding ground for cricketers of genius. In the middle of a sweltering afternoon, you may have sore feet and be wondering how to combat the West Indians' spectacular play. Just as suddenly they can play with an indifference which can put you in with a chance. They are often bored by half measures and that is part of their cricketing charm. They play the game their way, just as we do ours, and over the years it evens itself out. It will be a different game out there but it would be just as easy for a West Indian to be non-plussed by a wet English summer until he learns the ropes.

So don't despair and keep bowling to a line and length. Get in line when you're batting. Have a marvellous time on a beautiful island with lovely, laughing people, blue waters, waving canefields, exotic birds and unforgettable sunsets. Make the best of the chance of a lifetime.

Thanks to Manor Cricket Club for their help with my Benefit Year – 1985 will be a year for all of us to remember.

Cricketing Thoughts

'I have frequently been asked if I was born a cricketer. 1 do not think so, because I believe that cricketers are made by coaching and practice, and that nerve, eyesight, physique and patience, although necessary, would not be much use alone.'

W. G. Grace

249

"It's a thinking game is cricket If tha' doesn't use thi' brains, tha' might as well give up."   Wilfred Rhodes

"I don't think these Bajans are really fast, do you?"

Famous Barbadians include … The 3 W's – Frank Worrell, Everton Weekes, Clyde Walcott; Wes Hall, Charlie Griffiths, Seymour Nurse, Cammie Smith, Conrad Hunte, and the incomparable Sir Gary Sobers.

> Thank God who made the British Isles
>   And taught me how to play
> I do not worship crocodiles,
>   Or bow the knee to clay!
> Give me a willow wand and I
>   With hide and cork and twine
> From century to century
>   Will gambol round my shrine!
>
> Rudyard Kipling

"There are several ways of looking at the game of cricket; first, and probably best, it is a game played for enjoyment. It is an art, rich in the expression of subtle technical skills, where grace and strength may be magically blended. It is a long picturesque romance, as rich in comedy and character as *Don Quixote* or *Pickwick Papers*. It is also a fascinating form of controversy. It is spectacle, it is drama, it is good fun. It is undoubtedly an art; an art that can give pleasure to those who practise it and to those who watch."   A. A. Thomson

Itinerary

Saturday, 19 October	Arrive Barbados
Sunday, 20 October	At Leisure
Monday, 21 October	Match v Harrison College and Princess Margaret
Tuesday, 22 October	At Leisure
Wednesday, 23 October	Match v Foundation School and Ellersley
Thursday, 24 October	Water Sports
Friday, 25 October	Match v Lodge School and St. James Secondary
Saturday, 26 October	At Leisure
Sunday, 27th October	At Leisure
Monday, 28th October	At Leisure
Tuesday, 29 October	Match v Ellersley School and Foundation
Wednesday, 30 October	At Leisure
Thursday, 31 October	Match v St. Michael's School and Lodge
Friday, 1 November	Trip on 'Jolly Roger'
Saturday, 2 November	Depart Barbados
	matches commence at 1.30 p.m.

It is anticipated that some of the 'Leisure Days' will be taken up by further matches and also trips to Banks' Brewery, a plantation, and the Barbados Government Offices.

Accommodation List
(...or Who's been sleeping in my bed?)

Rockley Beach Club	Rockley Resort
David Shannon	Richard Ironside
Andrew Bamford	David Spolding
Simon Wall	Tim Medcraft
Chris Mitchell	Andrew Crofts
Mark Pearson	Andrew Creasey
David Gray	Graham Lomas
John Payne	Lee Marriott
Tim Kirk	Roger Suttle
Anthony Holmes	Mr. D. Clarke
Neil Bradbury	Mr. B. Alien
Sean Hoole	Mr. P. Tonge
Tim Hollinshead	
David Ward	Rockley Resort (families, etc.)
Paul Pollard	Mr. and Mrs. O. Wright
Robert Edwards	Mr. and Mrs. P. Marriott and Wayne
Mr. R. Ironside	Mr. and Mrs. P. Crofts
Mr. R. Suttle	Mr. and Mrs. B. Lack and Darren Crofts

A History of Manor Cricket Club

1981   First Season, 15 matches played, some boys played in white trousers!

1982   Three teams played in the North East Derbyshire League and the Chesterfield Under 13 League.

It was an enjoyable season and results improved

1983   School became a Community School and with three teams still playing – now in whites and cricket boots!

The idea of a pavilion was conceived.

1984   Thanks to help from Somersall Rangers FC and Mr Stan Lomas, the Cricket Pavilion was built and sited on our Ashgate Avenue pitch.

Still three teams – good season and hot!

1985   International Year of Youth.

Sent 24 boys to Barbados after a season of 60+ matches at Under 11, 12, 13, 14, 15,16, 17 and 18 levels.
Included indoor game against England Ladies and outdoor games against Hilversum (Holland), and Derbyshire Colts.

Square was marked.

1986   Sight Screens?

West Indian Flavour

What is it that makes West Indies cricket so different from the other cricketing nations? Most people will tell you that it is because they are un-inhibited, natural, flair players. They have not had their aggression coached out of them and on the whole that is true. However, as a coach I would not support any coaching scheme that "coaches aggression out".

To understand their attitude to cricket it is necessary to look at the climate in which they live, the pitches on which they play and their whole philosophy of life. Overall the pitch has probably had the greatest effect on the development of the most successful type of player. In addition, the fact that the West Indian of African descent tends to be a tall, well muscled, loose Jointed athlete has been a significant factor in producing numerous world class fast bowlers over the years. Wes Hall, Michael Holding, Vanburn

Holder, Joel Garner are all in this mould.

West Indian pitches, though not always quick, usually give the fast bowler sufficient bounce with the new ball to encourage him. The crowds also encourage bowlers to produce fast balls which bounce high as this in turn provides exciting cricket There tends to be much less movement off the pitch and therefore the medium pace seam bowler is not as great a wicket taker there as in other countries. Bowlers and teams are coached to increase speed of delivery and worry about line and length later. In England where our pitches are so much slower, line and length are of paramount importance and some coaches may, with the best of intentions, hold back the development of potential quick bowlers by stressing it to the detriment of an increase in pace.

English players worry about lateral movement off the pitch and this figures largely in their discussions. Abroad one must recognise that bounce is every bit as important, particularly when looking at spin bowlers. The most successful wicket taker in West Indies cricket is Lance Gibbs with 309 Test wickets and he delivered the ball from a very high position indeed, achieving an awkward bounce even on English pitches. To digress for a moment, the reason Iveson and Cleeson, with their unorthodox grips, were not as effective in England as in Australia was the lack of bounce.

When comparing other world class batsmen with those from the West Indies, the most striking difference is their attitude to the playing of strokes which may get them out. The ball is bowled to be struck and they attack when many batsman would be content just to play the ball. It is a philosophy which produces exciting cricket but also can contribute to the loss of wickets at vital stages of a game. It is the exact opposite of the approach of some England openers such as Boycott and Tavare whose style is built on the principle of sound defence first and foremost.

There is a theory in cricketing circles that it is easier to bowl at an attacking batsman because he gives you a chance. I wonder what Hendrick's

Gary Sobers meets Tim Hollinshead in Sheffield

answer to that would have been following his last over to Viv Richards in the Prudential four years ago? What is it that makes Richards so good? Apart from his records and his obvious general all-round ability as a batsman, I believe it is his willingness to take the bowler on. He puts the bowler on the defensive and wins the psychological battle by making the bowler worry about bowling to avoid being hit instead of trying to bowl him out. For those who would analyse his style a clue to his continued success is in the position of his head. All the great batsman have had their heads in good positions when making contact with the ball. Despite Viv's apparent unorthodox or improvised strokes, his head is, almost always, in the correct position. Couple that with the narrow athletic waist, the powerful shoulders and forearms and you have a very formidable batting machine indeed.

One final point. Do not attribute the distance Richards and Lloyd hit the ball to the very heavy bats they use. Remember they are very powerful men indeed and can get their ponderous bats moving quickly. If you are built along the lines of Alvin Kallicharan a "willow wand" which you can move with the speed of a rapier will be more likely to produce the magical results you seek.

Bob Carter
Worcestershire C.C.C. and National Coach (Midlands)

Cricket, lovely cricket

Two teams of young cricketers from Manor School Chesterfield, were given a civic send-off by Mayor Coun Tom Whyatt last night as they prepare for a two-week tour of Barbados as part of International Youth Year.

Twenty-three players have each paid £100 towards the £13,000 tour, the Borough Council and local firms have contributed, and fund raising ventures have helped meet the cost.

Coach Dick Suttle, a native of Barbados, took a young team from Loundsley Green, Chesterfield, over there four years ago.

The two teams, who fly out on Saturday, are to play a ten-game tour of seven colleges in Barbados. Seven medallions will be presented to the college by courtesy of Chesterfield Borough Council.

Manor continue cricket tour

With their first two matches washed out by rain last Monday, the Manor Cricket Club from Chesterfield, England, are expected to continue their tour of Barbados today, when they meet teams from the Foundation School and Ellerslie at the home team's respective grounds, commencing at 12.30p.m.

The Manor team consist of players under the age of 18, with Tim Hollingshead as the captain of one team, while Tim Kirk is the skipper of the other team. On any given play day, both teams can be seen in action. Kirk is the tour captain, while Hollinshead is the tour vice-captain.

Barbadian-born Richard Suttle is the coach of the team, and being the coach of an English youth team in Barbados is no new experience to him. Suttle was here back in 1981, as coach of the Loundsley Green cricket team.

Manager of the team, Ralph Ironside said yesterday that he was looking forward to his team's performances against the Barbadian youngsters as his

The civic send-off by Mayor Coun Tom Whyatt

Members of the team from Manor School which toured Barbados in October 1985

Members of the Manor Cricket Club's contingent are shown in this Grantley Sealy photograph, as they get together for a group shot at the Rockley Resort, at Christ Church yesterday.
Front row, L to R:- Ben Lack (umpire), Anthony Holmes, Brian Allen (Assistant Manager), Graham Lomas, Richard Suttle (Coach) and Tim Hollingshead.
Second row, L to R:- Ralph Ironside (Manager), Andrew Bamford, Sean Hoole, Paul Pollard, Tim Kirk, Robert Edwards, Neil Bradbury, Richard Ironside, David Spalding and Andrew Crofts.
Back row, L to R:- Simon Wall, Lee Marriott, David Gray, Chris Mitcheli, Dave Shannon, Andrew Creasy, Roger Suttle, Dave Ward, Mark. Pearson and John Payne.

side boasted some fine players who could make careers out of playing professional cricket back in England.

Among those who should perform well on this tour is Paul Pollard, who represents Nottinghamshire's second eleven in England. Pollard has also represented the young England team, against Zimbabwe, Scotland and Wales. This young, versatile batsman has a wealth of experience, having faced such West Indian fast bowling greats as Courtney Walsh and Eldine Baptiste.

Their all-rounder captain Kirk, will also be made to pull his weight, as he is hopeful of making it professionally sometime in the future. The 16-year-old is presently with the Derbyshire Colts team when he is at home. This is his first time playing cricket in Barbados.

The assistant manager is Brian Allen, while the English lads have also brought an umpire to Barbados, Ben Lack, Coach Suttle said yesterday: "We are hoping for a change of weather, as my players are indeed anxious to, match their skills with the Barbados schoolboys."

The two-week long tour will continue on Friday, with matches against the Lodge School and St. James Secondary. The visitors will again be matched against Ellerslie School and Foundation on Tuesday, October 29, and will end their tour of Barbados with engagements against the St. Michael School and Lodge on Thursday, October 31.

Barbados Advocate Wednesday, October 23, 1985

Cricket visitors lose to St James school

The visiting Manor youth cricket team from Chesterfield, England, crashed to yet another defeat on their two-week tour to Barbados, when they went under to St. James Secondary School by four wickets at the St. James Secondary School's grounds yesterday.

Batting first, the visitors could only manage 81 runs for the loss of nine wickets in their innings, which lasted 30 overs. Andrew Crafts topscored with a well played 25, while Tim Hollingshead got 22 and Robert Edwards 13. Michael Hinds had a good day with the ball for the home team capturing four wickets at a cost of nine runs,

St. James Secondary took only, 18 overs to make the required runs finishing with 86 for six wickets when play was called to an end. Rafael Reid was the high scorer for the winners with 19, while Michael Hinds contributed 13, Glyne Small 12 and Rodney Gilkes, an undefeated 10.

Mark Pearson and Tim Medcraft collected two wickets each for 17 and 20 runs respectively.

The English lads were also on the receiving end last Wednesday, as they went under against Ellerslie and the Foundation schools. Ellerslie convincingly beat Manor by 57 runs at Ellerslie, while Foundation snatched a three wicket victory at Foundation.

Against Foundation, Manor again had first knock, but their batsmen found form on this occasion, as they were 112 for two wickets after the match was reduced to 28 overs for each team.

Tim Kirk topscored with 36, while Neil Bradbury was 31 not out. Paul Pollard and David Shannon each got 11, with Shannon as the other not out batsman. For Foundation, Dave Greenidge got both wickets for 22 runs.

Barbados Advocate Saturday, October 26th, 1985

Bajan boys win

A combined schools XI defeated the touring Manor Schools of England by 50 runs in a 35-overs a side cricket match at Kensington Oval yesterday.

Scores: Combined Schools 158 for nine off 35 overs (Richard Hinds 64. Sherwin Campbell 51. Floyd Reifer 12; Robert Edwards 5/31). Manor Schools 108 off 32·5 overs (Sam Wall 24, Roger Suttle 20; Vasbert Drakes 3/12, Scofield Hewitt 2/21, David Roach 2/31).

Daily Nation Monday, October 28th, 1985

Cricketers return from two week tour of Barbados

Manor Cricket Club has returned from a two week tour in Barbados to mark the International Year of Youth.

All through the summer they had to contend with rain as money was raised for an International experience of a lifetime and Barbados – chose to do the same.

Fourteen matches were arranged but only five played. The opposition was strong and all games were lost. They were however close encounters and in no way were the teams disgraced. Mr. Ralph Ironside, Tour Manager, commented "In cricketing terms, the tour might be thought to have been less than successful. In youth terms however, it was a marvellous experience. The attitude and behaviour of the group was excellent despite the frustration of the rain. It would rain for half an hour before the game, but the rain was of monsoon proportions. We were soon back to hot sun but the damage was done and games were called off."

"The highlight was the 'Test' at the Bridgetown Oval against the Barbados Representative Schools' XI," said Richard Suttle, Club Coach. "To play on the Test ground was a privilege and we played particularly well on this occasion. The fielding and bowling was first class and when we batted we found the heat, the pace of the wicket and the bowlers just a bit too much. That proved to be our last game, but the boys were adjusting and I'm sure that a victory was due."

Joining the group for the second week. Jim King, Headteacher at Manor School, was also impressed with the spirit of the cricketers and the party who travelled. "It is a beautiful island. The Bajans are very friendly and we made many good friends. We visited most parts of the island and we were amazed at the heat, the range of vegetation, the range of living conditions. I bought a poppy for Remembrance Day. The schools emphasise cleanliness, religion and a good education. I was surprised to find nodding donkeys pumping oil out of the ground right in the middle of the sugar cane. We appeared on the Barbados Television and our games were reported in the press. Having been to the Caribbean I am sure we will all appreciate David Gower's problems in trying to win a Test series. I was disappointed with the rain, but felt that the experience was unforgettable, exciting and a credit to all who were involved in the project. I would like to thank everyone who helped the group and hope to share some of our adventures with a slide show early in the New Year."

21st November 1985

Veteran Suttle smashes Works
Chesterfield A.G.D. 143 for 8
Staveley Works 94
(Bassetlaw IE)

Veteran all-rounder Richard Suttle steered Chesterfield A.G.D. to victory against Staveley Works on Bank Holiday Monday.

Batting first, A.G.D. had an opening partnership of 58 runs before wickets began to fall.

Richard Suttle produced the stability in the middle order batting with a well compiled 40 runs, the team total reaching 143.

Staveley Works opening partnership reached 41 before the introduction of an all spin attack.

Right arm off spinner Richard Suttle troubled all the batsmen with his variation of flight and spin to capture seven wickets for 25 runs, with the left arm slow bowler Brian Medlam collecting three wickets for 22 runs.

Derbyshire Times Friday, May 29, 1987

Chesterfield A.G.D. 1st XI 197-4
Staveley Works 1st XI 55
(Bassetlaw IE)

Requiring 72 points from their last six games, Chesterfield defeated Staveley Works with 13 balls remaining, to keep their promotion hopes alive.

Having been asked to bat first on a wet wicket at Calow, A.G.D. built their victory platform on a substantial score of 197 runs for the loss of only four wickets.

Paul Foster, with 53 runs, his third 50 this season, was the top scorer with contributions from Roger Suttle (16), Brian Medlam (44), Neil Collings (24) and veteran Dick Suttle 43 not out.

Staveley Works survived 43 overs and five balls, before A.G.D. achieved their eighth victory.

Leading wicket taker Nell Collings claimed another haul of six wickets for 18 runs in 19 overs to make his tally for the season to 31 wickets.

Peter Williams proved an admirable foil, bowling 20 overs for a return of three wickets for 27 runs.

A last wicket stand occupied seven overs before the introduction of the off-spinner Dick Suttle bowled the last batsman.

Dramatic finish as Manor C.C.
Defeat Chesterfield Unemployed Centre C.C. by 11 runs
Scores: Manor C.C. 86 off 35 overs
Chesterfield Unemployed Centre C.C. 75 off 33·3 overs

On Saturday 20th June, Chesterfield Unemployed Centre C.C. captained by Paul Ozenbrook, met Manor C.C. led by Dick Suttle at Loundsley Green, on a sun-drenched afternoon, as Ozenbrook won the toss on a rain-affected wicket and sent in the opposition to bat.

Manor were all out for 86 runs off their allotted 35 overs. Thanks to some resolute batting from Dick Suttle and John McEvity who scored 18 runs each. Hussain at no 9, boosted the total with a useful 14 with Sharif undefeated with 5.

Bowling for the Unemployed team, medium pacer Ozenbrook bowled well and took 3 for 7, John Hornsby 4 for 28, John Johnson 2 for 17 and Colin Hampton 1 for 4.

In reply, the Unemployed team were all out for 75 runs off 33·3 overs. Thanks to an opening stand of 22 between Colin Hampton and Alan Hoskin who scored 11 and 8 respectively. After that, the middle order batting collapsed to the pace of Nissar Sulleman; but skipper Ozenbrook, who came in at No 7, played a splendid innings to top score with 23. With 9 balls left and 12 runs needed, and one wicket to fall, 14 year-old Simon Sheppard took a brilliant slip catch to dismiss Mark Boswell off Sulleman for thedreaded cipher, to win the match. Bowling for Manor N. Sulleman took 5 for 9, M. Hussain 2 for 6, D. Suttle 2 for 15, and F. Sharif 1 for 9.

Barbados Overseas Cricket Association
Defeated Chesterfield Unemployed Centre C.C. by 70 Runs
Scores: Barbados O.V.C.A. 193 for 7 off 30 overs
Cheterfield Unemployed C.C.C. 123 for 7 off 30 overs

The Chesterfield Unemployed Centre Cricket Club captained by Dick Suttle, travelled to London on Tuesday and were well entertained by the Barbados Overseas Cricket Association, astutely led by Martin Forte at the Civil Service Ground Eltham and lost by 70 runs.

Skipper Forte won the toss on a perfect wicket in glorious sunshine, elected to bat and at the end of their allotted 30 overs, they were 193 for 7.

Skipper Forte, who opened the innings, topscored with an aggressive 34, while consistent contributions came from T. Forte 27 not out, B. Allette 24, A. Bacchus 24, J. Ramsay 23 F. Skinner 22.

Bowling for the Unemployed team, Dick Suttle took 3 for 58, Roger Suttle 2 for 51, John Johnson 1 for 17 and Steven Sharpe 1 for 58. In reply, the visitors scored 123 for 7 off 30 overs. Thanks to an opening stand of 69 between Brian Medlam and Steven Sharpe. First to go was Medlam for 20. Wickets began to fall, as the middle order batsmen tried to force the pace against accurate bowling, Sharpe who batted with controlled aggresion, was bowled by Sealy for a well played 56. The only other batsman to reach double figures was Roger Suttle with an undefeated 20. Bowling for the home team, K. Sealy took 3 for 14, L. Batson 4 for 13 to win by 70 runs.

(a Home Fixture will be arranged shortly).

30/6/87

Haringey C.C. 110 for 7
Chesterfield Unemployed Centre C.C. 103 for 6

Chesterfield skipper Medlam won the toss on an astro turf wicket with the skies heavily overcast and sent in the opposition, led by Ryland Gibson to bat.

After their 25 overs, Haringey were 110 for 7. S. Bastein top scored with an aggressive 33, while good supporting inning's came from T. Rajapaska 31. S. Mohammed 16. and A. Winston 14 not out.

Bowling for the Unemployed, medium pacer John Johnson ended with the splendid analysis of 5 for 19 in five overs as his team's fielding left much to be desired.

With 111 runs required for victory, the Chesterfield batsmen made a gallant effort to win the match but failed by eight runs as they were 103 for 6 at the end of their alotted 25 overs.

The bespectacled Hornsby who came in at number eight, topscored with an undefeated 28 and was ably assisted by his captain Medlam with an undefeated 20, while useful contributions came from Dick Suttle with 18 and Paul Ozenbrook 11.

Bowling for the London team, Numan Sadiq took 3 for 9 in 5 overs. Sean Mohammed 1 for 30 in five overs to win the match by the narrow margin of seven runs.

Hoaxer bowls a bouncer

Unemployed Chesterfield cricketers are blaming a hoax caller for trying to stump a big match in London.

The squad from the town's Centre for the unemployed had to borrow a man from their opponents for Tuesday's game against the Barbados Overseas Cricket Association after the mystery caller telephoned some players and told them the game was off.

Alan Hoskin, Chesterfield centre orgainser, told the *Derbyshire Times* he suspected that three players who did not turn up had been called. This left the team with only 10 men to make the trip south.

To get a fixture against a team from London took a lot of hard work and organising, and it brought bit of excitement into the centre.

"I know most of the lads were very disappointed that they didn't have a full side."

Mr Hoskin said the calls were a complete mystery, but this week National

Cricket Association coach Dick Suttle, who does voluntary coaching for the Chesterfield team, linked them with the disappearance from the centre of a list of the team's names, addresses and phone numbers.

Despite the calls, the centre's players were not completely bowled over. They made 123 for 7 and lost by 70 runs.

Derbyshire Times 3/7/87

Chesterfield Unemployment Centre 140-7, Haringey 141-8

Having won the toss. Haringey skipper Chase sent in the liome team to bat in glorious sunshine on an easy paced Tube Works wicket, and after their allotted 50 overs, the Chesterfield team were 140 for 7.

Opening batsmen, Roger Suttle and John Allan, put on 48, before the latter was bowled by Abdul for six, while his partner went on to score a well played 46.

Paul Ozenbrook batted with controlled aggression, to finish with an undefeated 45, while Dick Suttle and Dennis Sawdon scored 18 and 10 respectively.

Bowling for Haringey, Marsh took 2 for 23, Chaser 2 for 26, Abdul 2 for 35 and Atherley 1 for 13.

In reply, Haringey began to lose quick wickets to Roger Suttle, but Holoman, who opened the innings scored 17 before being bowled by John Allan.

Abdul batted soundly for 36 before he was caught by wicket-keeper Dennis Sawdon off Williams' bowling.

John Johnson had George also caught by Sawdon for four.

The catch of the day came with the score at 60 for five when Knight was brilliantly caught on the deep long-on boundary by Frank Portas off Dick Suttle's bowling, but unfortunately Portas injured his back in the process and had to leave the field.

With the score at 70 for six and 20 overs left, Dick Suttle struck again by bowling Tariq for ten.

Next was skipper Chase, lbw to Allan for seven, but Atherley and Somerville batted well and saw their team safely home with 25 and 15 n.o. respectively.

Bowling for the Chesterfield team, Roger Suttle took 2 for 32 in 18 overs, John Allen 2 for 14 in four overs, Dick Suttle 2 for 41 in eight overs, while John Johnson and Paul Williams took one each for seven and 28 respectively.

No fewer than six catches went a-begging as Haringey consolidated their victory by two wickets.

Straight bat for charity

Big-hearted cricketers are hoping their efforts have raised £500 to help send a two-year-old girl with a rare chromosone deficiency to America for treatment.

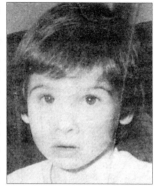

A charity cricket match in Queen's Park, between Spital C.C. and a team raised by local cricket coach Dick Suttle, involved players being sponsored for the number of runs, wickets and catches they made.

Organisers originally hoped to raise £200 – but Mr. Suttle said afterwards: "It went marvellously well and we are hoping the total will be nearer £500. One player alone was sponsored for £80, and another for £6(). The raffle made £40."

In the match on Sunday – played on the ground's Astroturf wicket after Saturday's heavy rain – Dick Suttle's XI made 141-8 and beat Spital, 83-8, by 58 runs in the 30-over a side game.

The money will go to the Nicola Scanlon Appeal, a fund set up to provide cash to send Nicola, of Grampian Crescent, Loundsley Green, Chesterfield, to the Institute of Human Potential in Philadelphia.

Richard Suttle N.C.A. (Cricket Coach
16 Pennine Way,
Loundsley Green,
Chesterfield,
Derbyshire.
S40 4ND

18/8/87

Dear Sir/Madam,

This is to inform you that a party of local cricketers have offered their time and expertise to help raise some money on behalf of the " Nicola Scanlon Appeal Fund " in order to send her to America for special treatment.

May I take this opportunity to thank you for any help for this deserving cause.

As I await your reply, I thank you.

Yours sincerely,

Richard Suttle

N.B. The match will be played at Queens Park on Sunday 20th September 1987 between Spital C.C and a Dick Suttle's XI.
Play starts at 2 p.m
30 overs per side.

Locals

No treatment is available in this country but local people have already raised over £5,000 to send Nicola and her mother Gail to the Institute for assessment later this year.

Nicola was born with a chromosome deficiency which restricts her mental and physical development. The older she gets, the more she falls behind other children of the same age.

Trophy in memory of cricketer Ian

A new trophy for outstanding fielding has been launched in memory a north Derbyshire cricketer who died tragically.

Chesterfield's cricketing fraternity was shocked to hear that Ian Suttle, a popular member of the A.G.D. team, was found hanged at his home earlier this summer.

But his father, Chesterfield cricket coach Dick Suttle, has ensured his son's memory will live on through the presentation of the trophy each year.

Said Mr Suttle: "I would like to thank all the people who have given donations to make the award possible."

It will be awarded at the A.G.D.'s annual presentation evening to the

Ian's brother, Roger Suttle, an all-rounder with the A.G.D., hands the trophy to Mr. Ron Lovegrove, secretary of the A.G.D. Cricket Club

player who has been the club's most outstanding fielder during the season. The cricketer will also receive a minature trophy to keep for good.

Derbyshire Times 21/8/87

Liz wins in Loundsley opener

Elizabeth Pearson of Eckington won the first Loundsley Green ladies single-wicket tournament.

She beat Sue Ball in the final, scoring 34 not out in her three allotted overs and dismissing Sue for four with the first ball in the second over. The fielding prize was won by Nasreen Fazil.

Results of the final stages:

Third round: Naomi Fulwood 18, Carol Herring 2, Elizabeth Pearson 20, Jaime Smith 0, Nasreen Fazil 4, Maria Clifford 5, bye; Sue Ball. Semi-final: Fulwood 0, Pearson 1, Ball 15, Clifford 4. Final: Pearson 34, Ball 4.

` *Sheffield Star* 28/8/87

Winner Liz Pearson is third from the right on the back row. Other competitors are:
Back row L to R: *Susannah Overton, Sue McLaren, Rachel Hill, Susan Ball, Emma Cocker and Olivia Cox.*
Front row L to R: *Carol Herring, Jaime Smith, Maria Clifford, Nasreen Fazil, Naomi Fulwood*

Ladies also play

A 17-year-old Derbyshire girl has been selected for the Young England Women's cricket squad from which the national team for next summer will be chosen.

Liz Pearson, of Lightwood Farm, Marsh Lane, near Eckington will spend alternate weekends throughout the winter training at Bedford, with 15 to 20 other teenage girl cricketers.

A pupil of Eckington School, Liz has been playing cricket for three years. "My brother Mark was coached by Richard Suttle at Chesterfield college and Richard was keen to get a girls team going, so I went along", she said.

"I quite fancied it – I suppose I am a tomboy at heart – and I really enjoy the game".

Liz, a medium pace swing bowler, plays for Notts Ladies during the summer. Her ambition is to earn selection for the England team.

Cricketing talent runs in the family – elder brother Mark, 18, plays for Derbyshire Colts. Younger brother Terence, 11, is just taking up the game.

And Liz is hoping to follow in the footsteps of another girl who was one of local coach Richard Suttle's protegés … seven years ago Denise Leary, from Calow, played for England on their under-25 tour to India.

Said Richard: "Liz has a lot of talent. I've coached her for the past three years and she has always been very interested and there is a lot of cricket potential there."

Editors note: Liz is the sister of Mark who is on this tour.

October 1987

Cricket boost for boy 9

A nine-year-old Derbyshire boy cricketer has been chosen for special coaching by the M.C.C. at Lord's because of his outstanding potential.

Ryan Williams, of Nottingham Close, Wingerworth, near Chesterfield, was among 40 boys from all over the country in his age group selected to go for trials, and so impressed M.C.C. coaches that he is one of only three who have been recalled for more tuition.

His mother, Mrs Susan Williams, said: "He wants to be a professional cricketer – that's all he has ever wanted. I can remember when he was only just walking, he was always waving a little cricket bat around."

He was originally coached by Benita White when he was six and spent two hours a week in her nets at Clay Cross.

He is also tutored by Chesterfield cricket coach. Dick Suttle, who said: "Ryan is a very exciting prospect. For his age, he has enormous potential and the coaches at Lord's say they'll be paying special attention to him."

Ryan, an all-rounder who bats and bowls, plays for a local junior team and has already had a taste of representative cricket – having played for Derbyshire Cricket Association under-11s last season.

Yorkshire Post Tuesday, January 5th, 1988

Denmark trip for cricketer

A local cricketer is hoping to bring home the bacon for Derbyshire C.C.C. when he makes a trip to Denmark.

Ryan Williams, nine, gets in a bit of practice at his home yesterday in readiness for his special coaching at Lord's

St. Peter and St. Pauls School Cricket Club at Queens Park Leisure Centre in February 1988 under the supervision of N.C.A. coaches.
Back row L to R:- *Jon Hornsby, Paul Ozenbrook and Dick Suttle*

John Allan (38) has been selected from 135 candidates to teach our national game to budding Danish cricketers – and he has high hopes of discovering another Ole Mortensen.

John leaves on April 7 and returns to Britain in July, bringing back with him a Danish touring team.

John, who recently completed his National Cricket Association Award course, has played for a number of Chesterfield-area teams, including Holmewood, Chesterfield Taverners and Sheepbridge.

The team he returns with in July will play a series of matches against English teams, and he has high hopes of introducing some Danish hopefuls to county sides.

"I have heard that there are a couple of them who are hoping to get to county standard and I would be rightly delighted if I could find another Ole Mortensen for Derbyshire," he explained.

John praised local cricket coaches Dick Suttle and Mick Roe far encouraging him to apply for the position.

The Gazette 31st March, 1988

Chesterfield Unemployed Workers Centre 86 for 9
Barnsley Unemployed Workers Centre 55 all out

Chesterfield were asked to bat, and on a firm pitch against some accurate bowling they lost two quick wickets with only five runs scored.

Allan and D. Suttle put on 24 for the third wicket before Allan was caught behind for 12, then after sharing a stand of 16 with Farnsworth, Suttle was eventually caught on the boundary for 16.

Although Chesterfield lost wickets at regular intervals in seeking to put runs on the board, E. Grant took on the Barnsley bowlers with a will before he was run out for 23.

Then a scintillating last wicket stand took the score to 86 for nine off the allotted 30 overs.

Barnsley in reply lost a wicket in the first over to E. Grant, but Green (19), M. Pickersgill (11), and S. Brown (19) led the spirited recovery.

However, once these three had departed the rest of the Inning collapsed to end on 55 off 14 overs.

Once again E. Grant produced an excellent spell of bowling and finished with two for 11 off six overs, while D. Walker polished off the tall to end with three for one off 1·4 overs.

This was another hard earned but well deserved victory for the Chesterfield side, and in travelling to play in matches of this sort the players, on and off the field, are proving to be excellent representatives for the town.

20th OCTOBER – 5th NOVEMBER 1988
Foreword Jim King

To go on a cricket tour to Barbados is an exciting international experience. I am sure that the senior cricketers writing in this brochure will refer to Barbadian cricket skills and ways of coping with the pace bowlers and free scoring batsmen. I know the cricket will be challenging but there will be so much more to discover.

Barbados is a beautiful island with a fascinating history. There should be plenty of opportunity to sample the cheap bus service and speed back to the Atlantic Coast or explore the beautiful beaches by the Caribbean Sea. I hope the group will take time to meet and talk with their cricketing friends after the matches and learn about Bajan homes, schools, hopes and aspirations. It will be interesting to compare Newspapers, Television and Radio perspectives of World News when you are so close to the Continents of North and South America. Remember to find a 'bearded tree', taste the sugar cane and enjoy a coconut or three!

If I could offer advice it would be to be open, sensitive, enquiring and lively. All your senses will be sharpened by this vivid place and if it is to be a once in a lifetime experience then make the best of every moment of your tour.

You immediately become ambassadors for your country, our county, our town. I know you will be well led by your management team. It gives me great pleasure to wish the party every success on the 1988 Tour to Barbados.

Jim King
Manor Cricket Club

Tourists pip Dick's celebrity team
Celebrity XI 161 for 7
Chesterfield and District Cricket Touring Team 163 for 5

On a slightly overcast Sunday afternoon at Queen's Park, Tim Kirk, captain of the Chesterfield and District Cricket Touring Team, due to tour Barbados in October, met a Celebrity XI led by Dick Suttle in a 40 over sponsored match, which ended in a victory for the touring team by five wickets with six balls to spare.

Skipper Dick Suttle won the toss with ideal conditions prevailing and decided to bat on a perfect wicket and after 40 overs the Celebrity team were 161 for 7.

Opening batsman Jim Brailsford, topscored with a classical 67, which included one six and five fours, while useful contributions came from Dean Hopkinson with an undefeated 35 and Dick Suttle 24.

Bowling for the touring team, John Johnson took 2 for 20 In four overs, Roger Suttle 2 for 26 in eight overs, Neil Johnson 2 for 34 in eight overs and Tim Kirk 1 for 14 in four overs in reply the touring team scored 163 for 5 in 39 overs.

Tim Kirk top scored with a splendid 32, Steve Sharpe 29, Roger Suttle 28 not out, Paul Williams 20 and Andrew Walker 16, to give their team victory by five wickets.

Bowling for the Celebrity XI Richard Dibbs took 2 for 18 in seven overs, Dean Hopkinson 1 for 15 in eight overs and John Allan 1 for 17 in three overs.

Meet the management

Ralph Ironside (Manager).
This is his second trip to Barbados, having previously been in 1985. He was a steady batsman and wicket keeper with Chesterfield C.C. until his retirement through ill health in 1981, since when he has concentrated on the organisation of local Junior cricket including tours such as this.

Richard Suttle (Club Coach).
An allrounder who has just completed twenty years with the A.G.D. Cricket Club. He has scored over 5000 runs. Highest individual score was 103 not out against Kirkby Wyvern, Notts in 1974 and last season took 7 for 26 with his off-spinners against Staveley Works at Staveley. Received the 1974 Service Cricket Award from the Chesterfield Cricket Lovers' Society. Gained the N.C.A. Coaching Award in 1975 and took his Advanced at Scarborough in 1978. Coached professionally in the Netherlands and Scotland in 1975 and 1977 respectively. Toured Barbados as team coach with the Loundsley Green Cricket Club (1981) and Manor Cricket Club (1985). Dick's present appointment is a part-time coach at Queen's Park Sports Centre and Chesterfield Centre Unemployed Cricket Club.

His latest book, *Caribbean Mission Accomplished* has been well received internationally.

Frank Orrill (Umpire).
Frank is a very well-known and respected Umpire in the Bassetlaw League

Pictured is the Touring Team that will visit Barbados next month.
Back row: *P. Ozenbrook, M. Pearson, L. Henshaw, S. Sharpe, N. Johnson and R. Suttle.*
Front row: *P. Williams, I. Stockdale, T. Kirk (captain), J. Johnson and A. Walker.*

Chesterfield Celebrity XI (Capt. by Dick Suttle) v the touring team at Queen's Park on 4/9/88.
Back row L to R:- *R. Dibbs, J. Revill, P. Foster, J Brailsford, J. Allan, W. Felix and C. Baxter.*
Front row L to R:- *S. Revill, D. Hopkinson, D. Suttle (Capt), D. Atkins and C. Mitchell.*

Derbyshire. He has always been a keen and dedicated follower of the game. He spent over twenty years as an Umpire in the North Derbyshire League before joining the Bassetlaw League for the past ten years. Frank is overwhelmed with the opportunity given to visit the "Caribbean".

Sean Dunford (Baggage Manager).
An ardent supporter and committee member of the Chesterfield & District Cricket Touring Team. Sean organised our first fund raising event, 'A Disco' at the Aquarius. He has always supported the club's, financial appeals and is looking forward to a successful and enjoyable tour of Barbados.

Chesterfield's Caribbean Connection
by Dick Suttle
I am extremely pleased to be chosen as cricket coach for the Chesterfield and District Cricket Touring Team due to tour my home land, Barbados, in October with such keen and enthusiastic youngsters, some of whom are making their first trip to the Caribbean, where I resided for three decades, before coming to the United Kingdom. I spent seven years in London before being transferred to Chesterfield, where I started coaching in 1968 for the A.G.D. Junior Cricket Club. I sincerely hope these youngsters will gain valuable experience from this tour and enjoy themselves, while sowing seeds of friendship in order to produce a good sporting atmosphere in general, amidst traditional rivalry.

May I take this opportunity to thank all those who have sponsored us or helped in any way to make this tour a success. Finally, thanks to our tour organisers "Kestours" as well as parents, players and committee for all the hard work done to achieve such a venture. Last, but by no means least, our Hosts, who made us so welcome on two previous visits to the lovely and idyllic isle of "Barbados" often referred to as "Little England".

Harold Rhodes former England & Derbyshire player
During one's cricketing lifetime, perhaps one of the greatest and hardest places to tour is the West Indies. I was very fortunate to have done that at a very early stage of my career. The experience, I feel, not only showed me what I had to do to reach the top but emphasised the importance of fitness. English County Cricket is without doubt the hardest system to play in but generally speaking we play in a mild climate and on grounds which do have some 'give'. In most cases the opposite is true in the West Indies. Very hard grounds are nearly always found, very little grass on the wicket or outfield and after a long day in the field you are always ready to put your 'feet up'.

As a bowler you are faced with a very small margin of error and therefore concentration is an absolute necessity. After a day's play the West Indian people are great hosts and it is very easy to get carried away and forget tomorrow. Have a good time and play well.

Proposed itinerary for Barbados tour

Thursday 20th October	Depart London Heathrow for flight to Barbados. Transfer to accommodation.
Friday 21st October	Free Day.
Saturday 22nd October	Trip around the Island.
Sunday 23rd October	Free Day.
Monday 24th October	Cricket Match v Harrisons College.
Tuesday 25th October	Cricket Match v Foundation School.
Wednesday 26th October	Free day or Water Sports.
Thursday 27th October	Cricket Match v Combermere School.
Friday 28th October	Cricket Match v Lodge School.
Saturday 29th October	Free day or visit to Banks Brewery.
Sunday 30th October	Cricket Match at Kensington Oval.
Monday 31st October	Cricket Match v Coleridge.
Tuesday 1st November	Free day or Water Sports.
Wednesday 2nd November	Cricket Match v Ellerslie School.
Thursday 3rd	November Trip on Jolly Roger.
Friday 4th November	Depart Barbados for Port of Spain and then onward flight to London Heathrow.
Saturday 5th November	Arrive Heathrow approx 0730 hours.

NOTE: This itinerary is subject to amendment in the light of circumstances prevailing at the time but will be adhered to as far as possible.

Improve your game – on tour

by Keith Andrew – Chief Executive National Cricket Association

I am delighted to have this opportunity to write about cricket prior to your tour, which must, indeed, be a great thrill for everyone.

I have been privileged to be associated with cricket in many countries, both as a player when touring with M.C.C. and as Manager of the Young England side. I have also played with and against many of the magnificent individual overseas cricketers that play regularly in this country. With this background allied to my position here at Lord's as Director of Coaching, I feel I may be able to make some comment on how you young fellows may benefit your game on tour.

Firstly, you can be certain that the warmth of foreign climes will only be matched by the warmth of your welcome. As such, the problems of maintaining fitness will not be so difficult to overcome as they are when faced with your first game or two here in England in May. In this respect, I strongly advise you to set yourself targets of fitness prior to the tour, as there is no doubt that a fitter cricketer is a better cricketer.

One of the attributes of cricketers from abroad that may well be copied by us, is the whole-hearted attitude and freedom of expression that they give to performing the skills of the game.

Another near certainty, apart from the weather, is the fact that the pitches on which you play will be very "flat". It is important, therefore, that bowlers concentrate on accuracy, as anything less I can guarantee will come in for considerable punishment. By accuracy, I mean not only length, but perhaps more importantly, direction. West Indian and Pakistan batsmen, unlike the average Englishman, play shots at the wide ball, regardless of its length, and having been brought up on true surfaces, it pays.

Batsmen must again adopt a different attitude, as compared to what they would have in this country. They must continually think in terms of a very big score made in an attacking frame of mind. To become "bogged down" will give tremendous psychological advantage to the opposition. I think it is worthwhile mentioning also, that whilst encouraging attacking cricket, you will notice that the best players hit the ball very hard, but hardly ever in the air – certainly not until they are in three figures.

And now to fielding. This is where I suspect you can come into your own and obtain some very good results to bring back home. I am sure that continual practice before and between games will pay dividends. The light is different in the bright sunshine and the ball seems to travel much more quickly through the air. Field placing becomes a vital part of match winning tactics and the team should give their all in supporting the captain at times when luck is swinging against them. A brilliant run-out or a catch at this stage, as you know, can turn the game.

Whoever is your wicket-keeper I wish him well and if I mentioned concentration before, this is the fellow who will have to set an example in this respect as much as anyone.

A cricket tour in the continuous sunshine against good opposition will be one of the great experiences of a life-time. Above all, in its enjoyment, I ask you to fly the flag for all that is best in our great game, regardless of what others do. Only by maintaining the traditions of cricket and adding to them, can we then look back with pride. A tip I have not mentioned that I have found normally always pays off – that is, make certain that all members of the team take the opportunity of practising their batting.

Almost certainly, the contribution of the batsmen from number six to number eleven at a vital period in a match, will win it.

Other tips that spring to mind: -

1. Wear loose clothing and shower as much as possible after a perspiring

session.

2. Really HIT the loose ball HARD.

3. Try hard ALL the time – encourage one another – nobody likes a "moaner".

4. Batsmen – remember, twenty is NOT a big score, so do not change your style of play when you think you have made a good score.

5. Fielders – the biggest psychological blow you can strike for your team is to run out a good batsman – practice an EARLY RELEASE of the ball when picking up and throwing – NOT two minutes practice – TWO HOURS.

On tour, there is much to interest you away from the cricket ground – take a camera and record the experiences of a lifetime – you will never regret it.

I wish you all a happy tour – enjoy it. I wish I was with you!

K.V. Andrew

I regard it a privilege to be asked to write a brief passage on behalf of Spital Cricket Club. I sincerely hope that the forthcoming Tour of Barbados is as successful as the first two. Dick Suttle is once again on his daily rounds working to attain the goal of another visit to his beloved Barbados. I am sure he will achieve this alongside his fellow Tour committee workers.

I would also like to take this opportunity to thank Dick for all his efforts in fund raising for the 'Nicola Scanlon' appeal fund, which raised £595.

Dave Jones, Spital Cricket Club

English Cricketers on 3rd Visit

The Chesterfield and District cricket team from England began their third biennial tour of Barbados last Saturday.

The touring party of 24 will spend two weeks in the island. During this time they will play a number of matches against local schools and clubs. The first game is carded for today when they play against Harrison College at the College grounds.

The visitors will play Foundation tomorrow, Combermere on Thursday and Lodge on Friday. They will oppose Pickwick at Kensington Oval next Sunday, and Coleridge and Parry next Monday. The English team will round off the tour on Wednesday, November 2nd, with a match against Ellerslie. The visiting squad comprises players from various teams in the Chesterfield area. They usually meet about twice a month and travel around England to

Members of the Chesterfield and District Cricket Team are:-
Squatting from L to R: *Dick Suttle (Coach), Paul Williams, Tim Kirk (Capt.), John Allan (Manager), John Johnson and Lee Henshaw.* Middle row: *Carol Herring (Secretary), David Bartram (Treasurer), Paul Ozenbrook, Ian Stockdale, Steven Carlisle and Wes Felix (Asst. Manager);* Back Row: *Sean Dunford (Baggageman), Andrew Walker, Stephen Sharpe, Neil Johnson, Toby Newson and Richard Branagan.*
Missing from the photo are Roger Suttle and Mark Pearson

play other teams. They have a very good record, having lost just one match since the last tour of Barbados in 1985.

Chesterfield and District are managed by John Allan who was appointed just three months ago after the death of his predecessor. Allan was coaching and playing in Denmark when he was asked to take over. He said he was very happy to make the trip and is looking forward to enjoying both the island and the cricket.

Barbados-born Dick Suttle is again coach of the team. Suttle, who left Barbados in 1960, is the only member of the squad who has made all three trips to Barbados with the team. He is also accompanied on this trip by his 20 year-old son Roger.

The Barbados Advocate Monday 24th October 1988

Tourists claim three wins from five games
Chesterfield and District's touring cricket team returned from Barbados

having won three of their five matches

In the first game, they defeated Harrison College by 24 runs.

Chesterfield reached 101-9 with Andrew Walker topscoring with 18 and Lee Henshaw hitting 13 not out.

Harrison was bowled out for just 77 runs,

Neil Johnson, Tim Kirk and Mark Pearson took three wickets each as Chesterfield raced to victory.

Rain helped the tourists win their second match against Foundation School.

Chesterfield rattled up 120-9 in 35 overs and Foundation had reached 90-6 when bad light stopped play

Roger Suttle was top scorer with 26. Tim Kirk and Toby Newson both hit 22.

Both John Johnson and Mark Pearson took 2-17 for Chesterfield.

Combined Schools beat Chesterfield by 115 runs in the third game.

The home side went in first and ended with 188-7; Roger Suttle captured 2-32 and Neil Johnson 2-35.

In reply, the tourists could only muster 73-8. Leading the way was Andrew Walker with 21, while Steven Sharpe hit 17 and Toby Newson 11

In their fourth game, Ellerslie raced to a 132 victory over Chesterfield with Barbados youth team player Philio Wallace slamming a magnificent 127.

Ellerslie finished on 207-7; Mark Pearson captured 2-43 and Neil Johnson 2-47

The tourists were only able to reach 75 before being bowled out.

In the final game of the tour. Chesterfield coach Dick Suttle's team enjoyed a four wicket victory over Ellerslie Old Boys.

The home side batted first and Dick Suttle finished with the figures of 4-15 while John Johnson took 2-11.

Suttle's team coasted to victory as Toby Newson (17,) Gary Grant (16), John Johnson (19) and James King (10no) hit the runs.

Man of the series was Neil Johnson, of Ashgate Valley Road. Chesterfield.

The Derbyshire Times 18/11/88

Cricketers shine in Barbados

By Mike Taylor (Vice Principal Chest College of Tech)

Tour Manager John Allan had the pleasure of presenting Chesterfield's Neil Johnson with the Man-of-the-Series Trophy whilst coach Dick Suttle received general acclaim for his work both on and off the field.

The only disappointment of the tour was a close encounter with Gloucestershire which failed to result in a match at a time when the West Country County were struggling against local opposition. Fortunately some considerable solace was forthcoming on the team's return to Chesterfield with the news from Lords that they had been invited to play the prestigious Cross Arrows team next summer.

Chesterfield Gazette 23/11/88

Catching the cricket bug

Budding Bothams, blossoming Borders, rookie Richards and embryonic Embureys are forgetting the winter chill and turning thoughts to summer down at Queen's Park Sports Centre in Chesterfield, where indoor cricket nets are being held every Saturday until March 12.

Local cricket coach Dick Suttle, the man responsible for grooming the blossoming talent, forecasts some of his young charges could go a long way in the game and even emulate some of those famous names we just mentioned. (For the uninitiated – Ian, Allan, Viv and John, Test Match stars of England, Australia, West Indies and England respectively).

The nets are held from 1pm-3pm each Saturday except for next week, January 9, when they will be moved forward to 9am-11am to allow the leisure centre's sports hall to be used for a gymnastics tournament.

Ian Blackwell is 3rd from the left in the front row.

December 1988

Cricket Coaching at Lea Green

Eleven cricket mad youngsters from a Derbyshire school enjoyed an out-of-season coaching course when they visited Matlock's Lea Green Centre.

Coaching the youngsters from Wirksworth's Anthony Gell School were (pictured left, left to right): Hugh Nichols, Jamie Perkins, Vernal Cooper, Brian Wright, Alison Body, Nigel Bowmer, Mark Wakefield, Carl Parkin, Robert Fuller and Gerry Nunn.

Those taking part in the N.C.A. examination from Chesterfield Unemployed Workers Centre were Robert Fuller, Gerry Nunn and not pictured, Paul Williams.

The Derbyshire Times 23/12/88

HND for Roger

A former Chesterfield School pupil has been awarded a Higher National Diploma in Science (Applied Biology) at Sheffield City Polytechnic. (See colour picture page 8).

Roger DeVere Morris Suttle, of 12 Hambledon Close, Loundsley Green, Chesterfield, completed the two-year BTEC approved course at the college in July.

Roger (21) attended Brockwell Junior and Newbold Green schools before going on to Chesterfield School, where he gained an A-level in biology and four 0-levels.

Initially, Roger said he hoped to become a National Health Service laboratory technician, but is now considering taking a degree in biology.

A keen cricketer, he has attained a national coaching certificate at junior level, and hopes to go on to coach at club level.

The Derbyshire Times 30/12/88

Foreword by Leslie McCulloch
Cllr & Ex. Mayor (Tour Manager)

I am sure that all who are going on the Chesterfield & District cricketing tour of Barbados in October 1993 will get more and more excited of the visit as the date becomes closer.

All members can expect a real Caribbean welcome and also some hard times on the field of play, the Barbadians love their cricket.

Barbados is a beautiful island and if time permits visits to Gun Hill for its spectacular views, Harrisons Cave for the stalagmites and stalactites or even a dive in a submarine to see the colourful fish and coral are not to be missed.

Remember that you will be representing your town of Chesterfield and your country, play hard and clean and you will return with memories that will last a lifetime. Good luck to all on the tour.

Les McCulloch
Tour Team Manager

Ann Wells
(Secretary / Treasurer)

Ann was born in Surrey. She came to live in Chesterfield twenty years ago.

She is a Senior Security Officer with Chesterfield Borough Council. She became a member of the Chesterfield & District Cricket Touring Team, and later took over the position of secretary / treasurer.

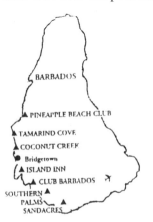

Her son, Douglas is looking forward to play some matches in England, before the team, leaves for Barbados; while her daughter, Sally and fiancé, Andy will be accompanying the party to the Caribbean. Ann who spent a delightful holiday in Barbados in 1984, has two beautiful grand daughters, Louise, four and Katie, two and she wishes the team every success on their second tour of Barbados.

Barbados lies 13° 4- N and 50° 37- W. It is 21 miles long, 14^1/2 miles at its broadest and has an area of 166 square miles, roughly the size of the Isle of Wight. The population of 240,000.

The highest point is Mount Hillaby (1.100 feet), near the centre from which the land falls gently on all sides towards the sea.

Coral reefs surround much of the coast, in some places extending three miles to the sea.

Ralph Ironside

This following picture illustrates a tribute to Mr Ralph Ironside, who was the founder of the Chesterfield & District Cricket Touring Team 1988. (See colour picture page 8).

He designed the touring teams' emblem, which is worn with pride by all the members of the 1993 tour of Barbados.

He passed away on Saturday 24th July, 1988. On Sunday 4th September the same year, a celebrity XI, captained by Dick Suttle against the Chesterfield & District Cricket Touring Team led by Tim Kirk, held a minute silence in his honour at Queen's Park, Chesterfield.

Morris Rowland

(Official Umpire) Born Scotland Yard, Palterton (13/3/28)

After leaving school, Morris was opening batsman with Palterton in the Derbyshire Miner League. After 4 years the team played in the Mansfield & District League, in which he won a cricket bat for the best allround cricketer in all seasons. Several occasions thereafter, he won the Batting & Bowling averages. After playing for the League team in both areas,

Morris moved to the Bassetlaw League with Glapwell and later with Bolsover (16 yrs.). The last three years, he played for the second team as well as umpired the U-21's in midweek.

Morris just completed nine years umpiring in the Bassetlaw League of which he has become a full member of the Association of Cricket Umpires.

Morris and his wife, Kitty, are looking forward to their first tour of Barbados.

Ben Lack
(Umpire)

Ben Lack aged 70, Vice Chairman of the Cricket Umpires Association (North Derbyshire League).

Ben started his cricket career at the age of 16. He played for Oxcroft Colliery C.C. and Bolsover Tradesman, as an opening left handed batsman. He won the batting averages on three occasions.

After retirement, Ben took up umpiring in the North Derbyshire League for fifteen years and still umpires in the Chesterfield & District Works League.

He also toured Barbados with Manor C.C. in 1985, accompanied by his wife, Madge and family. They are both looking forward to the forth coming tour of Barbados in October 1993.

Chesterfield and District touring team 135-7
Budleigh Salterton C.C. 137-3

Pictured above are the Tourists' before their journey to Devon.
Photograph by Doug Fearn

Chesterfield's nomadic cricket team, which plans to tour Barbados next October, travelled to Devon to meet Budleigh Salterton last weekend. The game was organised by Dick Suttle, the 64 year old retired cricket coach, who found himself in the Budleigh team because a player was absent.

Tim Wilson's Chesterfield team batted first and found themselves tortured by Dick Suttle's off spinners.

Veteran Dick took 2-16 in 6 overs, including the wicket of his own son!

Jack Wheeldon topscored for the tourists while Burden hit a controlled and aggressive innings of 45, including five fours.

Budleigh knocked off the required runs with more than five overs remaining.

M. Pearson took 1-13, T. Pearson 1-27 and John Johnson 1-28 as the home team won by seven wickets.

Steven Bennett also caught Ames brilliantly at mid-on.

Tourists' secretary/treasurer Mrs. Ann Wells invited Budleigh Salterton to visit Chesterfield next summer and the home captain was presented with a plate with the emblem of the Crooked Spire.

The Derbyshire Times 2/10/92

Chesterfield District Cricket Touring Team Barbados 1993

Summer Fixtures for the Chesterfield & District Cricket Touring Team

DAYS	DATES	TEAMS	VENUES
1. Sunday	13th June & District C.T.T.	Hasland v Chesterfield (2.00pm.)	Hasland
2. Sunday	11th July & District C.T.T.	Robinsons v Chesterfield (2.00 p.m.)	Walton Dam
3. Sunday	15th August & District C.T.T.	Wilmslow v Chesterfield (2.00 p.m.)	Cheshire
4. * Sunday	12th Sept. & District C.T.T.	Chatsworth v Chesterfield (1.00 p.m.)	Chatsworth
5. Sunday	19th Sept. C.T.T. v Budleigh Salterton	Chesterfield & District (1.00p.m.)	Queen's Park

N.B.

* The Duke and Duchess of Devonshire have been invited to attend the fixture on Sunday 12th September to meet the Touring Team and the Chatsworth XI.

Growing in Stature While Looking To The Future

Dick Suttle (N.C.A. Coach) Age 64

With three previous tours to my homeland, Barbados, as cricket coach, I can look back with much pleasure and gratitude, as many youngsters have done extremely well under my guidance, as I try to help them to overcome their hidden fears.

Some have gone on to reach great cricketing heights in County Cricket and have been able to represent their local clubs at the highest level.

I do believe that such tours to the Caribbean can give young players a great deal of confidence and best of all, help them to develop into splendid ambassadors for their country. This can only be achieved through hard work and personal dedication to gain the necessary experience required to have the ability to overcome failure.

To name but a few are: Damian D'Oliveria and Dave Banks of Worcestershire in 1981 with Loundsley Green C.C., Paul Pollard of Notts in 1985 with Manor C.C. Chris Adams of Derbyshire in 1987 with Repton C.C. and Tim Kirk and Lee Henshaw of Derbyshire in 1988 with Chesterfield & District Cricket Touring Team, while others have grown in stature as they have learnt to cope mentally and attune themselves to the rigours of the game.

Last summer, 18 year old, Lee Henshaw, who bowls left arm medium pace took 8 for 48 in 19 overs against Hosiery Mills in the Bassetlaw League Div. 1A at Queen's Park, Chesterfield. This performance speaks for itself. Unfortunately, after playing and coaching for 22 years non stop, I was forced to retire in 1989 with Osteo-arthritis. However, it gives me great pleasure that I can still encourage youngsters to enjoy one of the greatest games ever played, because of its character building influence and team participation.

As I look forward to a happy and enjoyable tour of the lovely and idyllic isle of Barbados often referred to as "Little England", in October 1993, under the leadership of our Councillor and Ex-Mayor, Les McCulloch. I take this opportunity to thank Mrs. Ann Wells (sec./Treas.) and all those who have contributed in any way to make this tour a great success.

Proposed itinerary for Barbados Tour 1993
Holiday No: BG118
Outward Flight No. AMM107 Inward Flight N. AMM108

Monday 4th October	Depart Manchester Airport for flight to Barbados 9.40a.m. to arrive at Barbados 15.55pm. (Transfer to accommodation)
Tuesday 5th October	Free Day
Wednesday 6th October	Free Day (Short practice for Touring Team)
Thursday 7th October	Harrison College v Chesterfield & District C.C.T. at Harrison College.
Friday 8th October	Foundation Sec. v Chesterfield & District C.T.T. at Foundation.

Saturday 9th October	Free Day. (Excursions, Water sports if required.)
Sunday 10th October	Free Day. (Excursions, Water sports if required.)
Monday 11th October	Combermere Sec. v Chesterfield & District C.T.T. at Combermere
Tuesday 12th October	* Combined Schools X1 v Chesterfield & District C.T.T. at (Kensington Oval. Test ground)
Wednesday 13th October	Free Day (Excursion to be arranged.)
Thursday 14th October	Lodge School v Chesterfield & District C.T.T. at Lodge School.
Friday 15th October	Visit to Banks Breweries at Wildey.
Saturday 16th October	Free Day
Sunday 17th October	Free Day (to wind down. take it all in)
Monday 1Bth October	Depart from Grantley Adams Airport Barbados 17.25pm.
Tuesday 19th October	Arrive at Manchester Airport U.K. 10.40a.m.

NOTE: This itinerary is subject to amendment in the light of circumstances prevailing at the time but will be adhered to as far as possible.

Chesterfield hosts the first big match in September 1757

Not many cricketers know that the first recorded cricket match played in Derbyshire took place at Chesterfield in 1757 and surprisingly did not involves a Chesterfield team. *The Derby Mercury* of 9th September 1757 reported the game and there are several interesting facts. The stake money of £50 was a considerable sum; the teams from Sheffield and Wirksworth travelled similar distances, not an easy journey in those days, to meet on neutral ground; the size and varied social composition of the crowd for a 'midweek fixture' seem to have impressed the reporter; Wirksworth at the time, before the industrial revolution, was the third largest town in Derbyshire grown wealthy on the profits from its lead mining industry, which was long established in the town.

Todays cricketers will recognise the nature of the dispute that led to an early finish!

Derby Mercury 1757

'On Thursday last a match at Cricket was played at Brampton Moor by eleven young men from Wirksworth against the same number from Sheffield for fifty pounds a side. At the latter end of the game the Wirksworth players were a considerable number of notches ahead of the others when a dispute arising about one of the Sheffield players being our some of them desisted playing again, whereby it was left undetermined, but we hear it has been since been given in favour of the Wirksworth players and the money has been paid them.

The match was played with the greatest spirit and activity on both sides which afforded the highest satisfaction to a larger concourse of persons than were ever seen in this Country on a like occasion.'

By Roy Pearce 1992

Town tributes to ex-mayor

Tributes have been pouring in this week following the sudden death of a leading Chesterfield politician and former mayor.

Les McCulloch, who was Chesterfield's mayor between 1989 and 1990, was found dead from a heart attack at his home on Ling Road, Walton on Friday. His last public appearance was at current mayor Terry Kendellen's farewell dinner at the Winding Wheel on Thursday evening.

Although it was Cllr McCulloch's second heart attack and he was diagnosed as having diabetes at the end of last year his family and friends have been left shocked by his sudden death.

Fellow Conservative councillor Terry Barlow said he will be sadly missed for his knowledge and personality.

"He was a small man in stature but a large man in his actions, " he said.

Mayor and deputy leader of the Labour group, Cllr Terry Kendellen said be had a hard act to follow.

"Cllr McCulloch was an extremely popular mayor. He brought to the mayoralty a refreshing and infectious sense of humour and always had a deep interest in all the organisations and functions he attended."

Liberal democrat leader Cllr David Stone said he was shocked and saddened by his opponent's death.

Cllr McCulloch moved from his home town of Manchester in 1963 to take up the post of head of catering at Chesterfield College of Technology. Three years later he joined Chesterfield's Conservative party and in 1973 he won his first seat on the council representing the Newbold ward. In 1979 he switched to the Walton ward where he remained until his death.

The highlight of his political career was when be became the town's mayor four years ago. He carried out more than 300 engagements and welcomed numerous visitors to the town, including the Princess Royal and the Duke and Duchess of Kent.

Cllr McCulloch had his first heart attack 18 years ago so he used the opportunity of his mayor's appeal to buy life-saving equipment to be used by ambulance crews.

In 1985 he became leader of the Conservative group on the borough council, a post he held until his death.

He was involved in numerous organisations, include Old Whittlngton care group, Scarsdale Probus Club and Chesterfield victim support group. He was also joint president of the Chesterfield Conservative Association together with the Duke of Rutland.

Away from the political arena his main interests revolved around sport, wine and his grandchildren.

A Manchester United fan, he used to referee in Sunday league games. His other main sporting interest was cricket, having played for the College, the A.G.D. and Chesterfield Casulas. Later this year was due to go to Barbados as manager of the Chesterfield and District cricket touring team.

A widower following the death of his wife Joan in 1983, he leaves two sons, William and John, a daughter, Chris and six grandchildren.

A service at Chesterfield Parish Church is due to be held tomorrow (Friday) at 1.15pm followed by cremation at Chesterfield at 2pm. Donations can be handed in to the British Heart foundation on the corner of Knifesmithgate, Chesterfield in lieu of flowers.

The Derbyshire Times Thursday, April 28, 1993

Caribbean trip for cricketers
By Les Payne

There can be fewer greater attractions for any cricketer than playing in the West Indies and a group of Chesterfield cricketers are currently preparing for a trip to the Caribbean.

Under the guidance of Barbadian Dick Suttle. Chesterfield and District Touring Team will put Barbados on their list later this year.

The effervescent Suttle, a National Cricket Association coach and a former player, is the driving force behind the tour which lasts two weeks and takes in a possible eight matches.

"I do believe that such tours to the Caribbean can give young players a great deal of confidence and, best of all, help them develop into splendid ambassadors for their country," said Dick, now 64 but still inclined to turn out if required.

Experience

'It is a great experience and we have taken several with us on 3 previous tours who have gone on to higher things and the tours help players to grow in stature and to cope mentally and attune themselves to the rigours of the game," he adds.

Dick notes Chris Adams of Derbyshire. Notts' Paul Pollard and Damien D'Oliveira are among those who have been on previous Caribbean trips and his squad this time has a wide range of ages and, therefore, abilities.

They are taking some schoolboys as well as experienced local cricketers, including Tim Kirk, a regular with Derbyshire 2nds and Derbyshire Colts captain.

The squad comprises players from various teams in the Chesterfield area and their itinerary includes meeting about twice a month and travel around the country to play matches.

Hard work

"A lot of people have put, and are putting, plenty of hard work into the trip and all of us going are indebted to the people who have helped, not least our secretary and treasurer Ann Wells who has done so much," said Dick, who left Barbados in 1960.

The touring team has a number of fund-raising events organised throughout the summer including five matches with the first of them at Hasland on Sunday. June 13 and their own tour brochure entitled *Barbados Bound* – they will be on October 4!

Sheffield Star 13/5/93

School's Cricket (under 12)
Holme Hall School defeated Highfield Hall School by 7 wickets
By Dick Suttle
Scores:- Highfield Hall School:- 44 for 7 off 10 overs.
Holme Hall School:- 47 for 3 off 9·2 overs.

On Thursday 20th July 1995 Julian Wall, captain of Highfield Hall School, won the toss on a sundrenched afternoon at Holme Hall School and decided to bat on an easy paced wicket, but after their allotted 10 overs, the visitors were 44 for 7.

Matthew Booth, who came in at No. 6, topscored with an undefeated 16, which included three fours, while Rachel Holmes at No. 9, was also undefeated with 5, in which, she struck a boundary.

Bowling for the home team, Alex Furniss took 3 for 3, Joe Carney 1 for 1, Adam Barker 1 for 6 and skipper Daniel Lukic 2 for 8, with Barker, taking a splendid catch to dismiss Thomas Swift for 3.

In reply, Holme Hall scored 47 for 3 off 9.2 overs. Alex Furniss topscored with an undefeated 21, which included two fours, while Lukic and Barker scored 6 and 3 not out respectively.

Highfield's most successful bowler was Matthew Booth, he took 2 for 2, while Julian Wall took the other wicket for 9 runs to give Holme Hall victory by seven wickets.

Umpires:- Messrs. Steven Lee & Dave Connock.

Miss Louise Brocklehurst presents Umpire George Holmes of the Bassetlaw League with a gift during the pre-tour match between Hasland C.C. and the Chesterfield & District Cricket T.T. at Eastwood Park, Hasland, Chesterfield.

Caribbean-bound, that's the cricketing group above. They are the Chesterfield and District Touring Team who continue their build-up to-morrow towards the trip to the West Indies in October.

The team play Robinson's C.C. at Walton Dam, Chesterfield, tomorrow 2pm) as part of their fund-raising programme of matches and events aimed at boosting funds for the Caribbean trip.

Their first match ended in defeat at Hasland who on a rain-affected wicket, reached 130-9 off 40 overs (Glen Bramwell 27. Dean Holland 24).

The tourists' reply, with Roger Suttle making 66 which included a six and even fours, fell short at 119. Suttle enjoyed a stand of 77 for the sixth wicket with Richard Gratton, 21.

Before the match, both sides held a minute's silence in memory of Les McCulloch, former Mayor of Chesterfield, who was to be manager of the tour but who died recently.

Tourists tune up

Chesterfield & District Cricket T.T. 86-7, Robinson C.C. 89-3

Robinson C.C., captained by Charles Walker, entertained the Chesterfield & District Cricket Touring Team, due to tour Barbados In October, led by Tim Kirk, in their second pre-tour match at Walton Dam.

After winning the toss on an overcast afternoon skipper Walker sent in the Touring Team to bat on a dampish wicket which produced some uneven bounce and after 40 overs the visitors were 86-7.

Andrew Pearce, of Wirksworth C.C., topscored with 20 but had to retire hurt, aftar being struck on his forearm by a lifting delivery from Richard Boyle while 12-year-old wicket keeper batsman, Andrew Rogers was undefeated with a well played 16.

Roger Suttle and Tim Kirk scored 12 and ten respectively.

Bowling for Robinson, Kerry Spray took 2-10, Eddie Grant 2-17, while Adam Moon, Jon Grant and Richard Boyle took one each for five, 13 and 17 respectively.

In reply Robinson scored 89-3 off 23 overs. Opening batsman Marcus Hindle top scored with 33, while Jon Grant scored 16 and skipper Walker 12 not out

Bowling for the Touring Team, Peter Pollard, Stuart Baddeley and John Johnson took one each for nine, 13 and 29 respectively to give Robinson victory by seven wickets.

The event was videoed by the Pollards and after the match, Mrs Jan Hession presented a trophy to Andrew Rogers for his all round performance and a medal to Marcus Kindle for his batting.

Cash boost for cricket touring team

A cheese and wine party held by local Vauxhall dealers, The Blake Group of Chatsworth Road, Chesterfield, raised £80 towards the cost of Chesterfield and District Cricket Touring Team's forthcoming tour of Barbados.

The Blake Group's marketing manager David Creed, is pictured handing over the cheque to Mrs. Ann Wells, treasurer of the Chesterfield and District Cricket Touring Team. Also pictured are guests who attended the cheese and wine evening.

Guests were welcomed by group managing director, Mr David Merrifield and a buffet followed a guided tour of the service area and workshops at the Chatsworth Road, premises.

Treasurer of the Touring Team, Mrs. Ann Wells drew the raffle and the winner of the Immobiliser Security System, supplied by The Blake Group, was Mrs Joyce Cooper of Mansfield Woodhouse.

Mrs Wells thanked the management and staff of The Blake Group for their hospitality and those who attended the event before receiving the donation to the Touring Team from Mr David Creed, marketing manager of The Blake Group.

The Gazette 23 June 1993

A.G.D. 2nd 104-9
Marshalls 2nd 105-1
(Bassetlaw 2E)

The return fixture between A.G.D. 2nd XI and Marshalls 2nd XI resulted in a nine wicket victory for Marshalls C.C. ably led by Tony Guilliat at Gainsborough, Lincolnshire last Saturday afternoon with ideal conditions

Marshalls won the toss and sent in A.G.D. to bat on an easy-paced wicket, but after 34 overs, A.G.D. were 59-6.

Veteran Dick Suttle, in tigerish form despite his 64 years, came in at number eight and top scored with a swashbuckling 40.

His big-hitting innings included three massive sixes and three fours, while useful contributions came from Graham with 19, Chris Slack 17 and Martin Lomas 14 to take the score to 104-9 off 46 overs.

For Marshalls, Keith Limb, who bowled unchanged, ended with the rewarding analysis of 7-57 in 29 overs, while Mick Hewson took 2-24 in 17 overs.

In reply, Marshalls scored 106-1 off 20·4 overs.

Ged Hudson topscored with a splendid and undefeated 45 and was well supported by Steve Hadfleld with an undefeated 29, while Danny Nelson who opened the Innings, was bowled by Graham for a well played 23.

Rae Graham took the only wicket to fall for 11 runs in seven overs, to give Marahalls victory by nine wickets and consolidate their sixth victory of the season.

The Derbyshire Times July 22, 1993

Pre tour entertainment was provided by Connection Duo comprising Ian Jones and Ian Moss both of Chesterfield. Ian Jones was featured on TV in *Stars in their Eyes* as George Michael and is currently working as a Class 1 HGV driver and semi professional entertainer. Ian Jones was a tourist with the Loundsley Green C.C. and is registered with Spital C.C. for whom his father Dave Jones was associated for many years.

Holme Hall's three wicket victory
St. Peter & St. Paul School 59·2, Holme Hall School 61-7

Holme Hall Primary School Cricket Team
Back row L to R:- *R. Suttle (N.C.A. Coach), C. Barker, G. Collins, J. Sketchley, J. Brown, L. Watson, C. Bewley, John Brown (Derbyshire County Youth Coach)*
Front row L to R:- *B. Shepherd, M. Ryalls, B. Bahlaj, C. Hickton, A. Fareham (Capt.), C. Cowley, D. Hodby, M. Kirk, M. Allen*
Missing from the photograph: Darren Platt

St. Peter & St. Paul School, captained by Ross Sylvester, met Holme Hall School, led by William Buckingham at Newbold Community and resulted In a victory for Holme Hall School by three wickets.

After winning the toss, skipper Buckingham sent in St. Peter and St. Paul to bat on the Astroturf wicket and after 20 overs, they scored 69-2.

Ross Sylvester topscored with 16 while Edward Crowther scored 14 not out.

Bowling for Holme Hall, William Buckingham took 2-16 in eight overs.

In reply, Holme Hall scored 61-7 off 14 overs. Lee Miller was the only batsman to reach double figures. He scored 12 before being run-out.

Bowling for St. Peter and St. Paul 11-year-old Ross Sylvester with his medium pacers, took 8-7 in three overs while Simon Calow took 1-7, Edward Crowther 1-6 and Charles Summut 1-11. (See colour photos on page 10.)

The Derbyshire Times Thursday July 22, 1993

Touring team clinch shield

Clowne Town C.C. held its 10th annual cricket tournament under the supervision of Mr. Roy Burgin.

Teams taking part were: Marshalls, Clowne Town, Manton, Anston Greenlands, and the Chesterfield and District Touring Team – the sixth team, Grenoside, were unable to take part.

After a series of 12 over matches, using a round robin system which were keenly contested, Manton and the Chesterfield and District Team emerged winners of their respective groups and resulted in the final of the Pettinger Shield which ended in a nine wicket victory for the Touring Team over Manton, who have won the shield for the past three years.

The scores were: Manton C.C. 46-8 off 12 overs; Chesterfield and District T.T. 50-1 off 8·2 overs.

Tim Kirk, captain of the Touring Team won the toss and sent in Manton to bat, ably led by Roger Lee on a lively wicket and after 12 overs, they were 46-8.

Skipper Lee topscored with 20. John Johnson took 3-20, Simon Richardson 3-8 and Tim Kirk 1-5, which was backed up by splendid fielding and brilliant wicket keeping by 12-year-old Andrew Rogers.

In reply the Touring Team scored 50-1 off 8·2 overs.

Roger Suttle 27 not out and skipper Tim Kirk 21 not out, to win the final by nine wickets.

Nigel Keywood took the only wicket to fall for five runs in three overs.

After the match, Mr. Chris Woods, treasurer of Clowne C.C. thanked all those who participated in the tournament and then presented the Pettinger Shield to Tim Kirk, whilst Roger Lee received the runners-up trophy.

David Mannifield of Manton won the batting average, whilst Richard Gratton on the Touring Team won the bowling average. He took seven for 18.

Mrs. Ann Wells, secretary and treasurer of the Touring Team ended the day's activities with a vote of thanks.

Suttle is star in Shield

After a splendid day's cricket – lasting over ten hours in glorious weather – the Chesterfield and District Touring Team made it a successful trip to Clowne.

They won the Pettinger Shield in the Clowne Town tournament when they beat Manton in the final.

The teams had won through a round robin competition of 12 overs matches and in the final Chesterfield triumphed by nine wickets.

Manton were held to 46-8 with Simon Richardson taking 3-8 and John Johnson 3-20 and then Roger Suttle, 27 not out, and Tim Kirk, 21 not out, steered the tourists home to 50-1 after only 8.1 overs.

Chesterfield's Richard Grattan won the bowling award for the day and the batting award went to Dave Mannifield of Manton.

The Chesterfield lads continue their fund-raising efforts throughout the Summer in preparation for their trip to Barbados and in a week's time travel to Wilmslow.

The Derbyshire Times 7/8/93

Captain Kirk leads from the front
Wilmslow 128-8, Chesterfield Touring Team 129-4

Wilmslow C.C., winners of the Cheshire League Cup final entertained the Touring Team, Pettinger Shield winners, in a 30 over match and lost by six wickets.

Tourists' skipper Tim Kirk, won the toss on a damp and overcast afternoon and sent in Wilmslow to bat.

Bowling for the visitors, Neil Bradbury, who took a brilliant catch at short mid wicket, took 8-26 in six overs while Tim Kirk took 2-18. Martin Milner 1-21.

Steven Lee 1-21 and Stuart Baddeley who took a brilliant catch at deep long off, took 1-23.

In reply, the Tourists scored 129-4 off 29.2 overs. Tim Kirk topscored with an undeateated 54 which included four sixes and four fours while Neil Bradbury scored 24, Andrew Rogers 14 and Steven Lee 18 not out.

After the match, tour organiser, Dick Suttle thanked everyone for making the event a success, before asking Mrs. Rosemary Newson to present the individual trophies to Martin Stills of Wilmslow and Neil Bradbury for their outstanding performances.

The winner of the cricket bat in the programme raffle was Peter Feather, programme number 62.

The Derbyshire Times 15/8/93

Barbados bound!

Chesterfield cricketer Peter Feather is off to the Caribbean next month with a new addition to his armory when he takes on the West Indies due to tour Barbados with the Chesterfield and District Touring team and he won a new Magnum bat in one of the team's fund-raising prize draws, held while Peter was playing for the team in Wilmslow, Cheshire.

Chesterfield cricket captain Ansil Roach (left) is pictured handing over the prize.

The Derbyshire Times 9/9/93

Mrs. Rosemary Newson presents Neil Bradbury with a trophy for his outstanding performances of 24 and 3 for 26 at Wilmslow C.C. on 15th August 1993.

Test for Touring Team

Chesterfield and District Touring Team, captained by Steven Lee, met Budleigh Salterton C.C. at Queen's Park on Sunday 19th September 1993.

Having won the toss, skipper Lee sent in the visitors to bat on a perfect wicket and after their alloted 40 overs, Budleigh Salterton were 203-8.

Australian born Ross Toohey and Neil Murrin of Devon produced an opening stand of 130, before Toohey was brilliantly caught at mid-off by Lee, off Baddeley's bowling for a splendid 90, which included one six and 12 fours, while his partner went on to score a valuable 58.

The only other batsman to reach double figures was Paul Escott with 25.

Eighteen-year-old Andrew Pearce was the Touring Team's most successful bowler, he took 5-22 in eight overs with his leg spinners, while Richard Gratton took 3-35 in six overs.

In reply the Touring Team were all out for 190 in 39·3 overs.

Opening batsman Andrew Pearce topscored with a well played 76, which included 12 fours, while Neil Bradbury and Alan Haggo contributed splendid innings of 48 and 34 respectively.

Bowling for Budlejgh Salterton, Ross Toohey took 4-5 in 4 overs with his fast medium pacers while Ray Dawson took 2-27 in five overs, Rob Newing 2-36 in eight overs, while Neil Rice and Graham Vanstone took one each for 31 and 36 respectively to give their team a victory by 13 runs with three balls left.

Mrs. Ann Wells, Manager of the Touring Team presented a bat autographed by England and West Indian Players to Brian Atkinson who won it in their Grand Summer Raffle with ticket no 0851, while Trophies were presented to Toohey and Pearce for their outstanding performances by Mrs. Lovegrove and Miss Julie Weston, while Mr. Derek Harris from Devon won the Crystal Decanter donated by Dema Glass of Chesterfield with programme No. 100 as the shadows of the pavilion lengthen to remind us of the passing of yet another Summer. (See colour photo page 11.)

Umpires: - Messrs. R. Lovegrove & M. Rowland.

Cricketing trio's England trials

Three young north Derbyshire cricketers are being groomed as stars of the future.

Andrew Rogers, Steven Dolling and Alan Gofton, who all play for Sheepbridge Cricket Club, have been invited to take part in England Schools' U13s trials at Blackburn this month.

Andrew, of Heaton Street, Brampton; Steven, of Hollythorpe Close, Hasland; and Alan, of Brent Close, Newbold, have all represented Derbyshire at junior level and the trio are expected to impress the selectors in Lancashire.

A member of Dick Suttle's touring team, Andrew is due to play in Barbados later this year. He is pictured above, left, Steven (middle) and Alan (right) are also pictured on the previous page.

Rain stops play for Touring Team

The Chesterfield and District Touring Team, under the captaincy of Roger Suttle, deputising for skipper Tim Kirk, who was representing Chesterfield 1st XI in the final of the Tomlin Cup, met Chatsworth C.C., led by Jeff Madin.

Play began on a slightly overcast Sunday afternoon at Chatsworth, but the match was abandoned after an hour and 20 minutes because of rain.

Skipper Madin won the toss and sent in the visitors to bat on a wicket which produced variable bounce and after 21·5 overs, Andrew Pearce and Andrew Rogers took the score to 69 without loss and were undefeated with 46 and 20 respectively when rain stopped play at 3pm.

An early tea was taken, but at 4pm the match was abandoned due to heavy showers.

Bowling for Chatsworth David Robinson took 0:12 in five overs. Richard Ashcroft 0:15 in seven overs, Neil Whitham 0:20 in six overs and Harry Jones 0:21 in 3·5 overs.

Richard Gratton won the bottle of whisky donated by Mr and Mrs Lack with programme number 11.

Pre-tour match ends on a high note

An England Ladies eight-a-side team met the Chesterfield and District Cricket Touring Team on Sunday at Sharley Park Leisure Centre, Clay Cross, where the Touring Team won their final pre-tour match by 12 runs.

Ann Woods won the toss and sent the Touring Team – led by Steven Lee – in to bat, but after 9·3 overs, the Tourists were all out for 107, thanks to some briliant catching and fielding by the England team astutely led by Ann Woods.

Andrew Pearce topscored with 36, while Richard Gratton and Roy Burgin scored 28 and 24 respectively.

Gwyn Morris, who won the bowling award, took 3:11 in three overs, while Wendy Watson and Jane Cheney took one each for six and 22 respectively.

In reply, England Ladies scored 95 for one off their allotted 12 overs.

Evette Burton topscored with 27 not out, Wendy Watson 25 not out and Kim Robertson who scored 15 was caught by Baddeley off Roy Burgin's bowling. He took the only wicket to fall for 20 runs in three overs to give his team victory by 12 runs.

The Chesterfield and District Touring Team will leave for their tour of Barbados on Monday after a final farewell celebration at The Bradbury Club, Chesterfield.

The team invite everyone to the Grand Finale, a fun packed evening at the Bradbury Club on Thursday September 30 at 7pm, which will include music, dancing, raffle draw, auction, quiz and presentation of awards by a cricket celebrity.

Tickets are available, priced £4 adults, £2 children under 16, from Dick or Ann. (See colour photo on page 12.)

Tour Manager Mrs. Ann Wells, thanked everyone for their support before asking Mr. David Morley and Mrs. Trudie Turner to present Miss Gwynn Morris and Andrew Pearce with trophies for their outstanding performances, while Miss Angela Walmsley, of Speeds of Chesterfield, presented ties to Messrs Ron Lovegrove, Morris Rowland, Ben Lack and Jack Wilson (Umpires). Mrs. Nellie Lovegrove (Scorer) received a bouquet of flowers, which was presented by Miss Amy Rogers. Winning programme was no 77 as the final pre-tour match ended, before the Chesterfield and District Touring Team leaves for Barbados on Monday 4th October 1993.

England Ladies 8-a-side v **Chesterfield & District Cricket Touring Team 8-a-side**

1) Ann Woods (Capt.) (wkt)
2) Jo Chamberlain (World Cup player)
3) Karen Smithies (World Cup player & Capt.)
4) Wendy Watson (World Cup player)
5) Jane Cheney
6) Kim Robertson
7) Evette Burton
8) Gwynn Morris

1) Tim Kirk (Capt.)
2) Steven Lee
3) Stuart Baddeley
4) Richard Gratton
5) Andrew Rogers (wkt)
6) Peter Pollard
7) Neil Bradbury
8) Andrew Pearce

Reserves
Enid Bakewell (International player)
Karen Leppard

Reserves
1) John Johnson
2) Peter Feather
3) Roy Burgin
4) Allan Haggo
5) Roger Suttle

Dick Suttle (N.C.A. Coach)
Umpires:- Ron Lovegrove & Morris Rowland
Scorer:- Mrs. Nellie Lovegrove

N.B.
All are welcome to come along and support both teams. Do not lose your programme. It could be the one to win a Moulinex Mini Processor donated by Mrs. Ann Wells.

Barbados here we come!

Chesterfield's cricket touring team jets off to Barbados on Monday.

And the players will take with them a special plaque presented to the team by the mayor of Chesterfield Cllr, George Wright.

The tourists are expected to play five matches in the Carribean during their two week stay on the Island.

Pictured is touring team captain Tim Kirk receiving the plaque from Cllr. Wright surrounded by team members.

Photograph by Andrew Eyley.

The Derbyshire Times

Trans-Atlantic journey for the fourth time
By Dick Suttle

On Monday, 4th October, 1993, the Chesterfield & District Cricket Touring Team, under the management of Mrs. Ann Wells and yours truly, commenced its second tour to Barbados at 5 a.m. from Bolsover via Calow Lane, Devonshire Arms, Hasland, Storforth Lane, reaching Chesterfield Town Hall at 5.30 a.m. on a cold but dry morning, where the main size of the party of officials, players and spectators finally boarded the coach, bound for Manchester Airport.

Before reaching the Airport, we enjoyed a very pleasant and peaceful journey as we travelled through Baslow, the High Peak District as the Autumn sun came up, displaying the beautiful stone walls of Derbyshire, onto Chapel-en-le-Frith, the new Stockport dual carriageway, via Cheshire, through the tranquil suburbs of Manchester during that time of the morning and finally arriving at ten past seven at Terminal 2, where our Scottish guest player and statistician Allan Haggo, accompanied by his wife Fiona and

eleven-month-old daughter Samantha were awaiting us, thus completing our touring party of 37, bound for the Caribbean.

Before commencing our 4,500 mile journey, we spent approximately $2^1/2$ hours going through the usual, but important routine, of having our passports and luggage thoroughly checked before boarding at 9.40 a.m. on Flight AMM 107 on a Boeing 757 via Banger, Maine and then Grantley Adams Airport, Barbados.

On previous occasions, I could recall many people commenting at the

L to R: *Tim Andrew, Neil and Roger are awaiting the repairs to be done to the plane before re-embarking on the flight for Barbados*

point when the plane took off, but on this occasion, it took off so smoothly that many of us did not realise that we were airborne.

After about ninety minutes, and beginning to relax and enjoy the $8^1/2$ hour flight, we were informed by the pilot that we were over the Atlantic, but due to a malfunction in one of the hydraulic systems, he would have to return to Manchester Airport to have some repairs done; but there was no need for anyone to panic.

Just imagine what an experience this must have been for those who have never flown before. However, Captain Andrew Crofts reassured us that everything was under control. Fortunately, we touched down safely with the Fire Tenders, Ambulance Services and First Aiders all in attendance, but thankfully, they were not needed.

The repairs took approximately $3^1/2$ hours, during which we were provided with free refreshments, before we were re-embarked and finally airborne on our journey to Barbados. This turned out to be a wonderful flight, but unfortunately we arrived some $7^1/2$ hours late, thus missing most of the representatives from the Barbados Board of Tourism, who had come to welcome us at Grantley Adams Airport. To complete our journey, it took us $3/4$ hr. by coach to the Europa Hotel, which is situated in St. James safely; but obviously very tired and we needed a few days to overcome jet lag.

Howzat for a wedding!
Couple say 'I do' on calypso cricket tour

301

All-rounder Stuart Baddeley finally bowled his maiden over in the sunshine of the Caribbean. (See colour photo on page 13.)

A local minister visited the apartments where they were staying during a cricket tour of Barbados to seal the match between himself and his fiance of five years, Caroline Gregory.

A cricket bat guard of honour, formed by Stuart's playing colleagues, was awaiting the couple after the cermony,

"We decided about three months before the tour to marry on the island. We thought it would be romantic and something we would never forget.

"It was a gorgeous day and it was absolutely marvellous," said Caroline (24), a postal officer at the Postal Finance Department, Chesterfield.

The marriage took place in St James, Barbados, during a visit by the Chesterfield and District Touring Team. Caroline was one of the supporters in the 38 strong party.

She took her full length ivory wedding dress over from her parents' home at 40 Gower Crescent, Loundsley Green, Chesterfield, for the ceremony which was attended by her mother, Pearl.

Stuart, of 1 Elvin Way, New Tupton, a buyer for Sheffield Children's Hospital, plays league cricket with Pilsley C.C. and friendly matches with YYZ.

Celebrations in Barbados have been followed by others at the Van Dyk Hotel, Clowne, and Winding Wheel, Chesterfield.

The couple are now living at North Wingfield.

The Derbyshire Times Thursday, November 4th, 1993

Tour Match
by Dick Suttle – Played at Kensington Oval

Scores: Chesterfield & District C.T.T. – 140 for 4 off 40 overs
Barbados Combined Schools   – 143 for 2 off 31 overs

On Wednesday, 13th October, Chesterfield & District Cricket Touring Team, ably led by Tim Kirk, met Barbados Combined Schools XI, captained by Donovan Lopez, at Kensington Oval, where the match resulted in an eight wicket victory for the Combined Schools, with 9 overs left.

After winning the toss, skipper Lopez sent in the tourists to bat on a shirt front wicket, with ideal conditions prevailing, and after 40 overs, the Tourists were 140 for 4. The bespectacled Andrew Pearce, who opened the innings, topscored with a splendid 49, which included six fours. Allan Haggo at No. 3 struck one six and three fours in his 42, while skipper Kirk was undefeated with 26.

Michael Dunner took 2 for 35, while skipper Lopez and Ryan Hurley took one each for I7 and 27 respectively,

In reply, Combined Schools scored 143 for 2 off 31 overs. Allrounder Ryan Hurley topscored with an undefeated 58, which included seven fours, while useful supporting innings came from Ryan McCarthy 41, David Sealy 13, and Dwain Gill 16 not out.

Bowling for the Tourists, Tim Kirk and Roy Burgin took one each for 21 and 31 respectively,

After the match, short speeches and introductions were made by Keith Boyce (coach of Combined Schools) and Dick Suttle (Chesterfield). Mrs. Ann Wells (Manager of the Touring Team) presented Ryan Hurley with Man of the Match award before presenting a Hand Painted Shield, which was sent by the Mayor of Chesterfield to Mr. Wes Hall (Minister of Sport) who received the gift. He also spoke in glowing terms of his friendly involvement with sport and contacts around the world, before presenting two books on Tourism to Mrs. Wells for the team and the Mayor of Chesterfield.'

Skipper Lopez rounded off the evening's activities with individual mementos to members of the Touring Team.

Final tour match October 1993
By: Dick Suttle
Scores: Banks C.C. 191 for 7 off 30 overs
Chesterfield & District Touring Team 83 for 8 off 30 overs

On Friday 15th October, Banks C.C., ably led by Steve Linton, at Bridgetown Barbados entertained the Chesterfield & District Cricket Touring Team, Captained by Allan Haggo deputising for skipper Kirk at Banks Breweries, where the tourists last match ended in a victory for Banks C.C. by 108 runs in their friendly fixture, which was videoed by the Pollards, who have covered the entire tour.

Steve Linton won the toss on a perfect wicket in brilliant sunshine and decided to bat and after their allotted 30 overs Banks were 191 for 7. Michael Maynard topscored with an aggressive 45, while good supporting contributions came from Steve Holder 35, Luther Wiltshire 33, skipper Linton 21, Winston Greene 21 and Ronnie Gittens 15.

Bowling for the Touring Team, Steven Lee took 2 for 17, Dick Suttle 2 for 46, Morris Rowland 1 for 14 and Richard Gratton 1 for 37, during the abscence of some of their front line bowlers who were enjoying a day's excursion on the "Jolly Roger" in the idyllic waters of the Caribbean.

An innings of sound unfaltering concentration by 12-year-old wicket keeper batsman, Andrew Rogers, the last wicket to fall in the 29th over, top-scored with 28 and was ably assisted by Allan Haggo with 25, leaving

Richard Gratton and Dick Suttle to play out the remaining overs as they were both undefeated with 0 and 3 respectively and took the score to 83 for 8 off 30 overs.

Bowling for Banks, Linton took 2 for 9, Wiltshire 2 for 7, while Lovell, Graham, Holder and Gittens took one each for 0, 11, 15 and 28 respectively to give their team victory by 108 runs as the Chesterfield and District Cricket Touring Team ended their final match of the tour in gathering gloom.

Umpires:- Messrs. Ben Lack & Jack Wilson.

1993 tour results in Barbados

Chesterfield & District Touring Team:- 87 for 7 off 20 overs
A. Haggo 24. T. Kirk 18, S. Baddeley 12 not out, K. Burke 3 for 10, K. Lucas 3 for 9, I. McAlister 1 for 8.

Harrison College 16 for 2. off 5 overs. K. Harrison 9, S. Codrington 4 not out, John Johnson 1 for 11. Roy Burgin 1 for 5. (Abandoned because of rain.)

Chesterfield & District Cricket Touring Team:- 133 for 8 off 30 overs
A. Pearce 26, A. Haggo 33, S. Lee 18.
Matthew Moore 3 for 24, A. Branch 1 for 18, David Sealy 1 for 25, D. Clarke 1 for 25, P. Rock 1 for 30.

Foundation:- 119 for 6 off 30 overs
Matthew Moore 34, Allan Branch 32, David Sealy 19 not out, Roy Burgin 2 for 19, Neil Bradbury 2-for 15, John Johnson 1 for 17, Richard Gratton 1 for 27.

Combermere V Chesterfield & District Cricket Touring Team.
Chesterfield & District Cricket Touring Team 6 for 1 off 3 overs Derek Pilgrim 1 for 3. Abandoned because of rain

Chesterfield & District Cricket Touring Team 140 for 4 off 40 overs.
Andrew Pearce 49, Allan Haggo 42, Tim Kirk 26 not out, Michael Dunner 2 for 35, Ryan Hurley 1 for 27, Donavan Lopez 1 for 27.

Combined Schools:- 143 for 2 off 31 overs.
Ryan Hurley 58 not out, Ryan McCarthy 41, David Sealy 13. Dwain Gill 16 not out. Tim Kirk and Roy Burgin took one each for 21 and 31 respectively

Chesterfield & District Cricket Touring Team 87 all out off 33·5 overs,
Roger Suttle 28. Allan Haggo 16. Jerome Gittens 4 for 13, Davis, Lewis, Hackett Ellis. O'Neil took one each for 7, 5, 18, 22 and 6 respectively.

Lodge 90 for 4 off 17·4 overs
Jerome Gittens 52 not out A. Beckells 16, Tim Kirk 2 for 18, Johnson 1 for 7.

Banks Cricket Club 191 for 7 off 30 overs.
Micheal Maynard 45, Steve Holder 35, Luther Wiltshire 33, Steve Linton 21, Winston Greene 21. Ronnie Gittens 15, Steve Lee 2 for 17 Dick Suttle 2 for 46, Morris Rowland 1 for 14 & Richard Gratton I for 37.

Chesterfield & District Touring Team 83 for 8 off 30 overs, 12 year old Andrew Rogers 28, Allan Haggo 25, Steve Linton 2 for 9, Luther Wiltshire 2 for 7.

Chesterfield & District Cricket Touring Team Barbados 1993
Tour statistics
By Allan Haggo
Played - 6, Won - 1, Lost - 3, No Result - 2 (abandoned)
Runs scored by Chesterfield - 536. Wickets lost - 38
Runs scored by Opposition - 559. Wickets lost - 21

BATTING

Player	Matches	Innings	Not-outs	Runs scored	Average	Highest score
Tim Kirk	4	3	2	51	51-00	26 no.
Allan Haggo	6	5	-	140	28-00	42
Andrew Pearce	4	4	-	85	21-25	49
Stuart Baddeley	6	6	3	42	14-00	12 no.
Roger Suttle	4	3	-	29	9-66	28
Andrew Rogers	5	4	-	32	7-00	28
Steven Lee	6	4	_	28	7-00	18
Peter Feather	4	2	1	7	7-00	6 no.
Roy Burgin	5	2	1	6	6-00	3 no.
Peter Pollard	5	2	-	4	2-00	3
Richard Gratton	6	4	1	5	1-66	5
Neil Bradbury	3	3	-	2	0-66	1

ALSO BATTED

John Johnson - 8, Richard Suttle - 3 no. Andy Roberts - 1, Geoff Pollard -1, Rob Parker - 0

PARTNERSHIPS

Wickets	Total Partnership	Batsman	Opposition
1st	11	A. Rogen & S. Lee	Banks Brewery
2nd	78	A. Pearce & A. Haggo	Combined Schools
3rd	68	A. Pearce & A. Haggo	Foundation
4th	47	A. Haggo & T. Kirk	Harrisons
5th	40	T. Kirk & S. Baddeley	Combined Schools
6th	8	S. Lee & S. Baddeley	Lodge School
7th	16	P. Pollard & R. Suttle	Lodge School
8th	22	R. Suttle & S. Baddeley	Lodge School
9th	8	S. Baddeley & Haggo	Lodge School
10th	21	T. Kirk & A. Haggo	Lodge School

BOWLING

Player	Matches	Overs	Maidens	Wickets	Runs	Best Bowling	Average
Neil Bradbury	3	4	-	2	15	2-15	7-5
Steven Lee	6	3-1	-	2	21	2-17	10-5
Tim Kirk	4	14	-	3	39	2-18	13-00
Maurice Rowland	1	3	-	1	14	1-14	14-00
John Johnson	5	15-4	3	3	46	1-7	15-33
Richard Suttle	1	5	-	2	46	2-46	23-00
Roy Burgin	5	24	2	4	112	1-5	28-00
Richard Gratton	6	19	1	2	90	1-24	45-00
Andrew Pearce	4	2	-	-	15	0-15	-
Stewert Baddeley	6	9	-	-	70	0-11	-
Roger Suttle	4	13	-	-	73	0-6	-

FIELDING

CATCHES Roger Suttle - 2, Roy Burgin - 1, Alan Haggo -1, Andrew Pearce -1, Andy Roberts - 1, Stewart Baddley - 1

WICKET KEEPING

CATCHES Neil Bradbury - 2, Andrew Rogers - 2

Letter from John Deane

As a parent of two young cricketers who have benefited from the coaching of Richard Suttle, I write to express my gratitude to Richard.

Both my sons have represented Derbyshire at second XI level, Geoffrey at the age of twenty and Michael at age seventeen.

Michael in particular is a quick bowler and a hard hitting batsman whose approach to batting is very much in the West Indian mould, he delights in cutting, hooking and pulling and he is himself grateful to Richard whose tuition in those departments he acknowledges.

Geoffrey is an opening batsman who is now averaging around 45 runs per game throughout the season in 1994 and he too remembers Richard's words of advice and his delight at the success of those he has helped.

Nothing, except the game of cricket has been of such influence in Richard's life and he has kindled that same love in the hearts of many others.

I know that life has its ups and downs and I suspect that Richard discovered at an early age that cricket and life have much in common.

Cricket has been his life and his life has been around cricket, youngsters around Chesterfield look at him carrying his cricket bag and say "It's Mister Cricket".

How right they are.

From a grateful parent.

306

Mrs. Ann Wells, Manager of the Ches. & Dist. Cricket Touring Team presents a gift to the mayor of Chesterfield Cllr. Wright with a book from Barbados, sent by the Rt. Hon. Wes Hall, former West Indies fast bowler.
Looking on from L to R are:- *Dick Suttle, Ben Lack, Morris Rowland, Mary Ryan & Madge Lack*

Sobers makes tourists'day

By Les Payne

Talking of fund-raising, the cricketers from Chesterfield who worked their socks off in the past year to pay their way to play in the Caribbean, have returned telling of a wonderful trip.

And it was 'made' when two cricketing all-time greats – one of them arguably THE greatest – came walking across the outfield on one of the world's Test grounds to meet them. (See colour photo page 14.)

It happened at the Kensington Oval, Barbados, and the group was delighted when none other than Sir Gary Sobers and Wes Hall met the group and chatted with them.

It was a special moment for the local cricketers but especially for their organiser Dick Suttle. A Barbadian but for a long time living in Chesterfield, he was a former Sobers teammate from years ago in Barbados.

The Derbyshire Times Thursday, October 28, 1993

Allan, Fiona and Samantha – Barbados 1993

Cricket – Wickets were a lot slower than expected – outfields were poor as were a lot of the facilities. The hardness of Barbados cricket was displayed during the final match against Banks where we saw the difference between

307

Club and School's cricket.

Cricket Highlights – Beating Foundation whilst not ably led by Tim Kirk, playing at the Kensington Oval, and Roger's cover drives against Lodge.

Most Memorable Match – Most certainly this one against Foundation when a tremendous all round team effort won us the game against the odds.

Disappointments – The lack of local boys playing cricket on the beach and in the streets. Barbados did not live up to this reputation.

Players for the Future – Jerome Gittens, Ryan McCarthy and Ryan Hurley of the Barbadians. Andy Rogers and Andy Pearce of the Tourists.

Best Tour Batting Performance – Jerome Gittens' 54 not out for Lodge School.

Best Tour Bowling Performance – Roy Burgin's spell of 2 for 19 from seven overs against Foundation.

Best Tour Fielding – Stuart Baddeley throughout.

Best Drinking Performance – John Johnson's (surprise, surprise) Nine Bank's Beers during happy hour.

Best Eating Performance – Tim Kirk's demolition of an enormous curry at Angry Annies, he even licked the plate.

Tour Highlights – Meeting Sir Garfield Sobers for the first time, meeting Roger Suttle for the third time, and the wedding of Stuart & Caroline.

Tour Lowlights – The abandonment at Harrisons and Combemere, making fools of ourselves at Lodge, and drinking Tiger Malt at Bank's Brewery!

Humorous Moments – J.J. recalling how he defeated the Barbados darts champion and bemoaning the fact that he was using only bar darts. Maurice Rowland's straight face, after I asked for the sightscreen to be moved at Kensington Oval. (The screen is a 24 inch thick wall).

Signing Off – Fiona, Samantha and I had a brilliant two weeks in good company, really nice people. We hope to meet everyone again in Scotland in 1994 and look forward to beating the Tourists at Prestwick.

Finally, thanks are due to Ann and Dick without who the trip would not have been possible. Their organisation made sure the tour was successful and they were tireless workers before and after.

Deane a danger

The M.C.C. side due to face Rocester's Abbotsholme School cricket team today (Tuesday) could find things tougher than they expected thanks to Michael Deane.

Deane (18) – who has played several games for the Derbyshire Second XI – has been in cracking form so far this term, taking 14 wickets in the first three matches.

He also played a major part in last week's hefty defeat of Thomas Alleyne's High School, Uttoxeter, taking eight for 20 in just 35 balls.

June 1995

My experience of a cricket tour to Barbados

The chance of a cricketing tour to Barbados was an opportunity of a life time, which I could not refuse. In cricketing terms there can be no stiffer challenge than to face a side from the West Indies. This challenge proved to be an excellant test for the whole of the Chesterfield and District Touring Team as I personally enjoyed immensely.

Added to this, there is of course Barbados itself, a beautiful Island where locals are warm and welcoming and proud of their Island, which has so much to offer besides the cricket, there are many places of interest to visit for people of all ages and sceneries to take your breath away. On top of all that, there is of course the climate a great plus for some one used to the normal British summer.

Peter Feather

New cricketing experience

The experience which I gained during the two week cricketing tour of Barbados was something money could not buy.

I will never forget those burley West Indian Bowlers towering down on me, sending the ball whistling past my nose.

It was at this particular time, I remembered my dad saying to me

'Did you give me thought whilst you were enjoying yourself?' said dad. 'Yes.' Dad said, 'When did you think of me?'

I told him, I thought of him when I received 4 bouncers in the first over around my head, against Bank's Breweries. I also thought I would never see him again.

This tour will forever live in my memory as the company of the players and their families made the trip enjoyable and a memorable one.

I will always be extremely grateful to Dick Suttle and Ann Wells for giving me the chance of a lifetime.

Andrew Rogers (aged 12)

Umpiring in the Caribbean

Having Umpired in Barbados was quite an experience. The pitch completely different in texture to ours (back home) in the United Kingdom. The grass is a rough rye nature there is very little of it. Looking at the pitch was like looking at straw being rolled into soil, noticably the bowlers foot marks were far less than our own pitches.

The ball became rough more quickly, line and length becoming more important as the movement of the ball is very little if any.

Good points regarding umpiring-broken lines at right angles to the bowling and popping creases the length of the pitch indicating the ten feet pitch width secondly, lines marked at the back and at right angles to the redundant bowling crease. One foot either side of the middle stump, a guide to bowlers infringing the danger area of the pitch.

A good experience and one I should like to repeat.

Maurice Rowland

Caribbean dream which came true
By Richard Gratton

Destination Barbados, The Caribbean, the many thoughts of it provokes visions of blue skies, heat, clear seas,palm trees, sand. So when I was asked to go there as part of the Chesterfield and District Touring team I couldn't quite take it in. The holiday of a lifetime and the chance to play cricket, two weeks simply wouldn't be long enough.

As we arrived the first thing to wonder at was the heat 27°C at 11pm! We sped down road bristling with the sound of crickets surrounded by the tropical heat. It was still all a dream, yet here I was 4,000 miles away from home. The holiday flashed by. Days lasted for minutes, the sun had no sooner risen above our chalet, than it was setting over the Caribbean silhouetting the palms, waking the crickets as if to act as a reminder to us that we were still in Barbados.

Looking back its hard to imagine being there, golden sands, unbelievable heat, tiny lizards with huge gazing eyes. Touring the Island brought us further magics, we saw the contrast between the lazy Caribbean and the harshness of the mighty Atlantic, wandered dreamily through magnificant caves and found harmless black furry bees as big as golf balls, it was like something from an adventure fiction novel, a fantasy land.

The cricket was an experience which can never be forgotten. Playing on the Kensington Oval, meeting Sir Gary Sobers, trying to run about in temperatures unheard of in England. The difference in standards between school sides out there and ours in England was frightening at fifteen we're still learning what bails are, whilst they're playing reverse sweeps and bowling googlies. Yet viewing all these dream-like experiences, now one thing in particular strikes me as something to remember, the commitment of two people, Dick Suttle and Ann Wells organising accomodation, transport and fixtures from over 4,000 miles away is a feat which should be acknowledged and admired. Dick, who taught me how to play the game when I was just seven-years-old, symbolised everything about cricket, enthusiasm, wit and sternness when needed, Ann stepped in as Manager in unfortunate circumstances keeping the tour together.

It was a holiday of a lifetime meeting Sir Gary Sobers and Wes Hall, playing on the Kensington Oval,swimming in seas as clear as snow suggested it is a memory I shall never forget. It was the experience of experiences but if it wasn't for the excellence of Dick Suttle and Ann Wells this dream would never have become reality.

A Cricket Fan of Derbyshire C.C.C.

I have long been a cricket fan.

Derbyshire are of course my team, but the game is what really matters to me.

I had a full 40 years playing the game which I love, mainly with Oxcroft, but I did get around. Somehow, the serenity of cricket put the working week into perspective. Life is to be lived, and the beautiful sound of willow on leather, the sunshine, (even the 'rain stopped plays') but especially the people, made you realise just how good times really can last the whole summer.

Now I'm into my autumn, and my days of running between the wickets are long gone. But now, it's my turn to give something back. I have umpired for about 20 years now, and the thrill of the game, the beauty and the peace are still there. People are friends in the pavilion, and as I stand firm against the bowlers call of 'owzat', see the almost pleading look on the batsman's face, weigh it all up and speak with all the authority I can muster – "not out". I feel like I'm in my spring again.

That's what my friend Dick Suttle is all about. He's a people's person and a cricketer's friend. His enthusiasm rubs off on all who meet him. He's been an inspiration to man and boy alike for a long time now, see a cricket match – Dick's there. All who know him, all the kids he's coached, all the players who have gone abroad on his tours – even me, an old man in a white coat owe him a debt of thanks, for keeping the game alive, and for keeping us all in our summer.

Ben Lack

An invitation to Prestwick's 40th Anniversary

After an absence of 18 years, I returned to Prestwick Cricket Club, Ayrshire, Scotland, accompanied by Mrs. Ann Wells, Secretary and Treasurer of the Chesterfield and District Cricket Touring Team, to celebrate the Club's 40th Anniversary, which was held at Western House, Craigie Road, Ayr.

We were warmly welcomed as we attended the Dinner Dance which was well organised as everyone thoroughly enjoyed themselves. It was on this unforgettable occasion, where we renewed many old acquaintances and made new ones.

The following day I was selected to play at Prestwick Oval were we played in a 40 over celebration match. I was very pleased to meet several of the Youth and Junior players of the Club, some of whom I coached in 1977 during my six month contract.

I was also informed that two of them are now international cricketers, in the persons of David Haggo, who is a (wicket-keeper batsman) and Andrew Tennant who is an (Allrounder).

School's cricket (Under 12)
by Dick Suttle

Scores: Highfield Hall School – 44 for 7 off 10 overs
Holme Hall School – 47 for 3 off 9·2 overs

On Thursday 20th July, 1995, Julian Wall, captain of Highfield Hall School, won the toss on a sun-drenched afternoon at Holme Hall School and decided to bat on an easy-paced wicket. After their allotted 10 overs, the visitors were 44 for 7.

Matthew Booth, who came in at No. 6, topscored with an undefeated 16, which included three fours, while Rachel Holmes at No. 9, was also un-defeated with 5, in which she struck a boundary.

Bowling for the home team, Alex Furniss took 5 for 51 Joe Carney 1 for 1, Adam Barker 1 for 6 and Skipper Daniel Lukic 2 for 8, with Barker taking a splendid catch to dismiss Thomas Swift for 5.

In reply, Holme Hall scored 47 for 5 off 9·2 overs. Alex Furniss topscored with an undefeated 21, which included two fours, while Lukic and Barker scored 6 and 3 not out respectively,

Highfields most successful bowler was Matthew Booth. He took 2 for 2, while Julian Wall took the other wicket for 9 runs, to give Holme Hall victory by seven wickets.

Umpires: Messrs. Steven Lee and Dave Connock.

Tourers beat the ladies

Chesterfield and District (Junior) Cricket Touring Team, ably led by Steven Dolling, entertained the East Midlands Women's Cricket Association XI, captained by Australian born Ann Woods at the Civil Services Sports Club, Duckmanton Lodge, where the match ended in victory for the Touring Team by 120 runs.

Having won the toss, Ann Woods sent in the opposition to bat on a placid wicket and after their allotted 40 overs, they were 231 for seven.

Fifteen-year-old Nathan Dumelow produced an opening stand of 87 with

West Indies Cricket Tour
UNITED KINGDOM
1995

AUTOGRAPHS

Captain –	Richie Richardson	
Vice-Captain –	Courtney Walsh	
	Curtly Ambrose	
	Carl Hooper	
	Brian Lara	
	Jimmy Adams	
	Keith Arthurton	
	Junior Murray	
	Winston Benjamin	
	Ian Bishop	
	Kenny Benjamin	
	Shivnarine Chanderpaul	
	Stuart Williams	
	Rajindra Dhanraj	
	Sherwin Campbell	
	Courtney Browne	
	Ottis Gibson	
Manager –	Wes Hall	
Coach –	Andy Roberts	
Physiotherapist –	Denis Waight	

Team Headquarters: Westbury Hotel, Conduit Street, London W1A 4UH.

Gareth Palmer who scored 16, while Dumelow went on to topscore with a splendid 109, which included two sixes and 16 fours. Other useful contributions came from Allan Moss with 46 not out and Jonathan Stapleton 15.

Bowling for the East Midland's team, Stephanie Powell took three for 46, Kate Scott one for 43, Nicola Shaw one for 44 and Helen Pugh who took one for 28, also ran out skipper Dolling before he had scored with a direct throw.

In reply, the visitors scored 111 for four off 40 overs. Wendy Watson and Angela Carter produced an opening stand of 78, before the former was brilliantly caught at short square leg by Gavin Young off Paul Goodwin's bowling for 27, while Carter went on to topscore with a flawless and undefeated innings of 59, which included four fours.

Bowling for the home team, 12-year-old Paul Goodwin took two for seven in 3 overs and Nathan Dumelow two for 12 in five overs to give their team victory by 120 runs.

After the match, Steven Dolling presented Ann Woods with a miniature cricket bat, after which she thanked the organisers for a wonderful match.

To round off the day's events, Katie and Louise Wells presented Ann Woods with a bouquet of flowers.

Chesterfield Advertiser 6th September 1996

Town Hall 'fixture' for cricket team
Chesterfield & District Junior Cricket Touring Team, due to leave for the Caribbean on October 1, took on an East Midlands Women's Association XI, at Duckmanton Lodge on Sunday. The tourists won the match by 120 runs. Their next 'fixture' is a civic reception at Chesterfield Town Hall on Thursday, September 12th at 6.45pm. Pictured are Katie and Louise Wells presenting flowers to the East Midlands Women's captain Ann Woods.

Sandals reception – Nottingham

I met Dick Suttle about 2 or 3 years ago, obviously because of our involvement in the great game of cricket, and since then we have had some very interesting discussions regarding the game and the politics of the game.

Due to our interest in the game, I assisted him in a very minor part I might say in organising his book and the 1996 Cricket Tour to his beloved

Barbados. As a result of this Dick was good enough because of his friendship with the great Wes Hall, the West Indian Tour Manager, to arrange for my son and an invitation to the Sandals Reception held at the Albion Crest Hotel, Nottingham on Tuesday, 8th August, 1995, two days before the 'test match' between England and the West Indies.

At the reception, which was lavish with West Indian food and drink, we were escorted by Wes Hall and introduced to a number of the West Indian Team, all of whom were at the reception.

I must make the point of the warmth and kindness shown to our party by Wes Hall and the West Indian team during the unforgettable evening will live with my son and me for a very long time. (The rum is very strong).

If this is a taste of the reception which we can expect on our arrival in Barbados then 'roll on' October 1996, and I would like to add my son's and my thanks to Dick and Ann for the terrific commitment of work, time and organisation which goes into a trip of this magnitude.

Thanks again Dick.

John A. Palmer

Results of pre-tour cricket matches 1996

Date   Results

6.5.96   Ches. & Dist. Touring Team-178 for 4 off 40 Overs
N. Dumelow 52, D. Eckersley 56 not out, D. Ireland 50 not out, S. Dolling 26, G. Palmer 14
Bowling for A.G.D. – P. Ward 2 for 57, R. Suttle 1 for 27, H. Smith 1 for 27
A.G.D. – 72 all out in 21.1 overs
R. Suttle 25, M. Preston 14, P. Passey 15
Bowling for Ches. & Dist. T.T. - G. Young 6 for 50, R. Casson 2 for 8, G. Anthony 2 for 9
Ches. & Dist. won by 106 runs at Duckmanton Lodge

10.6.96   Ches. & Dist. C.T.T. 158 for 7 off 40 overs
S. Dolling 56, N. Dumelow 58
Bowling for Mount St. Marys: J. Horan 2 for 7, R. Butler 2 for 18, A. Fitzgerald 2 for 21
Mount St. Marys 141 for 5 off 28·5 overs
R. Harrison 76, J. Moran 57, A. Fitzgerald 15
Bowling for Ches. & Dist. C.T.T. : N. Dumelow 1 for 14, G. Anthony 1 for 18, D. Ireland 1 for 54
Mount St. Marys won by 7 wickets at Mount St. Marys

14.7.96   Ches. & Dist. C.T.T. 195 for 7 off 40 overs
D. Eckersley 67, S. Dolling 56, G. Young 51
Bowling for A.G.D. : J. Johnson 2 for 55, P. Ward 1 for 25, M. Jelley
1 for 27, Goodwin 1 for 57
A.G.D. C.C. 160 for 8 off 40 overs
P. Ward 56, J. Johnson 27, A. Powell 18, M. Jelley 15, B. Skidmoor
10
Bowling for Ches. & Dist. C.T.T. : D. Ireland 5 for 28, G. Anthony 2
for 22, M. Preston 1 for 5, J. Stapleton 1 for 25 and R. Casson 1 for
50
Ches. & Dist. C.T.T. won by 35 runs at Duckmanton Lodge

18.7.96   Miners C.C. vs Ches. & Dist. C.T.T. at Dema Glass, Sheffield Road
Ches. & Dist. C.T.T. 70 all out off 20 overs
G. Palmer 18, M. Preston 12 not out, D. Eckersley 10, S. Dolling 10
Bowling for Miners C.C. : N. Bradbury 2 for 57, T. Bowyer 2 for l6.
S, Horton 2 for 5, D. Holland 2 for 6, A. Elks 1 for 9
Miners C.C. 71 for 3 off 13 overs
B. Brace 25, G. Lowe 18, S. Woodbine 17
Bowling for Ches. & Dist. C.T.T. : R. Casson 2 for 27, D. Ireland 1
for 3.
Miners won by 7 wickets

11.8.96   Ches. & Dist (Snr) C.T.T. vs Barbados Overseas Cricket Association
at Queen's Park, Chesterfield. (See colour page 5.)
Barbados O.C.A. 198 for 5 off 40 overs
M. Forte 51, J. Holder 43,, A. Broome 34, N. Puckerin 22 not out
J. Lashley 13
Bowling for Ches. & Dist. (Snr.) Team
T. Kirk 2 for 18, I Smith 2 for 23, R. Dumelow 1 for 40
Ches. & Dist. (Snr) T.T. 131 all out off 40 overs
D. Eckersley 31 not out, T. Kirk 25, S. Dolling 19, S. Lee 15,
Bowling for Barbados O.C.A.
F. Smith 3 for 27, G, Skinner 2 for 18, N. Puckerin 2 for 22
D. Foster 2 for 29, T. Riggot 1 for 29
Barbados Overseas Cricket Association won by 67 runs

1.9.96   Chest. & Dist. (Jnr.) C.T.T. vs East Midland Ladies at Duckmanton
Lodge
Chest. & Dist. Jnrs 231 for 7 off 40 overs
N. Dumelow 109» A. Moss 46 not out, G. Palmer 16, J. Stapleton 15

Bowling for East Midland Ladies: S. Powell 3 tor 46, M. Pugh 1 for 28, K. Scott 1 for 43, K. Shaw 1 for 44
East Midland Ladies 111 for 4 off 40 overs
A. Carter 59 not out, W. Watson 27
Bowling for the Ches. & Dist. (Jnr.) C.T.T.
P. Goodwin 2 for 7, N. Dumelow 2 for 12
Ches. & Dist. (Jnr) Cricket Touring Team won by 120 runs

Whither women's cricket

Women cricketers drive further was the message on a sticker produced to promote the 1988 World Cup, the pun, illustrating one of the recurring problems caused by the minority sport nature of the current English women's game. At present there are only about 60 affiliated clubs in the whole of England and the success of the national team on home soil in the 1993 World Cup did not catch the public imagination sufficiently to inspire many girls and women to take up the game. There are signs, however, that progess is being made in some areas and flurries of activity in Surrey, Derbyshire and South Yorkshire, for example, have resulted in the formation of new clubs. Women's clubs are keener to work alongside the men than they were in the past, and this has yielded many

benefits, particularly in the form of assistance with umpiring and coaching and the provision of facilities. Prejudices on the other side are also being slowly broken down.

There is much to recommend in women's cricket, not least in that on-field behavior upholds the traditional values of the game. At county level and above, there is a high level of skill. the players concentrating on being technically correct in batting, in particular, to compensate for strength deficiencies. The bowling obviously lacks the pace. bounce and greater "tweak" that can be obtained by men, but tends to be naggingly accurate instead. Players are generally more aware of fitness, too, with impetus being provided by the Sports Science Support Project which has supported the national team throughout the '90's.

Kwik cricket in primary schools and clubs has provided a boost for cricket in general and has been responsible for giving many girls an introduction to the game. In common with the men's game. however, problems occur when the children move into secondary school and many are lost to our sport through lack of opportunity and poor facilities. It is to be hoped that the recent change in emphasis of government education policy and the creation of increased playing opportunities that should result from the National Junior Sport Programme and from the injection of finance from the National Lottery will provide more opportunities and allow the slowly growing interest in women's cricket to snowball.

Ann Woods (February. 1996.) N.C.A. Advanced Coach
& Regional Cricket Development Officer for East Midlands Region

Barbados bound
By Dick Suttle

On a dry and pleasant autumnal morning on Tuesday 1st October 1996. The Chesterfield and District (Senior and Junior) Cricket Touring Teams, departed from Chesterfield Town Hall, where the main body of the party, embarked on Branson's Coaches at 6.45am via Gatwick Airport on their third tour of the Caribbean, under the supervision of Mrs. Ann Wells (Secretary and Treasurer) and Dick Suttle (N.C.A. Coach) and Organisers of the trip, which was booked through Mrs. Michelle Allsop and her staff at Soluna Travel of Hasland.

The party consisted of 94 people, 26 of whom were selected as cricketers to nine matches. Five senior games and four junior games.

The journey to Gatwick Airport (Surrey) took just over five hours as we stopped at various "pick-up-points" to collect passengers from Trowell Station, The Hilton Hotel, Keyworth (East Midlands) and Leicester Forest, before taking a half hour meal break at Newport Pagnell, where Mr. Don Brophy took a photograph of the entire group, under a cloudless sky. (see colour photo page 15.) After this we continued our journey to arrive at 12.03pm at the south terminal entrance at Gatwick Airport, where an additional 15 passengers were waiting to complete our party of 86, and also another eight people who had already arrived in Barbados on Sunday 29th September to give us a final party of 94.

Before boarding our Transatlantic flight (BY 1.70 A) on the New Boeing (767-200) piloted by Captain Campbell. We had our luggage checked and sorted by the Airport Officials before leaving at 2.10pm bound for Barbados.

The flight lasted $8^1/2$ hours; as beautiful sunshine prevailed throughout the journey as everyone enjoyed the flight tremendously as we landed safely at 5.45pm at Grantley Adams Airport where we were met by Mr. Winston Carter, from the Barbados Authority of Tourism and Lisa a Representative of Thomsons Tour Operators, before being transported to our respective destinations which included East and West Wing at St.

Lawrence Gap, Sandy Beach Island Resort and finally the Pirates Inn, thus ending a long and exciting journey to begin our two week holiday.

Our only victim of the trip was Gavin Young, who lost his baggage through a mistake, but was collected by Thomsons Representative the following day.

Banks Holdings Sports and Cultural Club
Wildey, St, Michael, Barbados. - Tel: 429-2113. Fax: 427-0772
1996 October 8

Mr Dick Suttle
East Wing
St Lawrence Gap
CHRIST CHURCH

Dear Dick

Regarding the playing conditions of our playing field I and my team are extremely sorry that the outfield was below the usually very high standards which we strive to attain: and which you have usually enjoyed during your visits to our wonderful cricket loving island.

However, as I explained to you and your secretary the rain fell very heavily for two weeks and consequently we were unable to undertake the usual preparation. This was compounded by the break-down of our tractor when we did get the preparation under way.

Hence the unusually tall grass had to be cut the said day that the match was played. Inspite of our herculean effort we did not get the outfield up to standard. However I understand that the wicket played very well and the cricket was competitive. For this we are grateful.

I hope you continue to enjoy your tour and that our club continue to find favour with your tour committee when considering future tours.

BANKS HOLDINGS SPORTS & CULTURAL CLUB
Tennyson C Beckles
President

Harrison College defeat Tourists by 41 runs
Scores:- Harrison College 129 for 9 off 38 overs
Chesterfield and District (Junior) Cricket Touring Team 88 for 6 off 38 overs
On Thursday 3rd October, Harrison College Cricket Team ably led by Neil Benn entertained the Chesterfield and District (Junior) Cricket Touring Team, captained by Steven Dolling in a 38 over match which was played

under sun drenched conditions and resulted in a victory for Harrison College in the opening match of the tour.

Skipper Benn won the toss and elected to bat on an easy paced wicket and after 38 overs, the home team were 129 for 9. Jason Haynes topscored with 59, which included two sixes and four fours, while Kerry Cummins and Steve Cumberbatch scored 11 and 10 respectively.

Bowling for the Touring Team Allan Moss 2 for 15, Danny Ireland 2 for 30 and Nathan Dumelow 2 for 29.

In reply the Touring Team scored 88 for 6 off 38 overs, topscoring for his team Steven Dolling played a disciplined and undefeated innings of 47 and Nathan Dumelow who opened the innings scored 12.

Bowling for the home team, Ken Clarke took 3 for 16, Che Cumberbatch 2 for 22 and Sean Boyce 1 for 17 to win by 41 runs.

Banks Cricket Club won by 2 wickets
Scores:-
Chesterfield and District Cricket Touring Team 112 for 8 off 35 overs
Banks Cricket Club 113 for 8 off 31·4 overs.

On Friday 4th October Banks Cricket Club ably led by Orlando Greenidge entertained the Chesterfield and District Cricket Club captained by Tim Kirk at Banks Brewery on a sunny afternoon; but early morning showers made playing conditions difficult as freshly mown grass covered the outfield restricting proper stroke play.

Having won the toss, Tim Kirk elected to bat and after 35 overs the Tourists were 112 for 8. Of these, skipper Kirk 32, Ian Smith 18, Sid Horton 17 not out, Mick Barratt 14, and Gloustershire wicket/batsman, Reg Williams 12,

Bowling for Banks C.C, Sean Armstrong 3 for 19, David Corby 2 for 10, Ricardo Best 1 for 18, Orlando Greenidge 1 for 5 and Winston Green 1 for 38.

In reply. Banks C. C. scored 113 for 8 off 31·4 overs, Anthony Stuart 32, Sean Armstrong 26, J. Connell 14 and Winston Green 12.

Bowling for the Touring Team, Martin Cheshire took 3 for 29, John Branson 2 for 15, Ian Frost 1 for 11 and Phil Adamson 1 for 32 as the home team won by 2 wickets.

Tourists soundly beaten as Foundation win by 10 wickets
Scores:-
Chesterfield and District (Junior) Cricket Touring Team 47 off 18·5 overs.
Ch. Ch. Foundation School 48 for 0 wickets off 13·2 overs.

On Monday 7th October, Foundation School, astutely led by Quame Millar met the Chesterfield and District (Junior) Cricket Touring Team captained by Steven Dolling at Foundation School, where the match ended in a convincing victory for the home team.

Skipper Millar won the toss and sent in the Touring Team to bat on a softish wicket which was affected by early morning showers. The visitors started disastrously, as two wickets fell before a run was scored. Danny Ireland who came in at no. 5 batted superbly, to topscore with a well played 15 and Richard Casson scored a useful 9, while the rest of the batsmen were unable to cope with the turning ball in the prevailing conditions.

Kurt Wilkinson Foundation's leg-spinner took 4 for 12 off 5 overs. Phillip Browne took 2 for 6, Ryan Austin 2 for 12, while Jedson Yarde and Kevin Roach took I each for 2 and 6 respectively.

In reply Foundation scored the 48 runs required for victory without losing a wicket in 13·2 overs as skipper Miller and Junior Franklyn were both undefeated with 12 and 31 respectively to give their team victory by 10 wickets. (See colour page 5.)

Exciting finish
Scores :- Dover C.C. 198 for 6 dec off 28 overs
Chesterfield & District (Senior) Cricket Touring Team 185 for 4 off 35 overs
On Monday 14th October Dover C.C. captained by Trevor Clarke, entertained the Chesterfield and District Touring Team led by Tim Kirk at Dover and after 28 overs, Dover declared with the score at 198 for 6. Bernard Chase topscored with 104, which contained 11 sixes and four fours. Robert Braithwaite 29, David Lucas 20, Sylverton Weekes 14, McNeil Brewster 10. Bowling for the Touring Team Jon Branson took 2 for 11, Tim Kirk 2 for 15 and Phil Baker 1 for 62.

In reply the Touring Team scored 185 runs off 35 overs. Opening Batsman Robert Dumelow topscored with a chanceless 67, which included four sixes and four fours. M. Barratt 31, M, Cheshire 27, Reg Williams 26 not out. Bowling for Dover C.C, D. Lucas took I for 23, R. Braithwaite 1 for 36, Clarke 1 for 24, J. Kirton I for 14 to give Dover Victory by 13 runs.

Presentation
After the Dover C.C. match on Monday 14th October at Dover, a Presentation was held at the West Wing St. Lawrence Gap, Christ Church where Mrs. Ann Wells (Secretary and Treasurer) introduced Mr. Darnley Marshall, Principal of St. Lawrence Composite School, in place of Miss. Annette Beckett from the *Voice of Barbados* to present the prizes.

Mr. Marshall made a short speech before presenting ties to Messrs. George Holmes, Morris Rowland and Tim Crossley who umpired the matches. Mr. Marshall also presented each member of the touring teams with badges donated by the Barbados Tourism Authority. Mrs. Wells also introduced the Managing Director of Dardale Distribution Services Limited, Mr. Michael Brennan who donated and presented the (Senior) Award to Robert Dumelow and the (Junior) award to Danny Ireland for their outstanding performances on the tour. Mr. Brennan also presented a clock, encased in a mahogany frame to the Organisers of the Tour Ann Wells and Dick Suttle. To round off the evening's activities, Tim Kirk (Captain of the Senior Team) presented the above mentioned organisers with a thank you card, signed by all the players and a figurine of a cricketer with best wishes for the future.

N.B. Before leaving Barbados, Mrs. Ann Wells (Secretary and Treasurer) of the Touring Team refunded each of the Senior players $132.00 for 3 matches which were cancelled and $36.00 to the Junior players who had one match cancelled.

Six-a-side match at Dover Tuesday 15/10/96

Nathan Dumelow's Team 96 for 2 off 15 overs,
Natham Dumelow – 33 not out,
Gareth Palmer – 33.
Richard Casson – 12 not out,
Nicholas Brennan – 8

Bowling for Steve Dolling's team

Gareth Anthony took 1 for 14.
Graham Dolling took 1 for 27.
Steve Dolling's Team - 52 for 5 off 7.3 overs.
Gareth Anthony 16.
Graham Dolling 18.

Bowling for Dumelow's team

Richard Casson took 5 for 4 in 1·5 overs, including a hat trick which included the wickets of Graham Dolling, Gareth Anthony and David Eckersley while Nicholas Brennan took 1 for 19.

After boarding the Booing 767-200 from Grantley Adams Airport, Barbados via Gatwick Airport, Captain Tony Newport made an announcement about Richard Casson's hat trick for which he received a hat trick tie from N.C.A. Team Coach Richard Suttle at 35,000 feet above the Atlantic, followed by loud applause from the passengers bound for the U.K.

P.S. Due to adverse wet conditions, the Senior team was unable to play Pickwick C.C. on Tuesday, 8th, Wednesday 9th and Friday, 11th October 1996, at Kensington Oval.

An invitation to The V.O.B. Barbados

L. to R are:- Steven Dolling (Capt. Jnr. Team), Tim Kirk (Capt. Snr. Team), "Shell" Harris (Interviewer) Dick Suttle (N.C.A, Coach and Organiser of the Tour)

On Saturday, 12th October, 1996, the Chesterfield & District Cricket Touring Teams were invited to the Barbados Radio Station and were interviewed on the *Voice of Barbados* by Mr. Erskine King, Miss Annette Beckett and my P.E. teacher, Mr. "Shell" Harris, at 1.15 p.m.

The broadcast was transmitted throughout the Caribbean.

Those who were interviewed were: L. to R. Steven Dolling (Capt. of Jnr. Team), Tim Kirk (Capt. of Snr. Team), Richard Suttle (N.C.A.) Coach & Organiser of the tour, and "Shell" Harris (Interviewer).

A group of 1996 Tour Supporters included Jack Hole, Roddy Nicol, Graham Dolling and Clive Wesson at the East Wing, St. Lawrence Gap, Christ Church, Barbados.

Other officials who attended the studio were:

Ann Wells (Sec. & Treas.) Nicola Kirk (Sect. of the Sen. team), Clive Wesson (Manager of the Jnr. team), & John Palmer (Statistician), while other supporters included:

Maggie Ireland, Tony Casson, Mick Brennan, Phil Adamson, Graham Dolling and Barrie Spice (Photographer & Video Operator).

1996 Tour of Barbados

Chest & District Cricket (Senior) Touring Team

(1) Tim Kirk (Capt) (Chesterfield C.C. & M.C.C.).
(2) Mick Barratt (Victoria C.C. Notts).
(3) Robert Dumelow (Ticknall C.C. Derby).
(4) Gareth Palmer * (Whitwell C.C.).
(5) Allan Moss * (Victoria C.C. Notts).
(6) Martin Cheshire (V/Capt) (Thoresby Colliery C.C.).
(7) Dave Hallam (Thoresby Colliery C.C.).
(8) Ian Smith (Thoresby Colliery C.C.).
(9) Steven Lee (Y.Y.Z.C.C.).
(10) Peter Feather (S & J Kitchin C.C.).
(11) Jon Branson (Clay Cross C.C.).
(12) Phil Adamson (A.G.D. C.C.).
(13) Phil Baker (Bolsover C.C.).
(14) Ian Frost (Pretoria O.B.C.A. & Tunbridge Wells C.C.)
(15) Richard Williams (Gloucestershire C.C.). (WK)

Chest & Dist Cricket (Junior) Touring Team

(1) Steven Dolling (Capt) (Holmewood & Heath C.C. & Derbys Un 16)
(2) Nathan Dumelow (V/Capt) (Ticknall C.C. & Derbys Un 16)
(3) Gavin Young (Matlock C.C.).
(4) Richard Casson (Newton C.C. & Derbys Un 16).
(5) Andrew Phipps (Sheepbridge C.C.)
(6) Gareth Anthony (Ilkeston & Rutland C.C. & Derbys Un 16).
(7) Nicholas Brennan (Victoria C.C. Notts).
(8) David Eckersley (Trent College C.C. (WK) & Derbys Un 16).
(9) Daniel Ireland (Sheepbridge C.C.).
(10) Jonathan Stapleton (Matlock C.C. & Derbys Un 16)
(11) Matthew Preston (Baslow C.C.).
(12) Clive Wesson (Manager).
(13) Dick Suttle (N.C.A. Coach).
(14) Ann Wells (Secretary & Treasurer).

* This indicates players who are also members of the Junior Touring Team.

Students rewarded

Manor College held its second celebration evening in honour of those students who gained a qualification during the previous academic year.

The event was held at the Winding Wheel to accommodate the growing number of students and achievements.

Frank Lord, a corporation member presented the certificates to 105 students.

A special presentation was made to Jane Hughes a student on the centre's extended Education Course, for completing the Breakthrough to Education Course.

Frank Lord presents English and maths student Marva Suttle with her certificate 1999

THE FINAL CHAPTER

With the passing of time, I can now look back with great pleasure in my retirement, to enjoy my son, Roger's progress and enthusiasm in taking up, where I left off, in helping and encouraging the up-and-coming youngsters to enjoy and achieve great heights in the cricketing arena.

I wish him, my six-month-old grandson Isaac and my daughter-in-law Rachel best wishes and every success in the future. (See colour photo page 16.)

After experiencing some very devastating and emotional shocks in my life, which have been mixed with some inspirational enjoyment from my humble cricketing background, I have entitled this book *The Vicissitudes of a Cricketing Motivator* – in simple terms refers to the ups and downs of one's life in general, I sincerely hope my effort in producing this book with the help of family, friends and colleagues to whom I owe a debt of gratitude, will not only give individuals great pleasure in reading its contents,, but also encourage them to overcome the inevitable obstacles which life can some-times impose on us and our loved ones.

Finally, if it be God's will, I have just two cricketing ambitions left. They are to have the opportunity to visit the cricketing fields of Australia, New Zealand and South Africa and be able to extend an invitation to the Combined Schools' Team (Under 18's) of Barbados to tour Chesterfield and other parts of Derbyshire.

Thanks once again to all those who have contributed in any way to the publication of this book.

ACKNOWLEDGEMENTS

Mrs. Ann and Miss Sally Wells
Mr. and Mrs. R. Lovegrove
Mr. and Mrs. T. Kirk
Mr. amd Mrs. M. Rowland
Mr. and Mrs. B. Lack
Mr. and Mrs. D. Haggo
Mr. and Mrs. J. King
Mr and Mrs G Newson
Mr. and Mrs. J. Brailsford
Mr. and Mrs. A. Hession
Mrs. Joan Dolling (secretary)
G. & J. Holmes
Mr. Geoff Holden
Mr. Andrew Jarvis
Mrs. Betty Beet
Mr. Doug Herring
Mr. Colin Hampton
Mr. and Mrs. M. Taylor (photographer)
Mr. B. Spice (photographer)
Ultimate Signs

INDEX

Elliott, Robert 156
Elliott, Sally 177
Ellis, Mrs. 52
Ellis, Robin 49, 62, 83
Elmers End C.C. 27-28
Emmens, Mick 179
Englefield Green, Surrey 137
English Schools Cricket Association 87
Escott, Paul 295
Esveld, Van 158
Evans, Andy 230, 232, 235
Evans, David 164, 165
Evans, Philip 141
Evans, Stephen 54, 82, 92, 95, 99, 100-103, 106-107, 110-111
Eynsford, Kent 97
Eyre, Alan 123
Fairholme Guest House, Christchurch 205
Fairs, Martin 45, 47
Farquahson, Ian 167
Farrell, Jeffrey 11
Fazil, Nasreen 265
Fearn, George 38
Feather, Peter 294-295
Ferguson, Doug 178
Fergusson, Alston 13
Fidler, Ernie 144
Fidler, Richard 192
Field, Tony 102
Fielding, Colin 49
Fishwick, Nicholas 121, 143
Flavell, David 101
Fleming, A.W.P. 170
Flemming, Fergusson 13
Forbes, David 184
Forbes, Mark 113
Forde, Anthony 27
Forde, Ernest 24
Fordham, Stephen 137
Forrest, Duncan 203
Forte, Martin 97, 100-101, 107, 260
Foster, Beverley 9
Foster, Bob 38, 61
Foster, Paul 222, 259
Foster, Stephen 143
Francis, George "Cudjoe" 7

Francis, Ian 115-116
Franklyn, Junior 321
Frecheville C.C. 99, 121, 143
Frecheville Junior C.C. 101
Frost, Ian 320
Frost, Peter 143
Fuller, Robert 279
Fuller, Stephen 116-117
Fulwood, Naolmi 265
Furness, David 111
Furniss, Alex 288, 312
Gamble, Marva 24
Garner, Rawle 14
Garnes, Annette 10
Garnes, Desmond 9
Garrison Savannah, Bridgetown 17
Garvey, Jim 13
Gaunt, Alf 175, 190
Gay, Eroll 10
Gayton, Graham 228
Gibbions, Shaun 183, 186-187
Gibson, George 11
Gibson, Ryland 261
Gilchrist, Simon 236
Gilchrist, Tim 232
Gill, Darrell 17
Gill, Dwain 303
Gill, Rudolph 10, 17-18
Gillham, Charlie 61
Gilthorpe, Andrew 192
Gilthorpe, Johnathan 192
Gittens, Clifford 10
Gittens, Ronnie 303
Gittens, Winston 10
Gittins, Barry 202
Gladwin, Brian 175
Gladwin, Cliff 50, 145
Glapwell 188
Globe, Austin 144
Goddard, D 18
Goddard, E 19
Goddard, Noel 16, 17, 20
Gofton, Alan 297
Gofton, Paul 192
Goldstraw, Jane 238, 243
Goldstraw, Stan 239
Goldwell C.C. 228-229, 231, 236
Goodridge, Eroll 10

Goodwin, Paul 314
Gordon, George 27
Gowling, Jim 138
Graham, Norman 51, 58, 64, 82, 99, 127, 222, 230, 237
Graham, Rae 292
Graham, Terry 204
Grainger, Michael 192
Grant, Eddie 290
Grant, Frank 13
Grant, Gary 277
Grant, Jon 290
Grassmoor 49
Gratton, Richard 289, 294, 296-297, 303-304
Graveney, Tom 172
Graves, Mark 202
Gray, David 192
Greatbatch, Paul 121
Greaves, Gordon 46
Greaves, Neville 17
Greaves, Tony 178
Green, Penny 177
Green, Winston 303, 320
Greenidge, Dave 257
Greenidge, Keth 13
Greenidge, Orlando 320
Gregory Cup 75, 81-82, 93, 100, 125
Gregory Cup Final 46, 99
Gregory, Caroline 302
Griffith, Charlie 16, 189
Griffith, Michael 10
Griffiths, Debbie 184
Grocock, Andrew 101
Guilliat, Tony 291
H. L. Brown Cup 168
Hadfleld, Steve 292
Haffajee, Babu 178
Haffenden, Paul 38
Haggo, Allan 161, 163-164, 167, 296, 299, 302-303
Haggo, David 163, 166-167, 312
Haggo, Douglas 149, 168
Haggo, Mrs. Fiona 299
Haggo, Samantha 300
Hague C.C. 135
Hague, Richard 107
Hales, Kevin 236
Hall, Harold 10